T0319528

A
Political Explanation of
Economic Growth

State Survival, Bureaucratic Politics, and Private

Enterprises in the Making of Taiwan's

Economy, 1950–1985

Harvard East Asian Monographs 246

The Asia Public Policy Series

The Asia Public Policy series seeks to promote interdisciplinary research on key challenges facing the region. Specifically the series focuses on the provision of public goods and services, the health of financial systems, and regional security.

Anthony Saich
General Editor

A
Political Explanation of
Economic Growth

State Survival, Bureaucratic Politics, and Private

Enterprises in the Making of Taiwan's

Economy, 1950–1985

Yongping Wu

Published by the Harvard University Asia Center
Distributed by Harvard University Press
Cambridge (Massachusetts) and London 2005

© 2005 by the President and Fellows of Harvard College

Printed in the United States of America

The Harvard University Asia Center publishes a monograph series and, in coordination with the Fairbank Center for East Asian Research, the Korea Institute, the Reischauer Institute of Japanese Studies, and other faculties and institutes, administers research projects designed to further scholarly understanding of China, Japan, Vietnam, Korea, and other Asian countries. The Center also sponsors projects addressing multidisciplinary and regional issues in Asia.

Library of Congress Cataloging-in-Publication Data

Wu, Yongping, 1962–

    Political explanation of economic growth : state survival, bureaucratic politics, and private enterprises in the making of Taiwan's economy, 1950–1985 / Yongping Wu.

       p. cm. – (Harvard East Asian monographs ; 246. The Asia public policy series)

    Includes bibliographical references and index.

    ISBN 0-674-01779-x (cloth : alk. paper)

    1. Taiwan--Economic policy--1945- 2. Taiwan--Economic conditions--1945- 3. Industrial policy--Taiwan. 4. Taiwan--Politics and government--1945- I. Title. II. Series: Harvard East Asian monographs ; 246. III. Series: Harvard East Asian monographs. The Asia public policy series. IV. Series.

    HC430.5.w848 2005

    330.95124'905--dc22

2004029883

Index by the author

☉ Printed on acid-free paper

Last figure below indicates year of this printing

15   14   13   12   11   10   09   08   07   06   05

For
my mother,
Huang Xiurong,
and in memory of my father,
Wu Maoxing

Acknowledgments

A major reason for the stunning export performance of small- and medium-sized firms in Taiwan, one of the major themes in this book, is their global industrial connections. Not surprisingly, this book itself is a product of global academic connections as well. The research and revisions have been carried out in four locations on three continents, thus mirroring the increasing global integration of academic circles. I began the project and completed my doctoral dissertation from which this book emerged in Leiden. Field research was conducted in Taiwan. Major revisions were completed in Boston. The manuscript was finalized in Beijing. In the course of this journey, I benefited from the help and advice of many people and the hospitality of a number of institutions. Without their assistance, the completion of this book would have been impossible.

First and foremost, I thank Tony Saich and Richard Boyd, my teachers at Leiden University. Each provided indispensable intellectual guidance over many years in ways that can never be reciprocated. Tony Saich encouraged me to shift my research focus at a time ten years ago when Taiwan studies did not exist at Leiden University. After Tony went to Beijing to take up a position at the Ford Foundation, Richard guided me through the writing of the dissertation. Throughout this work, they provided standards of scholarly excellence that will be of lasting help during my professional career.

I also benefited from discussions with and comments from Leo Dow, Barend ter Haar, Ricky Kersten, T. W. Ngo, Axel Schneider, and Eduard Vermeer. Wilt Idema's support was crucial, as was that of James C. P. Liang, Magiel van Crevel, and J. L. Blusse during the last months of the project. In addition, Kristofer M. Schipper's profound knowledge of Taiwan provided inspiration.

My entrée to the premier academic circles on Taiwan enabled me to study with a group of scholars in the fields of history, political science, sociology, and economics whose knowledge greatly deepened my understanding of the subject. My special thanks go to Huang Chun-chieh and Hsiao Hsin-huang, whose help went far beyond academic encouragement. I also thank Chang Mau-kuei, Chu Wan-wen, Chu Yun-han, Hsieh Kuo-hsing, Hsu Sung-ken, Lai Shin-yuan, Lin Man-houng, Liu Su-fen, Shiau Chyuan-jeng, Rex Wang, Wu Rong-I, and Yang Ya-hwei.

In addition, I owe a great debt to Chao Ci-chang, Li Kuo-ting (K. T. Li), J. K. Loh, Sun Chen, Wang Chao-ming, Wei Yong-ning, and Ye Wan-an for providing crucial information that helped me understand the nature of the policy network in Taiwan's industrial transformation from the perspective of insiders in the policy process. Similarly, I also thank Kevin K. W. Chow and Laurence M. Yang for their views as business people about the economic development of Taiwan.

As the first graduate student with a PRC passport to visit National Taiwan University, I encountered many difficulties in applying for a research visa in 1996. Professor Lin Yaofu, then Dean of the Faculty of Liberal Arts of National Taiwan University, and his assistant, Joyce Ho, worked patiently and persistently to help me obtain the visa. The director of the Department of History, Professor Ku Wei-ying, also provided a great deal of help and encouragement. Professor Ku's successor, Professor Lee Tong-hwa, continued to support me during my fieldwork research, contributing to the productivity of my stay in Taipei. Zhuang Shuhua and Wu Jinyan assisted me in using the Li Guoding Archives, as well as other archives preserved at the Institute of Modern History of the Academia Sinica in Taipei.

In the United States, I especially thank Steve Goldstein of Smith College and Bill Kirby of Harvard for their comments and criticisms of my talk at the Taiwan Studies Workshop of Harvard's

Fairbank Center for East Asian Research, where I first introduced the major findings of this book.

Furthermore, I owe a great deal of thanks to a number of institutions. The School of Asian, African, and Amerindian Studies (Research School CNWS) at Leiden University provided support for my Ph.D. work, as did the Sinological Institute at Leiden. National Taiwan University (NTU) and the Institute of History of NTU accepted me as a Ph.D. student. This was indispensable in gaining access to libraries and archives during the field research. The major revisions to my thesis were completed at the Asian Program of the Center for Business and Government of the John F. Kennedy School of Government, Harvard University. The School of Public Policy and Management at Tsinghua University, where I presently teach, allowed me a leave during my first semester in order to complete the final manuscript. The Institute for Taiwan Studies at Tsinghua University was generous in providing ample time to allow me to concentrate on the finalization of the book.

I would like to extend special thanks to Edward Steinfeld of MIT and Tak-wing Ngo of Leiden University for their useful criticisms of an earlier manuscript of this book. Their comments and suggestions helped sharpen the arguments and improve the final product. Nonetheless, I alone remain responsible for all its shortcomings.

Many friends and colleagues contributed to the project at different stages of the research, writing, and revisions. They include Illona Beumer-Grill, Fransisca Bijkerk, Elizabeth Bulette, Sarah Cao, H. E. Chan, Julian Chang, Edward Cunningham, Jacob Eyferth, Peter Ho, Anne Sietske Keijser, Kuo Wen-hua, Stefan Landsberger, Ma Yiu-man, Daniel Russell, Masayuki Sato, Nicole Schouten, Wilma Trommelen, Willem Vogelsang, Joyce Wu, Yin Cunyi, and Yuan Bingling.

Special thanks go to Nancy Hearst, whose contribution went beyond careful copyediting to rescuing the manuscript from many factual errors. I also thank Xiong Nijuan for checking the notes and the bibliography.

This work was financed by the Netherlands Foundation for Advanced Tropical Research (WOTRO). The Chiang Ching-kuo

Foundation for International Scholarly Exchange kindly provided financial support during the last year of the project. The Cho Chang Tsung Foundation of Education also granted financial support, and the Pacific Cultural Foundation awarded a research grant. Finally, the United Daily News Foundation and the Lo-Hsu Foundation financed the fieldwork for my thesis.

Over the past years my daughter, Yubai, encouraged and supported me enormously in the course of the writing of this book with her patience and understanding. My only regret is that this experience has discouraged Yubai from pursuing an academic career.

The book is dedicated to my mother, Huang Xiurong, and to the memory of my father, Wu Maoxing.

Y.P.W.

Contents

Tables and Figures

Tables

Figures

Abbreviations

AID	Agency for International Development
APCG	Agricultural Planning and Coordination Group
BOT	Bank of Taiwan
CDC	China Development Corporation
CEC	Central Executive Committee
CEPD	Council of Economic Planning and Development
CIECD	Council for International Economic Cooperation and Development
CPC	China Petroleum Corporation
CSC	Central Standing Committee
CUSA	Council for U.S. Aid
DLF	Development Loan Fund
DPP	Democratic Progressive Party
DSMB	Department of Small and Medium Business
EOI	export-oriented industrialization
EPB	Economic Planning Board
ERSO	Electronics Research Service Organization
ESB	Economic Stabilization Board
FETCC	Foreign Exchange and Trade Control Commission
GTC	general trading company
IC	integrated circuit
ICA	International Cooperation Administration

IDA	International Development Association
IDB	Industrial Development Bureau
IDC	Industrial Development Council
IFC	International Finance Corporation
IPCG	Industrial Planning and Coordination Group
ISI	import substitution industrialization
ITRI	Industrial Technology Research Institute
KMT	Nationalist Party
LEs	large private enterprises
LTC	large trading company
MAAG	Military Assistance Advisor Group
Mission	U.S. Aid Mission to China
MOEA	Ministry of Economic Affairs
MOF	Ministry of Finance
MSA	Mutual Security Administration
NDCC	National Distillers and Chemical Corporation
NRC	National Resources Commission
SAJCRR	Sino-American Joint Commission on Rural Reconstruction
SMEs	small and medium-sized enterprises
SMTs	small and medium-sized trading companies
SOE	state-owned enterprise
STAG	Science and Technology Advisory Group
TAC	Technical Advisory Committee
TPB	Taiwan Production Board
TPCG	Transportation Planning and Coordination Group
TSMC	Taiwan Semiconductor Corporation
UMC	United Microelectronics

A
Political Explanation of
Economic Growth

State Survival, Bureaucratic Politics, and Private

Enterprises in the Making of Taiwan's

Economy, 1950–1985

CHAPTER I

State and Market: Reinterpreting
the Taiwan Experience

Taiwan is a classic case of export-led industrialization. But unlike
South Korea and Japan, two East Asian countries in which large
firms are the major contributors to exports, before the late 1980s
Taiwan's successful exporters were overwhelmingly small and
medium-sized enterprises (SMEs),[1] and large firms provided products and services for the domestic market. The SMEs were not
only the major exporters but also, ultimately, the engine of the entire economy by virtue of their backward linkage to the upstream
state-owned enterprises (SOEs) and intermediate-stream large private enterprises (LEs). Through this linkage, these unwieldy or po-
tentially inefficient behemoths were subject to the discipline of the
global market. Thus, the starting point for any examination of
Taiwanese development is to account for the unique division of
industrial labor between large and small firms.

There are two paradoxes in Taiwan's development. The first is
the conflict between the state's efforts to promote exports as a
means to advance the economy and the state's actual tolerance and
even encouragement of large enterprises entrenched in the domestic market. The state saw exporting as a solution to Taiwan's economic problems, in particular the balance-of-payments problems
and the dependence on U.S. aid. In the late 1950s and early 1960s, it
implemented a series of measures to encourage firms to engage in
exporting. The state initially regarded the large enterprises as potential exporters, yet it continued to implement protectionist poli-

cies to increase domestic supply. These policies had the effect of discouraging large enterprises from export activities and undermined the state's efforts to achieve its export goals. If the state is a reasonable actor, how can its unreasonable behavior be explained? The other paradox is that the SMEs became exporters even though the state did not devise an industrial policy for them until they had already begun exporting successfully to world markets. Why did the state ignore those firms that responded to its call to develop exports and that helped to realize this goal? Economic logic would also characterize this behavior as irrational.

The question that arises is What enabled the SMEs to succeed in the export markets even though the state did not have an SME-specific industrial policy? Of course, there were many reasons for the impressive performance of the SMEs. This book argues that the key to their success in export markets was Taiwan's singular industrial structure. One peculiarity of this structure was a strict division of labor: the SOEs monopolized the upstream industries, the LEs were entrenched in the intermediate-stream industries, and the SMEs focused on downstream activities. Further, the SOEs and LEs jointly monopolized the domestic market, whereas the SMEs had free run in the export markets. This structure was a critical precondition for the success of the SMEs. Thus, we need to ask, among other things, How did this industrial structure come into being? and What role did the state play in its formation and persistence?

All these phenomena had political origins. Political calculations came into play when the state set public policy toward the private sector. The first paradox arose because of the KMT's (Nationalist Party) top priority: holding on to power. For the KMT, an émigré regime that had lost the civil war on mainland China, winning political support from large firms was critical for the continuance of its rule on an island populated mostly by native Taiwanese. On the other hand, the KMT's substantial insecurities about its rule led it to restrict the large firms in order to prevent the rise of political rivals. Understandably, economic considerations were often subject to political concerns. Although it was economically irrational for the KMT to discourage LE exports, it was politically expedient. The second paradox was a consequence of the same political logic.

Because of their size and fragmentation, the SMEs had little political might and presented no threat to KMT rule. Their treatment by the state matched their political and economic status: they were neither protected nor restricted.

The industrial structure also had political origins. It resulted from the state's public policy toward the private sector. Public policy is determined by political strategies for managing societal forces. But the consequences of political strategies and public policy are often unintended. Indeed, both the witting and the unwitting interactions of the state and the private sector shaped Taiwan's unique industrial structure.

These facts suggest the importance of exploring the political basis for the state's choice of an industrial policy and of examining the role of politics in economic development. Taiwan's economic development cannot be adequately explained without taking the political factors into account. Therefore, this book addresses the political dimension of Taiwan's development.

This chapter has five sections. The first assesses the statist account of Taiwan's development. The second introduces the propositions and hypotheses of this book. The third clarifies the issues of institutions, bureaucratic politics and leadership, and economic policy. The fourth outlines the relationships linking the regime, political strategies, public policy, and industrial structure. The final section focuses on the provision of industrial finance as an element in the formation and persistence of the industrial structure.

The Statist Account of Taiwan's Development

Both state and market hold a central place in explaining economic development in East Asia. Except for market fundamentalists, the debate has moved far from the view that holds a free market responsible for the economic achievements of East Asia. Even the World Bank, a hub of free-market advocates, changed its long-standing views in 1993 and admitted the centrality of state-led policies in the East Asian economies.[2] Others have argued that the developmental state is the source of East Asia's, including Taiwan's, unprecedented economic and industrial success. In their view, the state had the right institutional mix and the steering capacity to sustain and implement its industrial policies. But we have to ask Was this really the case?

Industrial Policy

The statist account of Taiwan's industrialization focuses on strategic intelligence and assumes that the KMT government's industrial policy explains Taiwan's successful industrialization. According to Robert Wade, "a sectoral industrial policy aims to direct resources into selected industries so as to give producers in those industries a competitive advantage."[3] Wade's argument is based on the belief that this type of industrial policy achieves better results than an unguided industrial policy and that the economic successes of both South Korea and Taiwan can be attributed to such policies. Certainly, the successes of the petrochemical, semiconductor, and textile industries in Taiwan owed much to government industrial policy, but there were some equally spectacular failures. The automobile industry is a clear instance, as is the government's effort in the late 1970s to eliminate petrochemicals as a strategic industry. The statist account does not explain why some industrial policies succeeded and others failed.

Moreover, many industrial successes are not related to industrial policy. The major lacuna in the statist account of Taiwan's industrial success is the outstanding performance of the SMEs. During the late 1970s and early 1980s, the SMEs employed over 50 percent of all workers and were the major producers in terms of the value of production. In 1976, they were responsible for 44.9 percent of the total value of production, and in 1984, for 47.6 percent. The SMEs were not only major exporters but also the engine—more tugboat rather than locomotive—of the entire economy by virtue of their backward linkage to the SOEs and LEs. The SMEs accounted for over 60 percent of the value of exports from 1981 to 1985.[4] Their tugboat role resulted in a "buyer-driven" economy. In a "production-driven" economy, the larger firms in manufacturing networks create demand for smaller firms outside the networks.[5] In "buyer-driven" economies, big businesses are upstream suppliers of intermediate goods and services in response to demands generated by manufacturing networks of SMEs, which are, in turn, re-

sponses to the demands of buyers external to the producing networks. Production in these networks relies on external markets.[6]
Taiwan's LEs are not organizing nodes in these commodity chains.

These statistics are significant in themselves. If we compare
Taiwan to South Korea and Japan, however, the significance of the
SMEs in Taiwan's economy is even more striking. In Japan and
South Korea, the conglomerates contributed the greater part of
GNP and provided most of the final products for export. In South
Korea, for example, 70 percent of exports were generated by the
top ten business groups in 1983.[7] Given the significance of SMEs in
Taiwan, the analytical challenge is to explain their success.

Conspicuously, the SME sector was not strategically designed
by the state. The market in which it existed was not a governed
market. Wade himself admits that "Taiwan's industrial policies affect firms in the small-scale sector very little."[8] Apparently, the
SMEs' success cannot be attributed to the government's selective
industrial policy. The industrial structure is not in itself, however,
the explanation for the SME success. Rather, the SMEs' success can
be attributed to the development by Taiwan's SMEs of an industrial production system predicated on the existence of an array of
societal goods and the ability to mobilize these goods to offset the
disadvantages they otherwise would have faced in terms of capital
shortages and the like.

These examples suggest that industrial policy is insufficient to
explain Taiwan's industrial success. What, then, were the determinants of the successes or failures of Taiwan's industrial policy?
What contributed to Taiwan's industrial success, in particular that
of the SMEs? If the state's role in economic development cannot
adequately be explained by its industrial policy, how did it influence economic development? Did the state influence private LEs'
decision to focus on the domestic market and the SMEs' on export
markets? If so, in what way and how far?

The Right Institutional Mix

The assumption of a monolithic, meritocratic, and capable economic bureaucracy is essential to the statist account.[9] The evidence
shows, however, that in the case of Taiwan this institution-based

account of the economic bureaucracy is inaccurate and apolitical. As T. J. Pempel has pointed out, the bureaucracy premised in the developmental state thesis is based on Weber's idealized bureaucracy and is viewed "as totally depoliticized, socially disembodied, and in rational pursuit of a self-evident national interest."[10]

In reality, the economic bureaucracy in Taiwan was full of conflicts of interest, ideological divisions, rivalries, personality differences, factional struggles, and clashes of opinion. Personal competition was an inherent part of Taiwan's bureaucracy, and factional division was a conspicuous phenomenon. Basically, the economic bureaucrats were divided into two factions, the presidential residence faction (so-called because of their close relationship with the Chiang family) and the non–presidential residence faction. The financial and monetary officials belonged to the first faction. Trusted by the Chiang family, they were used as a check on the economic bureaucrats. Two major figures in this faction were Xu Boyuan and Yu Guohua, both longtime governors of the Central Bank of China.

Differences over economic policy among the leading bureaucrats often constituted the major sources of conflict among the agencies. Before the mid-1960s, established bureaucracies like the Ministry of Economic Affairs (MOEA) and the Ministry of Finance (MOF) played a less important role in economic policy making than did economic planning agencies financed by U.S. aid, such as the Industrial Development Council (IDC, 1953–58), Economic Stabilization Board (ESB, 1953–58), Council for U.S. Aid (CUSA, 1959–63), and Council for International Economic Cooperation and Development (CIECD, 1963–73). All these agencies initiated plans for industrial development, and the MOEA and MOF did no more than accept or oppose these plans.[11]

For several reasons, however, we should be cautious when assessing the role and functions of these economic planning agencies. First, they were short-lived (the IDC, ESB, CUSA, and the Economic Planning Board [EPB] for five years and the CIECD for ten years). Thus, the institutional continuities were fragile, and these organs were ephemeral. It was not until 1985 that the first institutionalized economic planning organ, the Council of Economic

Planning and Development (CEPD), came into being. In contrast to Japan and South Korea, where the pilot economic planning agencies achieved a stable existence, the highest leaders in Taiwan scrapped the economic agencies at will. An institution could be set up if the president thought there was a need, but it could also be dismantled if the president decided that he disliked it. The classic instance is the replacement of the CIECD by the EPB in 1973. Differences between Chiang Ching-kuo and the bureaucrats in the CIECD over economic issues were the major reasons for his dismissal of this body.[12]

Second, the functions of these organs depended on the strength of the person heading them. Their roles increased under the leadership of a strongman and decreased under a weak chair. Under the leadership of Yin Zhongrong, for example, the IDC was active and efficient, but it was much less so under Jiang Biao, because of his conservative style and the consequent low morale of the staff.[13] A newspaper headline such as "To strengthen its administrative functions, the vice premier assumes the chair of the CIECD [from the premier]" may seem absurd, but the CIECD was strengthened when Chiang Ching-kuo, then vice premier, replaced Premier Yan Jiagan as its head in 1969. The power and function of the IDC, ESB, and CUSA increased once Yin Zhongrong took over as their leader. The MOEA and MOF became more active when they were under the leadership of K. T. Li.

Third, the autonomy of these organs from the highest levels of the leadership was precarious. To some extent they were immune to pressure from other parts of the state, mainly the military, intelligence, parliament, and the party, but they were sensitive to the will of the top leaders.[14] Further, there was a difference in the degree of autonomy enjoyed by bureaucrats under Chiang Kai-shek and Chiang Ching-kuo. Chiang Kai-shek allowed them more discretion in routine matters, whereas his son was inclined to meddle even in the specific details of economic affairs.[15] According to K. T. Li, Chiang Ching-kuo trusted bureaucrats less than did his father.[16] However, Chiang Kai-shek had the final say over all important economic policies. Without the president's sanction, institutions were meaningless. Pempel's criticism of the developmental state thesis's view of the bureaucracy is relevant here: "Few contend that bureaucrats take their orders from political officials (elected or otherwise)."[17]

Fourth, conflicts were pervasive among these planning agencies and ministries. Those between the MOEA and MOF were typical.

Steering Capacity

Statism also assumes that the steering capacity of the economic bureaucracy in Taiwan was strong. But case studies reveal just the opposite. The state did demonstrate such a capacity in some cases, for instance, in the textile industry in the 1950s, but not in others. The assumption is too simplistic, and the issue of state capacity needs to be explored further.

Studies on the failure of the state's effort to promote the automobile industry blame the institutional arrangements of the economic bureaucracy, for example, bureaucratic conflicts between the MOEA's Industrial Development Bureau (IDB) and the CEPD (the two organs often advocated contradictory policies and frequently clashed over policy issues). The heads of the two organs had different personalities and very different opinions about the project. In addition, neither the expertise nor the staff required for such complex techno-economic changes was available. Finally, the inability to insulate policy making from fierce lobbying by domestic and foreign auto manufacturers also contributed to the failure.[18] A case study of Hua Tung Heavy Trucks reveals the range of elements in the policy process: diverse goals pursued by various groups within the government, patterns of coalition and opposition among these groups, and alliances based not only on bureaucratic position but also on such factors as personal ties and educational background.[19]

The government's decision to reverse an earlier resolution on the status of the petrochemical industry is another example. In 1973, Chiang Ching-kuo had designated petrochemicals a key industry. In 1981, acting on the suggestions of academics, the Sun Yunxuan cabinet suspended further expansion of the intermediate-stream sectors of the petrochemical industry, because the costs of its oil requirements and pollution were too high. This decision, however, was reversed by the Yu Guohua cabinet in 1984 due to pressures from vested interests and Yu's own close connections to the SOEs in this sector. The petrochemical industry thus regained its status as a key industry.[20]

There are a number of lacunae in accounts in the literature on Taiwan's experience. This book attempts to reinterpret this experience.

Propositions and Hypotheses

This study argues that the key to understanding the two paradoxes of the state's industrial policy and the origins of Taiwan's unique market, which provided the SMEs with space to perform in export markets, is the role of politics. Without a doubt, the state had economic goals and pursued these goals. But the state's economic goals were often subject to its political goals. When the two matched, the economic objectives were pursued. When the two diverged, however, the economic goals were compromised. Furthermore, when the political goals changed, the economic goals changed as well. Neglect of the crucial impact of politics on economic development is a major weakness in the literature on Taiwan's development.

This book brings the political dimension into the analysis by focusing on two issues. First, it addresses the political origins of Taiwan's market—a unique industrial structure that defined the role of the three key players in Taiwan's economy: the SOEs, LEs, and SMEs. This industrial structure determined the division of labor among the three players and constituted the marketplace for the SME-led export-oriented industrialization. The book argues that the state contributed to the formation and persistence of this structure and that its political strategies and public policy toward the private sector were the major determinants of the industrial structure, but the results were not always those it intended.

A second focus of the book is the political basis for the state's industrial policy. Contrary to the statist apolitical account of a monolithic and unitary economic bureaucracy, I argue that Taiwan's economic bureaucracy should be understood in terms of bureaucratic politics and that industrial policy was a product of these bureaucratic politics. This book uses a political perspective to explain the economic bureaucracy.

These propositions are based on seven hypotheses. The first is that the noneconomic goals of a state have consequences for economic development and that political and other actions by the state have consequences on the formation of the marketplace. It is too narrow to understand the economic role of the state merely in terms of its economic goals. Other state goals may also come into play. It is also too narrow to understand the economic role of the state simply in terms of policy. The economic influence of the state extends far beyond policy. Economic policy can be a result of various motives, and the entire process, from the initial awareness of the need for economic reform to the formation of a political response—the need for economic adjustments translated into effective political demands for policy change—is political.[21] In effect, market intervention can become political control.[22] The magnitude of state influence is far more than simple "intervention," which refers mainly to economic behavior and therefore is inadequate to characterize the scope of state actions. In this book, "action" refers to state behavior that is more encompassing than mere economic behavior.

The second hypothesis is that the impacts of state actions on economic development are not always intentional. Conventional wisdom on East Asian economic development assumes that actual economic performance is a result of state intention. However, state intentions and the outcomes are not always congruent. Some goals may not be realized, and some outcomes may be unanticipated. Interpreting the role of the state in economic development only in terms of its intentions is as misleading as attributing economic successes only to the intentions of the state.

The third hypothesis is that the outcome of the interplay of the state and private actors is far more than a matter of "cooperation" or "coordination" between the two. Cooperation or coordination implies direct and formal links. In fact, there are also indirect and invisible interactions between the state and private actors, and these can affect the evolution of economic performance. The impact of many government policies, for instance, devaluation of the currency and adjustment of interest rates, on the economy cannot be measured in terms of cooperation or coordination, but the interplay between the state and the private sector with respect to these policies helps shape the marketplace. Therefore, this book proposes that "interplay" and "interaction" replace "cooperation" and "coordination" in describing state–private sector relations. This interplay includes both cooperation and indirect interactions.

The fourth hypothesis is that the existence or absence of a free market and the intention of the state to conform to the market are less significant in economic development than the particular configuration of the marketplace that emerges from the interaction of the state and private actors and the kind of opportunities that this configuration affords the economic actors. The nature of the marketplace and the opportunities that result are significant for their capacity to facilitate the development of a production system that is able to mobilize "societal goods." Therefore, the prerequisite of economic success in developing countries is the existence of a marketplace that encourages the mobilization of societal goods and enables the entrepreneurship of private actors to come into play. But such a marketplace does not emerge by itself. It is a result of state actions and the interplay between the state and private actors.

The fifth hypothesis is that the role and function of the economic bureaucracy in the formulation and implementation of economic policy hinge not on coherence but on mechanisms that can solve differences within the state. It is misleading to assume that institutions are coherent and unitary. As is pointed out above, Taiwan's economic bureaucracy was far from coherent. Internal struggles, ideological conflicts, differences in interests, and factional rifts were common within the economic bureaucracy throughout the period under study. Many economic policies emerged as a result not of "coherence" but of compromise. The ideology of the bureaucrats, differences in interests among government departments, factional backgrounds, and even personalities influenced the policy-making process. What is decisive for policy success is whether mechanisms can be developed to solve these problems. Among the leaders, such mechanisms include shared ideologies or common backgrounds. Or they can even be particular persons, with special abilities to coordinate the efforts of diverse actors. The mechanisms vary from country to country and even within a single country from situation to situation.

A corollary of the fifth hypothesis is that the state's steering capacity may depend on the rule of a strongman. In the case of Taiwan, the economic bureaucracy was poorly integrated. Its internal conflicts and struggles highlighted the importance of coordination among the different agencies. As we have seen, the economic planning agencies were fragile and weak, and their existence depended on the will of the political leaders. This situation created the conditions for the emergence of a strongman who played a leadership role in policy formulation and implementation because he could resolve the coordination problems. In turn, a precondition for the role of the strongman was political support from the highest-level politicians. With this political capital, the strongman was able to overcome obstacles and put his ideas into practice. His charisma greatly facilitated his exercise of leadership. It was the strongman, not the institutions, that played a leading role in resolving the coordination problems. Thus, the issue of leadership is critical to our understanding of the role of the state in economic development in East Asia.

The last hypothesis is an attempt to explain the success of the SMEs. State action and the interplay of the state and private actors resulted in a unique industrial structure that enabled the SMEs to develop an industrial production system predicated on the existence of an array of societal goods and an ability to mobilize these goods to offset the disadvantages they otherwise faced, such as capital shortages. This explains the unusual success of Taiwan's SMEs. The existence of the industrial structure was a precondition for the performance of the SMEs, but this industrial structure was not designed to create a marketplace in which the SMEs might flourish, even though this was indeed its effect. The role of the state in Taiwan's industrial structure was critical but not always intentional—much of the industrial structure resulted from the unanticipated consequences of the political strategies of the state. A capital-substituting production system drawing on societal goods developed and enabled the SMEs to operate as competitive exporters.

In the following chapters, I verify these propositions and hypotheses based on an empirical study. The relationships among institutions, leadership, and bureaucratic politics are keys to understanding the economic bureaucracy in Taiwan.

Institutions, Bureaucratic Politics, and Leadership and Economic Policy

As institutionalism has become a dominant approach in the social sciences over the past two decades, we have seen a rapid rise of institutionalism in comparative studies of political economies. Institutionalism provides a useful approach for explaining economic, political, and social phenomena. It is, however, problematic when comparing political economies; as in other fields, there is a tendency to view institutionalism as omnipotent. This risks simplistic accounts of social, political, and economic life. This trend is particularly conspicuous in attempts to explain economic policy. The question we must ask is Do institutions provide an adequate account of economic policy?

A second problem is the tendency to simplify institutions in institutionalist accounts of public policy. Although this approach nicely captures some elements of institutions, it ignores other elements. Both implicitly and explicitly, institutions are reduced to rules and organizations. But institutions are also made up of people, and they are for the most part ignored in institutionalist accounts. The people who operate the institutions are neglected, even though to a great extent their ideologies, preferences, and personalities determine the function and operation of the institutions. Without an understanding of the personalities involved in the institutions, it is difficult to understand the institutions and to explain economic policy. Thus, we need to bring the people back in. In short, the institutions need to be humanized.

As a result of this dehumanization, the institutional approach neglects the issue of leadership. Yet leadership is highly significant in the efficiency of institutions, and the role of an institution is largely dependent on its leader. A strong leader can strengthen the role of the institution, whereas a weak leader will have the opposite effect. A strongman can be a source of power and authority for an agency.

The influence of the head of an institution is determined not only by his personality, ideology, knowledge, and ability but also by his relationship with the political leader. Strong support from the top leaders can strengthen the role of the head of an institution, whereas weak support can undermine his role. The relationship between political leaders and the head of an institution is determined by many factors. This is a matter of bureaucratic politics.

Another problem in the institutional approach is the depoliticization of institutions, which leads to the ignoring of bureaucratic politics. In explaining the role of institutions, conventional wisdom tends to view the bureaucracy as coherent and monolithic. The success of a policy is attributed to this coherence, whereas policy failures are taken as proof of incoherence. This treatment depoliticizes the bureaucracy. I argue instead that the bureaucracy is a world of politics rather than a discrete, monolithic mix of rules, organizational structures, and organizations. Politics is about who gets what and how, *and* it is a struggle of "us against them."[23] It is similar to a market in which people engage in exchange. Its functional task is to settle conflicts among individual interests and values at several levels and not only within well-defined legal structures.[24] Hence, in addition to people, we must also bring politics back in.

In this regard, it is useful to recall Graham Allison's classic analysis of bureaucratic politics. Introducing his Model III to political science, Allison wrote:

The "leaders" who sit on top of organizations are not a monolithic group. Rather, each individual in this group is, in his own right, a player in a central, competitive game. The name of the game is politics: bargaining along regularized circuits among players positioned hierarchically within the government. Government behavior can thus be understood . . . not as organizational outputs but as the results of these bargaining games. In contrast with Model I (the Rational Actor Model), the Governmental (or Bureaucratic) Politics Model sees no unitary actor but rather many actors as players—players who focus not on a single strategic issue but on many diverse intra-national problems as well; players who act in terms of no consistent set of strategic objectives but rather according to various conceptions of national, organizational, and personal goals; players who make government decisions not by a single, rational choice but by the pulling and hauling that is politics.[25]

Despite criticisms of Allison's Model III and doubts about the role of bureaucratic politics in foreign policy,[26] Allison's emphasis on the importance of bureaucratic politics in policy analysis is useful, and the significance of such politics can be seen far beyond the field of international relations. Bureaucratic politics exists in economic policy making as well. The problem is not whether bureaucratic politics matters in the policy process but how bureaucratic politics is defined and how the factors that constitute and determine bureaucratic politics are viewed. Interests are core elements in bureaucratic politics, as indicated in Allison's Model III. Government agencies and persons in these agencies have their own interests. Ideology also plays a part in the operation of a bureaucracy.[27] Different agencies have different views and attach different priorities to economic issues. Government agencies often come into conflict over both interests and ideology. In addition, factions matter in bureaucratic politics. Interests and ideology are the main bases of factions. Bureaucratic politics is also shaped by political culture. Although the effect of political culture may vary from country to country, trust and loyalty play a significant role in bureaucratic politics. Other formal and informal norms and practices also play a part in the operation of a bureaucracy. Therefore, it is simply apolitical to assume that government agencies are coherent and monolithic. The key is to explain how mechanisms are developed to coordinate among the different agencies and how conflicts are resolved. A successful policy is always the result of successful coordination rather than of coherence. A good economic policy must be not only economically sound but also politically acceptable. Good economics must be good politics.

Whereas the need to humanize and politicize our understanding of institutions is a universal necessity, we must distinguish between the role of institutions in developed societies and the role of institutions in developing societies, since the latter are generally less institutionalized. The role of institutions in a society is also dependent on how well established institutions are. They play a larger role in societies with well-established institutions. However, even in developed societies, the role of institutions cannot be understood merely in terms of formal rules and organizations. Studies of the Japanese civil service system have found that cultural factors and historical contexts interact with formal rules and organizational structures to determine the efficiency of institutions. Thus we need to recognize the complexity of the institutional matrix.[28]

Recent evidence for the complexity of the policy process was the smaller-than-expected role of General Colin Powell in the Bush administration's foreign policy making. As a moderate and a pragmatist, Powell was highly respected both inside and outside the United States. However, after assuming the post of secretary of state in January 2001, he experienced a series of setbacks on major issues, ranging from policy toward North Korea to the Kyoto Protocol on global warming to the anti-missile defense system for a number of reasons relating to bureaucratic politics. The main constraints on General Powell generally came from two key figures in the Bush administration, Vice President Richard Cheney and Secretary of Defense Donald Rumsfeld, who are widely regarded as conservatives. Bureaucratic politics within Bush's foreign policy team revolved around ideological differences (Powell is a multilateralist and an internationalist, whereas Cheney and Rumsfield are unilateralists and advocates of "America first"), different ways of doing business—pragmatic versus idealistic—and personal relations and trust (Condoleezza Rice, the president's national security adviser and a key influence on Bush's foreign policy during Powell's tenure, and eventually Powell's replacement as secretary of state, has a close relationship with Bush and is highly trusted by him; in contrast, Powell's relationship with the president was less close). All these factors resulted in a marginalization of Powell in foreign policy making.[29] This case indicates the complexities and subtleties of the policy process—it is much more than rules and organizations. It also involves bureaucratic politics.

The significance of leadership and bureaucratic politics in societies in which institutions are not yet well established is noteworthy. Given the lower level of institutionalization in these societies, leadership and bureaucratic politics play an even greater role in the policy process. We would miss this point if we use the standards derived from developed societies to make sense of less-developed societies. This applies to the situation in Taiwan. The highly personalized power structure, the importance of trust in personal relations, and faction-based politics determined the remarkable role of bureaucratic politics in the economic bureaucracy. This book examines several cases to highlight the importance of bureaucratic politics and leadership in the formulation and implementation of economic policy in Taiwan.

Regime Nature, Political Strategies, Public Policy, and Industrial Structure

As noted above, Taiwan's economic "miracle" and its industrialization were driven by SME exports. The SMEs were successful because of Taiwan's unique industrial structure, which enabled them to develop a production system that mobilized societal goods, and this offset their disadvantages and facilitated entrepreneurship. The formation of this industrial structure was significantly influenced by the state's political strategies and public policy, which in turn were determined by the state's political agenda. Why were the state's political strategies a determining factor in shaping the industrial structure, and in what ways did they influence this structure? One answer to these questions lies in the nature of the KMT regime.

The Nature of the KMT Regime

As many researchers have pointed out, relations between the state and the private sector in Taiwan differed greatly from those in Japan and South Korea. The Taiwan state, for example, distanced itself from business, and there was almost no direct link between the state and the SMEs. This relationship is attributed to the regime's antibusiness ideology, its authoritarian nature, and its ethnic subdivisions.[30] What is overlooked in most of these studies is the KMT's status as an émigré regime and its implications.

The states in South Korea and Taiwan differed from their Latin American counterparts because of their essential concern with security.[31] Yet their differences were also significant: the KMT was an émigré regime; its South Korean counterpart was not. This difference played a significant role in determining the two states' public policy toward large enterprises and resulted in different patterns of industrialization: SME-led, export-oriented industrialization in Taiwan and conglomerate-dominated development in South Korea. Decolonization also had different political results in Taiwan and South Korea. Although decolonization weakened the state in South Korea,[32] a new state emerged from within the society. However, the state that followed decolonization in Taiwan was imposed from the outside. When the defeated KMT central government fled to the island in 1949, it faced a population 80 percent of whom were native Taiwanese. The February 28 Incident of 1947, during which an estimated 10,000–20,000 local people were killed by the KMT army, made them hostile to the regime, their unfair treatment by the mainlanders left them resentful, and the prevalent corruption of KMT officials generated contempt. Although the locals were excluded from politics, they constituted the majority of the private sector. The KMT regime's deep distrust of the locals determined its position toward large enterprises. In South Korea, the state forged an industrial alliance with the business groups (*chaebols*). In Taiwan, however, the KMT vigilantly monitored the LEs to prevent the emergence of political rivals. In contrast to the ruling parties in South Korea and Japan, the KMT claimed to be unique in three other respects: it possessed an antibusiness mentality, was a Leninist / quasi-Leninist party, and was an economic actor in its own right. The KMT's quasi-Leninist structure strengthened it organizationally, and running its own businesses enabled the KMT to be economically independent. All these factors explain the regime's arm's-length relationship with private business.

The unique characteristics of the KMT regime and its vulnerable geographical position pushed political concerns to the top of the state's agenda. Defense expenditures were geared primarily to the external political goals of the state and, above all, to securing the island against mainland aggression. Domestically, political rather than economic goals were paramount.[33] As we shall see, however, these domestic political goals had a great impact on economic development.

State Political Strategies Toward Society

The state's status as an émigré regime encouraged it both to dominate societal forces and to keep its distance from them. The main
components of its strategy of domination were an authoritarian
state structure and corporatist arrangements in the state's relationship with society.[34] These arrangements allowed the state to separate itself from the major social forces in order to avoid being captured by them and to maintain relative independence. These
political strategies had significant consequences for public policy
toward the private sector and the state's dealings with the economy.

The nature of the regime does not fully explain why the KMT
state adopted these strategies. State-society relations also played a
role. The Taiwan state differed significantly from those in South
Korea and Latin America in terms of relations with society and
foreign capital. In many Latin American countries, alliances were
forged between the state and either the working class or the capitalists involved in import substitution and foreign capital. These alliances were political as well as economic, and they determined the
pattern of economic development. In South Korea, industrialization was dominated by the conglomerates. In Latin America, the
triple alliance of the state, local capital, and foreign capital was responsible for the second import substitution industrialization
(ISI),[35] which contrasts sharply with East Asia's shift to export-
oriented industrialization (EOI) after ISI. After the 1961 military
coup in South Korea, the state fostered a few large conglomerates
and forged alliances with them in order to boost economic development.[36] Although the KMT regime had a close relationship
with a few mainland and Taiwanese capitalists and won support
from the peasants after land reform, before the 1970s the state in
Taiwan did not rely on social forces as much as its Korean and
Latin American counterparts did during comparable periods in
their development. Governments in South Korea and Latin America had to link themselves with one or another social class because
they were politically and economically weak. In contrast, in Taiwan the state's monopoly of the financial system, upstream industries, basic industries, and infrastructure enabled it to be economi-

cally and politically independent and to maintain its distance from societal forces.

State Public Policy Toward the Private Sector

The regime's political strategies encouraged the KMT to practice a policy of protecting and restricting LEs while neither encouraging nor restricting SMEs. The state fostered a number of LEs through protectionism during ISI. During the 1950s, by controlling imports and entry into business, providing credit through state-owned banks, and distributing foreign exchange, the state encouraged a number of private firms to become involved in import substitution production. These enterprises grew into large enterprises and business groups in subsequent decades. The motivations behind this policy of fostering and protecting were both economic and political. The KMT had to increase production to aid in the recovery from wartime damages, to meet the basic needs of a growing population resulting from the influx of two million immigrants from the mainland (which increased the total population to eight million), and to realize the goal of recapturing the mainland. In Taiwan the KMT found a society with no entrepreneurs because of the Japanese monopoly over the economy during colonial rule. Therefore, there was a need to foster a private sector.

The KMT's tactic for promoting the private sector was to select and encourage economic winners as well as political supporters among both mainlanders and locals. The enterprises chosen by the government were allowed access to state-owned resources, ranging from credit to foreign exchange, and thus joined the SOEs in monopolizing the domestic market. A few capitalists were recruited into the KMT's Central Standing Committee (CSC), and their membership established a close relationship between the state and their firms. This relationship can be considered "close" in comparison to that between the state and SMEs. But it was far from close when compared to similar relationships in Japan or South Korea. This relationship persisted until the mid-1980s, when it was replaced by a state–business group alliance as a result of the Taiwanization of the KMT, democratization, and the growing influence of the business groups.

On the other hand, the state remained watchful of the LEs and generally restricted them, largely because the majority of the LEs were owned by native Taiwanese. The state became increasingly wary of the LEs beginning in the 1970s when they first began to develop into business groups. It attempted to restrict them in three ways. First, the state limited the scale of enterprises through laws and regulations. The Company Act, for example, curbed the size of business operations by regulating reinvestment through equity flows between firms. These laws served to block industrial integration. Second, the export promotion policy was universalistic rather than particularistic. It kept barriers to entry low and made incentives universal. This differed from the situation in South Korea, where the state channeled resources—particularly cheap credit—to a few select conglomerates to make them export champions.[37] This policy of the Taiwan state also deviated from its promotion during the 1950s of ISI by fostering a number of private enterprises. Third, before the 1980s, the state blocked the LEs from expanding their operations to the upstream industries and from participating in certain key sectors such as petrochemicals, finance, and infrastructure. The upstream SOEs played a strategic role in this respect. This restriction prevented the LEs from becoming vertically integrated conglomerates and affected the size of the business groups. Compared to their Japanese and South Korean counterparts, the leading business groups in Taiwan were less vertically integrated and much smaller in size.[38]

Before the mid-1970s, state policy toward the SMEs was neutral. It did not encourage them, because the SMEs were not important, and it did not restrict them, because the SMEs did not threaten the regime. Because of their small size and lack of sophistication, the SMEs were excluded from some export promotion incentives. Even so, the entry barriers to export activities were low, and this policy was highly significant for the growth of the SMEs' export activities. It allowed other factors to stimulate entrepreneurship. Although the state regulated the unorganized financial markets, it attached no importance to improving the SMEs' financial market. As a result, the LEs became entrenched in the domestic market, and the SMEs focused on the export market. The rise of the SMEs in the export market was not the intent of the state. In fact, when the government began to promote exports in the late 1950s, it did not expect the SMEs to become major exporters because of economies of scale.[39] This is reflected in the Statute for the Encouragement of Investment, a major move in 1960 to promote exports. The statute limited SME incentives in two ways: the statute was applicable to limited-liability companies only, and it aimed at encouraging expansion of the scale of production by requiring a minimum level of productivity. The first restriction excluded the 73.3 percent of the SMEs that were sole proprietorships, and the second restriction excluded many of the rest.[40] These conditions clearly reflect the government's expectation that larger firms would be the major exporters.

The state's policy toward SMEs shifted dramatically after the mid-1970s. This change was triggered by the KMT's legitimacy crisis, demands for political participation following Taiwan's loss of its UN seat, and economic problems caused by the oil crisis, increasing international competition, and the growth in wages. To deal with these problems, the KMT regime suddenly discovered the SMEs. They could further its Taiwanization scheme—the regime's major tactic for thwarting political opposition. Their exports became increasingly significant to the economic growth that the KMT desperately needed as a new source of legitimacy in the wake of a series of diplomatic setbacks. The regime also viewed the SMEs as a significant force in its effort to check the growing influence of the LEs. Chiang Ching-kuo's repeated emphasis on the importance of promoting SMEs and his call for government officials and public banks to provide assistance to them were not prompted solely by economic considerations.[41] Politics also motivated the state to move from a policy of benign neglect to one of active encouragement. Consequently, it implemented a series of measures aimed at promoting SMEs.

Public Policy and Industrial Structure

As is apparent from the preceding analysis, state political strategies and public policy toward the private sector regulated and determined the industrial structure. In effect, the state designed and po-

liced the marketplace. This policy resulted in an industrial structure with a strict division of labor between upstream SOEs, intermediate-stream LEs, and downstream SMEs. This industrial structure obliged the SMEs to engage in exports since they were denied
access to domestic markets but offered a near monopoly of the export markets. The state policed industrial organization to preserve
this division of labor through a variety of instruments. These included a universalistic rather than a particularistic export promotion policy beginning in the late 1950s, state maintenance and regulation of an "unorganized" financial market that was the major
source of capital for the SMEs (which were denied access to the
publicly owned financial system), reinforcement of the LEs' domestic focus through "financial constraints" and the distribution of
other economic rents, strengthening of the SOEs' upstream monopoly, including restrictions on SME firm size and legal disincen-
tives to expansion that might create dangerous political rivals. The
consequences for the SMEs were highly significant: immunity
from competition from the SOEs and LEs, without the loss of access to the intermediate products of the LEs and SOEs, and a marketplace that promoted societal goods.

As noted above, much of the state's role was not economically
but politically motivated—it was the result of the regime's pursuit
of noneconomic goals (power, stability, defense, and so forth). The
industrial structure was not designed to provide a marketplace in
which SMEs might flourish, but this was its effect. Moreover, the
state's role in defining the industrial structure was critical but not
always intended. The state was not only the unwitting architect of
this unique industrial structure but also, when it realized the significance and utility of this industrial structure to its rule, the witting and watchful policeman guarding this division of labor. The
role of the state came about because of its dealings with private-
sector actors. The magnitude of these interactions, including indirect and invisible relations, was far greater than coordination
through institutional linkages.

The clear-cut cleavage between the two markets in which the
SOEs and LEs monopolized the domestic market whereas the
SMEs had a free run in the export markets was a striking feature of

Taiwan's political economy until the mid-1970s. I will argue that
the political strategies of the state changed at that time as it sought
a new basis for its legitimacy in response to U.S. recognition of the
People's Republic of China (PRC). The new strategy was Taiwanization and a concerted effort to link legitimacy to the success of
the SMEs. The promotion of the semiconductor and computer industries was the first example of a willingness both to target the
SMEs and to allow the LEs to expand into new economic activities.
The state became less and less the policeman of upstream economic
activities and more and more the champion of integrated industrial
development. One consequence was that the two-market division
was not replicated in new or high-tech industries. This new marketplace was an integrated market. Unlike the dual-market structure, which was largely an accidental consequence of state action,
the integrated market was an intentional policy goal. The changing
role of the state in the formation of the marketplace reflected
changes in the state's view of industrial development—it was increasingly committed to integrated sectoral development. It was
also a consequence of the changes in the state's political concerns
in response to shifts in the nature and structure of the state, as well
as in state-society relations and international circumstances. This is
not, however, to imply that a new institutionalized steering capacity had come into existence. The success of industrial promotion in
both the semiconductor and the computer industries was the work
of two remarkable men. Their leadership proved decisive.

The Role of SOEs in the Industrial Structure

The SOEs played a strategic role in the state's policing and design
of the marketplace. Statist analyses have noted but not fully inter-
preted the significance of the SOEs. According to Wade, the SOEs
were used by the state as a policy instrument for governing the
market. Whether this was a reason for or the result of the arm's-
length relationship between the bureaucracy and the private sector,
the heavy presence of SOEs helped cement cooperation between
the bureaucracy and private firms. The SOEs were also used to influence private capital by inducing private investment in new fields

with high entry barriers and to influence downstream industries through price policies.[42]

Taiwan is not unique in having SOEs. In all countries, the state acts not only as a regulator but also as a producer.[43] Furthermore, in many countries, the state plays the role of demiurge by becoming directly involved in productive activities in ways that not only complement private investment but also replace or compete with private producers.[44] The provision of infrastructure and other products and services is a traditional state role. Although the economic presence of the Taiwan state is among the highest in the developing economies,[45] the difference is one of degree, not of type. However, Taiwan is unique in that the state owned all upstream industries. The impact of this was far reaching. It affected not only policy instruments and public-private cooperation but the marketplace as well.

The upstream SOEs played a dual strategic role in the formation and persistence of Taiwan's industrial structure. First, the presence of the upstream SOEs was a precondition for the establishment of Taiwan's most important industries, such as petrochemicals, steel, and information. The establishment of the SOEs came in response to the development of downstream SMEs in fields such as petrochemicals and to the initiation of new industries, such as the information industry. Although the SOEs emerged in the petrochemical industry as a response to the backward linkage of the downstream SMEs, they induced the emergence of intermediate industries through investment by the LEs. The role of the naphtha-cracking plants built by the China Petroleum Corporation (CPC) are striking examples.[46] This model was repeated in the contribution of state-sponsored or joint state-private ventures—Taiwan Semiconductor, United Microelectronics, Industrial Technology Research Institute, and Electronics Research Service Organization—to the development of the semiconductor industry.[47] Without these upstream SOEs, the LEs would not have invested in this sector because the risks would have been too high.

But the significance of the SOEs goes far beyond intervention to having or not having certain industries. In this regard, judging the SOEs strictly in terms of efficiency is too narrow because it minimizes their significance in the economy. What is noteworthy in the case of Taiwan is that the SOEs helped solve coordination problems when market failures occurred in the steel, petrochemical, and semiconductor industries. During the initial stage of these industries, the LEs had no interest in investing in them. There was a market failure because market forces on their own did not lead to the development of these industries. Thus, there was a need for coordination to remedy the market failure. The SOEs played such a role by initiating new projects, often at the expense of efficiency. For example, in order to promote the intermediate petrochemical industries, the upstream SOEs sacrificed profits to fulfill their policy tasks.[48]

The Industrial Structure, Societal Goods, and the Production System

Taiwan's singular industrial structure is widely acknowledged. In Zhou Tiancheng's "dichotomous market structure," for example, the LEs are the major players in the domestic market, which is highly protected and characterized by monopolies and high entry barriers. Production and sales are equally important in the domestic market. The SMEs dominate the export market, which is highly competitive and rather open with low entry barriers.[49] However, Zhou's definition of Taiwan's industrial structure is incomplete. In this book, Taiwan's industrial structure is defined by the strict tripartite division of labor and the dualistic market structure analyzed above. The concept of a "dichotomous market structure" addresses only the division between the domestic market and export markets and fails to include the division of labor among the SOEs, LEs, and SMEs. Thus, this theory neglects the role of the SOEs in the economy.

The book addresses the critical significance of the industrial structure because it views that structure as a necessary condition for the success of the SMEs. This distinguishes this work from the existing literature on Taiwan. However, it is not my intent to suggest that the industrial structure in itself accounts for the success of SMEs. Rather, the industrial production system was able to mobilize societal goods to offset the SMEs' disadvantages and to maximize their advantages.

Societal goods and a production system exist in a particular marketplace, which can facilitate or constrain their mobilization. The operation of an industrial structure is dependent on a market configuration that allows for its existence and facilitates its functioning. The functioning of a production system depends in turn on whether it can mobilize societal goods to overcome disadvantages and maximize advantages. The industrial structure in Taiwan provided space in which the production system could operate. And the production system that emerged was able to mobilize a complex of societal goods. This complex facilitated the operation of the production system that was responsible for the performance of the SMEs. Together, the industrial structure, societal goods, and the production system formed the sufficient condition for the success of the SMEs.

The term "societal goods" closely parallels Aoki Masahiko's notion of "private institutions." According to Aoki and his co-editors,[50] private institutions include firms, trade associations, financial intermediaries, workers' and farmers' organizations, business customs, and so forth. What is critical for Aoki is that the institutions are privately sponsored rather than state sponsored. However, the social resources of importance to Taiwan's SMEs include but are not reducible to private institutions. Whereas Aoki's term nicely captures institutions such as the informal financial system, kinship, and the cooperative network, it excludes noninstitutional social phenomena, such as cultural and social traits, that permit and sustain cheap labor, flexible production, and industrial clustering. I thus prefer to refer to these as "societal goods." This broader term allows us to encompass the noninstitutional elements in our analysis. Moreover, their construction as "goods" permits us to distinguish between "goods" that are free (e.g., cultural traits and kinship) and those that are not (e.g., cheap labor and an informal financial system).

"Production system" refers to the system developed by Taiwan's SMEs in response to circumstances related to the capital shortage. It was in essence a "capital-substituting industrial system" in which at all stages, from product choice to technology choice, production methodology, management, and marketing, the goal was to reduce capital costs. This production system was the source of the SMEs' competitiveness because it minimized their disadvantages and maximized their comparative advantages.[51] This production system enabled the SMEs to operate as competitive exporters. Indeed, I shall argue that much of the SMEs' success can be attributed to their ability to mobilize societal goods in support of the industrial system, a system designed to compensate for and to overcome their disadvantages (above all, capital shortages and difficulty of access to capital). The pursuit of a solution to these financial problems was tantamount to the pursuit of efficiency.

Two caveats about the position taken in this book are in order. First, despite the emphasis on the consequences of state political actions for economic development, it is not my intention to minimize the importance of state economic goals. My thesis is that it is insufficient to view the role of the state in economic development solely in terms of its economic goals. In fact, it is often difficult to distinguish clearly between political and economic goals. The truth is that the KMT regime faced two sets of contradictions. The first was between the regime's political concerns and the need for economic development. As we will see, often the political concerns had top priority on the regime's agenda. This was clearly the case during the Chiang Ching-kuo era and was one outcome of Chiang's dominance over economic policy. Many economic policies arose because of political concerns, and this gave rise to tensions between the political leaders and the bureaucrats, who tended to view economic issues from an economic perspective. The second set of contradictions was between the bureaucrats' ideology and their commitment to economic development. Bureaucrats are not a group of value-free people. They have their own ideologies and preferences, which are not always consistent with their roles as regulators and promoters of the economy. As we will see, ideology often conflicted with the bureaucrats' commitment to develop the economy. In the early stages of industrialization in Taiwan, the command economy was the major ideology of the technocrats. But conflicts emerged between this ideology and the market economy. From the 1970s on, as the KMT became increasingly preoccupied with restricting the fast-growing business groups, the focus shifted to restraining the LEs and promoting new industries. This resulted in conflicts in both the petrochemical and the information industries. These two sets of contradictions illustrate the complexity of state goals and their impact on the course of economic development. The political factors in Taiwan's economic development have thus far largely been underestimated. I hope the effort in this book to address their importance will draw scholarly attention to the complexity of the role of the state in the process of economic development.

The second caveat concerns the KMT's restrictive and protective policy toward the LEs. Basically, KMT policy toward the LEs vacillated between protecting and restricting them, that is, between creating supporters and preventing the growth of rivals, throughout the entire period under study in this book. It is difficult to separate these two sets of contradictory policies since they often went hand in hand. The emphasis on one or the other varied over time according to changes in the regime's political and economic concerns and priorities, and these changing concerns and priorities determined the different directions and contents of state policy.

On the one hand, the state needed the LEs for both economic and political reasons. The state needed some firms to play certain economic functions, such as providing products that met basic needs or earning foreign exchange or developing industries that were viewed by the state as significant to the entire economy. But the state also needed political supporters. To meet these two goals, the state created and protected a group of LEs by providing a wide range of rents, including entry and import controls, quotas, foreign exchange, tax exemptions, loans, subsidies, and so forth. These rents were not, however, always "contingent rents"[52] or "performance-indexed rewards."[53] Rather, the provision of rents was often designed to serve a political goal—the rents were exchanged for political loyalty and support. Moreover, these rents resulted not in the expansion of exports by LEs but in the strengthening of the

position of the LEs in the domestic market. In other words, the
state in Taiwan did not set export performance as a requirement
for rents. This constitutes a sharp difference with the South Korean case; there the state mandated export performance as a prerequisite for cheap credit to the business groups.[54]

The state in Taiwan was always sensitive to potential challenges
from rivals, both because of its one-party rule and because of its
status an émigré regime. The KMT regime had a history of fearing
challenges from business.[55] As a result, the KMT did not forge alliances with capitalists.[56] The fact that the majority of capitalists that
the KMT faced in Taiwan were native Taiwanese reinforced these
traditional fears.

Another reason for the restrictive LE policy was the regime's
desire to maintain the SOEs' monopoly and to protect their interests. This motive was both economic and political because the huge
SOEs were major sources of the state's political influence and economic might. There were two main categories of restrictions: those
on strategic industries, including infrastructure, the banking sector,
and upstream industries; and those on firm size. These restraints
were consistent with Sun Yat-sen's ideology and political rhetoric:
to protect the interests of ordinary people, to maintain an equal
distribution of wealth, and to prevent a private monopoly over
key sectors.

However, these policies sometimes contravened the interests of
the regime. The state was never monolithic and centralized, particularly as the state machine grew and became more diversified,
vested interests formed within different state agencies, and relationships developed with business groups. For example, legislators,
who often had business or local political backgrounds, pursued interests that could undermine the state's efforts to restrict LEs.
SOEs, the state-owned banks in particular, grew in influence as
they became more independent. In explaining the banks' relationships with the LEs, we need to distinguish the impact of state policy and the banks' pursuit of their own interests. That is to say, in
explaining the concentration of loans from publicly owned banks
to LEs, we need to distinguish between state intentions and the
banks' actions to further their own interests.

The Provision of Industrial Finance
and the Industrial Structure

The provision of industrial finance played a particularly important role in the designing and policing of the marketplace by the state. As indicated above, Taiwan's industrial structure was supported by a dual financial structure: an organized, or formal, financial system and the unorganized, or underground, financial market.[57] The organized system was the major source of financing for the SOEs and the LEs, and the unorganized market for the SMEs. This book addresses the question of the role of the state in the formation of this dual financial system and the system's consequences for the industrial structure.

John Zysman views the discretionary allocation of industrial credit as a "particularly effective instrument" of industrial policy; indeed, he sees it as the single tool necessary for all state-led industrialization.[58] He describes two basic patterns of development: state-led and market-led and, accordingly, two basic financial systems: a credit-based system with prices administered by the government, and market-led financing based on capital markets, with resources allocated by prices established in a competitive market. Taiwan had the first kind of financial system. According to Zysman, three questions are relevant to the provision of industrial finance: (1) Do one or several financial institutions exert discretionary power over financial flows, that is, have the power to influence who uses funds and on what terms? (2) Is market power used selectively and intentionally to affect the decisions of firms or the organization of an industry? (3) Can the government employ the financial system or institutions as an instrument in its dealings with the industrial economy? (It can do this either by discriminating between firms or sectors in granting access to funds or by creating financial packages that can be used to bargain with companies.)[59]

Thomas Hellmann and his coauthors make an important distinction between financial repression and financial restraint. "Financial repression" refers to a regime in which the government extracts rents from the private sector by creating high inflation and generates rent-seeking activities in the private sector. By contrast, under financial restraints, the government creates rent opportunities within the private sector through its control over deposit and lending rates. Such controls affect the distribution of rents to the different sectors. The rents in turn strengthen the incentives for banks and firms to increase their outputs of goods and services.[60] The concept of financial restraint is particularly relevant to the bank-LE relationship in Taiwan.

Taiwan is well known for the rigidity and inelasticity of its state-owned financial system. Assessments of the effectiveness of this financial system have, however, differed. Whereas most observers view the system as inefficient in resource allocation, there are those who assume that it must have contained enough resilience and elasticity to meet the needs of the rapidly growing economy.[61] Others speculate that the factors that made the system rigid helped the government implement its sectoral industrial policies and promote economic development.[62] But most research ignores the linkage between the financial system and the industrial structure. Although there are studies of the relationship between a selective industrial policy and the selective allocation of credit, studies that examine the role of industrial finance in the promotion of strategic industries generally confine their observations to the sectoral level and view the effect of the provision of credit on the development of particular industries only in terms of the industries themselves. This is not sufficient to explain Taiwan's economic success. Nor is it sufficient to explain the success of Taiwan's industries from a horizontal perspective because that viewpoint ignores the vertical division of industrial labor. The horizontal sectoral perspective can explain only how the state used a policy of selective credit to promote particular industries, and it is inadequate to link the success of particular industries to the selective credit policy. Furthermore, this perspective cannot explain the success of the SMEs that were not recipients of the selective credit. Therefore, we must view the provision of industrial finance from a broader viewpoint that can explain the relationship between the provision of industrial finance and the division of industrial labor.

In particular, three questions need to be answered. First, what is the role of the state in the formation and persistence of the dual financial structure? Second, what is the relationship between the formal financial system and the industrial structure? Third, in what way has the state used the provision of credit to influence the division of industrial labor among the SOEs, LEs, and SMEs?

The literature answers the formation aspect of the first question, but it ignores the role of the state in the persistence of the dual financial structure. As I show in subsequent chapters, the state not only contributed to the formation of the dual financial structure but also safeguarded the structure through both intentional and unintentional measures. The formal financial system supported industries that served the domestic market.

The second question is widely neglected in the existing literature. Zhou Tiancheng is one of the few economists who has noted this linkage. He suggests that the formal financial system supports mainly those industries serving the domestic market whose operators are LEs.[63] But his point needs to be elaborated on with more evidence. The book looks further at this issue.

The third question is related to the selective industrial and selective credit policies, but it goes deeper. The book ties the provision of credit to the industrial structure and focuses particularly on the implications of the provision of credit by the state banks to the maintenance of the activities of the LEs in the intermediate-stream industries. As discussed in Chapter 6, the rent opportunities created by the financial restraints reinforced the intermediate-stream and inward-oriented activities of the LEs.

Chapters 2 and 3 examine the origins of state–private sector relations in postwar Taiwan. Chapter 4 looks at how the close state-LE relationship was formed under state protection during the 1950–56 period and studies its implications for Taiwan's unique industrial structure. Chapter 5 explores the conflict between the state's export goals and its efforts to discourage LEs from exporting and the effects of this paradox on the emergence of SMEs in the export market. Chapter 6 analyzes how public policy helped shape the industrial structure. Chapter 7 discusses the political and economic bases for the state's public policy toward LEs and SMEs and the consequences of this public policy for traditional markets and markets for new industries. Chapter 8 focuses on the relationship among state action, the market, and the success of the SMEs. Chapter 9 concludes the book by summarizing its major findings and discussing their implications for comparative political economy.

CHAPTER 2

Formation of the State: The Rebuilding of the KMT State on Taiwan

The KMT state on Taiwan was formed in special historical circumstances: under threat from its Communist rival, a huge state machine was established in the former Japanese colony. Because of the island's geopolitical significance, it was taken under the umbrella of U.S. protection. What kind of state was formed? What were its strengths and weaknesses? What impact did it have on society and the private sector? What were the regime's political and economic goals and its strategies for achieving these goals? This chapter focuses on these questions and examines the reconstruction of the state and its international context, the formation of the public sector and its implications for the state and the economy, the early goals of the state, the economic bureaucracy, and the issue of "trust" in the KMT bureaucracy. I argue that the nature of the rebuilt state on Taiwan determined the ways it managed the economy and the ways it dealt with the private sector during the next two decades. These actions in turn influenced the formation of Taiwan's industrial structure.

State Rebuilding

Taiwan became a colony of Japan in 1895 as a result of China's defeat in the Sino-Japanese war. In 1945, following Japan's defeat in World War II, Taiwan reverted to Chinese sovereignty. In 1949, the KMT central government, after losing the civil war, retreated to

Taiwan. At that time the island had almost no local industry and faced serious threats from the mainland forces on the other side of the strait. The outbreak of the Korean War in June 1950 led to the incorporation of Taiwan into the American anticommunist front in East Asia, and Taiwan became the recipient of some $100 million in U.S. aid per year from 1951 to 1965. As the primary resource available to the island (over and above routine revenues), this aid became increasingly important to Taiwan. Naturally and inevitably, the state came to have a dominant position over society. State-private sector relations were shaped by these circumstances.

After fleeing to Taiwan in 1949, the KMT regime faced the urgent task of rebuilding the state on the island against a background of mounting international and internal difficulties. Internationally, the Truman administration explicitly expressed a hands-off policy toward Taiwan.[1] Taiwan was thus highly vulnerable to an attack from the mainland. Internally, the state faced strong hostility from the Taiwanese because of the February 28 Incident. A sharp decrease in production and hyperinflation imperiled both the economy and the financial sector. The relocation of two million immigrants from the mainland, which increased the population from six to eight million, created chaos on the small island. The influx of so many immigrants led to American predictions of unrest.[2] In response, the KMT built a highly repressive state machine and imposed austerities in order to maintain and consolidate its rule. Under this system, the state's grip stretched from the political realm to society and the economy.

The KMT established a one-party political system on the island. Since most of the major KMT factional leaders on the mainland did not flee to Taiwan, there was a sharp decrease in intraparty power struggles, and the KMT was able to reform itself. President Chiang Kai-shek dissolved the KMT's Central Executive Committee in 1950 and in its stead set up the Reform Committee. He also placed his supporters in key party positions and gained control over the nominations for membership on the Central Standing Committee (CSC). This reform and reshuffling effectively reduced internal factional struggles. The Chiangs also monitored the factions through their intelligence agency and played them off one another. The huge public sector enabled the state to be economically and financially independent from society, especially from business. This allowed, and even encouraged, the state to practice political strategies aimed at dominating society and to avoid being captured by the main social classes. Through authoritarian and corporatist arrangements, the KMT regime came to control the society. These political strategies in turn determined the ways in which the state dealt with the private sector.

This rebuilt state shared several characteristics with the Japanese colonial regime it replaced. Japanese colonial rule had been highly repressive, and among its legacies to the KMT was a weak and fragmented society. The KMT regime continued the authoritarian tradition of Japanese rule. To govern this society, the state restructured and reformed the huge state machine that had previously ruled the mainland. The sheer size of this machine, with its complex structure and many personnel, led to the absolute dominance of the state over society.

The KMT also realized that lax discipline and rampant corruption had contributed to its failure on the mainland, and it conducted a thorough reform of the party in the early 1950s. As a quasi-Leninist party, the KMT established a hierarchy of party organizations to oversee government at each level and concentrated power in the CSC, which was controlled by the chairman of the party. State policy was completely subject to KMT policy. "No branch of the state apparatus, not even the judiciary, was immune from the penetration by the party organization or the influence of party bureaucrats."[3]

The KMT state used its unique history, the teachings of Sun Yat-sen, international diplomatic recognition, and the confrontation between the two sides of the Taiwan Strait to create a strong ideology in support of its rule.[4] With society under the tight and systematic control of the party, the KMT succeeded in weaving a huge ideological net that included a Chinese identity, its claim to be the sole legitimate government of all China, its history as a national revolutionary party, the worship of a paramount leader (Chiang Kai-shek), and reinforcement of the people's fear of communism.[5] This ideology forged a strong psychological buttress for KMT rule.

To these ideological supports, the KMT added a repressive machinery and imposed martial law. Proclaimed in May 1949, martial
law would last until July 1987, the longest such suspension of civil
rule in history. Under the resulting state of siege, almost all civil
activities were proscribed, and a huge security and intelligence system penetrated every corner of the government as well as the entire society.

The state's dominance of society paralleled the dominance of the
mainlander minority over the Taiwanese majority. This feature of
the state originated in part from the Japanese legacy. When the
KMT state took over the island from the Japanese, it also took
over a politically weak society and, like the Japanese, was able to
exclude the Taiwanese from the government.

The new state combined this legacy of Japanese rule with its
own reformed state machine. As an émigré regime, the KMT had
both strengths and weaknesses. Its strength was that it did not have
to answer to vested interests in the society and was thus able to
control it. Its weakness was its negligible social base. To overcome
this weakness and to secure its power and rule, the new state created two "infrastructural power"[6] relationships with society. The
first was a "clientelist relationship"[7] in which the state distributed
monopolistic resources among its followers, both mainlanders and
locals, to reward their loyalty. This became the state's chief
method for fostering supporters. The state also established corporatist arrangements to control capitalists, workers, farmers, stu-
dents, and other social forces. There were three major business associations: the National Federation of Industries, the National
Federation of Commerce, and the Chinese National Association of
Industry and Commerce. The KMT set up a hierarchy of organizations within these associations to correspond to each level of government, from the center to the local level.

As noted in Chapter 1, the émigré nature of the regime had
critical consequences for public policy toward the private sector
and the formation of the industrial structure. As a regime with a
weak social base, the KMT state faced a society in which the majority of the population was Taiwanese. In the mainlanders' view,
during their fifty years of enslavement the islanders had acquired

Japanese values and ideas, and because of both the February 28 Incident and the prevalent official corruption and inefficiency of the KMT, they were hostile toward the mainlanders. For its part, the state deeply distrusted the locals and felt insecure about its rule. Its repressive political arrangements and corporatist relations with society were designed to cement its rule, as were its restrictions on the scale of private firms and prevention of their participation in infrastructure, upstream industries, and the banking sector. With the economy dominated by locals, Sun Yatsen's opposition to big capital became a useful ideological tool to justify constraints on the scale of private firms. Limiting big capital in essence amounted to limiting local capital and forestalling the locals from becoming economically strong enough to threaten the KMT's rule. This was the real motive behind its restrictions on big capital. Fifty years of Japanese colonialism and the February 28 Incident had left the locals "leaderless, atomized, quiescent, and apolitical."[8] Under these circumstances, the new KMT state was able to dominate the society. Even so, the KMT never felt secure on the island because locals constituted the majority. This insecurity explains the party's efforts to establish a social base and to secure supporters among the local elite, in particular the capitalists. As we will see in subsequent chapters, the nature of the state and its relations with society dictated its attitudes and public policy toward the private sector and thus had an impact on the industrial structure.

The International Setting:
A Unique Geopolitical Context

The new KMT state on Taiwan benefited from U.S. hostility to mainland China and American efforts to form blocs to contain communism. This international context had not only political but also economic consequences. It is no exaggeration to say that the Korean War, which broke out on June 25, 1950, saved Taiwan. The war forced the United States to reaffirm Taiwan's strategic position in its containment policy and to end its hands-off policy toward Taiwan, a policy it had announced less than a year earlier. Taiwan began receiving U.S. aid in 1951, and the signing of the U.S.-China Mutual Defense Accord in 1954 brought Taiwan under U.S. military protection. As a key link in the global system to contain communism and as the recipient of U.S. aid, Taiwan was secured by external forces and defended by foreign protection. American diplomatic recognition, military protection, and economic aid transformed Taiwan's weaknesses into strengths and constituted a primary source of the regime's legitimacy. Nevertheless, becoming a part of a global system had costs. In exchange, Taiwan had to open itself to foreign influence, and, as we will see, the state's economic policy was largely influenced by the United States.

Furthermore, the U.S.-Taiwan alliance did not betoken shared aims. The KMT government's top priority was to accumulate military power so as to retake the mainland; the United States merely wanted Taiwan to be a link in its containment system. This difference was inevitably reflected in both economic policy and military strategy. Also, despite U.S. aid, the authorities in Taiwan could not resolve the island's mounting difficulties quickly.

Hostile relations with the PRC had two main consequences. On the one hand, Taiwan had to devote over 80 percent of its budget to defense and subject its economy to military goals. On the other, this situation gave the regime a legitimate excuse for its grip on society. The military situation structured not only the economy but also the entire society. This had an effect on state economic policy as well. As we will see, one of the key impacts was that the state did not have its own development strategy.

Shaping the Public Sector

The huge public sector had a significant impact on the formation of the industrial structure as well as on state–private sector relations.[9] First, it was an important source of funding for the state: in 1955, for example, the monopoly revenues and the surplus from public enterprises and public utilities constituted 17.6 percent of government revenues. Second, it was a policy instrument for steering the economy and influencing the private sector.

The proportion of the economy under state control is a remarkable feature of Taiwan's postwar economy. Taiwan had one of the largest public sectors outside the communist bloc. Throughout the

1950s, state corporations accounted for 50 percent or more of industrial production.[10] The average share of the public sector in gross fixed capital formation from 1951 to 1980 was 30.9 percent; among nine noncommunist countries surveyed by R. Short, only India had a higher percentage.[11] The public sector included financial institutions, infrastructure, and upstream industries. This sector originated in confiscated Japanese property, the transplanted mainland state-owned sector, and newly established SOEs. An examination of the immediate postwar formation of this sector is important to understanding the role of the state in economic development. This section examines its two major components: confiscated Japanese property and the transplanted state-owned sector from the mainland.

Confiscated Japanese Property

Japanese property constituted the primary part of the postwar public sector. Two laws, "Measures for Dealing with the Enemy's Property in the Recovered Areas," promulgated by the Executive Yuan (cabinet) in 1945, and "Rules to Take Over Japanese Property in Taiwan Province," promulgated by the Taiwan provincial government in 1946, declared that all properties owned by the Japanese colonial government and by Japanese firms and nationals in Taiwan belonged to the Chinese government. The Takeover Commission, set up under the Taiwan provincial government on October 25, 1945, had confiscated all properties owned by the Japanese Government-General by the end of 1945; the separate Council for Japanese Property was established under the commission in January 1946 to deal with privately owned Japanese property. The task was almost complete in early 1947. By the end of February 1947, the KMT government had assumed control of 593 units of public property (valued at NT$2.94 billion), 129 firms (NT$7.2 billion), and 48,968 units of private property (NT$0.9 billion).[12] All these Japanese holdings were nationalized as "enemy properties."[13]

Of the 860 industrial firms confiscated up to 1950, 775 were Japanese-owned (defined as a Japanese share greater than 50 percent), and 85 were Taiwanese-owned. According to the regulations,

Table 2.1
List of Publicly Owned Firms Restructured
from Former Japanese Firms

Former Japanese firms	Owner-ship	Publicly owned firms
Bank of Taiwan, Taiwan Savings Bank, Japan Sanho Bank	p	Bank of Taiwan
Japan Quanye Bank	p	Taiwan Land Bank
Taiwan Commercial and Industry Bank	p	Taiwan First Commercial Bank
Hua-nan Bank	p	Hua-nan Bank
Chang-hua Bank	p	Chang-hua Bank
Industrial Bank	p	Taiwan Co-operative Bank
Life insurance companies (15)	p	Taiwan Life Insurance, Ltd.
Goods insurance companies (13)	c	Taiwan Goods Insurance, Ltd.
Unlimited companies (4)	c	Taiwan Co-operative Savings Company, Ltd.
Petroleum and gas companies (6)	c	China Petroleum Corporation, Ltd.
Japan Aluminum Company	c	Taiwan Aluminum Corporation
Taiwan Electricity Company	c	Taiwan Electricity Corporation
Sugar companies (4)	c	Taiwan Sugar Corporation
Fertilizer companies (4)	c	Taiwan Fertilizer Corporation
Chemical companies (4)	c	Taiwan Alkali Corporation
Salt companies (3)	c	Taiwan Salt Corporation
Shipbuilding companies (3)	c	Taiwan Shipbuilding Corporation
Iron, machinery companies (3)	c	Taiwan Machinery Corporation
Cement companies (11)	c	Taiwan Cement Corporation
Papermaking companies (7)	c	Taiwan Paper and Pulp Corporation
Monopoly company (alcohol and cigarettes)	p	Taiwan Provincial Monopoly Bureau
Camphor bureau and company (2)	p	Taiwan Camphor Bureau
Agricultural and Forest companies (45)	p	Taiwan Agricultural and Forestry Corporation
Industrial companies (163 small companies in textiles, glass, mining, chemicals, printing, rubber, construction, etc.)	p	Taiwan Industrial and Mining Corporation

Table 2.1, cont.

NOTES: The privatization of the Taiwan Cement Corporation, Taiwan Paper and Pulp Corporation, Taiwan Agricultural and Forestry Corporation, and Taiwan Industrial and Mining Corporation, the "four big corporations," began in 1953 as part of the land-reform program.

"P" indicates a firm owned by the provincial government; "c," one owned by the central government.

SOURCES: Liu Jinqing, *Taiwan zhanhou jingji*, pp. 26–27; Taiwansheng zhengfu xuanchuan weiyuanhui, *Taiwan xianzhuang cankao*, pp. 1–32; Mingzhi chubanshe, *Taiwan jianshe*, pp. 408–548; Taiwan yinhang, Jingji yanjiushi, *Taiwan yinhang jikan* 1, no. 3, pp. 95–159; 12, no. 3, pp. 1–42; 13, no. 4, p. 151; idem, *Taiwan zhi gongye lunji* 2, pp. 14, 17, 61.

enterprises with over 50 percent Taiwanese ownership were to be sold to the local shareholders of the enterprises. Of the 775 Japanese enterprises, 376 were sold or were offered unsuccessfully for sale, and the other 399 were nationalized. There were four types of nationalized firms: central government–owned (state-owned); provincial government–owned; owned jointly by the central and the provincial governments; and owned by a city or county government. The first two types accounted for the majority. Half the firms sold to the private sector were small in scale or were inappropriate for state ownership.

Since the KMT central government did not move to Taiwan until 1949, the National Resources Commission (NRC) represented the central government in the appropriation of Japanese property and the running of important sectors. There was some controversy between the NRC and the provincial government led by Chen Yi as to whether confiscated Japanese firms were to be converted into state- or provincial government–owned firms.[14] As a compromise, the NRC agreed to limit its activities to ten sectors: it enjoyed monopolies in the aluminum, iron and steel, and petroleum industries; together with the provincial government, it ran the sugar, electricity, fertilizer, paper, cement, shipbuilding, and machinery sectors, holding 60 percent of the shares in each. There were 22 firms in the three state-owned sectors and 43 firms in the seven jointly owned sectors. Another 306 firms, in mining, agriculture and forestry, shipping, insurance, construction, and finance, were owned by the provincial government; after restructuring, nine firms were city- or county-owned (see Table 2.1).[15] This arrangement was the result of a compromise between the central government, which wanted

Taiwan to be a link in a division of labor of the mainland economic system, and the Taiwan provincial government, which wanted more economic autonomy.[16]

The ten sectors owned by the central government thereafter became a major force in the state-owned sector affiliated with the MOEA. Both the state-owned and state-provincial jointly owned firms were supported by the provincial government. In particular, the Bank of Taiwan (BOT), which belonged to the provincial government, lent large sums of money to these firms. As discussed in subsequent chapters, the provincial government–owned banks monopolized the financial and banking sector, which remained vital to the economy.

The provincial sector was further expanded by transportation and communications companies, namely, the Taiwan Railway Administration, the Taiwan Road Administration, the Taiwan Post Administration, the Taiwan Telecommunications Administration, and the Taiwan Shipping Company. Consequently, former Japanese property constituted the principal part of the public sector—both state- and provincial government–owned—in Taiwan's postwar economy and thus remained essential to the economy. Liu Jinqing describes the state as occupying the "high commanding position" in industry, finance, and trading.[17]

Relocating State-Owned Enterprises from the Mainland

Another major component of the public sector in Taiwan derived from the mainland state sector. Beginning in 1948, as the civil war on the mainland intensified and grew increasingly unfavorable to the Nationalist Party, public confidence declined. Many people began to move their money and property out of the war-ravaged mainland. Some of this property went to Taiwan. First and foremost among those transferring assets was the KMT government, which began to move large amounts of property to Taiwan as early as 1948. The state-owned firms in this transfer ran the gamut from finance and banking to the textile, steel, agrochemicals, coal, machinery, fishing, transportation, and defense industries. The two most important sectors were banking and textiles. In the financial and banking sector, five major units—the Central Bank, the Central Trust of China, the Bank of Communications, the Bank of China, and China Farmers Bank—moved to Taiwan. Although most of them did not resume operations until the late 1950s and early 1960s, once they reopened, they constituted part of the public-owned financial and banking sector. After reopening in Taiwan in 1949, the Central Trust of China played a key role in carrying out government economic policy by providing industrial loans. The state-owned textile mills dominated the textile sector in the early 1950s because private capital in this sector was still weak, but they soon declined in importance with the rapid development of privately owned competitors. Among the state-owned mills transplanted from the mainland were the China Textile Construction Corporation, Yongxing Textile Company, Zhongben Textile Company, and Taipei Textile.

The opening of these firms reinforced the existing public-owned sector taken over from the Japanese. There were three types of industries in the public sector: financial and banking institutions (including insurance), infrastructure, and basic industries (those dealing in energy, important raw materials, agriculture, machinery, and basic goods). All these industries were economically strategic. The share of the public sector in overall industrial production reached as high as 70 percent in 1947. The public sector was an important resource and a major strength of the state, allowing it to exert substantial leverage over the economy. Within the public sector, the banks and other financial institutions were particularly important to the subsequent development of industry.

The Japanese-owned banks were restructured as several new banks: the BOT, First Commercial Bank, Hua-nan Bank, Chang-hua Bank, Taiwan Land Bank, and Cooperative Bank of Taiwan (see Table 2.1). The restructuring was completed in March 1947. The three commercial banks—First Commercial, Chang-hua, and Hua-nan—continued to be organized as corporations, whereas the BOT, Taiwan Land Bank, and Co-operative Bank of Taiwan were noncorporate entities. The state owned over 50 percent of the shares in all six banks. The Japanese private financial and banking system was thus restructured as the KMT state's publicly owned system.

Before 1949, only the Central Trust of China had set up a branch in Taiwan. Other major mainland banks, such as the Central Bank of China, the Bank of China, the Bank of Communications, and the China Farmers Bank, did not move to Taiwan until 1949 and, as mentioned above, did not resume operations until the late 1950s and the early 1960s. Therefore, the restructured banks were dominant. The BOT played the de facto role of the central bank in Taiwan until 1961, the year the Central Bank was reactivated.

In short, the large-scale public-owned sector was formed under unique circumstances. The defeated Japanese left an enormous amount of property, and the incoming KMT government took over all their property. This huge public sector, combined with the other resources it already held, distinguished the newly emerging state in Taiwan both from the former colonial state and from the KMT-led state on the mainland. In a sense it was similar to the Japanese colonial state in terms of its monopoly over the economy. But there were also vast differences. The Japanese colonial government by no means monopolized the *entire* economy. Rather, private capital dominated the colonial economy. The economy was monopolized by Japanese, but not by the Japanese government. Out of a total of ¥26–27 billion of Japanese capital entering Taiwan during the fifty years of Japanese rule, only ¥3.5 billion, or about 13 percent, was state capital.[18] When the KMT government superseded the Japanese, however, both at the state and at the private level, it became the sole owner of all important, large-scale firms. Although the KMT government had governed the public sector on the mainland, the scale of its operations in Taiwan was incomparably larger. On a small island with a small economy, the large public sector gave the state unprecedented economic strength. In this respect, it was not the same state that had existed on the mainland. As we shall see in the following chapters, what is more important is that the public sector formed in the early days and the SOEs created in the 1960s and 1970s monopolized the upstream industries, contributing to a unique industrial structure that led to SME-dominated industrialization.

Tasks and Goals

A state's economic tasks and goals encompass not only economic policy but also its means for achieving these goals. In the first decade of its rule on Taiwan, the KMT set itself four goals: restoring production, earning foreign exchange, maintaining defense expenditures, and fighting inflation.

Restoring production. Taiwan's economy was seriously damaged by Allied bombing during World War II. At the end of the war, agricultural production was only 45 percent of that in 1939, the most productive year under Japanese rule, and industrial production only one-third.[19] Most sizable modern factories had been destroyed during the bombing—two-thirds of the factories were severely damaged.[20] In 1948, industrial production was only 59 percent of that in 1941. Due to a lack of capital and technology, economic recovery proceeded very slowly.

All this occurred during the process of state rebuilding. The top priority of the state was to maintain itself in power despite the threat from the mainland. In order to achieve this goal, the state had to impose an ironclad rule. Meanwhile, increasing production to meet the basic needs of the enlarged population after the devastation of the war was an urgent priority. Economically, the sequence of state priorities was stabilization, survival, and self-sustainability rather than development.

When Taiwan reverted to Chinese rule, the economic structure of the island remained unchanged. It was still a colonial economy, now subject to China, exporting rice and sugar to the mainland, mainly to Shanghai and other coastal areas, and importing industrial products. But in 1949, Taiwan's trade relations with the mainland, to which its entire economy had been tied since 1945, were suddenly severed. Taiwan was immediately transformed from a colonial into an independent economy. This abrupt and dramatic change forced Taiwan to become self-sustaining, even as mounting problems jeopardized its survival.

In testimony before the Legislative Yuan in 1954, Yin Zhongrong, the head of the IDC, described Taiwan's predicament:

After retrocession, Taiwan's economy was severed from the Japanese economy. Since then, it should have become part of the mainland economy. The mainland should have replaced investment and technology from Japan. Trade should have shifted from Japan to the mainland. But unfortunately, the Communists occupied the mainland. Taiwan changed from a dependent economy to an independent economy. Thus, it fell into dire straits—no market for exports, lack of foreign exchange for imports, shortage of capital for economic development, and wanting in technology and managerial personnel.[21]

Curbing inflation. The runaway inflation resulted from the sharp reduction in production, the abrupt increase in the size of population, an enormous supply of money, the inflow of mainland capital, and variable rates between the Taiwan dollar and the mainland currency before the KMT central government moved to the island.[22] Retail prices increased a thousandfold from 1946 to 1949. The arrival of the central government and exorbitant military expenditures led to a large government deficit, which in turn kept the inflation rate high. Retail prices increased 8.3-fold from 1949 to 1952. One-third of the government's gold reserves, which had been secretly shipped from the mainland, were sold to make up for the huge deficit. The printing and issuing of paper money became the main vehicle for this purpose. From 1949 to 1952, the money supply increased 12.3-fold. The high inflation and huge deficits formed a vicious cycle. Although the hyperinflation eased in 1952, chronic inflation continued throughout the 1950s. Because fighting inflation was a never-ending task for the bureaucrats, it had an immense impact on economic policy making.

Earning foreign exchange. Meanwhile, the foreign exchange reserves were exhausted. In 1950, in order to pay its foreign debts, the BOT had to borrow $500,000 from the Aviation Company. By the end of the next year, the BOT found itself in an extremely embarrassing situation—it had not only used up all its foreign exchange reserves but even owed $10,000,000 to foreign banks. As a result, foreign banks were rejecting the letters of credit (called "authorities to purchase" at the time) issued by the BOT. Without foreign exchange, imports virtually halted. Taiwan had truly come to the end of its rope. The balance of payments remained the top problem throughout the 1950s and became the major reason for controlling the economy during most of the 1950s. As we will see, it was also the main motivation for the regime's trade liberalization and the shift in emphasis to exports in the latter part of the decade.

Maintaining defense expenditures. Sustaining its huge defense expenditures was also a top priority of the government during this period. During 1951–65, defense expenditures consistently formed about 85 percent of the outlays of the national government and averaged from 9 to 11 percent of GNP.[23] This policy was based on two major goals: defending the island from attack by the Communists in the immediate term and retaking the mainland in the long term. To meet these two goals, the entire economy was restructured and mobilized on a wartime basis.[24] Economic recovery and economic development took place under the burden of heavy military expenditures. Indeed, the point should be made even more forcefully. Between 1950 and 1962, expenditures on defense and diplomacy averaged 76 percent, and on the economy and transportation 0.6 percent. Clearly, economic recovery and economic development occurred at the very margins of the state's concern (see Table 2.2).

The Economic Bureaucracy: Organization, Personnel, and Ideology

Economic recovery and economic development were dependent on the economic bureaucracy. The restructuring of this bureaucracy centered on realizing the state's tasks and goals, but these bureaucrats were not mere implementers of the state policy. The key bureaucrats and their economic ideas also had an impact on economic policy.

Restructuring the Economic Bureaucracy

During the 1950s, the economic bureaucracy comprised the MOEA, the MOF, the BOT (the de facto central bank until 1960 when the Central Bank was reactivated), and the Foreign Exchange and

Table 2.2

Yearly Expenditures of the Central Government by Category, 1950–85
(percentage of total)

Fiscal year	Total	General administration	Defense & diplomacy	Education, science & culture	Economy, transportation	Investment in business	Social welfare	Debt payments	Subsidies to local govts.	Other payments
1950	100.0	6.8	89.4	0.7	1.2	0.2	0.1	1.4	–	0.3
1951	100.0	9.6	80.3	0.7	0.4	2.2	0.1	6.4	–	0.1
1952	100.0	8.9	73.8	1.0	0.7	1.5	0.1	7.1	–	6.9
1953	100.0	9.9	63.0	0.9	0.5	1.3	0.2	2.9	20.8	0.5
1954*	100.0	9.9	65.4	1.4	0.6	0.7	0.1	2.1	16.2	3.6
1954	100.0	7.8	65.0	1.5	0.3	0.4	0.1	1.6	19.8	3.5
1955	100.0	10.3	80.7	2.1	0.7	2.7	0.2	2.0	–	1.3
1956	100.0	11.2	78.5	3.5	0.1	2.5	0.9	1.5	–	1.1
1957	100.0	9.9	78.7	3.2	0.5	2.4	0.4	1.1	2.8	1.1
1958**	100.0	10.1	74.9	2.6	0.5	2.3	1.9	0.8	5.9	1.0
1960	100.0	10.3	74.0	2.8	0.6	1.2	1.5	1.4	7.0	1.2
1961	100.0	11.0	76.3	3.0	0.7	1.5	1.8	4.3	0.7	0.8
1962	100.0	11.4	70.5	3.2	0.8	4.4	2.7	5.7	–	1.2
1963	100.0	–	86.2	2.8	0.9	3.4	2.7	3.6	0.4	0.0
1964	100.0	–	81.4	2.8	1.0	3.2	2.8	5.5	1.3	2.0
1965	100.0	–	71.8	2.5	0.9	13.9	2.3	6.2	0.7	1.8
1966	100.0	–	77.4	4.1	1.7	3.6	2.8	4.8	0.3	5.3
1967	100.0	–	65.9	3.8	1.4	13.9	7.3	7.3	0.4	–
1968	100.0	–	72.5	4.5	2.1	2.3	7.8	6.8	3.5	0.5

1969	100.0	—	5.3	2.2	6.6	9.4	9.7	1.9	4.8
1970	100.0	—	6.0	3.1	3.6	10.0	7.5	2.2	1.6
1971	100.0	—	6.6	1.8	6.0	11.0	10.0	1.0	0.9
1972	100.0	—	7.6	2.4	8.1	14.9	8.4	1.7	1.3
1973	100.0	—	6.8	2.2	13.7	12.8	6.4	2.0	2.4
1974	100.0	—	8.1	2.3	9.0	12.2	5.4	3.9	1.2
1975	100.0	12.4	5.7	2.3	15.7	11.0	3.6	5.9	1.2
1976	100.0	6.7	6.3	3.9	16.4	13.0	2.6	5.6	1.3
1977	100.0	7.8	6.4	5.5	15.7	12.2	2.0	4.2	1.0
1978	100.0	4.3	6.0	4.7	18.1	11.7	9.1	3.9	0.9
1979	100.0	4.2	6.6	5.3	18.6	12.2	0.4	4.6	0.8
1980	100.0	4.0	6.8	6.8	19.2	12.8	2.2	7.3	0.7
1981	100.0	4.1	8.3	12.8	15.1	12.5	1.8	4.9	0.7
1982	100.0	4.4	9.2	9.5	15.4	14.7	1.7	4.4	0.6
1983	100.0	4.7	10.7	7.8	9.6	15.7	2.0	4.3	1.6
1984	100.0	4.9	10.9	8.4	9.2	17.5	3.8	3.1	1.5
1985	100.0	5.2	11.5	9.5	8.4	16.7	4.5	3.4	1.1

NOTE: The figures shown are those given in the sources and may not total 100 percent because of rounding. A dash indicates that no figure was available.

*The data are for January–June 1954. Thereafter, the fiscal year was changed to July to June of the next year.

**Fiscal year 1958 ran from July 1958 to June 1959; there was no fiscal year 1959; fiscal year 1960 ran from July 1959–June 1960.

SOURCES: Calculated from Caizhengbu, *Zhonghua minguo jinrong tongji* (1967), pp. 36–37; and idem, *Zhonghua minguo jinrong tongji nianbao* (1986), pp. 116–17.

Trade Control Commission (FETCC). One might have expected these organizations to dominate policy making, but in fact they did not. Instead, the U.S. aid–financed councils outside the constitutional ministries played a crucial role in policy formulation and implementation.

Normally, the MOEA and its subordinate departments and the MOF should have had much say in industrial policy. However, they faced two types of restrictions. The first was internal—the lack of qualified staff. Either because of their disappointment with the KMT government or the attractions of the communist government's fresh image and ambitious goals, or because of the factional struggles within the KMT, many staff in these two ministries did not follow the KMT to the island in 1949. The NRC was a typical case. Most NRC staff members, including its heads, who had been trusted by Chiang Kai-shek, switched allegiance to the communist government. Only a few migrated to Taiwan. However, some bureaucrats with NRC backgrounds, who shared the idea of state control of the economy, such as Jiang Biao and Yin Zhongrong, remained key policy makers. This phenomenon reflects two facts: the NRC had recruited a group of gifted men, and the government had few options but to use those who accompanied it to Taiwan. Nor were the economics ministries unique in this regard; the lack of qualified staff was a common problem in central government departments.[25]

The second restriction arose from the lack of resources, mainly industrial financing. Taiwan was quite poor in the 1950s. The burgeoning private sector was still weak and needed government help. The government, however, was unwilling to spend money on the economy. The government often ran at a deficit, and the most it could do was to maintain its own survival. Furthermore, as noted above, Taiwan was highly militarized. The military was given top priority on the government agenda, and the economy was basically ignored.[26] Under the principle of military first, it was out of the question to ask the government to provide funds to support economic development. The government's emphasis on defense was not in line with the goals of a developmental state.

In contrast, the U.S. aid–related organs, such as the ESB, the CUSA, and the Sino-American Joint Commission on Rural Reconstruction (SAJCRR), had overwhelming advantages in terms of money and personnel. So, not surprisingly, these became the major players in economic policy formulation and implementation.

Until 1953, the Taiwan provincial government was in charge of almost all economic affairs, including finance and trade. The Taiwan Production Board (TPB, 1949–53) was the most powerful economic organ. Even the MOF had to ask the chief of the provincial Bureau of Finance for money.[27]

In 1953, in a move to enhance efficiency, over twenty agencies were amalgamated to form the ESB. This was the first economic planning institution to be in charge of general economic affairs. It replaced the TPB, albeit with a greatly expanded list of duties. According to regulations, the ESB's major functions were planning, researching, and coordinating economic affairs. However, throughout its existence, from 1953 to 1958, it was the most important and most powerful economic policy–making institution. The ESB was directly under the Executive Yuan. Its members were the heads of economic and financial departments in both the central and the provincial government. Since it was a major institution receiving U.S. aid both for its own operations and for the industrial projects it promoted, it invited the heads of America's Mutual Security Mission to China and other American agencies to its biweekly meetings. There were four departments, one subcommission, and one secretariat under the ESB.

The main task of the ESB, as its name implies, was to stabilize the economy. This was determined both by the specifics of the situation and by government priorities, as noted above. Its activities were financed through the Counterpart Funds, the Taiwan currency derived from U.S. aid. This made the ESB independent of the government budget and allowed it to recruit staff by offering much higher salaries than the government. However, although the ESB enjoyed a relative degree of noninterference from the KMT, lawmakers, and other government departments, as we will see, it was subject to control from the highest leadership and under extreme pressure from U.S. aid agencies.

The core of the ESB was the IDC. The council was created especially to plan and execute the industrial development program. It was not simply an advisory body with little power; nor was it an autonomous organ with freedom to undertake projects with designated sources of funds. Rather, it was an organization similar to the contemporary Cabinet Committee in the United Kingdom, which concentrated authority in the hands of those directly concerned.

The IDC consisted of five full-time members, appointed by the Executive Yuan, and five ex-officio members: the minister of communications, the minister of economic affairs, the secretary-general of the CUSA, the commissioner of the Taiwan Provincial Department of Reconstruction, and the commissioner of the Taiwan Provincial Department of Communications. The IDC had four divisions: general industry, chemical industry, transportation, and finance. The General Industry Section was in charge of electricity, iron and steel, shipbuilding, mining, machinery, and textiles. Its functions ranged from compiling the four-year plan for industrial development to studying industrial policy to examining industrial projects supported by U.S. aid and supervising their implementation. The IDC became the most important agency in economic planning and the chief executive body for industrial projects supported by U.S. aid. In general, in the provision of industrial finance and other resources for industry, the IDC was a key player.

The IDC funds were four times those of the other components of the ESB combined, and its staff numbered 45 in June 1958, two-thirds of the ESB total.[28] In later years, the IDC exceeded its nominal superior, the ESB, in terms of power, staff, and funds. Regular meetings were held every two weeks, and officials from U.S. aid agencies such as the International Cooperation Administration (ICA) were invited to attend as observers. The decisions reached at the IDC meetings were submitted to the ESB for further deliberation, and those approved by the ESB were then forwarded to the responsible administrative agencies for action.

The ESB was dissolved on September 1, 1958. The reason for its dissolution is seemingly not that given by Neil Jacoby: that inflation had been curbed, and development had come to the fore.[29] The government claimed that the ESB's functions overlapped with those of other government departments. This comment was provided in a report on streamlining the government made by the Administration Reform Commission, which was headed by Wang Yunwu, the deputy chairman of the Examination Yuan. Others have claimed, however, that the real reason for its dissolution was the envy of other bodies, which were jealous of the ESB's tremendous powers and outstanding achievements.[30] Although this is subject to further research, my guess is that the dissolution of the ESB was the result of power struggles within the government.

Except for planning, most of its functions were transferred to the CUSA. The dissolution of the ESB caused chaos in the government, because the formal ministries could not fulfill many of its tasks. Soon thereafter, it was realized that a planning agency like the ESB was essential. The CUSA had been founded on the mainland in 1948 to focus on the administration of U.S. aid–related affairs. After a short suspension, it resumed its functions in 1950 in Taiwan. But it remained an agency in charge of formalities. After the CUSA assumed most functions of the ESB, most ex-ESB staff joined it as well. Thus, after enlargement, the CUSA was restructured from an administrative agency to the most powerful economic agency, in charge of all economic development with the exception of agriculture. Since IDC staff played a major role in the CUSA, it was said that the IDC took over the CUSA and not vice versa.[31]

To fill the vacuum in planning caused by dissolution of the ESB, three new groups were set up: the Industrial Planning and Coordination Group (IPCG), the Agricultural Planning and Coordination Group (APCG) under the MOEA, and the Transportation Planning and Coordination Group (TPCG) under the Ministry of Transportation. The staff of these three groups came from the CUSA and the SAJCRR. For example, the IPCG was founded in 1958 to coordinate industrial development after the IDC was dissolved. It was created mainly to plan industrial development and investigate the use of capital and U.S. aid in important industrial plans. Although the IPCG was under the MOEA, the most important staff members had worked for the IDC. K. T. Li was the chairman. The IPCG had less authority than the IDC, however, since it was a ministry organ.

The strength of the three most important and powerful economic planning agencies in the 1950s, the ESB, IDC, and CUSA, was based on two sources—staff and funds. The role of these agencies hinged on a few leading strongmen. More discussion of this issue follows in the remainder of the book. The two sources either derived from or were associated directly with U.S. aid. This situation remained unchanged until the mid-1960s, when the U.S. aid was phased out (it ended in 1965). The personnel in the EPB, IDB, and CUSA spread to the ministries, and beginning in the mid-1960s they began to assume key positions. As we will see in Chapter 6, this change was furthered when Chiang Ching-kuo transferred much of the power from the economic planning commissions to the constitutional ministries as a way of increasing his own weight in economic policy making. Here again the United States had an impact on Taiwan's economic policy making in the 1950s. As shown below, one source of U.S. influence was the pro-U.S. bureaucrats in the U.S. aid–financed economic bodies.

In addition to these two sources of strength, political support from the highest leaders was vital to the importance of the ESB, CUSA, and IDC. The bureaucrats enjoyed the trust of the highest politicians.[32] (For more on the importance of trust in KMT politics, see the last section of this chapter.) This political capital authorized such officials to exercise authority and power, which enabled them to remove obstacles to the formulation and implementation of economic policy. Without a doubt, the ESB, CUSA, and IDC played much greater roles than the formal government departments.

Did the economic planning agencies have autonomy? To answer this question, we must clarify the meaning of autonomy. When statists describe Taiwan's economic bureaucracy as autonomous, they mean that the economic bureaucracy could make decisions independently, without interference from politicians, and could resist pressure from private actors. As we will see, although these economic planning agencies were immune to interference from the KMT, the military, and intelligence, the major players in politics, they had no autonomy from the highest political leaders, and they were not immune to pressure from the business lobbies. Since the leadership role of the strongmen was based on their political support, the economic bureaucracy did not enjoy autonomy from the political leadership. The division of "reign" and "rule" between politicians and bureaucrats in Japan described by Chalmers Johnson did not exist in Taiwan. For the most part, the efficiency of these agencies was attributable not to autonomy but to strong bureaucrats who enjoyed the support of the top political leaders.

The autonomy of the economic planning agencies from society was also not as great as is generally assumed. Although the state dominated society, this does not mean that the economic bureaucracy enjoyed the same level of autonomy from society. Evidence suggests that the economic bureaucracy was not unaffected by the rent-seeking activities of business. As discussed in subsequent chapters, the provision of a wide range of rents was a major way for the state to foster a group of large private enterprises for both economic and political considerations. These rents certainly provided fertile ground for rent-seeking activities by business. It is especially evident that during the period from 1957 to 1959, when the domestic market was saturated, lobbying by private enterprises for restrictions on the construction of new plants was mounting. The Provincial Association of Industries even appealed to the MOEA to permit firms to form a cartel to limit competition. This was not an isolated case. In fact, the government was "perplexed" during these years by "requests [from businesses] to restrict the construction of new factories in their sectors on the grounds that production had already saturated the domestic market."[33] One official (the first head of the Industrial Development Bureau) claimed that he often had to fend off requests by major businessmen to set restrictions on new construction of competing plants and to lift restrictions on them.[34] This situation does not suggest that Taiwan's economic bureaucracy enjoyed an environment free of rent-seeking.

The autonomy of Taiwan's economic bureaucracy from society has been exaggerated by conventional wisdom. This exaggeration is caused by confusion about the KMT state's political dominance over society and the economic bureaucracy's autonomy from society. A regime's political power over society is one thing; the economic bureaucracy's autonomy from society is another. Political dominance cannot guarantee bureaucratic autonomy. Apparently, the political dominance of the KMT state in Taiwan was not converted into the autonomy of the economic bureaucracy from society.

Personnel

Until the late 1970s, the functions of the economic bureaucracy were discharged by a few key, powerful officials rather than by the agencies per se. The U.S.-funded economic agencies were certainly important, but their effectiveness depended on their leaders. The pivotal factors in these men's power were the trust and political support of Chiang Kai-shek and his chief deputy, Chen Cheng. Also instrumental in their success were the forceful personalities of these leading economic bureaucrats, particularly Yin Zhongrong and K. T. Li, who are regarded as the main architects of the Taiwan economic "miracle." The combination of political support and strength of character made it possible for individual bureaucrats to play a leading role in economic affairs. To understand economic policy in Taiwan, we must know something about the backgrounds, ideologies, and even the personal styles of these bureaucrats.

Until his death in 1965, economic affairs were the domain of Chen Cheng. Compared to security, the party, and the military, economic affairs were of lesser importance to the state. After arriving in Taiwan, Chiang Kai-shek never interfered in economic affairs and barred the party from doing so. The powerful Kong-Song faction, which had controlled economic and financial affairs on the mainland, did not follow the KMT to Taiwan. Chiang gave Chen Cheng, his longtime right-hand man, the authority to run the economy. Chen Cheng served as premier (1950–54, 1958–63) and vice president (1954–65). Next to Chiang, he was the most powerful figure in Taiwan. Despite his military background and his general ignorance of economics, Chen Cheng was regarded as open to new ideas, confident in the abilities of the economic bureaucrats, and willing to support their policies even in the face of Chiang Kai-shek's opposition.[35] All the main economic policies during the 1950s and early 1960s—for instance, land reform, foreign exchange and trade reform, the nineteen-point reform package, and the Statute for the Encouragement of Investment—were formulated and implemented under his aegis. And all the key bureaucrats—Yin Zhongrong, K. T. Li, and Yan Jiagan—were his protégés.[36]

Yan Jiagan was a unique and key player on the economic policy team. He served as governor of Taiwan (1954–57), head of the CUSA (1957–58), minister of finance (1958–63), vice chairman of the CUSA (1963–65), head of the CIECD (1963–66), premier (1963–72), vice president (1968–75), and president (1975–78). He was highly trusted by the Chiangs and viewed as very open-minded. His background in the NRC did not prevent him from becoming an advocate of the market. On the economic team, he was known for his powers of persuasion. In meetings, Yan Jiagan would often present Yin Zhongrong's ideas in simple and clear language, making them much more understandable, convincing, and acceptable.[37] Most famously, he persuaded Chiang to freeze defense expenditures, thus paving the way for the adoption of the nineteen-point reform measures. Equally important, Yan Jiagan always supported Yin Zhongrong and K. T. Li's push for market-oriented policies.[38]

Yin Zhongrong was indisputably the key figure on the team. In contrast to Yan, Yin Zhongrong was fairly aggressive and arrogant and unable to convince others to adopt what were often good ideas. As Chen Cheng recounted, "It seemed as if only he [Yin] was right."[39] Yin had also served on the NRC. He had been Song Ziwen's (T. V. Soong) confidential secretary for economic affairs. Song recommended Yin to Chen Cheng. Song was Chiang Kaishek's brother-in-law, minister of finance in the late 1920s and early 1930s, and premier in 1945–47. Yin served as the vice chief of the TPB (1949–53)—which at the time was the most powerful economic organ—president of the Central Trust of China (1950–55), chairman of the IDC (1953–55), minister of economic affairs (1954–55), secretary-general of the ESB (1957–58), vice chairman of the CUSA (1958–63), head of the FETCC (1958–1963), and president of the BOT. With the exception of a short interruption (1955–57), when he was implicated in a case of alleged corruption (he was exonerated), he remained at the core of the policy team. In the late 1950s and early 1960s, Yin was the most powerful economic bureaucrat because of his control of finance, U.S. aid, foreign exchange, and trade. He was the economic tsar of his times, a title later given by the Western media to Vice Premier Zhu Rongji, who is famous for his strong style and who successfully led the overheated Chinese economy to a soft landing in the mid-1990s. As we will see, one reason that Yin Zhongrong was able to play such a significant role was that he had earned the trust of both Chiang Kai-shek and Chen Cheng.

K. T. Li is regarded as the second most important bureaucrat in postwar Taiwan. He served as a member of the IDC (1953–58), secretary-general of the CUSA (1958–63), secretary-general (1963) and vice chairman (1963–65) of the CIECD, minister of economic affairs (1965–59), and minister of finance (1969–76). Many important reforms, such as the Statute for the Encouragement of Investment, were realized either because of his involvement or under his leadership. After Yin Zhongrong's death in 1963, K. T. Li became the most important economic bureaucrat in Taiwan.

Nor were all the powerful economic bureaucrats Chinese. American advisers exercised considerable influence over Taiwan's economic policy making. There is no doubt that American aid helped consolidate and strengthen KMT rule on Taiwan. However, the KMT government's acceptance of aid and protection gave the United States considerable leverage. The KMT state had no choice but to depend on the United States in military, economic, political, and diplomatic affairs. A large number of American military and economic advisers accompanied the aid to the island, and inevitably, aid became an effective means of influence, and even control. Such dependence was quite different from that of the transnational corporations in Latin America.

According to Wen Xinying's research, the Americans used four methods to interfere in KMT government policy making: (1) laws—the China Aid Act of 1948 and the Bilateral Agreement of 1948 between China and the United States; (2) procedures—audits of how the funds were used; (3) acceptance of aid—threats and enticements; (4) personnel—the U.S. aid agency.[40] The U.S. leverage was typically and thoroughly demonstrated in the economic policy making.

The chief U.S. agencies on Taiwan were the U.S. AID Mission to China (hereafter, "the Mission"), the Military Assistance Advisory Group (MAAG), and the U.S. embassy. In economic affairs, the key players were the Mission, the embassy, and the J. G. White Engineering Corporation of New York—a consulting company hired by the KMT government on the recommendation of the U.S. government to examine and supervise the economic aid programs.

The tasks of the Mission ranged from working with the CUSA to help Taiwan government agencies improve economic planning to the collection of economic data for the U.S. government to use in formulating the aid plan. It was in fact a U.S. economic intelligence center. The director of the Mission was extremely powerful and influential because of his role as interpreter of U.S. policies and objectives to the KMT government, his large, de facto authority to select projects, and his influence over the direction of KMT development policies.[41] His impact on the formation of Chinese economic policies was strong and persistent.[42]

The U.S. agencies had direct access to the top authority, Chiang Kai-shek,[43] and used meetings jointly attended by officials from the two sides to express American positions. A major weapon in the U.S. arsenal was a promise to increase or a threat to reduce the level of aid.[44] Americans from the Mission and the embassy regularly attended ESB, IDC, and CUSA meetings. One man who often attended the IDC meetings recalls that the Americans were given to forthright expressions of their opinions, which were mostly positive.[45] "Many decisions were substantially influenced by the Americans," Ye Wan-an, then a staff member of the IDC, concluded.[46]

This influence was reflected in most of the economic policies adopted in the 1950s. The Industrial Plan of the J. G. White Corporation for FYs 1952–55 (draft) had an important impact on the First Four-Year Economic Plan.[47] The nineteen-point reform package, the most important policy in postwar Taiwan, which led to the liberalization of the economy, was initiated by Wesley Haraldson, the director of the Mission. In 1958 and 1959, Haraldson repeatedly criticized Taiwan's policies of deficit spending and limited investment and suggested eight points for reform, in particular, a decrease in military spending, the lifting of foreign exchange controls to promote exports, and a reduction in consumption and an in-

crease in investment. Haraldson linked further U.S. aid to his suggested reforms.[48] His blunt criticisms shocked Taiwan's leading
economic officials and caused them to rethink economic policy.
Consequently, Haraldson, the economic counselor at the U.S. embassy, Yan Jiagan (minister of finance), Yin Zhongrong (CUSA
vice chairman), and K. T. Li (CUSA secretary-general) met with
Chen Cheng to discuss economic issues. Based on their discussions
and Haraldson's suggestions, the CUSA drafted the nineteen-point
reform package.[49] American influence on Taiwan's economic policy was realized through the interaction between the aid agencies
and a group of competent pro-America bureaucrats. The U.S. aid
groups, ESB, IDC, and CUSA, centering around a core group of
bureaucrats under Chen Cheng, remained the most powerful economic policy agencies until the mid-1960s.

Economic Ideology: From Command
Economy to Market Economy

A regime's economic ideology to some extent determines its economic policy. Economic ideology can, however, be affected by the
regime's tasks and goals, and the dominance of a particular ideology may be a response to economic realities. Hence, the acceptance
of certain ideas by a regime is a matter not only of economics but
also of other factors, especially politics. During the 1950s, the
KMT's economic ideology shifted from adherence to the planned
economy to a focus on the market. This shift paved the way for
the reforms of the late 1950s that liberalized the economy and
stressed the importance of the private sector in economic development. This section discusses the history of this shift. Chapter 5
examines the policy process of the reforms.

Solving political problems. The final factor behind the acceptance
of a "planned free economy" as the official ideology was political.
Chiang Kai-shek's and Chen Cheng's support for the reform bureaucrats was pivotal. Chiang was convinced by the bureaucrats
that the reforms would help solve Taiwan's most serious economic
problem, its worsening balance of payments, and enable Taiwan
to forgo American aid and become self-reliant. The balance-of-

payments problem had become so serious that at the end of 1957 Chiang named a nine-person committee to deal with it. Chiang also faced substantial pressures from the United States to adopt the reforms, including a threat to reduce aid levels. Moreover, the reforms would not affect military spending, the issue of greatest concern for Chiang. According to K. T. Li, this is why Chiang agreed to the nineteen-point reform plan.[50]

Since the economy was the most important battlefield in Chen Cheng's competition with Chiang Ching-kuo to succeed Chiang Kai-shek, Chen spared no efforts to establish his credibility in this area. When he was named premier in 1958, he put new people in key positions to replace those loyal to his predecessor, Yu Hongjun (O. K. Yui), or affiliated with the "presidential residence faction" (*guandi pai*). He provided full support to Yin Zhongrong and his colleagues.

The political consensus between Chiang Kai-shek and Chen Cheng and their support were critical to the acceptance of the reforms. Chiang's assent ended the fierce resistance from the military (because of the freezing of military expenditures) and from the government and public sector (because of the reduction in utility rates). The shift in Chiang's attitude also led to Xu Boyuan's resignation as minister of finance and chairman of the BOT in the late 1950s. The new team under Chen Cheng provided institutional backing for acceptance of the reform package. Thus, the idea of a market economy was adopted because it was seen as the solution to the economic problems of the regime, because the institutional configuration of the economic bureaucracy changed, and because it had the political support of the top leaders. However, as we shall see, the process of acceptance was quite complicated.

From planned economy to "planned free economy." Until the late 1950s, the planned economy dominated the KMT's economic ideology, although American pressures offset its influence to some extent.[51] This ideology was based on Sun Yatsen's Principle of the People's Livelihood, and its main embodiment was the "planned economy." Although the idea of a "planned free economy" appeared as "a glimmer of a new vision" in the late 1940s on the mainland,[52] it never became official ideology either on the mainland or on Taiwan before the late 1950s. Chen-kuo Hsu's assumption that the KMT adopted the idea of a "planned free market economy" as its official economic ideology after it took over Taiwan is erroneous.[53] The truth is that the former NRC staff members who dominated policy making in the early 1950s were for the most part engineers or even military men. They knew little about economics and treated the economy as an engineering project. They were steadfast adherents of the command economy and the view that a planned economy and state control of industry were the best ways to develop the economy. This school was associated with the concept of national socialism, which to a large extent originated in the collaboration between the Nationalist government and Germany during the post–World War I period.[54]

The origins of the KMT regime's economic ideology lie in the NRC. The NRC was established in 1938 under the MOEA. Its predecessors were the National Defense Planning Commission, which had been set up in 1932 under the Headquarters of the General Staff, and subsequently, in 1935, the Resources Commission under the Military Commission. Basically, its aim was to establish military-related industries to support the anti-Japanese war. By the end of the war, a total of 130 firms had been established under the NRC in the electricity, mining, metals, petroleum, steel, machinery, and chemicals sectors. This effort reflected a basic policy of the KMT regime—to build up state-owned infrastructure and heavy and chemical industries, and to leave light industries, with the exception of textiles, to the private sector. The NRC-led industrialization was strongly characterized by monopolistic state capital with military aims.

After the war, the NRC was responsible for taking over Japanese firms in the areas occupied by Japan. According to the "Measures for Dealing with the Enemy's Property in the Recovered Areas," all Japanese properties that resembled those in the existing state-owned sector run by the NRC were to be assigned to the NRC.[55] Thus, infrastructure and companies in the heavy industry and chemical sectors taken over from the Japanese were incorporated into the existing NRC-run firms. The wartime policy of developing state capital was extended to the postwar period and from the war-time rear areas to Japanese-occupied areas, including Taiwan.

Most NRC bureaucrats were deeply influenced by Sun Yatsen's ideas about developing industry and believed that the only way China could catch up with the advanced countries was to develop industry, especially heavy industry, and the infrastructure. The NRC's fundamental principle was that central planning was essential to industrialization. Weng Wenhao, a core leader of the NRC, believed that "a comprehensive and well-coordinated plan is always essential to the effective meeting of needs and realization of ideals."[56] Weng, a geologist, was named by Chiang Kai-shek (the chairman of the NRC) as its secretary-general. Because he had Chiang's trust and full support, he was extremely influential. The NRC bureaucrats strongly favored a command economy. The NRC, they suggested to the top authority, was the right institution to undertake the task of developing state capital.[57] This policy suggestion was echoed and adopted by Chiang Kai-shek.

The NRC's ideology remained Taiwan's mainstream economic thinking until the late 1950s. Almost all key economic officials came from the NRC. The chief members of the ESB, for example, were adherents of the planned economy. Even Yin Zhongrong, the only top official regarded by economists as having an appreciation of a market economy, "had his mind stuffed with the idea of a controlled economy" in the early years.[58] So the ideas of favoring state capital and controlling the economy continued to prevail in Taiwan and dominated government economic policy until the late 1950s.

Keynesianism also found adherents among some bureaucrats during this period. When the anti-Japanese war forced the Nationalist government to collaborate with the United States and Britain, American and British influence increased dramatically. Keynesianism came to prevail among the newly emerging bureaucrats who favored state intervention and a controlled economy. For instance, Zhang Zikai, BOT president between 1954 and 1960, was a strong proponent of Keynesianism. Nevertheless, the boundaries between economic schools and the factions behind the schools were not clear-cut. Both the conflicts and the collaborations among them had a strong impact on economic policy throughout the 1950s.[59]

However, a striking change occurred in the late 1950s. The conversion of some major bureaucrats to a pro-market ideology made the liberalization of the economy in the late 1950s and early 1960s possible. This, in turn, led Taiwan to move from import-substitution to export-oriented development and triggered the flourishing of the private sector in the 1960s. A close examination of this evolution will help us to understand what influenced this change and how it influenced economic policy making.

The adoption of new economic ideas is not merely about economic policy; it also involves political options. Empirical studies on the reception of economic ideas in many countries have shown that the acceptance involves economists, civil servants, and politicians. Based on comparative studies of the fate of Keynesianism in many countries, Peter Hall has argued that in order to be accepted, new economic ideas need to satisfy three criteria: economic viability, administrative viability, and political viability. This means that they must (1) have the capacity to resolve economic problems, (2) accord with the administrative biases of the officials responsible for approving them and be feasible in light of the existing capacity of the state to implement policies, and (3) have appeal in the broader political arena, to which the politicians who ultimately make policy are oriented.[60] Hall's findings are relevant to the acceptance of the planned market economy in Taiwan, and below I use this analytical approach to analyze how the notion of a planned market economy evolved from a heresy to the official ideology.

This shift can be illustrated by change in the thinking of Yin Zhongrong. As an engineer, Yin was a strong proponent of the command economy in the early 1950s. He did not believe in any economic theory. But his views began to change because of lobbying by economists and the practical difficulties he faced in his work.

A sign of the change in his thinking was a growing uncertainty about economic theory. In the mid-1950s, Yin said that he was not "bound to any single theory. The reality is volatile, and the problems cannot be resolved by any single theory or with an immutable method."[61] He elaborated his ideas in his four-volume *My Views on Taiwan's Economy*. But his main ideas were summarized in an important article published simultaneously in major local newspapers in 1953.

Under current circumstances, Taiwan's industrial development should be fast and resource-saving. However, these two goals cannot be achieved in a laissez-faire economy. They rely on the government's involvement in economic activities, sound plans, and supervision of the implementation of the plans. Nevertheless, here "plan" [refers to something] completely different from that found in the centralized planned economies in the communist countries, which manipulate all production tools and control all economic activities. Here "plan" means that after considering the whole situation and keeping its eye on the commonweal, the government decides the direction and goals of industrial development for a certain period. The government decides which industries should be given priority, and which are less important and therefore should be delayed. The government should also decide the extent to which a certain industry develops as well as the limits of its development. Meanwhile, each industry and each enterprise within the sector have ample freedom to perform. So it is a free market.[62]

To promote industry, Yin proposed using credits to determine the allocation of resources, giving priority to the distribution of foreign exchange (in order to import equipment) and to the allocation of materials, and offering technical guidance. He favored a private economy, a view that put him at odds with other bureaucrats in the ESB such as Jiang Biao, who was a strong proponent of a state-run economy. Yin Zhongrong was not, however, an advocate of the free market. He argued that the government should foster the private sector and protect domestic industries from international competition, but he also stressed that there should be reasonable limits on such activities. According to Yin, there were three reasons for government intervention. First, since Taiwan was an island with few resources, the use of resources needed to be well thought out. Second, industrialization was urgent, and time was limited. Third, the private sector was weak, and there were few entrepreneurs. Given their advantages of capital, human resources, knowledge, and efficient organization, the government and a few institutions, such as the banks, could do what the private sector could not do. Yin's ideas, based on the idea of a command economy, were shared only by his colleagues on the IDB.

In the late 1950s, Yin argued that what Taiwan needed was a "planned free market economy," or a market economy in which the private sector was the main player, but the state also played a role. Supported by the top leadership, this idea became the official economic ideology.

Lobbying by economists. Economists, both Chinese and American, played a crucial role in Yin Zhongrong's change of mind. Several, including Jiang (Tsiang) Shuojie and Liu Dazhong (Ta-chung Liu) (both of whom worked for the IMF and were "Chicagoists"), became economic advisers to the government in 1954 and were strong lobbyists for a free market. According to Jiang's recollections, in 1952 he gave Yin a copy of James Meade's *Planning and the Price Mechanism.* This was the first economics text that Yin had ever read. Yin was impressed by Meade's book, especially by the "price mechanism." He even recommended it to his colleagues on the IDC.[63] As followers of the Chicago School, Jiang Shuojie and Liu Dazhong were strong proponents of the free market. They were often invited to return to Taiwan for policy consultations. They suggested that the major economic issues, like exchange rates and interest rates, should be left to the market and price mechanisms.

Although the American advisers agreed that Taiwan should establish a free economic system, they argued that textbook theory was not appropriate for Taiwan at that time. The reality of the wartime economy and the incomplete market determined that a market mechanism could not work in Taiwan. In the mid-1950s, Taiwan's choice was between chaos and stability. Based on these divergent judgments, different policy formulas for specific policies, such as interest rates, were presented. These different policy suggestions incited heated debates among the government bureaucrats.

According to Xing Muhuan, Yin Zhongrong was one of the few bureaucrats able from the outset to understand the reform formulas on a wide range of issues, including foreign exchange rates, industrial protection, production limitations, and quotas for foreign exchange.[64] Even though Jiang's and Liu's free-market argument was regarded almost as a heresy among most bureaucrats as well as among local economists, Yin was willing to listen to their suggestions. Slowly, it seemed that Yin began to understand and partly accept these economists' suggestions, and he began to move away from the NRC's command economy perspective.[65] The evolution of interest rate policy from controlled to mildly liberalized is an example of the debate among the contending forces.[66]

Difficulties in practice. Yin's slow acceptance of a free-market ideology was ultimately accelerated by the practical difficulties of the controlled economy. The original aim in introducing multiple exchange rates was to control imports and to promote exports of agricultural and food products. This was an aspect of the command economy, and it led to hundreds of different exchange rates. The resulting difficulties led to inefficiencies in resource allocation, speculation in foreign exchange, and abuses of power. Because of these problems, Yin came to oppose the multirate system and was determined to change it. Jiang's and Liu's lobbying provided theoretical legitimacy for the need to change the system.

However, even though economists and the growing problems of the planned economy could change Yin's mind, they were incapable of changing official ideology. The chief obstacles were financial officials in the MOF and FETCC such as Xu Boyuan and politicians like Premier Yu Hongjun. Only after the administrative and political problems were resolved was it possible for Yin Zhongrong's ideas to become the official ideology.

The removal of administrative obstacles. The adoption of promarket ideas highlighted the difficulties in getting the bureaucracy to accept and implement new concepts. Not the least of the obstacles was the prevalence of the idea of state control of the economy in the early 1950s. Although Yin came to agree with the advocates of the free market, in 1954 he told Xing Muhuan, a leading local proponent, that the government should "go about things steadily and surely under the current circumstances. It will not help to be impatient."[67] His words acknowledged the dominance of economic planning. Apparently there was a serious theoretical clash between adherents of the market, on the one hand, and the pro–command economy bureaucrats in the ESB, MOEA, and FETCC, on the other. As is shown in Chapter 5, it was only after the bureaucrats who opposed the reforms were replaced with pro-reform bureaucrats that the reforms could be implemented.

The acceptance of the idea of a market economy as the KMT regime's official ideology also confirms Hall's assumption that the acceptance of new ideas relies on the resolution of conflicts between these ideas and the current political orthodoxy.[68] During the 1950s, orthodox political discourse was based on the doctrines of Sun Yatsen. The main argument of the pro–command economy bureaucrats was that only a state-run and state-controlled economy could allocate and use resources efficiently and thus realize the task of retaking the mainland. Therefore, they strongly opposed privatization.[69] The ideological basis for this argument was Sun Yatsen's teaching *Fada guojia ziben, jiezhi siren ziben* (Develop state capital, limit private capital). This teaching became an unchallengeable guideline. Because the idea of a market economy contradicted Sun's doctrine, it encountered resistance not only from officials but also from academics.[70] It appeared that only the top leader had the authority to resolve this conflict. Even Chen Cheng, the number-two figure in the KMT regime, was not in a position to override Sun. On a number of occasions, Chen Cheng argued for the development of a private sector. At the Third Plenary Session of the Seventh KMT Central Committee in December 1953, he stressed in his political report that "businesses that can be operated privately should be left as much as possible to the private sector. This is the framework of the national economy and the basic principle of the entire policy. It is also the most effective method to root out bureaucratic capital."[71] This did not, however, quiet the debate. The situation changed completely in the mid-1960s when Chiang Kai-shek commented publicly on Sun Yatsen's doctrine of state and private capital. At a conference, Chiang stated that he had never heard Sun say anything about rooting out or limiting private capital and that, as used by Sun, *jiezhi* meant to regulate and control, not to limit, private capital. The government should focus on regulating and controlling private capital in order to avoid monopolies that endangered state interests. The public and private sectors, Chiang said, should co-exist.[72] This comment was taken as the most authoritative explanation of Sun's doctrine and eventually ended the debate. Thereafter, the idea of a market economy gained legitimacy. Apparently, the conflict between political orthodoxy and new ideas could be resolved only by the top leader.

Two other factors were also important in the ultimate acceptance of the pro-market economy in Taiwan. First, the leading economic bureaucrats were politically sophisticated—both politically adept and politically "naïve." They were adept because they knew how to gain the trust and support of the highest politicians, and they were disciplined enough to distance themselves from the factional struggles. They identified themselves strictly as bureaucrats, and, very much aware of the seriousness of politics, they avoided becoming involved in it. Both Yin Zhongrong and K. T. Li followed this principle. Yin Zhongrong was not even a party member. Li was viewed as "knowing little about politics."[73] They were politically naïve in that they had no political ambitions and had no interest in politics. This boundary was crucial and was an important reason why the highest leaders trusted them. This trust was a precondition for acceptance and support of their ideas.

The second factor was the personalities of those involved. Yin Zhongrong was certainly an initiator and the most energetic promoter in the government of the "planned market economy." But his bluntness, aggressiveness, and arrogance often made it difficult for his colleagues, as well as for Chen Cheng, to accept his ideas. As shown in Chapter 5, it was Yan Jiagan who helped reduce the resistance caused by Yin Zhongrong's strong personality. In other words, Yan's strengths overcame Yin's weaknesses. Yan is thus widely viewed as having played a crucial role in the acceptance of the pro-market reforms. Although we cannot know if Yin's ideas would ultimately have been accepted, it is certain that without Yan Jiagan's mediation Yin Zhongrong would have encountered more difficulties in selling his ideas to his colleagues and to Chen Cheng. Contrary to the assumptions of a coherent and monolithic bureaucracy in the developmental state model, bureaucratic politics played a significant role in the policy process.

What roles did the KMT party, military, and security forces and the local factions that were the major political forces on Taiwan play in the economic policy process? The short answer is that they are conspicuous by their absence. Although the economic bureaucracy was subject to the highest political leaders, it enjoyed an impressive degree of autonomy from the political forces.

It had been a tradition since the first years of the NRC in the 1930s and 1940s that the technocrats were isolated from party cadres.[74] By 1949, when the KMT retreated to Taiwan, the technocrats had already won a large measure of independence from party and military control. This tradition remained unchanged in the 1950s. The trend was strengthened in the late 1950s when, because of the dearth of foreign exchange and the chronic negative balance of payments, economic affairs were given unprecedented emphasis. These economic difficulties as well as pressure from the United States forced Chiang Kai-shek to shift his short-term emphasis from retaking the mainland to improving the economy to serve his long-term goal of retaking the mainland by strengthening defense. With the exception of a short interval in the mid-1950s, Chiang Kai-shek's support ensured the independence of the economic bureaucracy. As has already been shown, U.S. aid significantly increased the power of the bureaucrats during this period. The fact that many former party ideologues did not come to Taiwan also contributed to the independence of the economic bureaucracy on Taiwan. During the Chiang Ching-kuo era, the bureaucrats enjoyed even more autonomy from the party and the military because of Chiang's dominance of economic policy.

In addition to the party and military and security forces, the economic bureaucracy was also immune to the influence of the local factions that were politically prominent before the mid-1980s. In the early 1950s, in order to overcome its lack of local support, the KMT began to nurture local factions in grass-roots elections by providing economic rents. However, in order to prevent the factions from spiraling out of control, the party prohibited them from competing at the county level until the 1970s. Thus, although these local factions were influential in local politics and financially powerful at the county level, they had little influence on the central government's economic policy. It was not until the lifting of martial law in the late 1980s and Taiwanization that the local factions became a powerful force in national politics.

The Importance of "Trust" in KMT Bureaucratic Politics

As is apparent from the preceding discussion, trust was an important element in economic policy making and its implementation. Sociologists define "trust" in a number of different ways. Basically "trust" applies to both persons and institutions. For Anthony Giddens, trust in persons "is built upon mutuality of response and involvement: faith in the integrity of another is a prime source of feeling of the integrity and authenticity of the self," whereas "trust in an abstract system provides for the security of day-to-day reliability, but by its very nature cannot supply either the mutuality or intimacy which personal trust relations offer."[75] In Niklas Luhmann's definition, "Trust remains vital in interpersonal relations, but participation in functional systems like the economy or politics is no longer a matter of personal relations. It requires confidence, but not trust."[76] With respect to the leadership of the KMT, the emphasis in this book is on the implications of trust in persons.

To use Francis Fukuyama's classification, Chinese society exhibits a low level of trust.[77] Lucian Pye reaches a similar conclusion based on sharp differences in Chinese and American responses to a survey about trust in people.[78] As a kind of cultural characteristic, the level of trust helps shape economic activities and organizations. The prevalence of small or family businesses in Italy and China is closely related to the lack of trust of those outside the family in Italian or Chinese society; in contrast, societies with a high degree of trust and social capital such as Japan or Germany can create large organizations without state support.[79]

The concept of trust plays a determining role in political behavior in China. The extension of the concept of family member/ outsider to political life has resulted in the phenomenon of political factions in both the KMT and the Communist Party. As Pye has observed of Chinese political culture, "The greater the manifest uncertainties in political life, the greater the sense of general distrust and the greater the search for more private and intimate association—that is to say, the greater the tendency to form factions."[80] Although Pye's observation is based on mainland politics, it can apply to KMT politics on Taiwan as well, since this remark speaks to the nature of Chinese political culture.

The KMT was never a coherent party, neither on the mainland nor on Taiwan. Instead, it fostered a faction-based authoritarian political system. At the top of the structure was first Chiang Kai-shek and then his son Chiang Ching-kuo. Despite an absolute ban against the forming of factions, under the paramount leader, there were several groups, such as the CC Clique, the Political Study Clique, the Youth Corps Clique, and the Military Intelligence Clique. The rule and power of Chiang Kai-shek were based on manipulating these factions and using them as checks on one another. Although most of the political factions were weakened after the KMT retreated to Taiwan because the KMT reformed itself and because some of the key figures in some of the factions did not follow Chiang Kai-shek to Taiwan, the ruthless power struggles within the KMT never ceased. When existing factions weakened, new ones emerged. As Chiang Kai-shek aged, the succession struggle between the old and the new factions led to a new struggle within the KMT. The patron of the new factions was none other than Chiang Ching-kuo.

The history of the power struggles in the KMT from 1949 to the mid-1970s is a history of the Chiang family excluding and defeating its rivals in order to establish Chiang Ching-kuo as his father's heir. The main strife took place between Chen Cheng and Chiang Ching-kuo. After a long build-up, Chiang Ching-kuo's supporters also divided into factions according to the length and origins of their associations with him. Chiang's factions consisted of three circles: inner, middle, and outer.[81] Chiang employed five strategies to consolidate and expand his power: he relied on his inner circle, compromised with his father's longtime associates, promoted his own people, co-opted people who sought an affiliation with him, and depended on other prominent leaders with their own independent power bases.[82] This faction-based power structure and the power struggle within the KMT had a significant impact on the economic bureaucracy, contrary to its general idealization in statist literature. The most important impact was that since political leaders had to distinguish allies and enemies, trust became a crucial condition in the leadership's selection and use of economic officials.

Political factions and leadership norms in the KMT state affected the selection and use of economic bureaucrats. In Chiang Kai-shek's consolidation of his power and in Chiang Ching-kuo's struggle to succeed his father, economic affairs held the lowest priority. Compared to security concerns, the military, the party, and the support of young people, economic affairs were less crucial. When the KMT replaced local rule on the island, Chiang Kai-shek wanted Chiang Ching-kuo to control these four areas through the General Political Warfare Department, the Political Action Committee, the Party Reform Commission, and the youth corps. Over the next two decades, Chiang Ching-kuo focused his attention on these areas as he took control of them step by step by defeating all his rivals. Since Chiang Ching-kuo did not extend his reach into economic or financial affairs, these areas were left to Madame Chiang's loyalists and to Chen Cheng's protégés. On the mainland, financial and economic affairs had been the domain of H. H. Kong and T. V. Soong. This faction was considerably weakened on Taiwan, since T. V. Soong did not go to Taiwan. However, Madame Chiang's people, the so-called presidential residence faction, still dominated financial affairs. Xu Boyuan and Yu Guohua were the two major officials. The financial presidential residence faction was used to check the economic bureaucrats. Chen Cheng, a key figure in the Whampoa Military School system, had no previous association with economic and financial affairs. But because the economy was the only arena in which he was allowed to participate and with which he might build up his credibility in his competition with Chiang Ching-kuo to succeed Chiang Kai-shek, he began to recruit his own people and put them in key economic positions. He focused on officials with fewer factional affiliations, for instance, Yan Jiagan and Yin Zhongrong. Their lack of a factional affiliation was a crucial precondition for acceptance by Chen Cheng and by Chiang Kai-shek, as well as for immunity from attacks by rivals. Yan and Yin were trusted by both Chiang Kai-shek and Chen Cheng.

Specifically, Chiang Kai-shek was impressed by Yin's clean record as a representative in the Chinese procurement office in the United States during the anti-Japanese war. Since the KMT regime's failure on the mainland was attributed to the cancer of corruption, Yin's rare clean record became a valuable virtue. Moreover, Yin was a close friend of Chen Cheng's brother-in-law and had been recommended to Chen Cheng by T. V. Soong, Chiang Kai-shek's brother-in-law. Yin had been Soong's personal secretary. Yin's nonmembership in the KMT also recommended him to Chiang Kai-shek and Chen Cheng.

When Chiang Ching-kuo became vice premier in 1969 and cemented his power in security, military, and party affairs, he shifted his focus to economic and financial affairs to obtain complete control of the state. These areas were becoming increasingly important as economic growth became a new source of legitimacy for the KMT regime. However, when Chiang Ching-kuo began to take over economic affairs, K. T. Li had already consolidated his reputation and position as the leading economic bureaucrat. He was so influential that there was a rumor of a "K. T. faction." Li thus became an obstacle and threat to Ching-kuo's efforts to build up his own forces. Chiang Ching-kuo's strategy when he assumed the office of vice premier was to reshuffle the bureaucrats by replacing the veteran K. T. Li with a younger bureaucrat. He first chose Tao Shengyang to replace Li as the minister of economic affairs, but Tao died a few months later. He then chose Sun Yunxuan as his protégé and successor.

In addition to trust, the selection and utilization of bureaucrats were also determined by the norms of the KMT political culture. They included loyalty, personal performance, lack of political ambition, and lack of a factional background.

Loyalty was the first precondition. Pye finds that the virtue of loyalty enjoys a loftier position in the Chinese political system than it does in liberal Western politics. In Western systems, loyalty, which is a value to be balanced with effectiveness, honesty, farsightedness, the appearance of high moral purpose, personal charisma, and a host of other values, represents no more than about 15 percent of the entire range of respected values in politics, whereas in China the comparable figure would probably be over 50 percent.[83] The highly personal nature of the faction-based KMT state thus elevated loyalty to an extremely important position. All the major bureaucrats had to prove their political loyalty. The main reason that Sun Yunxuan was chosen by Chiang Ching-kuo was that Sun's loyalty to Chiang had been proved over a lengthy period.

Personal performance is another source of trust. As noted above, Yin Zhongrong's clean record in the wartime procurement office in the United States played a key role in winning Chiang Kai-shek's trust. However, the classic case is Chiang Ching-kuo's examination of Sun Yunxuan. Chiang began to test Sun in the early 1970s. A fascinating instance occurred on a ship during an offshore inspection in 1978. A sudden storm arose, and Sun became seasick. Chiang was still sitting on the deck and asked Sun, "Are you all right? Do you need to go down to the cabin?" Sun held back from vomiting and said he was all right. According to Zhang Baoshu, secretary-general of the KMT, who was also on the ship, this was a crucial test for Sun. If he had failed, he would not have been named premier soon thereafter. In Chiang Ching-kuo's view, a leader of state had to shoulder everything. If Sun could not withstand the storm, how could he be a leader?[84] Chiang's view derived from his own personal experience in the Soviet Union when he defied death several times.

K. T. Li's role as a key economic official was also due to his good personal performance. His importance and influence was second only to that of Yin Zhongrong until Yin's death in 1963; he then became the most influential economic official until he was removed as minister of economics by Chiang Ching-kuo because Li's influence, reputation, and seniority constituted a great threat to him.

The case of Yan Jiagan is an interesting exception. Compared to other major economic bureaucrats, Yan Jiagan's performance was rather mediocre. Unlike Yin Zhongrong, K. T. Li, Tao Shengyang, or Sun Yunxuan, all of whom were promoted because of their ability, Yan's rapid advancement can hardly be attributed to his performance. The difference is due to the different virtues required of economic bureaucrats and those required of a loyal and docile figure at a time of a transition in power. The economic bureaucrats had to be capable and enterprising. But as a figure playing a role in the power succession from Chiang Kai-shek to Chiang Ching-kuo, loyalty was more important than ability. As a well-known "yes man," Yan Jiagan was the right person. Later developments confirmed the Chiangs' choice.

The lack of personal political ambition is another precondition for being trusted. In this respect, Yan Jiagan is a good example. He was cautious, maintained a low profile, and was good at mediating among bureaucrats. This convinced the Chiangs that Yan held no political ambitions and enabled him to win the trust of the Chiangs, even though he had earlier been connected with the Political Study Clique. Beginning in the late 1950s, Yan was one of the few persons who could make suggestions directly to Chiang Kai-shek. This position allowed him to play a crucial role in persuading Chiang to accept the economic reforms during the late 1950s and early 1960s. Because of his loyalty and lack of political ambition, Chiang Kai-shek chose him to play a transitional role between the elder Chiang and his son. Yan understood his mission and did exactly what was expected. After Chiang Ching-kuo served as Chiang Kai-shek's vice premier for three years, Yan recommended that he be chosen as premier in 1972. When Chiang Kai-shek died in 1975, Yan became president. He still clung to his mission as an interim figure. On the eve of the presidential election in 1978, when KMT chairman Chiang Ching-kuo sent an emissary to ask Yan's opinion about the presidential candidates, Yan showed him a letter that he had already written in which he recommended Chiang as the presidential candidate.[85] None of the other bureaucrats, such as Yin Zhongrong and K. T. Li, dared to cross the boundary separating the bureaucracy from politics. But Yan's lack of political ambition was a crucial factor in winning the trust of the Chiangs. Lack of political ambition was also a reason why Sun Yunxuan was chosen by Chiang Ching-kuo as his successor. When Sun suffered a stroke in 1984, Chiang had to choose Lee Teng-hui as his successor.[86]

Trust also required a lack of factional connections. With the exception of those who belonged to the Chiang family factions, such as Xu Boyuan and Yu Guohua, all other key economic officials (Yin, Li, and Sun) shared a common characteristic—they had no factional connections. One reason Chiang Ching-kuo chose Lee Teng-hui as his heir was that Lee had been an agricultural economist with no political connections.[87] The only exception is Yan Jiagan. Yan's previous connection with the Political Study Clique, which had been headed by the first governor of Taiwan, Chen Yi, did not prevent him from gaining the Chiangs' trust. First, after Chen Yi was executed by Chiang Kai-shek in 1949, the Political Study Clique declined in importance and was no longer a threat to the Chiangs. Second, Yan's personality compensated for his previous factional connections. Yan was a well-known "yes man" and was famous for shifting responsibility onto others. His political philosophy can be expressed as "on second thought, and be considerate." He did not want to take responsibility, and he lacked initiative. As governor of Taiwan, he has been described as "a good man but not a good official, a good citizen but not a good civil servant."[88] But this was the exact personality required of a transitional figure. The irony is that whereas Yan's performance as a bureaucrat has been criticized, his role in coordinating and mediating among the bureaucrats and in persuading Chiang Kai-shek and Chen Cheng to accept the economic reform policies has received high praise.

The personnel involved in the KMT economic bureaucracy are important for understanding Taiwan's economic bureaucracy, particularly the role of institutions, leadership, and bureaucratic politics in the policy process. As noted in Chapter 1, the study of institutions dominates the social sciences today. I am not arguing against this trend, but I would warn against the danger of dehumanizing and depoliticizing institutions. This warning is not new.[89] The findings in this book duplicate conclusions about the Japanese economic bureaucracy. The operations of Taiwan's economic bureaucracy were to a great extent about bureaucratic politics; the current analysis is an attempt to bring bureaucratic politics back in. Ideology, political culture, and formal and informal norms were, it is argued here, key determinants of bureaucratic politics. Although the trend was toward institutionalization as the economic bureaucracy was decentralized and the importance of bureaucrats' personalities decreased accordingly, the overall society was still run by a political strongman. The importance of individual leaders was crucial not only in politics but also in economic policy.

Therefore, the economic bureaucracy in Taiwan before the early 1970s cannot be reduced to institutions, because the role of institutions hinged on three parameters. First, the major bureaucrats—the strongmen—were crucial. Although the U.S.-funded economic planning agencies provided a stage for the leading bureaucrats, what these institutions did was largely up to individual bureaucrats. The power of a particular institution depended on its leader: a strong leader strengthened the institution; a weak leader weakened it. Second, the role of an institution depended on the relationship between the politicians and the bureaucrats. Chiang Kai-shek's and Chiang Ching-kuo's attitudes toward bureaucrats had an important impact on institutions. As in the Japanese civil service system,[90] this relationship determined the efficiency and functions of the economic bureaucracy. Third, political culture played an "invisible" role in the economic bureaucracy because, to a significant extent, it determined the role of individual bureaucrats. This factor has been downplayed in the existing literature on Taiwan's economic bureaucracy. However, these three parameters together determined the workings of the economic bureaucracy.

As this discussion has shown, the language of the developmental state captures something of the state's relations with society, but it is inadequate to deal with the complexities of policy making and the initiation of economic action within the state. These have to be understood in terms of bureaucratic politics or the politics of bureaucracy. Agencies were highly open to interference from above. They existed only as long as the top leaders allowed them to exist.

They competed to exert pressure on the center in order to secure an advantage.

Conclusion

The findings in this chapter dispute the statist account of the developmental state in Taiwan. First, the economic bureaucracy was not coherent and monolithic. It was riven by factional and ideological differences. Second, the economic bureaucrats had no autonomy from the highest political leaders. The bureaucrats had to sell their ideas to the political leaders, and only a winner could put his ideas in practice. Third, institutions were fragile. The economic planning agencies existed at the whim of the political leaders. Therefore they tended to come and go. What remained unchanged, however, was the informal behavior, norms, and practices, such as trust and loyalty. An institution-based explanation of the state neglects to take these into account.

Nor can Taiwan at this period be called a developmental state. Political leaders were preoccupied with security, military goals, and holding on to power. In fact, the state did not have a development strategy. Most economic bureaucrats focused on the balance-of-payments problems, and only a very few were concerned with economic development.

The role of the KMT state in economic development was related to the nature of the KMT regime. Special historical and international contexts helped the KMT build a unique state on Taiwan. The new state was politically strong (in terms of organization and ideology) and economically independent (because of the huge public sector), and it was an émigré regime. As noted in Chapter 1, unlike South Korea, where decolonization weakened the state, decolonization strengthened the state in Taiwan. These characteristics determined the KMT's public policy toward the private sector. Political strength and economic independence enabled the state to dominate society and to keep it separate from the private sector. Hence, the state did not rely overwhelmingly on the society politically or on the private sector economically. This allowed the state to have more room to maneuver vis-à-vis society. The émigré nature of the state encouraged it to keep a vigilant watch over large businesses, the majority of which were run by local Taiwanese. This had significant consequences for its political strategies and hence public policy toward the private sector.

Since institutions were fragile, it was left to individuals to play a leadership role in economic policy formulation and implementation. Political support from the highest leaders enabled individual bureaucrats to put their ideas into practice. Their initiative and personality were also important. In the final analysis, the role and function of agencies depended on their leaders rather than on their autonomy.

CHAPTER 3

The Emergence of the

Private Sector

The private sector is not a passive element but a vital actor in the shaping of the state's policy and strategy for dealing with it. This chapter examines the private sector under Japanese rule, its development during the early stage of KMT rule, its implications for the state and for state–private sector relations, and its impact on the evolution of these relations in the following decades. The first section of this chapter focuses on industrialization under Japanese rule; the second examines the privatization of four state-owned companies; and the third analyzes the influx of private capital from the mainland.

Industrialization Under Japanese Rule

The colonial legacy had a lasting impact on postwar Taiwan, both on the state and on the private sector,[1] and the Japanese policy of industrialization determined the fate of local capital under the KMT. As a result of its victory over China in the war of 1895, Japan took control of Taiwan and ruled it until the end of World War II. From the very outset, under the policy of "agricultural Taiwan and industrial Japan," Taiwan was run as a colony that produced rice, sugar, and other agricultural products for Japan. Before the early 1930s, the Japanese had no plans to develop industry in the colony, with the exception of sugar processing. Industry accounted for 32.1 percent of gross production in 1912 and 34.6 percent in 1927; although these are fairly high figures,[2] sugar refining constituted a high proportion of the industrial sector.

Food processing was the predominant industry. In 1920, 54.0 percent of factories engaged in food processing; in 1930, 64.5 percent; and in 1940, 65.4 percent.[3] In the 1910s and 1920s, food processing accounted for roughly 75–85 percent of gross industrial production (see Tables 3.1 and 3.2). This did not change until Japan began to implement its ambitious expansion plans in Asia. In 1931, the Japanese occupied northeast China and began to implement the "southward policy." Under this plan, Taiwan suddenly became a base for military expansion into southern China and Southeast Asia, and the discriminatory distinction between metropolitan territory and colony was discarded. As a result, after 1931 some industries, mainly in military-related sectors, were established in Taiwan. It is fair to say that in the absence of the southward policy, Taiwan's industry might have remained confined to food processing.[4]

The outbreak of the Sino-Japanese war in 1937 accelerated plans to make Taiwan into a base for military expansion. The subsequent industrial drive produced a rapid change in the economic structure (see Table 3.3). The share of industry in the economy began to rise after 1932 and surpassed agriculture in 1943, 51.1 percent to 37.3 percent.[5]

Starting with the building of the Sun Moon Lake hydroelectric project, the industrialization drive focused on military-related sectors. Among the new industries were cement, chemicals, fertilizer, papermaking, plywood, aluminum, alcohol, metalworking, machinery, and even shipbuilding and petroleum refining.[6] This military-oriented industrialization had three characteristics: a focus on electricity; reliance on Japanese capital and technology; and the establishment of heavy industries and defense industries with overseas resources.[7] Food processing remained the largest sector after 1931, however, accounting for 44 percent of gross industrial production in 1944, when the Japanese effort to industrialize Taiwan ended prematurely with the approaching end of World War II. Even so, industrialization was rather extensive. Existing industries

Table 3.1
Gross Industrial Production by Sector,
Selected Years, 1914–31
(percentage)

Industry	1914	1917	1920	1922	1925	1929	1931
Textiles	0.5	1.6	1.7	1.8	2.2	1.2	1.1
Metal- working	0.6	0.6	0.7	1.3	1.7	1.8	1.9
Machinery & tools	0.8	1.1	2.2	2.6	2.0	2.2	2.7
Mining	2.8	1.3	3.8	5.0	3.4	3.8	3.5
Chemicals	3.5	3.4	6.1	7.9	9.8	8.7	6.3
Food proces- sing	86.3	88.7	81.2	75.7	73.4	74.3	76.7
Others	5.5	3.3	4.3	5.7	7.5	8.0	7.8
TOTAL	100.0	100.0	100.0	100.0	100.0	100.0	100.0

SOURCE: Zhang Zonghan, *Guangfu qian Taiwan zhi gongyehua*, pp. 26–27.

Table 3.2
Gross Industrial Capital by Sector,
Selected Years, 1931–44
(percentage)

Sector	1931	1938	1940	1942	1944
Food processing	70	65	52	42	44
Electricity & gas	18	21	20	25	18
Chemicals	5	7	15	15	14
Others	7	7	13	18	24
TOTAL	100	100	100	100	100

SOURCE: Zhang Zonghan, *Guangfu qian Taiwan zhi gongyehua*, p. 207.

underwent rapid expansion, and some new industries, such as chemicals, metalworking, and machinery, emerged during the last decade of Japanese rule.

Two points about industrialization under Japanese rule are noteworthy for the study of postwar state–private sector relations. First, the entire colonial economy was monopolized by the Japa-

Table 3.3

Percentage Shares of Agriculture and Industry in the Taiwan Economy
During the Colonial Period, Selected Years, 1902–37

Year	Agriculture	Industry	Year	Agriculture	Industry
1902	78.0	16.8	1927	54.9	34.6
1907	81.7	14.1	1932	52.7	40.1
1912	63.4	32.1	1937	47.9	43.2
1916	46.8	37.3	1943	37.3	51.1
1922	52.6	37.8			

SOURCE: based on Zhou Xianwen, *Riju shidai Taiwan jingjishi (2)*, p. 62.

nese. The sugar sector is a typical case. Sugar refining, a pillar of
Taiwan's industry throughout the colonial period, was controlled
by several large Japanese companies. After 1940, the monopoly was
further concentrated in four large Japanese companies—Taiwan
Sugar, Meiji Sugar, Nittō, and Ensuikō Sugar. These four companies accounted for 99 percent of all sugar production in 1944.[8] This
sector was dominated by "capitalists living in Japan."[9] According
to a 1929 survey, the proportion of Japanese-owned capital in Taiwan's total industrial capital formation was 76.45 percent, whereas
Taiwanese-owned capital was only 21.89 percent.[10] Moreover, in
limited companies in 1929, Japanese-owned capital stood as high as
90.7 percent, and Taiwanese-owned capital at only 8.44 percent.[11]
Table 3.4 presents convincing evidence of the Japanese monopoly
of Taiwan's economy during the late colonial period.

Table 3.4 reveals that the percentage of capital owned by Japanese resident in Japan grew steadily over time, and the percentage
of capital owned by Japanese living in Taiwan increased only
slightly. This suggests an increasing concentration of capital in the
hands of domestic Japanese owners. Moreover, the larger the size
of the firm, the higher the percentage of capital owned by Japanese
living in Japan. This implies a Japanese monopoly. The share of
Taiwanese capital in companies with capital between ¥200,000 and
¥5,000,000 fell from 38 percent in 1938 to 25 percent in 1941, and the
percentage in companies with capital over ¥5,000,000 held steady
at around 3 percent. This suggests that Taiwanese capital was

Table 3.4

Japanese-Owned and Taiwanese-Owned Capital in Companies, 1938–41
(percentage)

Amount of capital (¥)	Year	Total capital (000 ¥)	Japanese			Taiwanese owned (%)	Others (%)	Total (%)
			in Japan (%)	in Taiwan (%)	Total (%)			
¥200,000– 5,000,000	1938	72,076	25.5	34.1	59.6	38.5	1.9	100
	1939	80,588	27.4	34.6	62.0	36.3	1.7	100
	1940	93,433	31.9	35.8	67.7	30.9	1.4	100
	1941	117,619	36.4	36.3	72.7	25.6	1.8	100
>¥5,000,000	1938	302,184	77.7	18.5	96.2	3.6	0.2	100
	1939	325,811	76.9	19.7	96.6	3.1	0.3	100
	1940	361,810	75.6	21.1	96.7	3.0	0.3	100
	1941	414,210	76.5	20.4	96.9	2.8	0.3	100

SOURCE: Zhou Xianwen, *Riju shidai Taiwan jingjishi* (2), p. 76.

almost completely excluded from the large-sized firms. Further-more, the drop in Taiwanese ownership leads to the conclusion that in the late colonial period the Japanese increasingly monopo-lized Taiwanese industry and the Taiwanese were driven out.

What was the fate of Taiwanese capital under these circum-stances? Traditionally, Taiwan's local capitalists had fulfilled a tri-ple function as landowners, merchants, and moneylenders.[12] Under Japanese colonial rule, local capital began to flow toward industry and modern banking. Before the 1930s, although small-scale local capital was suppressed by the colonial government and Japanese capital, a few traditionally prestigious families continued to pros-per and a few newly wealthy families emerged and joined this ex-clusive club. Chen Zhonghe of Gaoxiong and Lin Benyuan of Banqiao, heads of two of the older elite families, expanded their businesses into the sugar sector through close relations with the co-lonial government. Along with Lin Xiantang of Wufeng, they also entered banking, trading, and other sectors. Gu Xianrong[13] of Lu-gang and Yan Yunnian of Jilong joined this prestigious club by col-laborating with the colonial government and establishing close re-lations with private Japanese capital. The extended families of these five men were called the "five top clans" in colonial times. Al-though their relations with the colonial government varied, all five families were closely associated with Japanese capital, which col-luded with the colonial government to expand into Taiwan.[14] The diversified investments of the five families were facilitated by the colonial government or by private Japanese capital.[15] The scope of their businesses ranged from land to banking, insurance, mining, commerce, sugar refining, and monopolistic businesses (for exam-ple, salt and cigarettes). For a time, the five clans seemed likely to emerge as modern local capitalists under Japanese rule.

However, by the late colonial period, these families had gradu-ally been pushed out of most of their businesses. In 1935 members of Lin Xiantang's and Yan Yunnian's families were excluded from several companies in which they had held key positions and were replaced by Japanese. Lin Xiongzheng (from Lin Benyuan's family) suffered the same fate. In 1944, Lin Xiantang's and Yan's banks were merged with Japanese companies. The salt companies of the

Gu and Chen families were taken over in 1938. When the Chen family's sugar company was appropriated by a Japanese company in 1941, the Chens were driven out of the sugar sector.[16] The fate of the top five clans in the late colonial period was an inevitable outcome of the Japanese oligarchy.

In general, there was a division of labor between the Japanese and the Taiwanese during Japanese rule. The Japanese were engaged in industry, whereas the local people were confined to agriculture. Only three industrial sectors were open to the islanders: mining, tea processing, and sugar processing.[17] However, the large Taiwanese-owned firms were eventually merged with large Japanese companies. Tu Zhaoyan concludes that by the final stage of Japanese rule, except for the banking sector, in which local capital still held some shares, the influence of local capital had begun to decline; this was an unavoidable outcome of Japanese rule.[18] But the five top clans still held on to their land, which rooted them deeply in the island. This limited their options and made collaboration with Nationalists inevitable.

Industrialization under Japanese rule and the fate of Taiwanese capital strongly suggest that there was virtually no local private industrial sector on Taiwan when colonial rule ended in 1945. This is a key factor in the existence of a strong state and a weak private sector in postwar Taiwan. The KMT government replaced the Japanese as the new monopolists after expropriating all Japanese-owned property.

The second point about industrialization in Taiwan that merits attention is its wartime nature. After 1931 Taiwan became a wartime base for military needs, and this trend was reinforced after the outbreak of the Sino-Japanese war in 1937. The emphasis of Japanese colonial policy, as described by the then-governor-general, was "subject[ion of the Taiwanese], industrialization, and the southward policy." Under these circumstances, heavy industry and military-related industries received top priority, firm mergers were encouraged, and the state exercised increasing control over the economy. In short, the economy was militarized. Similar industrialization drives emphasizing heavy industry were launched in Korea and Japanese-occupied Manchuria for the same purposes at around the same time.[19] As a result, the colony's economic structure more and more came to resemble that of the metropolitan state. This accounts for the accelerated pace of monopolization after 1931 and the exclusion of local capital from many businesses in which it had previously been involved.

More important, the colonial wartime economy coincidentally paralleled the KMT government's wartime economy, which was established during the anti-Japanese war in the interior of the mainland. It was led by the NRC—the same agency that took charge of former Japanese firms in Taiwan.

Privatization of the Four Publicly Owned Companies: The Emergence of Local Capital

The Japanese shares in small-scale and miscellaneous firms sold to the private sector immediately after the war can be seen as the forerunners of the private sector in the postwar economy. Nevertheless, given the extremely small scale and primitive equipment of these firms, their economic function was generally negligible. In contrast, the local private capital that emerged from the privatization of four state-owned companies was significant.

This development was a by-product of a moderate land reform program. Learning a lesson from its bitter failure on the mainland and under pressure from the United States, the KMT government instituted a land reform program from 1949 to 1953. The reform sought to balance the interests of the state, landlords, and farmers.[20] As part of the "land to the tiller" policy—the third stage of land reform—shares in four state-owned companies taken over from the Japanese were used to compensate the landlords. Under this program, some 144,000 *jia* (one *jia* equals 9,699 m², or about 2.4 acres) of land was taken from 106,000 landlords. The compensation was calculated at 2.5 times the value of the annual yield of the land, and the total amount came to NT$2.2 billion.[21] About NT$1.5 billion, or the value of 70 percent of the land, was paid in crop bonds-in-kind (rice and sweet potatoes) maturing in ten years, and the remaining 30 percent (NT$600 million) was paid immediately with shares in the Taiwan Cement Corporation, Taiwan

Paper and Pulp Corporation, Taiwan Industrial and Mining Corporation, and Taiwan Agricultural and Forestry Corporation. In return, the recipients of land turned over 25 percent of their harvests for ten years to the government to a total value of NT$2.200 billion, which the government then used to redeem the crop bonds.[22] In privatizing these four public enterprises, the government's aim was not to foster local capitalists but to win the support of the peasantry.

Indeed, the land reform was not only economically but also politically successful. Empirical studies show that the peasants' morale was high and confidence in the future strong after land reform. The peasants had never expected to own their own land,[23] and their support was critical in stabilizing the KMT's rule. The land reform satisfied the majority of the population. However, the landowners suffered substantial losses due to the devaluation of the land and the overvaluation of the industrial shares they received. But the KMT had no intention of antagonizing them, and the compensation program represented a compromise with them. One consequence of the privatization of the four enterprises was the emergence of the first wave of local capitalists. This was an unanticipated result of the land reform.

The process of privatization was subtle and complicated. First, privatization contravened the principle of the state monopoly of the economy. The nationalization of Japanese property gave the state a monopoly and provided a solid foundation for the KMT regime. On the one hand, maintaining this monopoly remained vital to its rule. On the other hand, the state had to win the support of local landlords. Privatizing part of the public sector satisfied the landowners.[24] Due to the weaknesses of the public sector and under pressure from the United States,[25] the government had no choice but to privatize part of the huge public sector, even though this created a breach in the state monopoly system.[26]

Second, the scope of privatization and the choice of companies to be privatized represented a compromise between the state and the landlords. Initially, the landowners demanded company shares as compensation for 50 percent of their land.[27] But the government ultimately reduced this to 30 percent. The government's underlying principle for choosing the firms to privatize was "fewest in number and poorest in quality," which conflicted with the landowners' demands for more and better companies. The Taiwan Industrial and Mining Corporation and the Taiwan Agricultural and Forestry Corporation were the first two publicly owned companies singled out by the government. The reason was obvious. The two companies were the least profitable and were difficult to operate, given their small and scattered nature and poor equipment. The Taiwan Paper and Pulp Corporation was also put up for sale because of its declining profits. The landlords, however, were interested in two lucrative companies: the Taiwan Fertilizer Corporation and Taiwan Cement Corporation. An appraisal valued the five companies at NT$1.16 billion, far more than the NT$660 million due to the landlords. So the Taiwan Fertilizer Corporation was removed from the list by the government.

The land reform was in fact a compromise between the KMT and the landowners.[28] However, a few big landowners were the real beneficiaries of privatization. At the time, the four companies' prospects were uncertain, and their profitability was in doubt.[29] Furthermore, most landowners had no idea about how to run an enterprise, and so they saw no value in the shares they received. A small number of wealthy and influential landlords seized the opportunity to purchase other landowners' shares for a price 20–30 percent lower than the market value. According to a survey, 98 percent of the small and medium landowners and 90 percent of the big landowners sold their shares.[30] The shares became concentrated in the hands of a few big shareholders, and in the end the privatization program resulted in the emergence of a few leading landowners as capitalists. Most of the small landlords suffered a loss because of the land reform, and only a small group of the local elite joined the KMT ruling coalition politically and economically.

A closer examination of the major buyers of the four state-owned companies and their subsequent operation of these companies will help to clarify the significance of the privatization. The influential families that had been big landowners and engaged in business became the major shareholders in the privatized firms. For example, the privatized Taiwan Cement Corporation was controlled by the five top clans and a few other prominent local families. At its 1954 shareholders' meeting, members from four of the five top clans, the Gu, the Lin clan of Wufeng, the Lin clan of Banqiao, and the Chen, were elected high-ranking officers—president and trustees—of the corporation.[31]

After privatization, the Taiwan Paper and Pulp Corporation was in poor shape. In 1958 it was broken into four parts.[32] Zhongxing became the property of the provincial government. Xiaogang became part of the Taiwan Cement Corporation, which was controlled by the most powerful families. Xinying and Dadu remained part of Taiwan Paper and Pulp Corporation. The head of the corporation, Lai Senlin, appeared on the "business celebrity" list in a 1968 survey and also invested in Nangang Tire and Nanshan Life Insurance.[33] The backgrounds of the heads of the fourth part, Shilin Papermaking, are unknown.

The Taiwan Industrial and Mining Corporation also sold off parts of its holdings. Yongfeng Original Papermaking, which ranked as Taiwan's seventeenth largest corporation in 1985, was set up by the He family after it bought the No. 3 Papermaking Mill from this corporation. Xu Jinde, vice chairman of the provincial congress and a candidate-member of the KMT Central Committee,[34] bought Shilin Electrical Machinery, another subsidiary of Taiwan Industrial and Mining Corporation. His political background is thought to have helped him buy the firm.

It is clear that the more powerful and influential local capitalists shared the better part of the privatization pie. Because of their traditional economic power or political connections, only a few locals benefited from the privatization of the four firms. However, the implications of the privatization went beyond this.

The privatization was a significant starting point for local private capital. Liu Jinqing describes it as "the emergence of local capital."[35] It is noteworthy that the privatization effort became combined with the KMT regime's strategy of fostering a local elite. Due to its origins, the regime needed to build a local social base. The local elite was a natural choice. In late 1949, Chiang Ching-kuo held talks with major local landowners and asked them to support the land reform program. Chiang specifically asked Gu Zhenfu to help persuade other major landowners.[36] It is not clear how Gu "persuaded" the other landowners to "cooperate" with the KMT; his subsequent spectacular success in business and politics makes his unique and close relationship with the KMT understandable. As a reward for their "cooperation" in land reform, the KMT offered the big landowners economic rents in exchange for political support. The privatization of the four state-owned companies was one such program. As a result, the onetime large landlords (some of whom ran manufacturing businesses until late in the period of Japanese rule) were abruptly transformed into capitalists, and the collaboration between the state and the local elite was realized. The close relationship between the state and the newly emerging local capitalists became a stable axis of state–private sector relations.

This close relationship was not duplicated in the majority of small and medium-sized firms, however. Because the KMT government ignored them, they had to fend for themselves. Like the public sector, the large firms enjoyed monopolistic resources and a protected domestic market. These differences originated in the land reform and the privatization of the four state-owned companies in the early 1950s.

Several points need to be emphasized. First, the assertion of some observers that land reform and the privatization of the four state-owned firms resulted in the emergence of local capital through capital restructuring is correct.[37] The Japanese monopolistic system provided almost no room for local capital. Particularly in the late colonial period, local capital, including that of the top clans, was forced out of industry. In the immediate postwar period—1945–53—the KMT state monopoly replaced the Japanese colonial monopoly. There was still virtually no room for local capital. But the privatization of the four corporations thereafter provided local capital the opportunity to enter the industrial sector. Second, the privatization was significant because it established a special relationship between the state and the local elite. A group of former leading landlords emerged as new industrialists allied with the KMT regime. This unintended outcome of the land reform was politically and economically vital to state–private sector relations and to the overall economic structure of postwar Taiwan. Third, although it is true that in the 1950s the four privatized firms were the leading firms in the private sector—Taiwan Cement, Taiwan Pineapple, and Taiwan Paper were among the five largest private firms in 1958[38]—the privatization was only the first wave in the emergence of local private capital. Once these pioneers blazed a trail, more locals followed.

The Influx of Private Capital from the Mainland

The leading player in the private sector in the immediate postwar period was capital from the mainland. Although many mainland capitalists fled to Hong Kong, the United States, or Southeast Asia, some followed the KMT regime to Taiwan, particularly those who had close relations with the KMT government on the mainland. There are no exact statistics on the amount of private capital moved to Taiwan. Generally it can be classified into consumer goods capital, loan capital, and industrial capital.[39] Textile capital accounted for the principal part because of that industry's connections with the KMT. Therefore, an analysis of mainland textile capital can serve as an example of mainland private capital in the early 1950s.

Taiwan had no textile mills until 1941, the year the first Japanese factory was built.[40] The number of textile mills reached 109 in 1946,[41] but they were small in scale, and their equipment was rudimentary. Production capacity was limited; it could meet only 10 percent of demand on the island.[42] In 1946 the scattered textile mills were restructured into the Taiwan Industrial and Mining Corporation. The share of the textile sector in total manufacturing was never higher than 2.0 percent before 1949. But in 1950 the proportion rose sharply to 4.7 percent and reached 20.8 percent in 1953 (see Table 3.5).

The influx of mainland capital was mainly responsible for this sudden increase. Other than Taiwan Industrial and Mining Corporation, the only newly established firm was Hua'nan Cotton Mill, which was set up in 1948. But in 1949, four Shanghai-based cotton

Table 3.5
Share of Textiles in the Total Manufacturing Sector,
Selected Years, 1930–1953

Year	Percentage		Year	Percentage
1930	1.0		1950	14.3
1935	1.2		1951	18.3
1940	1.8		1952	17.5
1942	1.7		1953	20.8
1949	4.7			

SOURCES: Huang Dongzhi, "Taiwan zhi fangzhi gongye," pp. 5–6; Wang Hongren, "Zhanhou Taiwan siren duzhan ziben zhi fazhan," p. 26.

mills, Daqin, Yongxing, Yufeng, and Shenyi, moved to the island. By 1952, there were a total of twelve cotton mills. Seven of these were privately owned by mainlanders, four were state-owned, and only one (Taizhong) was owned by Taiwanese (see Table 3.6).

The textile capital from the mainland was either state-owned[43] or closely associated with the KMT government before moving to Taiwan. China Textile Construction,[44] Yongxing, and Taibei were financed by the Central Trust of China, Bank of China, and Bank of Communications. The Central Trust of China was a public bank with capital from the government. The Bank of China and Bank of Communications, both government-chartered banks, were originally privately owned, with four-fifths of their shares in private hands. However, they became public banks in 1935 when the state acquired a majority interest. These two banks were controlled by the KMT. Among the seven privately owned cotton mills with a mainland background, Daqin Textile Company and Shenyi Textile Company retained their original names. Their connection with the government is not clear. However, the main owners of the other five mills, Ni Keding of Hua'nan, Yan Qingling of Taiyuan, Song Renqing of Liuhe, Ma Junde of Zhanghua, and Xu Youxiang of Yuandong, had close relations with the KMT government. For example, Yan Qingling, brother of Yan Jiagan—Chiang Kai-shek's longtime trusted protégé and vice president (1966–75) and president (1975–78) of the ROC—was also the president of Yulong Auto,

Table 3.6
Dates of Establishment of Cotton Mills and Number of Spindles, 1946–53

Company	A	B	1946	1947	1948	1949	1950	1951	1952	1953
Taiwan Industrial & Mining	prewar	1946	9,548	14,564	14,988	15,667	20,668	25,668	25,668	25,708
China Textile Construction	1949	1951						10,608	10,608	10,680
Hua'nan	1948	1951			3,120	3,120	3,120	3,120	3,120	5,120
Daqin	1949	1949				5,000	13,992	17,932	29,400	29,652
Yongxing	1949	1950					7,200	12,600	19,576	21,560
Shenyi	1949	1950					5,040	5,040	5,040	16,240
Taibei	1950	1951						1,000	13,200	13,200
Taiyuan	1949	1951						10,368	10,368	10,368
Liuhe	1948	1952						3,200	10,000	10,000
Zhanghua	1951	1952							6,484	6,484
Taizhong	1952	1952							6,000	10,000
Yuandong	1952	1953								10,000
TOTAL			9,548	14,564	18,108	23,787	50,020	89,536	139,464	169,012

A. Year established. B. Year operations began.

SOURCES: Huang Dongzhi, "Taiwan zhi fangzhi gongye," p. 21; Liu Jinqing, Taiwan zhanhou jingji, p. 208.

which was financed in large part by Madame Chiang Kai-shek. Yu-long Auto had long been protected by the government but re-mained inefficient and unsuccessful.[45] Liu Jinqing sees 1949 to 1953 as the era of primitive capital accumulation for mainland capital, and he views this capital as restructured private capital.[46]

A few statistics will make the impact of this textile capital on the Taiwan economy in the early 1950s clear. First, as noted above, the textile industry accounted for an increasing share of the entire manufacturing sector from 1950 to 1953 (see Table 3.5). Second, whereas the public sector constituted two-thirds of the entire manufacturing sector, the share of private capital in the textile in-dustry reached 76.5 percent in 1953. Third, about 35 percent of the entire private sector was in the textile industry in the early 1950s.[47] Clearly, the textile industry accounted for the major part of the private sector in the early 1950s. Or, to use Liu Jinqing's phrase, private textile capital was the main pillar of the private sector.[48] Furthermore, private textile capital from the mainland was the leading force in the private sector of Taiwan's economy in the early 1950s. In fact, the textile firms originating on the mainland and the four privatized public enterprises (which only landowners were entitled to buy) were the only large-scale private enterprises in the early 1950s. The textile sector continued to play a major role in the economy, as did the wool industry.

However, this is not the whole story. After following the KMT to Taiwan, the textile barons restructured their capital and became leading industrialists, and the alliance between the KMT govern-ment and mainland textile capital was extended to Taiwan. The KMT needed supporters, and the mainland capitalists were un-doubtedly its most reliable allies. Following the KMT to Taiwan rather than relocating elsewhere was in their best interest. The two groups needed each other, and a close and firm relationship be-tween them was mutually beneficial. Once again, the state and the private sector formed an alliance, this time on Taiwan. This be-came a key element in state–private sector relations in postwar Taiwan. It also influenced the economic structure and the pattern of development. The KMT's relations with the private sector in

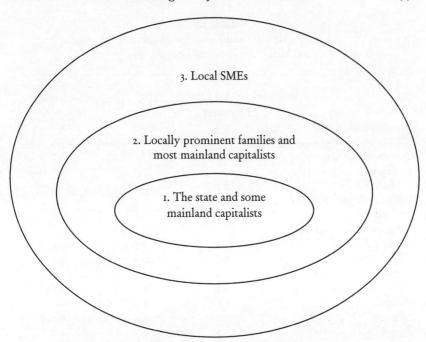

3. Local SMEs

2. Locally prominent families and
most mainland capitalists

1. The state and some
mainland capitalists

Fig. 3.1   State–private sector relations during the
early period of KMT rule on Taiwan

the 1950s are shown on Figure 3.1. The inner circle was the core
of the state-industry relationship—the alliance between the KMT
and the leading mainlander capitalists. The locally prominent families in the second circle were less close to the state. The local SMEs
in the outer circle had a rather distant relationship with the regime.

As an émigré group, the mainland capitalists were weak and dependent on the KMT government. Ironically, they played a leading
role in the private sector for years in postwar Taiwan since the local private capitalists were even weaker. Unsurprisingly, overall relations between the state and the private sector were characterized
by a strong state and a weak private sector.

State domination of the private sector was strengthened by
highly repressive political arrangements. Following the February
28 Incident, the provincial government under Chen Yi imposed
strict rule. Political control became even harsher after the KMT

Table 3.7
Japanese and Taiwanese Males
in Major Occupational Groups, 1940

Occupational group	(A) Taiwanese (000)	(B) Japanese (000)	Japanese as percentage of A + B (%)
Government workers	5.8	16.1	73.5
Technicians	5.0	11.0	68.8
Transportation	0.1	1.2	92.3
Mining & manufacturing	1.5	5.8	79.4
Agriculture, forestry, & fishing	1.4	2.5	64.1
Medicine	1.8	0.9	33.3
Professional workers	9.9	8.1	45.0
Clerical workers	40.4	21.3	34.5
Managers	8.6	1.9	18.0
Laborers	1,420.0	35.5	2.4
Others	1.6	0.1	5.8
TOTAL	1,491.1	104.4	6.5

NOTE: The table does not include people other than Japanese and Taiwanese.
SOURCE: Ching-yuan Lin, *Industrialization in Taiwan, 1946–72*, p. 228.

central government retreated to the island in 1949. These political arrangements stifled challenges to the state. KMT control over society was reinforced by its economic strength. Government revenues were equivalent to 22 percent of GNP. These revenues consisted of taxes (62.4 percent), income from monopolies (13.8 percent), the surpluses of public enterprises and public utilities (3.8 percent), and other (20 percent). KMT economic strength was reinforced by U.S. aid, which averaged about 6.5 percent of Taiwan's GNP from 1951 to 1965.

The dominance of the mainlander-minority state over the Taiwanese majority paralleled Japanese practices. During the colonial period, Taiwanese access to positions in the bureaucracy and professions was limited. According to a census of Japanese and Taiwanese males in major occupational groups in 1940 (see Table 3.7), the Japanese constituted nearly three-fourths of government workers. Taiwanese working for the government were limited to low-ranking jobs. The Japanese also held most of the technical jobs, particularly in transportation and mining and manufacturing. The exceptions were found in two sectors—agriculture, forestry, and fishing; and medicine. In the colonial era, agriculture and medicine were the two fields at Taipei Imperial University open to Taiwanese. Becoming a doctor was often the only avenue into professional ranks for a local youth. As Table 3.7 clearly indicates, most Taiwanese males worked as laborers (about 95 percent of all workers).[49]

After the retrocession, Taiwanese continued to be excluded from the government. In 1946, of the total of 296 officials at various levels of the provincial government, only 22, or 7.4 percent, were Taiwanese; the rest were mainlanders.[50] The widely held view that this reflects KMT discrimination against the Taiwanese is, however, wrong. More likely, it was a result of power struggles among the competing factions within the KMT government, which ceased only after Chiang Kai-shek and Chiang Ching-kuo restructured the KMT and cemented Chiang Kai-shek's paramount position.[51] Not only islanders but also mainlanders who were not members of the powerful factions were excluded from power.[52] Those few Taiwanese given positions in the government had strong connections with KMT factions. The cases presented in the following chapters demonstrate the complexity of the mainlander-islander relationship issue in state–private sector relations and should warn us against hasty conclusions.

Accounting for the near total exclusion of Taiwanese from the government is, however, less important than determining the consequences of having mainland administrators, professionals, and technocrats, not only entrepreneurs, replace the Japanese in almost all fields. Inevitably, the mainlanders' dominance had a decisive impact on the distribution of state-controlled resources to the private sector, especially such scarce resources as foreign exchange and credits. Mainland capitalists had relatively easier access to resources controlled by the government, because of connections formed on the mainland. Most Taiwanese business people were not so lucky. Only a few elite families, whether picked as "winners" or chosen as "supporters," were granted the privilege of sharing in the political and economic resources.

The private sector was weak in terms of other factors. Apart from resources, the state also monopolized knowledge and know-how. As discussed in subsequent chapters, these informational asymmetries gave the state an advantage over a private sector that suffered from a lack of technological know-how, market information, and even the English-language skills necessary for international commerce. This situation remained unchanged until the late 1960s.

Conclusion

History is always present and always plays a role in current circumstances. It deserves our particular attention in regard to Taiwan since the Taiwan experience has been romanticized as an ahistorical state by proponents of statist explanations and an ahistorical free market by neo-classical economists. The KMT state on Taiwan inherited a weak private sector and a huge public sector from the Japanese. Both the local capitalists who emerged after the privatization of the four public enterprises and the mainland capitalists who followed the KMT to Taiwan were congenitally weak. Even though the émigré KMT regime needed to win supporters and was ready to offer economic rents to do so, its huge and varied resources, reinforced by the repressive political arrangements, allowed it to dominate the private sector. This dominance was reinforced by economic ideology—the command economy formed during the anti-Japanese war remained in favor among bureaucrats until the late 1950s—and by the émigré regime's wariness of local capitalists. This complex situation lies behind the KMT's political strategies and its policy toward capitalists. This history had a far greater impact on postwar state–private sector relations in Taiwan than did institutions. No theory that tries to explain the Taiwanese experience solely in terms of institutional factors can capture the subtleties of the situation.

Steve Chan has argued that the state on Taiwan grew strong because of its weaknesses: the civil war, Japanese occupation, and external dependency.[53] In contrast, this book argues that history endowed the state with strengths, not weaknesses. Politically, the state inherited an enormous organizational and ideological endowment. Fifty years of Japanese rule created a weak and poorly organized local elite, and the absence of an effective opposition allowed the KMT state to fill the political vacuum, reform society, and rebuild the state.[54] Economically, history afforded the state strength and independence from society. The state inherited a substantial economic legacy from the Japanese. Surprisingly, history helped the state dominate the private sector in Taiwan by a dramatic economic restructuring after it lost the civil war on the mainland. In the case of Taiwan, the state's strength was thoroughly embedded in history.

CHAPTER 4

Relations Between the State and Large Firms, 1950–1960

For the KMT, an émigré regime that eagerly sought supporters, forging a relationship with large firms was a matter not only of economics but also of politics. In selecting firms to foster, the state attempted to pick firms that were both "economic winners" and "political supporters." This chapter examines relations between the state and large businesses in the 1950s. These relations were dictated by the nature of the state and of the private sector, as well by other circumstances. Basically, in the 1950s the economy was on a wartime footing. The state controlled a wide range of resources and policy instruments critical to the economy. State-LE relations were formed through the allocation of resources and application of the instruments. Several questions arise from the state's behavior. Did the state intervene in the economy with "market-conforming" or "coordination-complementing" intentions? Was the state's intervention in line with its political strategies? What were the consequences of the interactions between the state and the LEs for Taiwan's unique industrial structure? The first section of this chapter discusses the state's strategies in pursuing its economic tasks and goals. The second examines the instruments and resources available to the state, and the final section analyzes the formation of a close state-LE relationship under the auspices of the state.

Strategies for Realizing
Economic Tasks and Goals

Taiwan's development in the 1950s is usually characterized as a case of import substitution industrialization (ISI). This post-hoc label is convenient but risky. It implies—wrongly—that the government had a clear, well-thought-out development plan. In reality, the state adopted short-term measures to resolve immediate economic difficulties. Two factors contributed to the state's lack of interest in developing an economic plan. First, the economy was subject to military goals. The regime's paramount concern was to "recapture the mainland," and it envisaged Taiwan as a base for this purpose. All activities were subordinated to this central task.

Second, development was not a major theme of the state in the 1950s. As noted in Chapter 2, reviving production and stabilizing the economy were the top economic priorities of the early 1950s. Although inflation had eased and production had recovered to prewar levels by the mid-1950s, the priorities were stabilization, survival, and self-sufficiency rather than development. These tasks determined that the state's economic efforts were based on short-term rather than long-term considerations. The economic bureaucracy did not even engage in long-term planning. As late as 1964, Wang Zuorong, an outspoken economist and a major aide to Yin Zhongrong and K. T. Li, criticized the aimlessness of the government's economic policy that resulted from its military priorities.[1]

The state did, however, have a strategy for realizing its short-term goals. This strategy was determined by the nature of the wartime economy and the economy of shortages, and its core elements were control and protection of domestic industry. The state controlled almost all resources, ranging from credit to foreign exchange to key commodities such as cement and steel. Even some production goods like raw cotton were under state control. For the state, the distribution of these resources was an issue not only of economics but also of politics. For the private sector, access to these resources was a precondition for development.

The state's major policy instruments were:

Foreign exchange controls
Import controls
Credit—through state-owned banks
Allocation of U.S. aid
Interest rates
Factory licenses
Allocation of raw materials
Taxes
Allocation of industrial land

The economic planning agencies made extensive use of these instruments to promote targeted industries. The industries selected for promotion in the First Four-Year (1953–56) and Second Four-Year (1957–60) plans included cement, textiles, papermaking, plastics, man-made fibers, and glass. The reason for choosing these industries was to save precious foreign funds by meeting the demand for these goods domestically. Import substitution was a natural and logical response to the economic realities. So it is fair to say that the government's first concern in controlling the economy was economic. However, the choice of entrants to these industries was a political issue as well. Not only did the government pick "economic winners," it also chose "political supporters."

The adoption of these instruments was also influenced by the state's economic ideology. As discussed in Chapter 2, the KMT's dominant economic ideology before the late 1950s favored a planned economy. State control and state-run industries were regarded as two effective methods for developing the economy. This ideology dominated the entire economic bureaucracy. Economic reality and economic ideology thus determined government policy. Yin Zhongrong, who later promoted the market economy and favored removing these control measures, was the main designer of these instruments. In the early 1950s, all economic officials believed that such instruments were necessary and effective and that they were the only way to solve the economy's problems.

The measures the state adopted to promote targeted industries focused either on controlling imports or on controlling entry.

Given the serious shortage of foreign exchange and the need to protect the domestic market, rigorous controls were placed on imports. For this purpose, a complex set of multiple foreign exchange rates was introduced, and the Taiwan currency was overvalued to make imports more expensive. To avoid overinvestment, the government set up barriers to block new entrants to particular industries. This was an important method for regulating the economy. In the 1950s such barriers were most frequently used in the textiles and cement sectors. This form of economic rents insulated existing operators from domestic competition.

Thus, large businesses on Taiwan enjoyed protection from foreign and domestic competition. This would have a significant impact on their development as well as on the entire industrial structure. Although the government's reasons for "fostering and protecting" a few select private enterprises were both economic and political, the consequences of these measures were far-reaching and extended beyond the government's short-term goals. By distributing government-held resources to both the public sector and these few large enterprises, the government gave these firms a monopoly in the domestic market. Protected by import controls and entry barriers, these enterprises were insulated from foreign and domestic competition. Most of these businesses grew into large enterprises in the 1960s and business groups in the 1970s. As we will see below, this policy helped to forge a close relationship between the state and the LEs and had an impact on the LEs when the state began promoting exports in the late 1950s and early 1960s. The first consequence was intended; the second was not. Both consequences were significant to the formation of Taiwan's unique industrial structure.

Instruments and Resources Available to the State

In Taiwan as elsewhere in East Asia, the availability of a wide range of instruments was vital to the state's capacity to steer the economy. Statist theorists are correct on this point. In the case of Taiwan in the 1950s, the government either invented instruments and resources or utilized pre-existing or imported ones. The first group includes all the control instruments. The second consists mainly of resources held by the state, U.S. aid, and the financial system, which became available to the KMT because of special historical circumstances (the financial system) or the international environment (U.S. aid). The distinction between instruments and resources is not clear-cut. Some, such as the financial system and the U.S. aid, may be both. These instruments and resources enabled the KMT government to dominate the economy in the 1950s. How did the state deploy these instruments and resources? More important, what was the outcome of their deployment? In what ways did their use help form a marketplace for the private sector, and how did the private actors respond to them? Since the provision of industrial finance is a major concern of this book, I focus on that resource in this section.

In general, "industrial finance" refers to all funds needed to establish and operate a firm. In the wartime economy of 1950s Taiwan, capital was in extremely short supply. Industrial finance specifically consists of funds spent at home and those spent abroad. In Taiwan, the domestic funds went for building factories, paying salaries, purchasing materials, and so forth. Equipment and raw materials not available domestically were purchased abroad. Even though domestic spending accounted for the greater part of industrial finance, foreign expenditures remained a vital concern in the 1950s since they involved scarce foreign exchange. Taiwan had few exportable goods, and it had to use the bulk of its hard currency to finance imports of necessary consumer goods and industrial materials. Little was left to purchase the capital goods and technical services required for industrial development. Consequently, the government had to control foreign exchange stringently. Raising capital in Taiwan dollars was not always difficult for most private firms, but obtaining foreign exchange allocations from the government was. Foreign exchange thus often became a key element in industrial finance. All the cases presented below involve the allocations of foreign exchange.

Industrial finance denominated in the Taiwan dollar came either from the organized or the unorganized financial system. The organized financial system provided most of the capital for the public sector—over 92 percent from 1968 to 1975. By contrast, about 50 percent of the private sector's capital came from the unorganized financial system during the same period.[2] Although we have no statistics for the 1950s, the organized system probably supplied even less to the private sector during this period than it did in later years. In the 1950s the organized financial system consisted of the publicly owned banks. The great majority of loans by all public banks went to the public sector, whereas those to the private sector were minimal. Moreover, there were no money and capital markets in the 1950s; in the 1960s, they accounted for 20 percent of the capital formation in the private sector.[3]

Given the severe shortage of capital, aid from the United States was the major source of finance in the 1950s. During 1951–56, total U.S. capital assistance (both in U.S. dollars and in nonduplicating aid-generated NT dollars) amounted to about $810 million, or 31.09 percent of Taiwan's net domestic investment of U.S.$2,605 million.[4] Four-fifths of all U.S. capital assistance went to government projects and the public sector; less than one-fifth directly financed private enterprises. American capital aid financed more than one-half of domestic investment in the public sector, but less than one-eighth of investment in the private sector. Even so, aid-financed investment helped induce a large amount of private investment.[5]

One significant contribution of U.S. aid in the 1950s was that it augmented foreign exchange resources and enabled Taiwan to purchase foreign machinery and equipment that complemented domestic labor and materials. Taiwan thus transmuted domestic savings into productive investment.[6] The contribution of the roughly $100 million in annual aid is even more impressive when contrasted with Taiwan's exports. From 1950 to 1958, Taiwan exported products valued at only $120 million each year.[7]

Financial and Banking System

Until 1959, most of Taiwan's financial system was state owned. There were no privately owned institutions in the banking sector. During the 1950s, there were no trust or credit corporations, nor were there stock and bond markets. Banks were the major force in the financial system. With the exception of the Central Trust of

China, which resumed functions in Taiwan in 1949, all other banks were owned by the provincial government and restructured from expropriated Japanese banks and other financial institutions (see Table 4.1). It was not until 1959 that two privately owned banks began operations in Taiwan, the China Development Corporation and the Nippon Dai-Ichi Kangyo Bank. Of these two, only Dai-Ichi was truly a private bank. The China Development Corporation was a joint public and private operation (see below). Thus, throughout the 1950s, the state monopolized the banking system. There was, however, an unregulated market, which coexisted with the organized financial system. This was an important source of funding for the private sector, especially SMEs.

The Bank of Taiwan (BOT) was the bankers' bank, the de facto central bank between 1949 and the reactivation of the Central Bank of China in 1961. The BOT was the center of a financial capital group, linked by interlocking shareholdings.[8] According to Liu Jinqing's research, the group included the three commercial banks, Hua-nan, Chang-hua, and First Commercial. The BOT held shares in First Commercial and Hua-nan, and each of the three commercial banks held shares in the other two (see Table 4.1). Through personnel arrangements, the KMT government controlled the three commercial banks, and KMT officials held positions in each. Among the staff of eleven bank officers in the Hua-nan Bank, one represented the "government share," five the BOT share, one the First Commercial share, and four the private share. Because the banks' holdings were the public share, the ratio of public to private was 7:4. Of the eleven officers at First Commercial, six represented the government share, one the BOT, one the Hua-nan Bank, and three the private share; the ratio of public to private was 8:3. At the Chang-hua Bank, the ratio was 6:5 (five from the government share, one from First Commercial, and five from the private share). Thus, through the BOT and a system of interlocking holdings, a public financial capital group was shaped. Joined by the Land Bank of Taiwan and the Co-operative Bank of Taiwan, a large group owned by provincial government (with both public and business financial capital), the BOT group, was formed.

Table 4.1
Capital Structure of Banks, December 1964

Bank	Owner	Total financial assets (million NT$)	Public and private shares (%)				Date of establishment or reactivation
			Total	Government share	Private share		
Central Bank of China	State	1,000	100.0	?	?		June 1961
Bank of China	State	18,000	100.0	66.7	33.3		Oct. 1960
Bank of Communications	State	18,000	100.0	88.0	12.0		Feb. 1960
Central Trust of China	State	8,000	100.0	100.0	0		1949
Postal Savings System	State	–	–	–	–		June 1962
Bank of Taiwan	Province	30,000	100.0	100.0	0		1946
Land Bank of Taiwan	Province	4,000	100.0	100.0	0		1946
Co-operative Bank of Taiwan	Province	3,000	100.0	60.0	40.0		1946
First Commercial Bank	Province	6,400	100.0	74.5	25.5		1946
Hua-nan Bank	Province	6,000	100.0	58.2	41.8		1946
Chang-hua Bank	Province	6,000	100.0	56.2	43.8		1946
Overseas Chinese Bank	Private	10,703	100.0	0	100.0		March 1961
China Development Corporation	Private	12,000	100.0	19.6	80.4		May 1959
Nippon Dai-Ichi Kangyo Bank	Private	–	–	–	–		Sept. 1959

SOURCE: Liu Jinqing, Taiwan zhanbou jingji fenxi, p.287.

Furthermore, through shareholding, this group brought about the domination of financial capital over industrial capital.[9]

There was a division of labor among the banks in making loans. Before 1961, given its function as acting central bank, most BOT loans were to the public sector. This situation began to change after the Central Bank was reactivated in 1961. In 1963, when the Central Bank's branches were authorized to make loans, there was a dramatic increase in loans to the private sector. Throughout the 1950s, the provision of loans to the private sector was the business of the Hua-nan, Chang-hua, and First Commercial banks.

The financial system in Taiwan in the 1950s was not only a policy instrument but also an important resource for the government. Through this system, the government allocated financial resources to both public and private users.

Allocation of U.S. Aid

From 1951 to 1965, U.S. economic aid to Taiwan totaled $1.465 billion, an average of $100 million a year. The aid represented 5–10 percent of Taiwan's GNP in each year during this period. The aid averaged 34 percent of total gross investment and covered roughly 90 percent of Taiwan's net import surplus of goods and services.[10] The types of U.S. aid were complicated and changed over time. Although not strictly separate, the aid could be categorized as military aid or economic aid. The amount of military aid between 1951 and 1967 was $2.48 billion, equivalent to 1.65 times the economic aid.[11] There is no doubt that the military aid had an impact on the economy; it clearly increased military procurements, for example. However, since military aid is not the subject of this research, I focus on economic aid, particularly aid to industry.

For the most part, U.S. economic aid consisted of general economic assistance, surplus agricultural commodities provided under Public Law 480, and the Development Loan Fund. The fifteen-year U.S. assistance program can be divided into three phases. The first phase was from 1951 to 1956. Most of the aid during this period falls under the rubrics of defense support, technical cooperation, and direct forces support. The U.S. agency responsible for the program was the Mutual Security Administration (MSA). Most assistance was given through grants. The second phase ran from 1957 to 1960. The surplus agricultural commodities and Development Loan Fund were added during this period. The aid was administered by the International Cooperation Administration (ICA) and came in the form of both loans and grants. The third phase was from 1961 to 1965; during this time development assistance replaced general assistance, and loans were the major method of assistance. The program became the responsibility of the Agency for International Development (AID).[12]

The first two phases of U.S. aid, from 1951 to 1960, are covered in the following chapters. The aid recipients did not receive U.S. currency; rather, they were given commodities and services of an equivalent worth. Deposits of New Taiwan dollars were made to a special account in the name of the Government of the ROC for use on projects mutually agreed to by the United States and Taiwan governments. The local currency was derived from several sources: sales of commodities supplied by Public Law 480, Title I commodities, and commodities financed by the defense support program. The aid-generated NT dollars were known as the "Counterpart Fund." In local currency between 1951 and 1965, the total in the fund amounted to just under NT$33 billion, roughly U.S.$825 million.[13] About 64 percent of the available aid-generated local currency was used for developmental purposes; the remaining 36 percent was used to support the military budget.[14]

The local currency program played a vital role in Taiwan's development by raising the level of domestic investment. Most substantial aid projects were financed by a combination of U.S. dollars, aid-generated NT dollars, and funds supplied by the Taiwan sponsor from local resources. The significance of the Counterpart Fund to the Taiwan economy lay in its capacity to transform a great quantity of local savings into productive investment; this would not have happened in the absence of the U.S. dollar and aid-generated NT dollar aid.[15]

How was U.S. aid allocated? Who had a say in the allocation process? And how did the government use the aid as a policy instrument? An examination of these issues helps reveal the impact of U.S. aid on the state structure, the ways the state managed the

economy and dealt with the private sector, and the resultant implications for the formation of the industrial structure.

Roughly 80 percent of U.S. economic aid went to the government (90 percent if military assistance is included).[16] Table 4.2 illustrates the allocation of economic assistance between the public and
the private sectors. The public sectors received more aid for infrastructure, whereas aid to the private sector went more to the
commercial and mining sectors. It is striking that manufacturing
received over half the U.S. aid to the private sector.

For the Taiwan government, the enormous amount of U.S. aid
was both a vital resource and an important policy instrument. One
main concern was furthering the government's economic and
political goals through the distribution of assistance. The use of
U.S. aid was regulated by the bilateral agreements between the two
governments and by U.S. law—the aid was to serve American interests. These restrictions gave the Taiwan government only limited
room to exert discretion. However, within the scope of its permitted autonomy, the Taiwan government tried to use the distribution
of the aid to serve its economic and political goals.

The aid had a strong impact on state autonomy and capacity in
Taiwan. On the one hand, it helped strengthen the autonomy of
the Taiwan government from society by providing huge financial
and material support. On the other hand, the aid made the state
dependent on the United States, politically, militarily, and economically. In other words, the aid simultaneously increased the
state's internal autonomy and its external dependency. This para-
doxical impact was also reflected in the state–private sector relationship. The state was able to influence private sector investment
through allocation of the aid. In this sense, the aid bolstered the
state. But the state also had to satisfy U.S. pressure to promote the
private sector through improving the investment environment. To
some extent this compensated for the weakness of the nascent private sector.

The aid also influenced the state structure. As elaborated in
Chapter 5, the U.S.-funded economic agencies played a vital role in
economic policy formulation and implementation. The aid helped
increase their authority and power.

Table 4.2
Allocation of U.S. Economic Aid in the Fixed Capital
Formation of the Public and Private Sectors, 1952–58

Sector	Amount of aid (million NT$)	Share of the amount of aid in a single sector		Share of a single sector in all public/private sectors	
		Public (%)	Private (%)	Public (%)	Private (%)
Agriculture, forestry, & fishing	858	64.5	35.4	8.9	27.4
Mining	69	23.8	76.2	0.3	4.7
Manufacturing	1,760	66.1	33.9	18.6	53.8
Construction	14	100.0	0.0	0.2	0.0
Electricity, gas, & tap water	3,041	100.0	0.0	48.7	0.0
Transportation	818	100.0	0.0	13.1	0.0
Commercial	3	0.0	100.0	0.0	0.3
Services & administration	644	99.6	0.4	10.3	0.2
Others	152	0.0	100.0	0.0	13.7
TOTAL	7,359	85.0	15.0	100.0	100.0

SOURCE: Wen Xinying, *Jingji qiji de beihou*, p. 245.

The U.S. aid also contributed to the development of Taiwan's unique industrial structure. First, it helped reinforce the upstream SOEs, particularly those in the infrastructure. The fact that 85 percent of U.S. assistance went to the public sector reflected the common goals of both the U.S. and the Taiwan governments. Support for the public sector served to strengthen Taiwan as an anticommunist base, which was in the interest of both sides. Aid to the public sector concentrated on infrastructure, such as electricity, transportation, telecommunications, and tap water, both because the infrastructure had military significance and because improvements in these areas helped improve the climate for investment. Economic assistance also went to some sectors monopolized by the state, such as petroleum, aluminum, sugar refining, fertilizer, and tobacco, because American technology and capital goods best fit the needs of large-scale producers. Thus, U.S. companies could share monopoly profits through aid-financed procurement, technical cooperation, and loans.[17] Second, U.S. aid helped strengthen state-LE relations through the allocation of the aid among the LEs. During the 1950s, the state used U.S. aid as rents to foster its chosen winners and supporters.

The Formation of
Close State-LE Relations

Compared to its Japanese and South Korean counterparts, the Taiwan state kept large business at arm's length. As analyzed in the preceding chapter, a relationship began to form between the state and a few mainland and local capitalists at the very beginning of the KMT's rule on the island. Throughout the 1950s, the state continued to practice a policy of nurturing and protecting large business. In Chalmers Johnson's opinion, one of the major features of East Asian developmental states is their commitment to private property and the market.[18] The Taiwan state fits this description. Although it had a huge public sector and an anti–big business bias, it was well aware that it needed to rely on the private sector for the economic growth essential to its rule.

However, the KMT regime had a history of distrusting business people. On the mainland, its relations with business were based on manipulation rather than cooperation.[19] This tradition was reinforced by its nature as an émigré regime on Taiwan. Its distrust of capitalists became a distrust of the Taiwanese business people. This ran so deep that Chiang Ching-kuo extended his intelligence agencies into private enterprises. In the 1950s, Chiang stipulated that every major firm had to employ a retired military or intelligence officer in a high position in its personnel department.[20] Nevertheless, as an émigré regime with a weak social basis, the KMT had to foster support among capitalists. Because of these conflicting goals, the Taiwan state practiced a policy of both protecting *and* restricting the LEs. This policy differed considerably from the single-minded fostering of a few large business groups as engines of economic development in Japan and South Korea.

The policy emphasis varied over time in line with the regime's changing political and economic concerns and priorities. In the 1950s, the KMT nurtured a group of chosen private enterprises on the principle of picking winners and supporters by using its policy instruments and allocating its resources to the selected enterprises. The enterprises in question were the mainland companies that followed the KMT to Taiwan and the local firms formed from the privatization of public enterprises in 1954. In addition, a number of new enterprises, owned mainly by locals, joined the SOEs to monopolize the domestic market. These businesses were primarily in textiles, cement, and plastics. Among the new firms, the Tainan Spinning Group, Formosa Plastics, and Jiaxin Cement were prominent. Despite their small size, they still can be viewed as LEs since most of them grew substantially in subsequent decades and their relations with the state differed from those between the SMEs and the state.

There are a number of classic cases of state fostering of enterprises. The entrustment scheme in the textile industry, the Formosa PVC project, and the Xinzhu Glass Plant are prime examples. When Yin Zhongrong decided to develop the textile industry in Taiwan, he introduced a program whereby the government provided raw cotton to the producers, paid the workers' wages, and purchased the yarn. This risk-free arrangement induced a number of enterprises to enter this industry. Indeed, most of Taiwan's leading business groups began as textile companies. Another example is the case of the Xinzhu Glass plant. The Central Trust of China invested in the Xinzhu Glass Plant and sold it to private interests after it became profitable in 1953. The three case studies examined below illustrate (1) the ways in which the government deployed its resources and instruments to nurture private enterprises, (2) the policy process in the economic planning agencies, and (3) the government's criteria for picking enterprises to support.

Picking a Winner: The Formosa PVC Project

The Formosa PVC (polyvinyl chloride) project illustrates one form of state–private sector relations in the 1950s and the government's use of economic criteria to select investors. Both the First and the Second Four-Year plan singled out plastics for promotion. The IDC considered PVCs to be a promising sector for development on Taiwan. But several conditions had to be met: the investment could not be large, the plant had to begin operating quickly, the investment had to be efficient, and the products should find a ready market. Since these requirements could not be met by a public enterprise, the planned PVC project had to be undertaken by a private firm. Although U.S. aid had already been earmarked for the PVC project of the state-run Taiwan Alkali Company, Yin Zhongrong and the Chemical Industry Group of the IDC led by Yan Yancun decided to give this project to a private firm.

The IDC approached He Yi, owner of Yongfeng Original Papermaking, a firm that originated in the privatization of the four public corporations. He Yi and his brother agreed to take over the project, and U.S.$700,000 of foreign exchange from U.S. aid was allocated to him. However, on-the-spot investigations of PVC plants in the United States, Japan, and West Germany revealed that the scale of production contemplated for Taiwan was too small to be profitable—only four tons per day would be produced in Taiwan, compared to 40 tons elsewhere—and the project was withdrawn. However, the U.S.$700,000 in aid funds had already been allocated, and the IDC still believed that PVC was promising. So it decided that the project should go forward. Yi Zhongrong asked the BOT to check its depositors to find a potential investor. It recommended Wang Yongqing, a rice merchant who was anxiously seeking an investment opportunity and held NT$8 million in bank deposits. Ironically, Wang's earlier interest in plastics had received a cold shoulder from Yan Yancun, because of Wang's ignorance of plastics. Yan had also rejected his application for a project to manufacture tires. Yan reluctantly approached Wang and his partner, Zhao Tingzhen, about the PVC. Although the proposed cooperation between Wang and Zhao was not realized, Wang promised to take over the PVC project. Since Wang knew little about either PVC or plastics, Yan, who had a Ph.D. in chemistry, was hesitant to give the project to Wang. He warned Wang that the project required advanced technology and scientific methods,[21] but Wang agreed to accept the project without further consideration,[22] and Formosa Plastics Corporation was founded in March 1954 and began operations in 1957. Few would have predicted that this was the start of a plastics kingdom that would become the largest business group on the island and the largest producer of PVC in the world.

Unquestionably, the success of Formosa Plastics was due solely to the insistence of IDC bureaucrats that the project be privately run. In 1953, at a time when the idea of a state-run economy dominated the thinking of bureaucrats, it was a brave but difficult move for Yin Zhongrong and Yan Yancun to insist on giving the PVC project to a private firm, particularly since the initial applicant for U.S. aid for the project was the state-run Taiwan Alkali Corporation. Yin and Yan faced mounting pressure and had to prevail over dissenting views. After He Yi withdrew, voices in favor of a public-run project resurfaced. Yin still insisted that the project should be run by a private firm. Although from a professional and technical perspective Yan Yancun was initially reluctant to give the project to Wang Youqing, he shared Yin Zhongrong's view that it should be given to a private firm. After Wang took over the project, Yan helped him considerably. During its subsequent expansion, Formosa Plastics continued to receive support from the government. For its 1,200–ton expansion plan, Formosa also received support from Shen Jintai, director of the First Section of the IDC, in obtaining the necessary foreign exchange allocations.

The Formosa Plastics case reveals that during the early period of economic development the IDC was the key organ promoting the private sector. Some pro-market bureaucrats in the IDC gave promising projects to private firms because they believed that private firms were more efficient than public firms and they favored private ownership of industry. Their efforts led to the development of firms like Formosa Plastics Corporation and sectors like plastics. But opposition from their pro–state enterprise colleagues often triggered struggles. During the first half of the 1950s, the pro-market bureaucrats lost many battles. Yin Zhongrong had to step down in 1955, and soon thereafter Yan Yancun resigned over allegations of corruption in the Formosa Plastics project. Still, these key bureaucrats' personal preferences had a considerable impact on the development of the private sector. In the PVC case, Yin Zhongrong's insistence on private ownership led to the emergence of Formosa Plastics. Shen Jintai's support for its expansion plan proved important to the development of the company. Wang Yongqing himself admitted that without Shen's support, Taiwan's PVC industry would never have developed as it did.[23]

The fate of the private sector was tied to bureaucrats' personal preferences rather than to a specific policy. Under Yin Zhongrong, the IDC was successful in promoting the private sector. When Jiang Biao replaced Yin as chairman of the IDC, K. T. Li felt that it would be difficult to promote private industry because Jiang favored a command economy and was fairly conservative.[24] Yan Yancun was greatly at odds with Jiang, and he cited this conflict as an important reason for his resignation.[25]

If the Formosa PVC case supports the assumption of "market-conforming intervention," the next two cases challenge this assumption.

Picking *a Winner* and *a Supporter:* The Jiaxin Cement Corporation

Cement was one of the most profitable sectors in the 1950s and illustrates state–private sector relations during this period. Because of the military demand for cement, this sector was strictly controlled. Until 1954, the cement sector was monopolized by the publicly owned Taiwan Cement Corporation. Domestic production could not meet demand, and the government had to spend foreign exchange in order to import cement. To substitute for the imports, the government opened cement to the private sector. In 1952, ex–Shanghai capitalist Xu Youxiang, president of the Yuandong Textile Corporation, together with former Shanghai banker Chen Guangfu, applied for permission to set up a cement plant, but their application was rejected. In 1954, a group of mainland legislators and capitalists received approval to establish Jiaxin Cement Corporation. Xu Youxiang finally obtained permission for the Asian Cement Corporation in 1957 after he invited a legislator to serve as president. Another cement plant, the Universal Cement Corporation, was founded in 1960 by a group of local capitalists.

The story. The Jiaxin case illustrates relations between the state and mainland capitalists. As part of an expansion, Jiaxin Cement Corporation planned to buy a second unit of machinery and equipment from William and Hunt, an American company, and from the Kobe Steel Works of Japan. Since Jiaxin had to pay US$1.5 million for the equipment, it applied to the IDC for foreign exchange allocations and asked the BOT to issue a letter of credit for US$1.5 million before the deadline date of March 24, 1956. The IDC found the project to be economically and technically sound and in principle granted approval at a meeting on March 1, 1956. The IDC passed the Jiaxin case to Committee A of the ESB for financial screening, and that committee also concluded that the project submitted by the chairman of the board of Jiaxin should be approved in principle. It further suggested that the ESB be asked to designate a bank to guarantee the credit required for this project. On March 15, the ESB approved the project in principle but asked the IDC to check that the Jiaxin had insured its first manufacturing unit, which was worth NT$31 million. Thereafter, Committee A conducted a final review and concluded at a meeting on March 19 that the project already approved by the ESB should be implemented immediately. It specifically assigned the BOT to consider confirming a letter of credit. It stipulated that Jiaxin had to agree that the final decision on importing the equipment would be made by the government. This condition was stated in Jiaxin's letter to the BOT on the same day.

The project was presented to the FETCC meeting on March 23, 1956. It concluded that in pursuance with the ESB's decision reached on March 15, 1956, the necessary foreign exchange allocation should be granted and the BOT should be instructed to issue a letter of credit for the down payment before the deadline and guarantee the subsequent promissory notes. The BOT did so that same day. The project and the decisions made by these agencies were ratified by the ESB at a meeting on March 30, 1956.

The policy network for the Jiaxin case. The approval process in the Jiaxin case allows us to draw a policy-making map for the 1950s. Four government departments were involved: the IDC, Committee A of the ESB, the ESB itself, and the FETCC.

After reviewing the application, the IDC concluded that the project was economically and technically sound and that its prompt completion would help the country's foreign exchange situation by reducing imports and increasing exports of cement. These conclusions were cited by the other agencies in their discussions. The IDC's deliberations reflected its role, designated in the "Organization Rules of the ESB," in screening and promoting industrial projects.

Committee A of the ESB was responsible for the "planning and screening of monetary, finance, and foreign trade, and screening the united import plans supported by the government foreign exchange and the U.S. aid foreign exchange." In the present case, its role was to examine the financial aspects of the project.

The Jiaxin case demonstrates the ESB's special role in the policy network. It involved three of the seven functions assigned the board by the Executive Yuan: reviewing and coordinating monetary, finance, foreign exchange, and trade policies; reviewing and coordinating the use of U.S. aid and the Counterpart Fund; and reviewing and coordinating the plans for industry, transportation, and agriculture. Its decisions were forwarded to the departments responsible for implementation after they had been approved by the Executive Yuan. This was the administrative basis of the ESB as a supra-ministerial agency.

The ESB's organizational arrangements reinforced its role. Its members were drawn from the central government and the economic and finance departments of the provincial government. The chairmen of each of its committees and the IDC were the heads of the analogous government departments. For example, in 1956 when the Jiaxin case was under review, Committee A was chaired by Xu Boyuan, who was also the minister of finance and chair of the FETCC. The head of the IDC, Jiang Biao, was also the minister of economic affairs. These arrangements enabled the ESB to coordinate different departments and to make final decisions, thus ensuring the authority of the decisions made at the ESB meetings. It is therefore not surprising that the ESB was much more efficient than other government departments.

In explaining the policy process in the Jiaxin case, ESB documents refer to the discretionary power of the ESB. One clause of the ESB Organization Rules reads: "If the case is within the discretion of each responsible department, it can be forwarded to the related responsible departments for implementation and reported to the Executive Yuan for reference." The Jiaxin case was processed according to this clause since it was within the discretion of the government departments.[26]

Implications. Two other applications for large cement plants were sent to the IDC. Only Jiaxin's was approved, however. Why Jiaxin? All three projects would have satisfied the industrial development priorities of the First Four-Year Plan. Why, then, were the other two applications rejected? According to the IDC, Jiaxin won approval because its proposal was economically and technically sound and less costly in terms of foreign exchange. Was this claim true?

In fact, the IDC's conclusions encountered some opposition, and the application did not receive unanimous approval. Some of the members who reviewed the application raised objections. R. D. Smith and C. D. Jones, officials of the U.S. Aid Mission to China, questioned the IDC's conclusion that the project was economically sound. They said that "no information or data have been submitted to show that Jiaxin will be able to furnish the NT$19 million to be used on the second unit as well as the remaining NT$10.205 million still required for the first unit."[27] Martin Wang (Wang Peng), secretary-general of CUSA and a member of the ESB, echoed Smith and Jones: "The political sagacity of giving assistance only to one firm and not to other applications cannot be ignored, especially if the [firm's] financial soundness is questionable." He favored "giving assistance to another applicant before approving the second unit for Jiaxin."[28] V. S. de Beausset, a U.S. official, also suggested the possibility of assigning the second unit to another party.[29] Qian Changzhao, the secretary-general of the ESB, suggested adding two conditions to Jiaxin's approval. First, the second unit would be assigned to another qualified applicant if Jiaxin failed to satisfy the New Taiwan dollar requirements. Second, Jiaxin had to abide by government regulations on pricing and the allocation of output to civilian and military users.[30]

Subsequently, two further conditions were added at Committee A's meeting on March 19. First, the final disposition of the second unit of equipment was subject to future decisions by the government. Second, Jiaxin and other large cement manufacturers "should be immediately notified that in the future their product will be subject to government regulation with respect to pricing and allocation of sales quota for both military and civilian uses."[31] After approving the Jiaxin project in principle at the March 15 meeting, the ESB passed another resolution on the project at the March 30 meeting. In this resolution, two significant conditions were added. First, Jiaxin had to agree that the final use of the second unit of machinery was subject to government approval. Second, unless the financial arrangements satisfied the government, the second unit of equipment would be assigned to another appropriate manufacturer.

Obviously, the ESB's March 30 resolution incorporated the differences of opinion voiced in the other meetings. The document explaining the policy-making procedure stated that the purpose of the ESB's resolution was to implement the principles of the previous meeting's resolution.[32] Despite the eventual compromise, the doubts about Jiaxin's financial situation were not allayed, and the other two applications were not considered.

Why was Jiaxin favored over the others? The names of the officers of Jiaxin Cement Corporation supply part of the answer. The chairman of the board was Shu Yunzhang. Shu had been general manager of China Textile, chairman of the Commission of the Textile Administration under the MOEA, a member of the Legislative Yuan even before the move to Taiwan (a position he retained until his death in 1973), and chairman of the boards of China Textile, Yongxing Textile, and many other companies. He was also chairman of the Chinese National Association of Industry and Commerce from 1952 to 1961, chairman of the board of the China Productivity and Trade Center between 1956 and 1961, and chairman of the China Federation of Industry from 1957 to 1965. He thus had a strong political background, was trusted by the government, and enjoyed close relationships with the economic bureaucracy and key bureaucrats. Under the corporatist arrangements through which the KMT government controlled and communicated with business, Shu's chairing of two of the most important business associations, the Chinese Association of Industry and Commerce and the Chinese Federation of Industry, made him the most influential businessman in Taiwan during the 1950s. He was also a successful entrepreneur who ran a number of companies. In effect, he was a spokesman for the business community and frequently urged the government to support the private sector and improve the environment for industrial development. Shu's role as a bridge between the government and the private sector was vital both to the government and to business. It was Shu who communicated with government officials during the deliberations over the Jiaxin application. He had obviously been invited to chair the Jiaxin board because of his influence and the help he could give the corporation, especially during its start-up phase.[33] Considering Shu's background, the ESB's decision on Jiaxin's application is not surprising.

Why, then, did Martin Wang and the American officials suggest considering the other applications? It is understandable that the Americans advised careful scrutiny of Jiaxin's application and that they wanted equal consideration given to other applications. From their neutral position, they were able to treat the matter from a technical point of view and ignore political and other factors. However, the opinions of Martin Wang, who was secretary-general of the CUSA and who was regarded as unique among the bureaucrats for his anti-traditional, western-style manner, are noteworthy.[34] After he was dismissed as secretary-general of the CUSA, he was named minister counselor of the ROC embassy in Washington, D.C. Given his personality, Wang's blunt and outspoken comments on the Jiaxin application make sense. But the questions raised by the Americans and Wang reflect the influence of nontechnical and noneconomic considerations in the policy process.

From the Jiaxin case, we can draw two conclusions. First, political considerations were the major factor in the approval of the application. Later developments suggest that Jiaxin's financial situation was not as sound as stated by the IDC and ESB, thus substantiating the doubts raised by the American officials. Jiaxin was unable to take delivery of the equipment because of financial difficulties, and eventually, Asian Cement took the machinery.

Second, the economic planning agencies used foreign exchange and other resources as policy instruments to pick supporters by either blocking or allowing entrants to certain industries. Foreign exchange remained vital to the building of new plants in the 1950s. It was not only a resource and an instrument but also a source of economic rents for the government. Policy instruments allowed the government to intervene in the economy and to distribute rents among its supporters.

Another Winner and Supporter: The Universal Cement Corporation

The story. This case illustrates relations between the state and local capitalists. Universal Cement Corporation was founded by Tainan Spinning—the base for the Tainan Group—one of the most successful local business groups in Taiwan.

Tainan Spinning Corporation was founded by members of the Hou family of Tainan, an ancient city in southern Taiwan. Universal Cement Corporation was established by some of the major shareholders in Tainan Spinning. The timing of Universal Cement's application to the IPCG in 1960 was poor (the IPCG assumed the functions of the IDC after the ESB was dissolved). Yin Zhongrong and his associates thought there was excess capacity in the cement sector and that production should be limited and no new plants should be approved. Therefore, Yin rejected Universal's application. Wu Sanlian, the president of Universal, sought assistance from Wu Zhongxin, a senior KMT cadre. After Wu Zhongxin spoke with Yin, Yin reversed his decision and approved the project.[35] This approval was unexpected given the ban on new cement plants.[36]

The IPCG had no objections to the application in principle, even though it raised the issue of excess capacity. Not only was the application approved, but the project was given access to foreign exchange. As in the Jiaxin case, foreign exchange, which was in short supply at the time, was a critical factor for the project. The project required NT$100 million in capital. In contrast to Jiaxin, however, this amount had been subscribed by the shareholders (one of whom held 50 percent of the shares). But foreign exchange was required to purchase machinery from a Japanese supplier. The application for foreign exchange was approved by the FETCC, then led by Yin Zhongrong, at meetings on April 22 and April 29, 1960. Out of the total of $2.55 million in foreign exchange required for the project, $637,500 for the first and second payments was allocated. The remainder was to be paid later with foreign exchange earned by Universal's cement exports. The BOT agreed to be the guarantor by issuing a letter of credit for the entire payment.

There were some changes in the policy network between the Jiaxin and the Universal applications. The ESB and the IDC had been disbanded in 1958; most of the ESB's functions were transferred to CUSA, and the IPCG was established within the MOEA to replace the IDC. Thereafter, the IPCG played a key role in reviewing the applications for industrial projects. The FETCC was still authorized to approve foreign exchange allocations. Another important difference between the two cases was a change in personnel. Yin Zhongrong resumed office in 1958 after he was exonerated in a corruption case. He was named the vice-chairman of CUSA and appointed president of the BOT, and he replaced Xu Boyuan as the director of the FETCC. As economic tsar, he was the most powerful person in economic affairs and could thus give the green light for the project.

Implications. At a time when there was a ban on new cement plants, why was Universal Cement's application approved? In order to answer this question, we must understand Universal Cement's background.

After five years of operations, Tainan Spinning had accumulated considerable capital, and the major owners had capital to invest in new projects. With this strength, the capital in NT dollars for Universal Cement Corporation was easily provided by major investors. Hou Yuli, the major shareholder in Tainan Spinning and once the wealthiest person in southern Taiwan,[37] held 50 percent of the shares in Universal Cement. It is clear that the shareholders in Universal Cement were wealthy local capitalists.

Another significant point is that the president of Universal Cement, Wu Sanlian, was appointed mayor of Taipei (1950–51) and then became the first elected mayor of Taipei (1951–54) with the backing of the ruling party. He was a provincial lawmaker between 1954 and 1960. The fact that he was both appointed by Chiang Kai-shek to be mayor of Taipei and supported by the KMT to run in the election for mayor was unusual. Although this was part of KMT's strategy to gain the support of the locals, his selection reflected his prestige and influence among the local elite. Wu was among a handful of prominent Taiwanese used as "political window dressing" by the KMT to allay the locals' resentment against the KMT and to win them over. Although he was not a KMT member, he had good relations with the KMT government. That was the reason he was elected president of Tainan Spinning Corporation and why Tainan Spinning could beat other strong competitors despite the ban on new textile plants.[38]

Once again, the Universal case reveals the role of politics in state–private sector relations in the late 1950s. Like Jiaxin, Universal selected an influential person with a strong political network as president to lobby the bureaucrats to get around the government bans.[39] Universal's application was eventually approved after strong lobbying—Yin was persuaded by an influential KMT veteran. Unquestionably, as in the case of Jiaxin, political factors were vital. Politics, not economic or financial factors, led to the approval of Universal's application. It is true that unlike Jiaxin, Universal's financial situation was sound, and the IPCG and the FETCC meetings noted this. However, since its financial situation was equally sound when Yin Zhongrong rejected its application, its financial health was apparently not the major factor in the government's approval of the application.

In both the Jiaxin and the Universal cases, the BOT played a role as guarantor by providing letters of credit and loaned the foreign exchange required for the down payment. Its functions were key to both applications at a time when foreign exchange was tightly controlled by the government. In 1949, the Central Bank of China designated the BOT as the only bank permitted to deal in foreign exchange. Following this decision, it had become involved in foreign exchange–related policy making. In 1955, the FETCC was set up under the cabinet to replace the Group of Foreign Exchange to strengthen controls. The president of BOT was a member of the FETCC (Yin was the concurrent chairman of the FETCC), and the BOT implemented resolutions drafted by the FETCC. The BOT held and determined all uses of foreign exchange. This situation did not change until 1959, when a foreign bank, Dai-Ichi Kangyo, was allowed to open an office in Taiwan. From 1961 on, local banks were allowed to enter the foreign exchange business. In the allocation and use of foreign exchange in the 1950s, a key scarce industrial resource, the role of the BOT was twofold: to implement both foreign exchange–related policy and instructions of the FETCC and to provide foreign exchange to users. The BOT was an important part of the policy network through its provision of foreign exchange, which was a kind of industrial finance, in the 1950s.

Three implications can be drawn from the Jiaxin and Universal cases. First, political considerations were the most important factor behind the approval of their applications. This point is further confirmed by the Asian Cement case. Xu Youxiang's first application for a cement plant was rejected in 1952 when Chen Guangfu, a Shanghai banker, was his partner, but his application was approved in 1957 after he dropped Chen and invited lawmakers Wang Xinheng and Li Zemin to join him as partners. Wang Xinheng was named president of Asian Cement Corporation. The second unit of machinery ordered by Jiaxin in 1957 wound up with Asian Cement—it was transferred to the company by the ESB. These three cases demonstrate the importance of a strong political network—

regardless of whether the applicants were mainlanders or local people. Strong political connections were the most important condition in winning government approval. This was a matter of "picking supporters."

Second, the applicants had to be economically powerful. All three plants had been set up by capitalists who had accumulated considerable capital in the textile business. The major shareholders of Universal Cement were the owners of Tainan Textile, Xu Youxiang of Asian Cement was the owner of Yuandong Textile, and Jiaxin's major shareholder was China Yuexin Textile. Sound finances were a precondition for a successful application, although they were not the only condition.

Third, we should be cautious about claims that the government discriminated against local capitalists in allocating resources. Despite his mainland background, Xu Youxiang's first application was rejected. The approval of his second application can be attributed to a wiser selection of partners. And despite being a local project, Universal Cement was approved, due to its strong political network and sound finances. The cases of Asian Cement and Universal Cement show that political networks and economic strength were more important than geographic origins in winning government favor. This serves as a reminder to be careful when attributing geographic origins to state–private sector relations in postwar Taiwan.

Conclusion

As we have seen, a regime's policy toward the private sector is determined by multiple factors. Ideology, economic realities, the nature of the regime, and political considerations, as well as the personal preferences of individual bureaucrats, can all have an impact on public policy toward business. In the case of Taiwan, these factors determined the KMT's policies of both fostering and restricting capitalists. The findings of this chapter suggest that the goals and motives of government economic policy in Taiwan were multifaceted. The economic planning agencies did consider technical and efficiency factors (as in the case of Formosa PVC). However, often political considerations predominated, as in the cases of Jia-xin and Universal. This finding challenges the conventional wisdom about economic policy in East Asia—that state intervention was neither always market conforming, as statism suggests, nor always coordination complementing, as the "market-enhancing view" maintains.[40] Instruments and resources also served as sources of economic rents. Therefore, the state-business relationship cannot be reduced to an economic relationship. In particular, political factors should also be taken into account. The cases reviewed in this chapter show that political considerations were a major element in the government's fostering of private firms, be they mainlander or local. The state's strategy was not only to pick economic winners but also to find political supporters.

Second, the state's protecting and fostering of a few firms resulted in these privileged firms' jointly monopolizing the domestic market with the SOEs. This outcome would have consequences for Taiwan's industrial structure. As elaborated in the following chapters, because the LEs became accustomed to monopoly profits in the domestic market, they were less willing to enter the risky export markets when the state changed its policy emphasis from import substitution to exports in the late 1950s. In other words, the state-LE relations formed in the 1950s constituted one of the origins of Taiwan's industrial structure as it evolved over the following two decades.

Third, the significance of U.S. aid to Taiwan's development was greater than has previously been assumed. The findings of this book suggest that U.S. aid influenced the state structure by funding economic planning agencies and affected state-business relations by providing significant resources and instruments to the state. More important, the allocation of U.S. aid had an impact on the formation of the industrial structure by reinforcing the upstream SOEs and strengthening state-LE relations.

The Shift to Exports: Encouragement or Discouragement?

The late 1950s–early 1960s were a key period in the economic history of postwar Taiwan: under pressure from the United States, the emphasis shifted from a commitment to import substitution to a strategy of export promotion. This change established the basis for Taiwan's export-oriented industrialization. Paradoxically, even as the state strengthened its ties with the LEs, it did not encourage them to export. Rather, the relationship discouraged them from exporting. The policy-making process surrounding the shift in emphasis was full of conflicts, compromises, and calculated choices. Why did this change occur? How did the government promote exports, and how did the private sector respond? What was the outcome of the interplay between the state and private actors, and what were its implications for the formation of Taiwan's unique industrial structure? This chapter addresses these questions by analyzing the three economic reforms of the late 1950s and early 1960s, the establishment of the China Development Corporation (CDC) and its implications, and the Tangrong Iron Corporation case.

An End to the Wartime Economy and the Move Toward Exports

Taiwan's economy reached a turning point in the late 1950s. As the Second Four-Year Plan neared completion in 1960, severe production shortages had been alleviated. What had not changed, however,

was the wartime footing of the economy and the continuing inflation and international balance-of-payments deficit. The military
confrontation with mainland China on the offshore islands of
Jinmen and Mazu in 1958 highlighted Taiwan's military vulnerabil-
ity and economic weaknesses. This expensive artillery engagement
motivated KMT leaders to develop the economy.[1] Severe floods in
August 1959 worsened inflationary pressures. As the policy debate
among bureaucrats over state versus private running of the economy intensified, mounting pressures from the United States and
support from the top authorities strengthened the pro-market bureaucrats. This paved the way for the liberalization of the economy
and for the growth of the private sector.

Three actions in particular encouraged the development of the
private sector. The state's use of universalistic rather than particularistic incentives to promote exports created an opportunity for
SMEs to enter the export-oriented manufacturing sectors. With respect to industrial finance, the semi-public CDC was active in providing industrial finance to the private sector. The establishment of
the CDC, which combined state and private capital, signaled the
strengthening and expansion of state-LE relations. After Yin
Zhongrong replaced Zhang Zikai as president of the Bank of Taiwan, government monetary policy underwent a dramatic change—
from Keynesian to anti-inflationary. This shift had a dramatic impact on the private sector, as we shall see in the case of the failure
of Tangrong Iron Corporation.

Although Yin Zhongrong and his colleagues in the U.S. aid–
financed economic organs were pro-market bureaucrats, they did
not see the free market as a solution to Taiwan's economic problems, since Taiwan was still a backward society, its private sector
was in its infancy, and market mechanisms were weak. Rather, their
goal was a market economy, and they favored the intensive use of
policy instruments to steer the economy in this direction. This suggests that the transformation from import substitution to export-
oriented industrialization during the late 1950s and early 1960s was
driven by state policy. To what extent did the state design this transformation, and how did it police the marketplace? These are key issues for understanding the state's role in economic development.

Three Reforms

The shift from import substitution to exports and the government's commitment to promoting the private sector are exemplified in three reforms. The first, of foreign exchange and trade, occurred in 1958. The multiple exchange rate system previously in effect to control imports and to conserve foreign exchange featured literally hundreds of different exchange rates, depending on the commodity. This aspect of the controlled economy was intended to control imports and the country's balance of payments through supply and cost restrictions. However, the multiple exchange rate system was extremely difficult to implement in practice. Not only was it inefficient, but it also encouraged corruption by prompting speculation in foreign exchange and imported materials as well as abuses of power by the bureaucrats in the supervising agencies. Meanwhile, the balance-of-payment problems persisted.[2]

By the beginning of 1958, there was a growing consensus in business, the press, and the bureaucracy that the system had to be changed if the country's balance of payments and industrial structure were to be improved.[3] By the end of the year, the multiple exchange rate system had been simplified to a double exchange rate system. Rate A was applicable to the goods Taiwan was able to export at this time, including rice, sugar, and salt, as well as imported goods needed in the domestic market, such as machinery, fertilizer, crude oil, cotton, soybeans, and wheat. Rate B was applicable to all other goods. Rate A was U.S.$1.00:NT$24.78; rate B U.S.$1.00:NT$36.08.[4] The aim of the reform was to eliminate the multiplicity of exchange rates, reduce the strict controls on foreign-exchange allocations, and strengthen policy incentives in the export sectors.[5] The consequence of the reform was that it shifted the emphasis from restricting imports to encouraging exports.

The second reform was a comprehensive plan aimed at improving the overall environment for the private sector and foreign capital in order to boost exports. After receiving Chiang Kai-shek's approval, the Nineteen-Point Program of Economic and Financial Reform was implemented in 1960. This package consisted of four sections: economic development, budget, finance, and foreign exchange and trade. The first section contained initiatives to encourage savings, establish a stock market, lift restrictions on the private sector, privatize public firms, and simplify bureaucratic procedures for business. In the budgetary section, the most important action was that the government agreed to freeze defense expenditures as a percentage of the total budget. The finance section proposed a strengthened central banking system. The central bank would regulate interest rates, control the money supply, and supervise the commercial banks. Moreover, a tight credit policy would be put into effect in an effort to stabilize the economy. In the area of foreign exchange and trade, a single exchange rate system was implemented, and all restrictions on foreign trade were lifted. Measures encouraging exports were to be introduced, and procedures for settling exchanges of exports to be simplified.

There were two critical points in the package: promotion of the private sector and expansion of exports. The promulgation of the nineteen-point package signaled a dramatic shift in government economic policy. The encouragement of the private sector and the moves toward the global market represented attempts to avoid an economic crisis and to sustain continued economic growth. This change paved the way for the rapid expansion of exports in the 1960s.

The third reform was intended to implement the principles set out in the nineteen-point reform package. The nineteen-point reform package was a general statement of the principles of reform. Since it was a government circular, not a law, it had no legal binding force. Furthermore, because it had been drafted by the CUSA, there was resistance from other government departments. Thus, there was a need to legalize the reform measures. The key purpose of the Statute for the Encouragement of Investment, promulgated in September 1960, was to codify the reform measures. Existing legal restrictions constituted the main obstacles to the implementation of the reform policies. For example, establishing a factory fell under the Land Act, which was designed to ensure the principle of "land to the tiller." Reducing taxes ran counter to the Tax Act. The statute overcame these obstacles by legalizing specific rules. It lessened bureaucratic resistance by making export incentives legally binding.

The statute specified criteria for tax incentives for eligible products and firms. These criteria have been updated more than ten times since 1960 in response to changing circumstances. The statute provided a strong impetus for private firms to engage in exports.

The Policy Process of the Three Reforms

The policy-making process behind these vital reforms provides an important case to test assumptions about the state structure, bureaucracy, and autonomy of East Asian developmental states. Many observers have pointed to economic factors as the impetus for the reforms and argued that the changes reflected a saturation of the domestic market.[6] The military confrontation with the mainland in August 1958 and the severe floods of August 1959 exacerbated the economic crisis. The deteriorating balance of payments remained a major concern of both economic officials and top authorities. Constrained by the small domestic market and limited opportunities for new investment, further development depended on moving outward. However, the reforms were not driven solely by economic rationality. They also reflected a process of struggle and compromise among the bureaucrats in terms of both personnel and ideologies. The involvement of top leaders remained essential to resolving the differences.

Within the government, the heads of public enterprises and banks favored a second import substitution strategy relying on the public sector, whereas bureaucrats in the U.S. aid–funded economic planning agencies proposed an export-oriented industrialization led by the private sector. The latter was adopted after the intervention of Chiang Kai-shek. As we saw in Chapter 2, the main reasons for Chiang's approval of these reforms were mounting pressures from the United States and his conviction that they would help resolve the chronic balance-of-payments problem and enable Taiwan to forgo American aid and become self-reliant.

Although we know much about the policy process behind these reforms,[7] little attention has been paid to its implications. The first point to be noted is the role of the United States. The U.S. impact on the structure of the economic bureaucracy is rarely noted in the literature and raises the issue of the international autonomy of the

Taiwan state and the nature of the role of an economic bureaucracy dependent on U.S. aid.

The U.S. aid package underwent two significant changes in 1957. The emphasis shifted from military assistance to economic development, and grants were replaced by loans. This change resulted from both the global situation and domestic problems. Internationally, tensions with the Soviet bloc eased, and military confrontation did not seem imminent. The United States therefore sought to help recipient countries develop their economies so as to enhance their defense capacity and their ability to shoulder more of the military burden themselves. Subsequently, more emphasis was placed on the private sector. As a result, in 1958 the U.S. Congress passed a law establishing the Development Loan Fund. The fund was intended for private enterprises in the recipient countries in an effort to encourage U.S. firms to increase their investment abroad.

However, Taiwan's policy was inconsistent with the new U.S. policy: military, not economic, development was the KMT government's top priority. Private enterprises received less emphasis than the public sector. The United States used carrot-and-stick tactics to pressure Taiwan and to convince it by promises of gain. Soon after the August 23, 1958, military confrontation with the mainland, Secretary of State John Foster Dulles announced that the United States had no intention of helping Taiwan attack mainland China.[8] In the joint communiqué issued during Dulles's visit in October 1958, the KMT government stated for the first time that it would not use military force to attempt to retake the mainland.[9] Obviously, this statement was the result of American pressure.

In order to force Taiwan to change its economic policy to meet the changed American aid strategy, the United States increased its pressure. In June 1959 Wesley Haraldson, the director of the U.S. Aid Mission to China, harshly criticized Taiwan's economic policy. Moreover, in October the deputy U.S. secretary of state and in December the acting director of the ICA emphasized to Chen Cheng that U.S. aid had shifted from military support to the Development Loan Fund, and the focus was being placed on private enterprises. The United States had begun to encourage private investment abroad, and Taiwan was urged to improve its economic development environment so as to obtain more U.S. aid.[10]

Faced with this pressure as well as a number of economic problems, the KMT government had to take the changes in American policy into account. As a result, intensive discussions between CUSA and the MSA in Taiwan took place during December 1959. On June 19, 1959, Haraldson presented the Taiwan government an eight-point "Outline for Accelerating Economic Development." On December 30, Haraldson, Yan Jiagan, Yin Zhongrong, and K. T. Li engaged in discussions at Chen Cheng's residence. Chen Cheng stated that he accepted Haraldson's suggestions without reservation.[11]

Based on Haraldson's suggestions and the discussions at Chen Cheng's residence, a team consisting of Yan, Yin, Yang Jizeng (minister of economic affairs), and K. T. Li worked out a nineteen-point reform package, called the Plan for Accelerating Economic Development. On January 4, Chen submitted the plan to Chiang Kai-shek. On January 7, Chiang called in Chen Cheng, Zhang Qun (secretary-general of the President's Office), Yan Jiagan, Yin Zhongrong, and K. T. Li. After Yan Jiagan dispelled Chiang's doubts about the freeze on defense expenditures, he consented to the plan. Yan, a persuasive speaker, assured Chiang that the freeze meant only that defense expenditures would be indexed to inflation and that the percentage of the total budget devoted to defense expenditures would not increase. Yan's explanation allayed Chiang's fears about reductions in military expenditures, which were always his top concern and an untouchable part of the budget. Despite Yan's skills at persuasion, however, it is unlikely that Chiang would have agreed to curb defense expenditures absent the substantial U.S. pressure.

The role of U.S. influence in forcing the KMT government to shift its economic policy raises the issue of the autonomy of the Taiwan state. Although the United States was motivated primarily by self-interest, it successfully pushed for momentous changes in Taiwan's economic policy. The U.S. appeal for reform was echoed by pro-reform bureaucrats within the KMT government and reinforced the position of these bureaucrats. This was one reason why the top authorities came down on their side. In fact, however, the United States forced both Chiang and the bureaucrats to agree to the reforms. The Taiwan leadership exhibited little autonomy in this case. Chiang was compelled by the United States to accept limits on military expenditures. Even though the pro-market bureaucrats agreed with the United States on the goal of reforming Taiwan's economy, in terms of the content of the reform, they merely followed Haraldson's suggestions. Moreover, the fate of the reform proposal was up to the political leadership. The bureaucrats faced constraints from both the politicians and a foreign government.

In Latin America, governments to a great extent were limited in economic policy making by their dependence on transnational corporations. The constraints imposed on the Taiwan government may have been equally onerous. The difference is merely that the pressures on Taiwan came from a foreign government.

As noted in Chapter 2, U.S. aid greatly reinforced government autonomy in Taiwan from the private sector by providing enormous amounts of assistance. At the same time, however, the government's autonomy was substantially undermined by U.S. aid. In accepting the aid, the government had to accept U.S. influence as well. As a result, Taiwan's experience was unique. One cannot look only at the dimension of international capital to assess whether Taiwan's case was a classic or a deviant case of dependent development.[12]

The implications of the external association were greater in Taiwan than elsewhere. This association even had considerable influence on the state's structure. As we saw in Chapter 2, the U.S. aid–financed economic bodies dominated economic policy. The advantages these bodies enjoyed because of their funding and their talented personnel allowed them to exercise the state's limited steering capacity; other government economic agencies did not perform as well. In this regard, U.S. aid helped shape the internal structure of the state in Taiwan. Without the association with the United States, there would have been no U.S. aid. And without the U.S. aid, there would have been no economic planning bodies. Furthermore, the economic bureaucracy praised by statism would not have existed.

The level of foreign influence on state structure varies from country to country and over time within a single country. However, in an increasingly integrated world, foreign influence does matter. Therefore, it cannot be omitted from discussions of state structure and autonomy.

Equally noteworthy, the association with the United States considerably influenced state–private sector relations in Taiwan by providing the state with strategic resources. The allocation of U.S. aid allowed the state to forge links with the private sector. These links contributed to the "embeddedness" and to the completion of "shared projects." American pressure and influence, through the conditions attached to the aid and direct interference in the aid agencies, helped strengthen state–private sector relations, especially relations between the state and the locally owned private enterprises.

A second point concerning the policy process behind the reforms, as discussed in Chapter 2, is that the reforms resulted from the shift in the government economic ideology from a planned economy to a market economy. The acceptance of a "planned market economy" as the official economic ideology was due to the resolution of administrative and political problems. This change paved the way for the reforms. Without the shift in economic ideas, there would have been very little reform.

Another aspect of the policy process is that the reforms relied on personnel arrangements that were in turn determined by political decisions. As shown in Chapter 2, during the first half of the 1950s, a group of pro-market bureaucrats in the U.S. aid–financed economic bodies emerged as elite economic bureaucrats. Led by Yin Zhongrong, these liberal-minded bureaucrats became active in policymaking circles. However, in many ways Yin and his colleagues in the IDC were at odds with the mainstream pro-command economy bureaucrats in the ESB, the MOEA, the MOF, the FETCC, and other regular government economic departments who not only had ideological differences with Yin but also had vested interests in the control measures. The conflict evolved into a power struggle between the two factions. The main conflict was between Premier Yu Hongjun and Yin Zhongrong. Yin was forced to step down in 1955 following the Yangzi corruption case. This event was widely viewed as politically motivated—Yu wanted to use this case to remove Yin.[13] Yin was eventually exonerated, however, and resumed office in 1957. Yan Yancun, another major pro-private sector member of the IDC, who insisted that the proposed PVC plant be run by private interests, also resigned after being accused of corruption. As a proponent of the private sector, he was at odds with IDC chairman Jiang Biao.[14]

Opposition from other government departments posed obstacles to acceptance of the reforms. The liberalization of trade encompassed both reform of exchange rates and reform of the tax system. The FETCC and the MOF had the final say on these two issues. Although Yin Zhongrong strongly believed in the necessity for reforms in these two areas, as minister of economic affairs, he was in no position to carry them out in the mid-1950s. Xu Boyuan, at the time the minister of finance and chairman of the FETCC, favored a controlled economy and firmly opposed change in the existing system. Xu was more senior than Yin and belonged to the presidential residence faction. He was also backed by Premier Yu Hongjun.

The situation began to change in 1957. After Yin Zhongrong was cleared of corruption charges, he was named secretary-general of the ESB. This move signaled not only a personnel change but also a policy shift. Faced with stagnating production and a deterioration in the balance of payments and trade, the highest leaders were anxious to find a solution. At the end of 1957, Chiang Kai-shek asked Vice President Chen Cheng to form a nine-person team, including Premier Yu Hongjun, Minister of Finance and Chairman of the FETCC Xu Boyuan, Minister of Economic Affairs Jiang Biao, Secretary-General of the ESB Yin Zhongrong, and Chairman of CUSA Yan Jiagan, to work out a solution to the economic problems. But the committee soon split into two competing views. One side, represented by Xu, insisted on the continuation of import substitution policies and control over the economy. The other side, led by Yin, suggested lifting the restrictions and depreciating the New Taiwan dollar in order to encourage exports. It was left to the top leaders to find a way out of the stalemate.

Therefore, although the resolution of the economic problems depended on policy decisions, the adoption of a particular policy ultimately rested on political decisions made at the highest level, particularly those dealing with personnel. If Chiang Kai-shek had backed Xu instead of Yin, there would have been no reform. But Chiang eventually approved Yin's proposals, and in order to implement the reform he replaced Xu with Yin.

The subsequent unfolding of events is even more revealing. In April 1958, Xu resigned and was replaced by Yin. Yin was a protégé of Chen Cheng, who was quite open-minded about economics and had views similar to Yin's. In the debate between Yin and Xu, Chen favored Yin. But it was equally important that Xu was Chiang's favorite economic official. Much senior to Yin, he was also quite talented. In fact, he was the pre-eminent financial official at the time. He had been deputy minister of finance on the mainland, and after the retreat to Taiwan, he became president of the BOT, president of the Bank of China, and minister of finance. Chiang's confidence and trust in him were well known. But Xu strongly opposed liberalization, and the top leaders had to choose between him and Yin. Chen Cheng's acceptance of liberalization was critical. It was Chen Cheng who persuaded Chiang to accept Yin's reform policy. How he did so remains a mystery. When Chen told Xu of Chiang's decision, he asked if Xu were willing to implement the policy. Xu said that he could not and submitted his resignation.[15] This move was regarded as extremely unusual. In Chinese bureaucratic politics, barring a serious mistake or involvement in a political struggle, an official as high-ranking, senior, and trusted as Xu Boyuan would never have been asked to resign. In this case, policy determined the key economic officials, and the highest leaders did not hesitate to remove a favorite official.[16] Even forty years later, a former official still expressed amazement at this turn of events in an interview with this author.

Even more significant for the reform program, in 1958 Chen Cheng replaced Yu Hongjun as premier. Chen then named Yan Jiagan minister of finance. This cabinet reshuffling was essential to the acceptance of Yin's pro-market ideas because it removed those who had blocked their acceptance. As noted in Chapter 2, Chen

Cheng supported Yin Zhongrong and other pro-reform bureaucrats for political reasons. Yan Jiagan was viewed as open-minded and willing to accept the reform formulas proposed by Yin Zhongrong and K. T. Li. He played a key role in persuading Chiang Kai-shek and Chen Cheng to accept the reform plan. Meanwhile, Yin was named the governor of the BOT in 1958. With this position, as well as his posts as chairman of the FETCC and vice chairman of CUSA, between 1958 and 1963 he became the most powerful economic bureaucrat on the island. These personnel arrangements enabled Yin Zhongrong to play a leadership role and to push through his pro-market ideas.

The change in personnel also established an administrative basis for the implementation of the reform policy. When Yin sought to reform the foreign exchange system, he encountered resistance from vested interests within the FETCC who had benefited from the control measures. When Yin replaced Xu as head of the FETCC, he was able to overcome these administrative obstacles. Similarly, MOF officials had opposed the nineteen-point reform package and the Statute for the Encouragement of Investment, but Yan Jiagan was able to persuade his subordinates to accept the reform measure. The removal of these obstacles was critical to reaching a consensus and clearing the way for the implementation of the reforms.

Backed by the highest leaders, Yin Zhongrong began implementing his ambitious reform program soon after he took over the FETCC. There were two critical requirements for the implementation of the foreign exchange and trade reform: Yin's initiative and the top leaders' approval. The reform finally came about as a result of the combination of these two factors. Without Yin, there would have been no foreign exchange and trade reform. And without Chen Cheng's support, there would have been no reform. Sometimes, economic policy is the result of personnel arrangements rather than institutions. Key individuals can play a leading role, and the power of a leader does not depend solely on his office.

Furthermore, the realization of the reforms depended to a great extent on mechanisms derived from the roles of the individual bureaucrats who mediated within the policy-making team and coordinated the bureaucrats and the politicians. This is an issue of bureaucracy that goes beyond institutionalist explanations. It concerns the interworkings of the bureaucracy, personality, and human behavior. Like the commissions, councils, and ministries, this "invisible mechanism" is a part of the bureaucracy and plays an important role in its operations. But conventional wisdom tends to ignore this mechanism. As a result, analyses of the KMT's economic bureaucracy are often oversimplified. The case of Yan Jiagan demonstrates the significance and importance of the "invisible mechanism" in the economic bureaucracy.

Yan Jiagan played a unique and crucial role in the policy process behind the reforms. In the areas of foreign exchange and trade reform, he convinced Chen Cheng to support Yin Zhongrong. And he persuaded Chiang Kai-shek to agree to freeze military expenditures under the nineteen-point reform package. Yan's acceptance of the tax-reduction policy was a key to overcoming the unanimous resistance of the MOF to the implementation of the Statute for the Encouragement of Investment. As minister of finance, Yan Jiagan overrode all dissenting views and accepted the reduction. Almost forty years later, in an interview with this author, K. T. Li, a major drafter of the statute, praised Yan and expressed his gratitude for Yan's critical support of the reform.

Yan's role shows that the efficiency of the bureaucracy depends on the support of individual bureaucrats. The interplay and cooperation among the members of the team, which consisted of the heads of the economic and financial ministries and the U.S. aid–related councils, was decisive. Yin Zhongrong was certainly an initiator of the reform policy, but he was extremely outspoken and too arrogant and aggressive. During the meetings chaired by Chen Cheng, Yin's style made the other members uncomfortable and his ideas unacceptable.[17] Under the circumstances, Yan Jiagan's role was vital. Although he rarely initiated policy, he often supported Yin and shared his views. As noted above, his re-presentations of Yin's proposals clarified Yin's ideas and made them acceptable to Chen Cheng. In other words, Yan Jiagan was the mediator between the top authorities and the major bureaucrats, as well as among the bureaucrats themselves.

Yan Jiagan graduated from St. John's University in Shanghai in 1926. In 1938 he became head of both the Bureau of Construction and the Bureau of Finance in Fujian province. He became head of the Taiwan provincial Bureau of Finance in 1948. Thereafter, his career advanced rapidly. In 1950 he served as minister of the MOEA and deputy director of CUSA; in 1957 as the chairman of the Taiwan provincial government and director of CUSA; in 1958 as the minister of finance; from 1963 to 1972 as premier; from 1966 to 1975 as vice president; and from 1975 to 1978 as president. Due to his loyalty and tactfulness, he was trusted by Chiang Kai-shek and thus was able to play a unique role in postwar politics.

Yan Jiagan was one of the few people in the KMT regime who could make suggestions directly to Chiang that were acceptable. Chiang chose him as an interim figure in the transition of power to Chiang Ching-kuo. Yan Jiagan understood his mission and fulfilled it perfectly by finally handing over power to Chiang Ching-kuo.[18] Basically, he served as a caretaker president of the ROC between 1975 and 1978.

Yan's political role within the KMT enabled him to play a unique role in economic affairs. As we will see in Chapter 6, when Chiang Ching-kuo wanted to exclude K. T. Li from the economic bureaucracy, it was Yan Jiagan who protected Li and suggested to Chiang that Li be made minister of finance. He made a great contribution to the efficiency of the bureaucracy by mediating among the major bureaucrats in the 1950s and 1960s. This invisible role is difficult to document, but it was widely confirmed and highly praised in articles by insiders and in my personal interviews with retired officials. It was also acknowledged at a recent meeting held to commemorate Yan's contribution to Taiwan's economy. Although the participants praised his great achievements, few could name specific contributions. Even so, he was associated with almost all the important policies of his time.[19]

Yan's role among elite civil servants is relevant to a discussion of the bureaucracy in a developmental state. The economic bureaucracy in Taiwan is often assumed to be coherent and even monolithic. But Yan's part in the policy process refutes this simplistic assumption. Yan's critical contribution to the adoption of all the reforms clearly suggests that the economic bureaucracy was far from coherent and monolithic. His role is indicative of differences and conflicts within the bureaucracy and shows there was a mechanism that allowed elite bureaucrats to coordinate and balance different opinions and interests. To discover this mechanism, we need to penetrate the inner workings of the policy process. But first we must examine the composition of the bureaucratic elite and understand their views and personalities, as well as their political culture, norms, and rules. In short, we need to "humanize" institutions. Institutions are more than groups of units; they consist of people. The ways people run institutions determine their functions. Without an understanding of people's behavior within the institutions, any discussion of institutional efficiency is inadequate.

The policy process behind the reforms also raises the question of bureaucratic politics, in particular the relationship between the politicians and the bureaucrats. This relationship determined the role and function of the economic bureaucracy. Chiang Kai-shek's and Chen Cheng's attitudes were key factors in determining the fate of Yin Zhongrong's reforms. If the reformers could convince Chiang and Chen, their policy proposals would be adopted. In this regard, they were luckier than their successors during the Chiang Ching-kuo era. As we will see in Chapters 6 and 7, Chiang Ching-kuo dominated economic affairs and used only those bureaucrats who shared his views. K. T. Li, who had been active in economic policy making in earlier years, was sidelined by Chiang Ching-kuo because of his different views on the economy and because of his seniority. The differences in the relationship between the politicians and the bureaucrats during these two periods had decisive consequences for the role of the bureaucracy and economic policy.

Seemingly, Taiwan's economic bureaucracy is not what the statist account assumes. Institutions were fragile, and individuals were important. The institution-based account is thus inadequate to explain the nature of the economic bureaucracy. Politics—a kind of bureaucratic politics—was more important than institutions. To understand how Taiwan's economic bureaucracy worked, we must examine the bureaucratic politics of the KMT regime.

The Bureaucratic Politics of the KMT State

In statist theories, two central elements in a developmental state are the autonomy and capacity of the economic bureaucracy to formulate and implement economic policy. The autonomy and capacity of the economic bureaucracy arise because these institutions are depoliticized and insulated. Further, the economic bureaucracy is coherent and harmonious. Both implicitly and explicitly, Taiwan's economic success is attributable to the institutional arrangements of the economic bureaucracy. However, statism's monolithic treatment of the state has been criticized.[20] Walter Arnold's case study of the automotive sector shows that the economic bureaucracy was neither depoliticized nor insulated from political pressures and hence was ineffective in policy making.

In explaining the failure of the Big Auto Plant project, Arnold points to the institutional arrangements. The problems included bureaucratic conflicts between the MOEA and the CEPD, personal competition, an absence of the expertise required for complex techno-economic changes, a lack of qualified staff, and different ideas about the development of the automobile industry among MOEA and CEPD bureaucrats. In addition, the inability to insulate policy making from fierce lobbying by domestic and foreign auto manufacturers also contributed to the failure. The unsuccessful efforts of the economic bureaucracy are indicative of the ineffectiveness of the "developmental state" in economic policy making. Arnold's study demonstrates that an institution-based explanation of Taiwan's economic bureaucracy is not tenable. A number of questions follow from his findings. Was the failure to develop an automobile industry due to the inefficiency of the economic bureaucracy? Was this also the case in other industries as well? Was this the case in the 1950s and 1960s when the economic planning agencies were thought to be stronger than they were during the period of Arnold's study? If the economic bureaucracy on the whole was inefficient, what explains the success of other industries? Can the success of other industries be attributed to the efficiency of the economic bureaucracy? If not, what was responsible for their success?

My argument is that the statist institution-based account of the economic bureaucracy is inaccurate. Arnold's finding about the auto industry is not an isolated case. It was the general situation throughout the period under study in this book. The statist account of institutions ignores relevant facts about the Taiwanese state, especially the frequent change in economic planning agencies, which is evidence of the fragility of the institutions. Informal norms, informal practices and procedures, and the shuffling of officials were of particular and enduring importance. These did not change despite the rapid turnover in formal institutions. From the late 1940s to at least the late 1970s, institutional arrangements beyond these informal arrangements scarcely existed.

Statism also ignores questions of leadership. The institutions were not autonomous from the highest political leadership. In short, the history of the economic bureaucracy is not an institutional history but a matter of individuals and bureaucratic politics. Bureaucratic politics in the 1950s and the first half of the 1960s consisted of three layers (see Fig. 5.1). The first layer consisted of the president. The first president was Chiang Kai-shek, who was followed, after a brief interim, by his son Chiang Ching-kuo. The president was also the chairman of the KMT. He had the final say on key economic policies. However, Chiang Kai-shek and Chiang Ching-kuo had different styles. Chiang Kai-shek left day-to-day economic affairs to the economic bureaucrats. He steered economic policy making through trusted officials. Before 1965, Chen Cheng played a key role as a bridge between Chiang Kai-shek and the key economic bureaucrats. But unlike his father, Chiang Ching-kuo liked to interfere in economic policy. He not only determined overall economic policy on his own but also decided on specific economic policies, such as prices.

The second layer of bureaucratic politics consisted of the heads of the economic agencies. They pressed competitively upward to get their ideas across. A striking phenomenon is the role of the bureaucratic leaders. Yin Zhongrong and K. T. Li were the two most powerful bureaucrats in the postwar economy. The most important element in their success was political support from the highest

Fig. 5.1 The three-layer structure of Taiwan's bureaucratic politics

leaders. Chiang Kai-shek's and Chen Cheng's confidence in them provided them with the political capital to legitimize their leadership role in the economic policy network. Another element was political savvy. They knew how to win the trust of the highest politicians and were able to distance themselves from party and factional politics and insist on their independent technocratic role. This boundary was crucial in their role in economic affairs. A third element was their ability to take the initiative and shoulder responsibility. Both Yin and Li were extremely active in initiating economic policy and brave in accepting the political responsibility for their decisions. Neither was satisfied with the status quo and sought to change it. Almost all the principal economic reform policies were initiated by these two men. Yin's trademark phrase was "Carry on regardless," and he was famous for his fearlessness. At hearings of the Legislative Yuan, Yin always promised to take personal responsibility if his proposals were to fail. To those legislators who disliked his strong style and threatened to drive him from office, Yin proclaimed, "I am ready to leave office at a moment's notice."

A fourth element is charisma. Both Yin and Li were colorful characters who were outspoken, optimistic, sharp, and assertive. These traits were viewed as deviant in Chinese bureaucratic politics, where the standard norms are humility, politeness, and secretiveness. Yan Jiagan and another long-surviving politician, Huang

Shaogu, who was part of the Chiang family's brain trust, were widely regarded in political circles as master practitioners of this philosophy.[21] According to a longtime follower of Yin and Li, both had a tendency to offend others because of their strong and straightforward styles. A close friend of Yin advised him to "refrain from showing your abilities." Because these personalities were so unusual in bureaucratic politics, the two tended to have many political enemies; still, their strong styles also helped them win a lot of political support. Political support from the highest leaders largely offset the problems caused by their strong styles. Their styles also made them popular in the media and the private sector. Reporters loved Yin's vivid and colorful words and often quoted him directly. In order to provoke his witty remarks, reporters often would deliberately irritate him. Overall, the two men's charisma helped build public support for their ideas and policies. The "Yin Zhongrong style"—outspoken, upright, willing to shoulder responsibility and to take the initiative—is still remembered by those who lived through that period.

A final element in their success was their ability to assemble a group of capable aides. These aides were the backbone of the economic bureaucracy and played a significant role in implementing economic policy. Indeed, K. T. Li, who was promoted by Yin, was attacked by his enemies for forging a "K.T. faction," whose members spread into the MOEA, the MOF, and the Ministry of Transportation.

Conventionally, the word "strongman" refers to a ruler with a military background whose control over military forces is the source of his authority and power. In contrast, a civilian strongman has to rely on credibility and persuasiveness. To a great extent, ability and knowledge also strengthen his authority.

Bureaucratic competition and conflicts often erupted among bureaucrats at this level. Ideological differences, policy views, and personal and departmental interests were the sources of such conflicts. These were important parts of bureaucratic politics and often determined the fate of an economic policy. The competition between Yin Zhongrong and Xu Boyuan during the trade and foreign exchange reforms of the late 1950s and the conflict between Yu Guo-

hua, the head of the CEPD, and Minister of Economics Zhao Yaodong during the auto project in the early 1980s are two such examples. There was also competition and conflict surrounding Yin
Zhongrong and K. T. Li, both of whom had strong personalities
and styles, even though they held similar views about economic development. In 1951 Yin invited Li to be a full member of the newly
established IDC. Li thereafter became Yin's aide. However, when
Chen Cheng as chairman of the CUSA named Li secretary-general
of the newly restructured CUSA in 1958, Yin, the deputy chairman
of the CUSA, fiercely resisted this appointment. The dispute
reached an impasse broken only through mediation by Yan Jiagan
and another influential person, Ye Gongchao.[22] The dispute was indicative of the competition between the veteran Yin and Li—a rising
younger star who had come to the attention of the top leaders.

The third layer of the bureaucratic politics was the formal bureaucratic order—the agencies. The economic agencies consisted of
the constitutional ministries and the extra-constitutional planning
agencies. The constitutional ministries were the MOEA, the MOF,
and the central bank (initially the Bank of Taiwan and later the
Central Bank of China). The FETCC, a ministerial-level agency,
played a key role in the 1950s. A subministerial agency, the IDB
under the MOEA, was also important in industrial policy implementation. The functions and roles of these agencies varied over
time. Before the mid-1960s, the MOEA and MOF functioned
poorly because of a lack of resources and qualified staff. After the
mid-1960s, the two ministries seldom undertook more than routine
tasks. Until the CIECD's dissolution in 1973, it performed their
functions. More important, Chiang Ching-kuo began to dominate
economic policy from 1969, when he became deputy premier and
the head of the CIECD. The economic planning agencies thus
played a much larger role than the formal ministries. But how significant was the role of these institutions?

As noted in Chapter 1, all these institutions were short-lived.
Second, the performance of the institutions depended on the
power of those who led them. Their functions could increase under a strong leader or be reduced under a weak director. The IDC
under the leadership of Yin Zhongrong was active and efficient,

but it was much less so when Jiang Biao was in charge due to his personality and the low morale of the staff. The functions of the CIECD were strengthened when Chiang Ching-kuo, then deputy premier, replaced Premier Yan Jiagan as its head in 1969. These leaders owed their power not to their position per se but to their backers. The power and function of the IDC, ESB, and CUSA increased once Yin became their head. The role of the CUSA was largely reinforced when Li was secretary-general. The MOEA and MOF began to be active after Li took over.

Despite the apparent importance of the economic planning bodies, the agencies had next to no autonomy from political leaders. Seemingly, the outstanding performance of these economic planning agencies can be attributed to their talented leaders rather than to the institutions themselves. The power and authority of the institutions derived from the persons who headed them. Once the battles over leadership were over, the institutions did what they were told, as seen in the case of Yan Jiagan and the MOF regarding the Statute for the Encouragement of Investment. The life expectancy of these agencies was five to ten years. In this sense, Taiwan's economic bureaucracy was rather weak. This was a Chinese-style administration, a style colored by officials and mandarins.

Nor can this rule be characterized as a technocracy. A technocracy is marked by rule based on technical competence. It would be inaccurate to apply this description to Taiwan before the late 1970s. Instead, it can best be characterized as rule by strongmen. It was powerful bureaucrats, not the economic bureaucracy, who exercised power and demonstrated steering capacity. The locus of all authority was ultimately the president, who was also the chairman of the KMT. The bureaucrats were empowered by the president and were responsible to him. The personal power of an official was not a consequence of his office; rather, his power rested on the backing of the top leaders. The establishment or disbandment of an institution depended on the president. Without the president's sanction, institutions were meaningless. The strongman epitomized Taiwan's bureaucratic politics. He was also principally responsible for the success of its industrial policy. We will return to this topic in Chapter 7.

The Promotion of Exports and Their Significance for Taiwan's Industrial Structure

The three reforms dramatically changed the way the government managed the economy and led to a movement away from passive restrictions to positive encouragement. The liberalization measures signaled the end of the wartime economy. Starting in 1949, the controlled economy had been characterized by the setting of prices for important products and services, the control of imports and foreign exchange, and factory licensing. The aim of these policies was to stabilize the economy, curb prices, and realize a balance of payments. The origins of the idea of a controlled economy and the accompanying measures can be traced to as early as the beginning of the anti-Japanese War on the mainland in 1937.[23] The lifting of these restrictions marked the end of the era of the command economy and the start of a new period in Taiwan's postwar economic history. Inevitably, this change also influenced state–private sector relations.

The implementation of the three reforms varied. The first was successful since it was implemented through specific measures, such as unified exchange rates and the lifting of controls over trade. The third reform—tax incentives to promote business—was also a success since it was passed into law. However, the second reform— the nineteen-point program—was the least successful for two reasons. First, as already indicated, it was a government policy statement that lacked legally binding force. Second, the government departments were less willing to implement these reforms because they had been proposed by a U.S. aid–related agency and many officials feared that they would have inflationary effects.[24] As a result, although a supervisory group, headed by the deputy premier, was set up under the Executive Yuan, most of the nineteen-point reform package was not implemented. The only exception was the part dealing with capital formation, which was enacted in the Statute for the Encouragement of Investment. In addition to its legal status, according to K. T. Li, the success of this statute can also be attributed to the role of the Group for Industrial Development and Investment. The group was established in late 1959 under the

CUSA, and it was active in implementing the statute by removing obstacles to investment.[25] The setback to the nineteen-point program and the success of the foreign exchange and trade reform and the Statute for the Encouragement of Investment suggest that the effective implementation of the reforms hinged on legislative enactment and administrative guarantees.

As with any reform, there were both winners and losers. Likely losers included the administrative officials of the controlling agencies, such as the FETCC, and the firms that benefited from the controls. However, as I discuss below, the reforms made more winners than losers, mainly because of the co-existence of the particularistic measures for the LEs and the universalistic measures for the SMEs.

A neglected topic with respect to the reforms is their implications for the formation of Taiwan's unique industrial structure. This structure largely originated from the ways the state boosted exports in the three reforms and the state's continued strengthening of state-LE relations. As noted above, the purpose of the reforms was to boost exports by promoting the private sector. This was done in a universalistic rather than a particularistic fashion. This contrasts with the methods the government used to promote import substitution. As analyzed in Chapter 4, the government boosted import substitution by picking both winners and supporters. The state allocated resources—credit, foreign exchange, U.S. aid, and important raw materials—among a few select private enterprises and used a wide array of policy instruments to control imports and set entry barriers to limit foreign and domestic competition. Consequently, a close relationship between the state and a few private enterprises took shape. As we will see below, this close relationship was intentionally strengthened and safeguarded by the state throughout the postwar era. However, this is not the way the government promoted exports.

The government's chief method to promote exports was to establish an environment that induced and encouraged firms to produce exportable goods. The measures the state undertook to boost exports were nondiscriminatory. The primary measure was deregulation. That is, the state eliminated existing controls to create general incentives from which every export producer could benefit. These universalistic measures included unification of the exchange rates, depreciation of the currency, simplification of administrative procedures, liberalization of regulatory measures, tax exemptions and rebates for exports, and so forth. The state did not pick winners or supporters. Unlike the South Korean government, the state did not channel resources to foster a few enterprises as major exporters.

Strikingly, however, the state continued to strengthen its ties with a few privileged LEs. Most of the rents that the government adopted to foster and protect a group of "supporters" during the import substitution period were left in place. The change to a strategy of export promotion did not lead to a dismantling of the earlier incentives given to the domestic-market-oriented producers. Moreover, as is shown in the next section, even more rents were created for the latter through the setting up of the CDC. No matter how committed the state was to exports, this is evidence that the state did not encourage the LEs to engage in exports. Obviously, there was an inconsistency between state actions and state goals.

It may be an exaggeration to say that the state was undermining its own efforts and goals. But the state was unclear about which firms should be the potential exporters. Did the state expect the LEs to be the exporters? The economic bureaucrats had an understanding of economies of scale, and they must have expected that the larger firms would export.[26] But the coexistence of particularistic and universalistic incentives drove the LEs to opt for monopolistic profits in the domestic market over competition in export markets. In effect, the state discouraged the LEs from exporting. Meanwhile, the state did not believe that the SMEs were able to export because of their low level of competitiveness. As a result, many particular incentives adopted by the state to encourage exporting discriminated against the SMEs. For example, firms had to meet certain minimum size requirements to qualify for some incentives, such as tax exemptions and tax rebates. Furthermore, the first version of the Statute for the Encouragement of Exports in 1960 was applicable only to limited liability companies.

Even so, the universalistic method of facilitating exports *was* significant for the SMEs. First, despite the discrimination of particular incentives, the SMEs could benefit from the general incentives. Second, the state did not set up entry barriers to export manufacturing, and this paved the way for the SMEs to emerge as the major export manufacturers beginning in the 1960s. Although the state discriminated against the SMEs in terms of particular incentives for exports, the negative effects of this discrimination did not thwart them from benefiting from exporting. This contrasts with South Korea, where the state channeled all resources, mainly domestic and foreign capital in the form of cheap credit, to finance a few large firms as the main exporters.[27] The universalistic method of promoting exports is, however, evidence that the state did not encourage SMEs in particular to become exporters. The emergence of the SMEs in exports was an inadvertent consequence of state action, not an intention.

The Establishment of the China Development Corporation

The establishment of the CDC signaled the beginning of a new stage in state-business relations in postwar Taiwan. The CDC was a response to the shift in U.S. aid from military to economic development and the new emphasis on private enterprises. Its aim was to solve the problem of shortages of industrial finance in the private sector. It was thus an attempt by the government to strengthen relations with the private sector.

As early as 1957, when it became apparent that existing financial institutions were unable to provide sufficient credit to private firms, both the government and the private sector concluded that it was necessary to establish a financial institution for development. Yu Guohua, then chairman of the Central Trust of China, led a delegation to the United States on a three-month fact-finding tour in late 1957. In its extensive report, the delegation suggested that a stock market and a development company be set up. The contours of the CDC emerged from this report. Based on these suggestions, the Organizational Rules for the Promotion Committee of the Development Corporation were passed in November 1958 by the Executive Yuan, and the committee was established soon thereafter.

Huo Baoshu, a senior financial official, was appointed the chair of the committee, and Yu Guohua the vice chair. Zhang Xinqia was named executive secretary. Nine industrial and financial tycoons were appointed members in February 1959. The CDC was officially established the following May, with a registered capital of NT$80 million; the public shares accounted for NT$23.47 million and the private shares for NT$56.53 million. Lin Boshou became the president, and Huo Baoshu the general manager, and Zhang Xinqia and Pan Zhijia the deputy managing directors.

Following a heated debate over whether ownership of the CDC should be public or private, it was finally established as a private concern. The government wanted a development bank to help increase industrial funding. During the 1950s, the publicly owned banks provided only short-term funds to private enterprises. Long-term funds were unavailable. Thus, there was an urgent need for a development bank to provide long-term credit to private enterprises. However, the government wanted to keep the development bank under its control. During 1958 two new institutions, the Office of Private Enterprise and the Development Loan Fund, were established in the United States as part of the shift in emphasis to economic development in foreign aid.[28] Basically, the establishment of the CDC was a response to this shift in U.S. assistance. The goal was to facilitate access to U.S. funds and international financing resources. For this purpose, Huo Baoshu was named the general manager because of his familiarity with both finance and U.S. aid–related business. The Industrial Development and Investment Center was established for the same purpose at that time.

Although the CDC was privately owned, it was controlled by the government. A look at the list of major shareholders reveals how the government strengthened its relations with the leading private enterprises and controlled the company through personnel and share arrangements. Lin Boshou was a major capitalist and held important positions in both the BOT and the First Bank. Huo Baoshu, the general manager, had been a member of the united committee of the Central Bank, the Bank of China, the Bank of Communications, and the Farmers Bank during the anti-Japanese war. The deputy general manager, Pan Zhijia, was concurrently director of Section Four of the CUSA. Among the major shareholders, Yu Guohua was chairman of the Central Trust of China and governor of the Central Bank. Zhao Baoquan, one of the sixteen high-ranking officers of the CDC, was a leading figure in the Bank of Communications. Thus, they were all bureaucrats from government financial agencies or public banks.

As for shareholders with both official and private-sector backgrounds, Chen Guangfu was a member of the board of the Central Bank and the Bank of Communications and an executive member of the board of the BOT. He was also an influential figure in the private banking system and had served in many government financial and foreign exchange agencies. Bei Zuyi was president of the Shanghai Branch of the Bank of China and had served in various government financial and foreign exchange agencies as well. Lin Tingsheng, president of the Datong Iron Corporation, one of the leading private firms, held important positions in the BOT and the First Bank. Both Lin Boshou and Lin Tingsheng were business tycoons.

The representatives of the private sector, such as Chen Shangwen, Shi Fengxiang, Xie Chengyuan, Xu Jinde, Chen Fengyuan, Yan Qinxian, and Li Jianxing, were from the leading enterprises. They also had close ties with the government. For example, Shi Fengxiang, a textile magnate, was the adoptive father of Chiang Wei-kuo, Chiang Kai-shek's second son.

Thus, the personnel and major shareholders in the CDC were government financial bureaucrats, mainland businessmen or bankers closely connected to the KMT government, and leading native Taiwanese business people. This composition had two implications. First, the makeup of the CDC combined state capital and private capital. Second, the government controlled the corporation through its personnel. With public finance officials and government-appointed business people constituting the board of directors, and public finance officials holding managerial positions, the government was able to control the CDC. The government's dominance was further secured by the shareholdings of three public banks: Bank of China, Bank of Taiwan, and Bank of Communications. As shown in Table 5.1, the three public banks held 19.5 percent of the CDC's total shares. Since the private shares were scattered among various shareholders, the public shares were able to dominate the CDC's business.

Thus the CDC represented a combination of state, private, and foreign capital. Morgan Bank, an international banking giant, represented international capital. The private enterprises listed in Table 5.1, Datong Iron Corporation, Xinzhu Glass Corporation, China Man-made Fibre Corporation, Formosa Plastics Corporation, Nangang Tire Corporation, and Asian Cement Corporation, were all leading companies. They represented either mainland capital (China Man-made Fibre Corporation and Asian Cement) or local Taiwanese capital (Taiwan Cement Corporation and Formosa Plastics Corporation). Tangrong Iron Works, then the largest private firm, also was one of the shareholders of the CDC.

The government's control of the CDC provoked a polarized reaction during the preparatory stages and in its early stages of operations. For the government, its control assured that the CDC would coordinate government policy. Government officials stated explicitly that the corporation would and must follow government policy in expanding its business.[29] As a result, business and the media worried that the CDC would become another public bank with a bureaucratic style or a semi-official U.S. aid agency. The major shareholders' close ties with the government raised doubts about its private nature.[30]

The CDC's business ranged from loans to investments. It introduced foreign capital, issued bonds for companies, guaranteed the establishment of new factories, provided business management, purchased equipment for companies, helped with technical designs, and engaged in other investment and credit-related activities. But its main business was to provide medium- and long-term loans, to invest and foster new enterprises, and to provide guarantees for the purchase of equipment.[31] As noted by Liu Jinqing, "the CDC was not only the midwife and protector of the firms but also the producer and creator."[32]

Table 5.1
The Major Shareholders of the CDC, February 25, 1966

Firm	Name	Amount of funds (000 NT$)	Proportion of shares (%)	Accumulated proportion of shares (%)
Shanghai Commercial and Savings Bank	Chen Guangfu, Bei Zuyi	12,400	10.3	10.3
International Bank, Morgan Bank Group	Zhang Xinqia	12,250	10.2	20.5
Bank of China	Yu Guohua	10,000	8.3	28.8
Bank of Communications	Zhao Baoquan	10,000	8.3	37.1
Bank of Taiwan	Long Liyin	3,400	2.9	40.0
Taiwan Cement Corporation	Lin Boshou	7,500	6.3	46.3
Datong Iron Corporation	Lin Tingsheng	5,000	4.2	50.5
Xinzhu Glass Corporation	Chen Shangwen	5,700	4.8	55.3
China Man-made Fibre Corporation	Shi Fengxiang	3,750	3.1	58.4
Taiwan Pineapple Corporation	Xie Chengyuan	3,000	2.5	60.9
Formosa Plastics Corporation		1,500	1.3	62.2
Nangang Tire Corporation	Xu Jinde	750	0.6	62.8
Asian Cement Corporation		450	0.4	63.2

SOURCE: Liu Jinqing, *Taiwan zhanhou jingji*, p. 315.

Table 5.2
The Use of the CDC's Own Funds, June 1962

Use	Amount (000 NT$)	Percentage (%)
Loans to enterprises	24,600	20
Investment in enterprises	9,200	7
Purchase of securities	47,200	38
Payments advanced for the "August 7 flood" loans	2,300	2
Fixed deposits	37,000	29
Others (advance payments, fixed assets, etc.)	4,700	4
TOTAL	125,000	100

SOURCE: Jinghehui disichu (CIECD), "Zhonghua kaifa xintuo gufen youxian gongsi cha-zhang baogao," p. 73.

Notably, most of the firms listed on the stock market received financing from the CDC.[33] This shows that the CDC had special relations with the leading private enterprises. The disbursement of the CDC's funds of NT$125 million up to June 1962 is summarized in Table 5.2. The proportion of funds used for loans and investments to enterprises was only 27 percent, whereas those used for securities and deposits was as high as 67 percent. This reveals the conservatism of the corporation. The CIECD's 1968 accounting report stated that the CDC had sent its trustees or observers to all eighteen enterprises in which it had invested, as well as to the two listed enterprises it had acquired. The CDC saw these as long-term investments, and it intended to invest its funds in a few selected enterprises, sell the successful enterprises, and use the money to invest in new firms. In criticizing the CDC's conservatism, the CIECD accused it of being a "holding company" rather than a development company.[34]

As shown in Table 5.3, the chemical sector received 24.80 percent of the total amount loaned in NT dollars up to June 1968, the textile sector 18.45 percent, cement 16.55 percent, the food sector 13.62 percent, and mining 13.07 percent. All other industries received 13.51 percent. But these sectors were major industries in

Table 5.3
Sectoral Distribution of CDC Loans (until June 1968)

| Industry | NT$ | | US$ | | Number of loans |
	Number	Amount (000 NT$)	Number	Amount (000 US$)	
Chemicals	21	80,925	2	479	23
Cement	6	54,000	3	349	9
Textiles	15	60,220	–	–	15
Timber processing	3	15,500	2	153	5
Food processing	10	44,448	–	–	10
Iron & steel	2	10,400	1	98	3
Machinery	1	610	–	–	1
Electrical appliance	5	17,497	4	337	9
Mining	6	42,659	–	–	6
TOTAL	69	326,259	12	1,416	81

SOURCE: Jinghehui disichu (CIECD), "Zhonghua kaifa xintuo gufen youxian gongsi cha-zhang baogao," p. 74.

Taiwan during the 1960s. Compared to the corresponding figures for 1964—40.6 percent for textiles, 18.5 percent for chemicals, 9.7 percent for food, and 8.1 for mining[35]—the greatest difference was the sharp decrease in textiles and the considerable increase in chemicals. Except for food and some textile firms, most of the industries did not concentrate on exporting. In fact, the CDC did not see export promotion as a priority; rather, it tended to support the LEs' domestic activities.

The establishment of the CDC and its operations demonstrate that, in addition to the public banks, the government created a new type of financial institution to provide funds for private enterprises as a response to the changing conditions of U.S. aid. The main function of the CDC was to provide intermediate- and long-term credit to private enterprises. In this sense, the CDC complemented the public banks, which made only short-term loans. With the CDC, the government acquired one more vital policy instrument. The Tangrong case, analyzed below, reveals the role of the CDC in government policy considerations.

Through the CDC, cooperation took place between the state and large private enterprises with both mainland and local capital.[36] It is striking that the leading firms were also the main shareholders in and the major borrowers from the development corporation. In fact, the CDC was an exclusive club for a few privileged private enterprises that benefited from the CDC's services. As happened during the privatization of the four public corporations in the early 1950s, a large collective distribution of credit took place among the leading private firms, thus reinforcing the coalition between the government and the largest private companies. Unlike the earlier privatization, however, this distribution spread to both mainland and local capitalists. This had a far-reaching impact on the emergence of a dual industrial structure in which the SOEs and LEs jointly monopolized the domestic market and the SMEs moved into the global market. This unique industrial structure began to form in the 1960s.

Although the CDC was under government control, the leading firms had a say through their shareholdings and seats on the board of directors. This provided an unprecedented channel for the private sector to exert an influence on economic issues, and it inevitably increased the influence of the private sector on government economic policy.

Furthermore, the CDC reflected the tremendous influence of U.S. capital. One of the main reasons for establishing the CDC was to attract U.S. aid and private funds from U.S. capital and other international financial institutions. Indeed, the amount of foreign funds the CDC administered exceeded its own funds. By the end of June 1962, in terms of funds denominated in New Taiwan dollars, the amount from the Counterpart Fund was 2.5 times that of the CDC's own funds—NT$300 million to NT$120 million. In funds denominated in U.S. dollars, the total, including the Development Loan Fund (DLF) and the International Development Association (IDA), was U.S.$15 million. Liu Jinqing describes the CDC as a foreign comprador bank.[37] This not only provides further convincing evidence of the U.S. influence on Taiwan's economy during this period but also suggests that U.S. capital helped reinforce state-LE relations in Taiwan. Without a doubt, as a sort of state-business financial capital,[38] to borrow Liu Jinqing's term, the CDC provided the government a new instrument for influencing the private sector.

The Tangrong Iron Corporation: An Industrial Policy Success Story

The Tangrong case demonstrates how the economic planning agency used policy instruments to achieve its goals, as well as the complexity of relations between the state and a leading local enterprise. The most important consequence of the case was the government's success in regulating the unorganized financial market, which improved the availability of financial resources for export-oriented SMEs.

Tangrong Iron Corporation, Taiwan's largest private firm, faced insolvency in 1960. Despite its political connections within the government, which included support from Chen Cheng, the BOT refused to provide further loans because the company would not accept the conditions set by the bank. Consequently, it went bankrupt and, in 1962, became a publicly owned enterprise. The Tangrong episode illustrates government–private sector relations in the late 1950s and early 1960s and shows how the government used the provision of credit to serve its policy goals. The implications were not only economic but also political, involving factional struggles among the top leaders, government policy goals, the dual financial structure, and mainlander/Taiwanese relations.

Tangrong was no ordinary business. It was the largest Taiwanese-owned enterprise. Set up in 1940 by Tang Chuanzong and his father, Tangrong survived a severe financial crisis in 1949 because of the currency reform. Chen Cheng, then provincial governor of Taiwan, ordered that the public banks provide loans to Tangrong. Thereafter, it expanded quickly, and by 1960 it employed 4,500 workers, had over NT$10 million in assets, and produced over 60 percent of the steel made in Taiwan. It was the island's fifth largest firm in terms of turnover and taxes, trailing only the publicly owned Taiwan Sugar Company, China Petroleum Company, Taiwan Tobacco Company, and Taiwan Alcohol Company. In its heyday, Tangrong's bills of lading could be circulated as promissory notes, and as an attractive site for private deposits, the company accounted for 6.15 percent of all fixed deposits in 1960.[39] Without doubt, Tangrong was a successful model of a private business in the 1950s in Taiwan. From the vice president to the speaker of the legislature, politicians frequently paid visits to Tangrong and expressed their support.

Tangrong's financial crisis surfaced with a shortage of working capital in June and July 1960. In August 1960, three months after being established, the CDC chose Tangrong as its first firm to support by offering NT$50 million in loans. Tangrong declined this offer because it would not accept the CDC's condition that the CDC be allowed to appoint its general manager.

Yin Zhongrong, who had replaced Zhang Zikai as president of the BOT in July 1960, then met with Tang Chuanzong on September 8, 1960, and offered NT$50 million in loans to pay the interest on its private deposits. The next day the BOT set up a bank group consisting of the CDC and three commercial banks, Huanan, Chang-hua, and the First Bank, to provide NT$120 million in loans to Tangrong. After studying Tangrong's accounts, the bank group realized that Tangrong's situation had deteriorated seriously in 1960. Its indebtedness had increased by over 60 percent in just nine months, from NT$2.6 billion at the end of 1959 to NT$4.19 billion in September 1960.[40] As a result, the group tried to retract the loan agreement previously reached with Tangrong. After repeated requests from Tangrong and the intervention of Chen Cheng, then vice president and premier, the bank group devised a plan that included seven conditions.

Tangrong thought the conditions were too harsh and that its financial situation was not as serious as the BOT deemed. It thus refused to accept the conditions. The CDC investigation report was published in the newspapers on September 19, making Tangrong's financial situation public information. In testimony before the Legislative Yuan on September 23, Yin Zhongrong informed the legislators that the bank group's loan plan had not been accepted, and he released details about Tangrong's debt. This testimony caused Tangrong's creditors to pressure Tangrong for repayment.

Tangrong was unable to handle the situation, and, as it had ten years earlier, it asked the Executive Yuan for help. Citing a clause in the General Mobilization Law empowering the government to order the rescue of important enterprises, the government took the unprecedented step of saving a private enterprise.[41] The CDC was entrusted with the task of setting up a supervisory group to take over Tangrong during its reorganization. In 1962, the state's share in the restructured Tangrong Corporation surpassed the private share, and Tangrong was transformed into a publicly owned firm. The saga of Taiwan's largest private firm ended with a state takeover.

The point is, however, that Tangrong was not an ordinary business. First, as noted above, it was the largest private firm in Taiwan. In Tang Chuanzong's opinion, the larger the firm, the less likely the government would allow it to go under, since the bankruptcy of a large firm would affect many people. Continuous expansion became Tang's philosophy for survival.[42] Eventually Tangrong produced over half the steel in Taiwan and was the supplier for many big public works.[43] Second, Tangrong was an important business partner of the military. It was a major buyer of military scrap iron.[44] Third, Tangrong had strong political connections. Tang Chuanzong later admitted that since one had to rely on powerful officials to secure bank loans,[45] he had deliberately built up a huge political network. As a KMT member, he was asked by the party to fund numerous legislative campaigns.[46] He had good relations with many prestigious and influential local figures, particularly Zhang Daofan, speaker of the Legislative Yuan, and Chen Cheng. Unsurprisingly, he had many supporters in political circles. In fact, two provincial lawmakers acted as go-betweens in the initial talks between the BOT and Tangrong. When Tangrong's crisis erupted, Chen Cheng, Zhang Daofan, and other officials immediately tried to help.[47] Fourth, Tangrong had good relations with the banks, including all three major commercial banks. Given its scale, the banks were willing to lend it money.[48]

Then why did the government refuse to help the firm this time, as it had done ten years earlier? One explanation that has been offered is that Tangrong was a victim of one bureaucrat's personal ambition. According to Tang Chuanzong, Pan Zhijia, the deputy general manager of the CDC and the head of the supervisory group, coveted the position of general manager of Tangrong. The crisis was solely the result of a scheme on the part of Pan.[49]

Another explanation attributes the result to the power struggle between Chen Cheng and Chiang Ching-kuo. As the struggle between Chen Cheng and Chiang Ching-kuo to succeed Chiang Kai-shek intensified, Tangrong, it is alleged, became one of Chiang Ching-kuo's first targets.[50] Chiang Ching-kuo is variously said to have taken offense at Tangrong's rejection of his demand that it employ veterans[51] or at its support for Chen Cheng's attempt to prevent Chiang Kai-shek's re-election as president.[52]

A third explanation points to competition between Shanghai and Taiwanese business people or between the mainland business clique and the local business clique.[53] The evidence adduced for this argument is that Tangrong had negotiated a joint venture with Ford to manufacture cars, but the plan had not received government approval, because it was competing against the Yulong Corporation, a Shanghai firm linked to Madame Chiang that also wanted to manufacture cars.[54]

A fourth reason cites the government's political and economic ideologies. The dominant ideology was Sun Yatsen's doctrine of the people's livelihood, which was centered around "developing state capital and limiting private capital." Tangrong's rapid expansion triggered fears about its size among many government officials. Furthermore, steel was closely related to defense. So a government takeover was only logical.[55] Under the circumstances, it is not surprising that when Tangrong introduced a plowing machine from Japan and applied for government permission to build a plant to manufacture it, the contract was instead given to Yongfeng Original Papermaking Corporation, a company that had previously had nothing to do with machinery.[56]

A final explanation attributes the crisis to the change in economic policy. By the end of the 1950s, the shift from high to low interest rates led to a drop in the inflation rate. This became the major source of Tangrong's financial crisis.

Pan Zhijia's animus cannot be considered a valid explanation because of the consistent attitudes and policies of the BOT and the

MOEA and the semi-official nature of the CDC.[57] It cannot be denied that competition between mainland and native business interests was part of the reason, but it was clearly not the main reason. Political ideology can explain the government's attempts to limit the speed of Tangrong's expansion, but it does not tell us why the government withdrew its previous support for Tangrong and eventually took it over. The power struggle between Chen Cheng and Chiang Ching-kuo may explain why Yin Zhongrong, Chen Cheng's longtime protégé, did not follow Chen Cheng in supporting Tangrong.[58] Because of the lack of evidence, however, this theory can only be considered conjecture.[59] However, if the political explanation is valid, Tangrong was the victim of a political struggle.

Despite the political background of the Tangrong case, if it is viewed only from a political perspective, its implications will be oversimplified. Given its economic impact and consequences, we must look at the case in the context of the evolution of government economic policy in the late 1950s, the dual financial structure, and the general economic situation.

The dual financial structure was a primary factor in the Tangrong case. During the 1950s, the government's control of the financial system gave it a vital resource and strategic policy instrument. The publicly owned financial system mainly served the public sector. In addition, an unorganized, or private, financial market gradually formed. Some mainland capital and local capital accumulated by small and medium landlords during the land reform were the sources of this private market. Due to chronic inflation in the 1950s, this unorganized financial market was a major resource for the private sector.[60] This market had a contradictory impact on private firms: it helped firms solve capital problems, but at a heavy price, because its interest rates were much higher than those of banks (see Table 5.4).

Large borrowing from the private capital market was Tangrong's major strategy and remained vital to its rapid expansion. This led to a severe financial crisis in 1949, and as a result operations had to be suspended. Its total indebtedness to the private financial market was as high as NT$600,000. But due to direct

Table 5.4
Evolution of Interest Rates in the Private Capital Market and Banks, 1949–65
(% per month)

| | Private interest rates | | | | Bank interest rates | | | |
| | Taipei city | | Fengshan town | | Bank of Taiwan | | Other banks | |
Year	Credit loan	Collateral loan	Credit loan	Collateral loan	Credit loan	Collateral loan	Credit loan	Collateral loan
1949	17.4	15.0			3.90		9.90	8.40
1950	12.0	0.5			3.90		3.90	3.30
1951	10.5	9.0			4.80		4.80	4.50
1952	6.6	5.5	6.5	5.5	3.30		3.30	3.00
1953	4.3	3.5	4.0	3.0	2.40		2.40	2.25
1954	4.1	3.1	4.0	3.5	1.98		1.98	1.95
1955	4.5	3.6	5.0	4.0	1.86		1.86	1.80
1956	3.9	3.3	4.0	3.0	1.86	1.80	1.86	1.80
1957	3.6	3.0	3.5	2.5	1.86	1.65	1.86	1.65
1958	3.3	3.0	3.0	2.0	1.86	1.65	1.86	1.65
1959	3.9	3.3	3.0	2.0	1.74	1.50	1.74	1.50
1960	3.9	3.3	4.0	3.0	1.74	1.50	1.74	1.35
1961	2.7	2.4	3.5	2.5	1.56	1.35	1.56	1.32
1962	2.7	2.4	3.0	2.0	1.56	1.32	1.56	1.17
1963	2.4	2.1	3.0	2.0	1.38	1.17	1.38	1.17
1964	2.1	1.8	3.0	2.0	1.29	1.17	1.29	1.17
1965	2.1	1.8	3.0	2.0	1.29	1.17	1.29	1.17

SOURCE: Zhongyang yinhang, Jingji yanjiuchu, Zhonghua minguo Taiwan diqu jinrong tongji yuebao, Jan. 1965, pp. 67–68.

intervention from Chen Cheng, the BOT and other banks loaned Tangrong NT$335,000. These loans saved Tangrong from bankruptcy and strengthened its confidence in the government's determination to help important private firms. As a result, Tangrong continued to absorb huge private deposits to finance its rapid expansion.

By the end of 1960, Tangrong's debt had grown to NT$600 million. Borrowing from private sources accounted for NT$240 million of the total, twice the combined amount of long- and short-term debts owed financial institutions.[61] The banks' monthly interest rate was 17.5 percent, whereas the private monthly interest rate was 30 percent. Due to the relatively stable inflation rate during 1959 and 1960, the private interest rates were a heavy burden on Tangrong and led to a severe financial crisis. Tangrong had to seek more loans from the banks to pay the interest on its private debt. A study by a joint Japanese-American group (Investigation Report on Tangrong Iron Corporation), which had been invited by Tangrong to investigate the possibility of investing in it, concluded that the manager of Tangrong had misjudged the prospects for inflation and had borrowed to expand the company and to buy an excessive amount of real estate. This strategy had resulted in a shortage of working capital.

In Tangrong's view, the high interest rates in the private capital market would be offset by the high rate of inflation. Although private interest rates were much higher than bank rates (see Table 5.4), it could benefit from a large amount of borrowing.[62] Indeed, this strategy had been quite successful for years. In addition, the banks' elaborate procedures frightened Tang Chuanrong, another factor that led him to turn to the private market.[63] Although the inflation rate did not soar as high as anticipated during 1957–60, expectations remained strong, and Tangrong continued its heavy borrowing from the private financial market. However, the decline in the inflation rate in the late 1950s spelled disaster for Tangrong, and its debt situation deteriorated sharply. The firm eventually became insolvent.

The government's economic goals and policy during this period also contributed to Tangrong's crisis. The government became determined to fight high interest rates in the private capital market as a means of curbing inflation and diverting idle private capital to the public banks. After replacing Zhang Zikai as BOT president in July 1960, Yin Zhongrong abandoned Jiang Biao's Keynesian policy and adopted an anti-inflationary policy. There had long been a debate between Zhang and Yin over interest rate policy.[64] Yin favored Jiang Shuojie's suggestion to increase the banks' interest rates to attract more savings, whereas Zhang Zikai preferred to cut interest rates through government control. The low interest rate policy prevailed when Zhang served as president of the BOT. In 1960, Yin had the opportunity to put his own interest rate policy into practice. In various articles published in 1959 and 1960, Yin repeatedly emphasized his determination to fight inflation. Against this background, the *Bank of Taiwan Quarterly* published Jiang Shuojie's article "Taiwan's Interest Rate Policy." As noted in Chapter 2, Jiang was one of two economists who worked in U.S. universities and international financial institutions consulted by the government. Jiang's article suggested that interest rates should be subject to market mechanisms and the official interest rate should be raised substantially in order to reflect the market level. But as long as Zhang Zikai remained president of the BOT, Jiang's article was not published in the *Bank of Taiwan Quarterly*. As soon as Zhang was replaced, however, the article was published with an appended editorial expressing the views of the BOT about inflation and interest rates. The editorial note confirmed that interest rates should reflect the market level. But it argued that the issue had to be resolved in a more comprehensive way. First, the currency needed to be stabilized in order to fight inflation. Second, the entire economic environment had to be improved, so as to bring about a decline in interest rates. The views in the editorial reflected Yin's ideas. Given Yin's remarks on earlier and later occasions, it is obvious that a systematic government policy toward inflation and interest rates was already in place at the time of the Tangrong crisis.

Two important events facilitated the formation of Yin's inflation and interest rate policies: the huge defense expenditures associated with the Jinmen (Quemoy) military conflict in August 1958 and the reconstruction after the August 1959 floods. Both caused inflationary pressures, and the government tightened financial policy by increasing the rediscount rates to the commercial banks.[65] In response to the mounting pressure for a loosening of credit from the business sector, Yin stressed that one of the major tasks of the BOT, as a central bank, was to maintain the stability of the domestic currency, that is, to maintain price stability.[66] Yin saw the high interest rates in the private capital market as an obstacle to this goal. The total amount of deposits in public financial institutions was NT$9.679 billion. Estimated borrowing from the private capital market was NT$3 billion, about one-third of the deposits in the public financial system.[67] Despite the high interest rates, many firms still turned to the private capital market because it was difficult for the private sector to access the public financial system, which served mainly the public sector and government institutions. From the government's point of view, however, some firms had become dependent on continued inflation, which allowed their assets to increase in value compared to their debt. Without inflation, these firms would encounter financial difficulties. Yin called these firms "unsound," and the government had to choose between maintaining economic stability or maintaining these unsound firms.[68]

Yin granted the necessity of a short-term capital market that responded to market demands. It had its own function and importance, and it could not be replaced by the banks. However, because it threatened economic stability, it had to be regulated.[69] Tangrong's financial crisis offered a perfect opportunity to implement such regulation. Seemingly, the economic considerations of the authorities in the Tangrong case are evident, and this is why it is risky to oversimplify the Tangrong case and see it as only politically motivated.

Although Yin did not specifically characterize Tangrong as unsound, he clearly viewed it as a typical case of a firm using inflation to expand. Tangrong was a large borrower in the private capital market. According to a September 10, 1960, debtor list, Tangrong owed NT$279 million to private lenders and had 4,262 creditors in Taipei and Kaohsiung.

Yin acknowledged that Tangrong was "in fact like a bank."[70] Compared to the total deposits in all financial institutions

(NT$4,536 million), Tangrong had NT$279 million in borrowings. Tangrong's borrowing amounted to a tenth of the estimated total of NT$3,000 million of "idle funds" in the black market. And finally, in 1960, private deposits in Tangrong equaled 35 percent of the total deposits of the BOT.[71] These data demonstrate the importance of Tangrong in the financial market during this period. The government clearly had to do something to influence the private capital market and to realize its policy goal of forcing the private financial market to reduce its interest rates.

Despite Tangrong's strong political connections and its large scale of operations, the government eventually chose to sacrifice Tangrong to its own larger policy goals—cutting interest rates in the private funds market and attracting private funds to the banks.[72] Yin's strategy was to pressure the black market to cut its interest rates,[73] and Tangrong could be used to educate both borrowers and lenders in the black funds market. Through it, the government could demonstrate its determination to stick to a tight financial policy and to fight inflation and thus reduce inflationary expectations.[74] A close look at the government's methods for dealing with Tangrong will clarify the implications of the case.

The government used Tangrong to reduce private interest rates by providing loans. Among the conditions attached to the BOT's NT$120 million loan to Tangrong was that Tangrong reduce the monthly interest rates it paid in the private capital market to 17 percent for one-year loans, 19 percent for two-year loans, and 21 percent for three-year loans. Creditors who did not accept the reductions could withdraw their deposits from Tangrong.

In a report to the Ministry of Finance about the Tangrong loan case, the BOT spelled out two goals that it hoped to achieve: to solve Tangrong's financial problems and to force the private capital market to reduce its interest rates.[75] Given the general policy on inflation and interest rates, it is not difficult to see that the second goal was the major one. However, the loan plan did not come about, since Tangrong did not accept the conditions.

Tangrong eventually yielded to pressure and had to accept the BOT's conditions. After the CDC's report on Tangrong's financial situation was printed in the newspapers on September 19 and Yin publicly released data on Tangrong's debt in the Legislative Yuan on September 23, Tangrong could not handle the mounting pressure from its creditors demanding repayment. On September 24, it had to ask the Executive Yuan for urgent assistance. In return, Tangrong had to agree that the Executive Yuan would send staff to supervise Tangrong; guidance would be provided to improve Tangrong's operations; the deposits of the president of Tangrong and his lineal relatives and the president's personal property would become company property; the company's affiliated investments and units would be sold to reduce its debt; and the average monthly interest rate Tangrong paid would be lowered to 20 percent. In return, the BOT provided NT$120 million to compensate for depositors' withdrawals from Tangrong and supply Tangrong with working funds.

It is interesting to consider why the interest rate was set at 20 percent. In Yin's view, a reasonable interest rate for the private capital market was 22 percent. In a speech before the provincial legislature on September 2, Yin calculated this rate from the difference in the foreign exchange rates between the official and black markets, which was 10 percent. Thus, if the BOT's interest rate were 20 percent, the 10 percent difference worked out to a 22 percent interest rate in the private market.[76] This rate was subsequently granted to firms that applied for loans from the BOT, and they had to "reduce the monthly interest rate of their borrowings from the private capital market to under 22 percent."[77]

The policy was quite successful. Table 5.5 shows that the interest rate gap between the private funds market and the banks narrowed by 12.6 percentage points in 1961, from 28.8 percent in 1960 to 16.2 percent in 1961. The difference between the two was also reduced from an average of 26.15 percentage points in the 1953–60 period to an average of 14.03 percentage points in the 1961–68 period. This policy success is also reflected in the flow of funds from the private capital market to the banks. In a January 17, 1961, editorial, the *Credit Information News* reported that a number of large public and private firms had begun, or were ready to begin, to reduce interest rates for private borrowings. The interest rates in the private market had already declined, and a 20 percent monthly rate could be expected.

The revelations about Tangrong in the newspapers contributed to this change. Private enterprises were alerted to what might happen if they borrowed too heavily in the private funds market. Firms looking to borrow from the general public could no longer set their own rates, since higher interest rates were not protected by law.[78] Yin Zhongrong also confirmed this result of the Tangrong case. He attributed the increasing month-by-month shift in deposits from firms to banks to the psychological influence of the Tangrong event.[79] Thus, Tangrong can be regarded as a watershed.

Fixed deposits in banks increased by NT$2.9 billion in one year alone. This large increase was a rare event in Taiwan's postwar monetary history, until 1963–64 when bank deposits were swollen by the expansion in export income.[80] Because of a lack of information on the exact amount of private funds shifting to bank deposits after the Tangrong event, we cannot know how much of this increase can be attributed to Tangrong. Ching-yuan Lin estimates that the figure might have been as high as NT$1 billion.[81] The significant point is that the shift occurred without a rise in nominal interest rates, and the transfer of funds from the informal private capital market can be seen as a shrinking of the private capital market.

Thus, one may question what the implications were for the SMEs. It is hard to estimate the real impact. My judgment is that the sources of capital for the SMEs may not have been influenced too much. This is because most of the funds that shifted to the banks was sums lent to large firms like Tangrong. The main consideration of the owners of these funds was not the high interest rate but security. They had lent money to the large firms because these firms could pay the higher interest rates and they had greater credibility. They moved their money because the banks were able to provide more security after the monetary authorities decided to reduce the interest rates in the informal capital market. The flow of money had little impact on the SMEs. The SMEs benefited from this situation, however, because of the reduced interest rates in the regulated private capital market.

Table 5.5
Interest Rates and Prices Between 1946 and 1971

Year	(1) Retail inflation rates	(2) Commercial banks' interest rates	(3) = (2) – (1) Commercial banks' real interest rates	(4) Private capital market interest rates	(5) = (4) – (1) Real private capital market interest rates	(6) = (4) – (2) Difference between the banks and the private market
1946	2810	16.4	−2793.6	171.6	−102.4	155.2
1947	274	16.4	−257.6	300.0	−196.0	201.5
1948	496	98.5	−397.5	208.8	−4444.2	108.0
1949	4653	100.8	−4552.2	144.0	−348.0	104.4
1950	492	39.6	−452.4	126.0	77.0	72.0
1951	49	54.0	5.0	79.2	56.2	43.2
1952	23	36.0	13.0	51.6	32.6	24.6
1953	19	27.0	8.0	49.2	44.2	26.2
1954	5	23.0	18.0	54.0	46.0	32.4
1955	8	21.6	13.6	46.8	33.8	25.2
1956	13	21.6	8.6	43.2	34.2	23.4
1957	9	19.8	10.8	39.6	36.6	19.8
1958	3	19.8	16.8	46.8	39.8	28.8
1959	7	18.0	11.0	46.8	32.8	28.8
1960	14	18.0	4.0	32.4	29.4	16.2
1961	3	16.2	13.2	32.4	29.4	16.6
1962	3	15.8	12.8	28.8	22.8	14.8
1963	6	14.0	8.0			

1964	3	14.0	11.0	25.2	22.2	11.2
1965	-5	14.0	19.0	28.8	33.8	14.8
1966	1	14.0	13.0	25.2	24.2	11.2
1967	3	13.3	10.3	25.2	22.2	11.9
1968	3	13.3	10.3	28.8	25.8	15.5
1969	0	13.3	13.3	28.8	28.8	15.5
1970	3	12.6	9.6	22.1	19.1	9.5
1971	0	12.0	12.0	21.6	21.6	9.6

SOURCE: Fan Qinping and Liu Sufen, "Minguo sishi niandai Tangrong yu minjian daikuan," p. 34.

The immediate implications for government policy were that the monetary authorities were able to expand credit to the private sector substantially in 1961, as well as adjust nominal interest rates incrementally downward in subsequent years without serious inflationary repercussions; and that the government's anti-inflationary policy succeeded in eradicating the deep-seated inflationary psychology that had prevailed since the immediate postwar years.[82] Thereafter in the 1960s, Taiwan moved into a period of price stability and rapid growth. Despite the lack of explicit evidence that links this change directly to the Tangrong case,[83] the change did begin with that event.

Although Yin's goal was to use the Tangrong case to stabilize the economy by curbing inflation and reducing interest rates in the private financial market, the significance of his efforts reached far beyond this goal. They were extremely important for the emergence of the SMEs. The key point is that Yin recognized the necessity for a private financial market. What he wanted to do was to reduce the high interest rates of this market because he saw them as a threat to the government's goal of stabilizing the economy. As shown in Table 5.5, private interest rates dropped substantially after 1961. It is significant that the government continued to maintain the private financial market and to regulate it through interest rates.

As we have seen, a dual financial structure had been in existence in Taiwan since the early 1950s. The publicly owned financial system provided credit only to the public sector and the LEs, whereas the private financial market provided credit to the SMEs. The CDC case and the subsequent chapters demonstrate the close relationship between the state-owned banks and the LEs. The LEs obtained their initial capital or fixed capital from the banks. But the SMEs were denied access to the banks because of their small size, unsound accounting practices, and the banks' demand for collateral. As Chapter 8 shows, the SMEs had to resolve their capital problems in the private financial market. Therefore, the private financial market remained important for the launching of the SMEs. The drop in interest rates in the unorganized financial market that began in 1961 coincided with the SMEs' emergence in the export markets. Despite the lack of explicit statistics, I believe that these two events are linked.

Four points are relevant in the Tangrong case. First, it is a typical case of the government using policy instruments to achieve its economic goals. The bureaucrats successfully used financial policy not only to influence the market but eventually to regulate the market and lead it in the direction desired by the government. In this regard, Yin Zhongrong was correct to state in 1961 that this was the first time since the KMT regime retreated to the island that the government had successfully used long-term financial policy to fight inflation.[84]

Second, the case reflects the complexity of the policy-making process. It involved political intervention by Chen Cheng and other politicians, strong lobbying by Tangrong, and the policy goals of the bureaucrats. The bureaucrats did not exist in a political vacuum, a fact that suggests we should be careful about the theory of bureaucratic autonomy. Not only were the bureaucrats unable to insulate themselves from societal and political interference, but they were unable to overcome the pressures. What mechanism allowed Yin Zhongrong and his colleagues to attempt to resist the pressures? To answer this question, we would need to understand the extent to which Chen Cheng intervened in this case. Did he refrain from further interference and finally leave the matter to the financial bureaucrats? Or did his intervention have no effect? Did Yin, Chen Cheng's long-time protégé, ignore Chen Cheng's opinion and handle this matter with his own policy goals in mind, or was his decision a result of a shift in political loyalties? Unfortunately, the answers to these questions remain unknown.

Third, once again, as in the case of foreign exchange and trade reform, the Tangrong case highlights Yi Zhongrong's key role in economic policy making. Yin demonstrated his strong style throughout the event. This confirms that economic policy depended greatly on the personal views of bureaucrats. Yin was adamantly opposed to inflation. Zhang Zikai was a Keynesianist. If Zhang had continued as the president of the BOT, would he have adopted the same policy? Probably not.

Fourth, the decrease in interest rates was a result of an interaction between the state and private actors. The goal of the monetary and financial authorities was realized only when other big firms reduced the interest rates they paid private creditors after the government showed its resolve in the Tangrong case. This indicates that the scope of the interaction between the government and the private sector was far more than an example of Peter Evans's suggestion of "cooperation" between the state and the private sector to realize a "shared project."[85] Seemingly, Tangrong's failure was attributed to a misunderstanding of the government's economic goals and a lack of cooperation with the bureaucrats. In an economy like that of Taiwan in the late 1950s and 1960s, the government had both a desire and the instruments to police the marketplace in which private enterprises operated. A firm that could not understand the government's goals and follow them, even one as large as Tangrong, would not be successful. Tang Chuanzong was an astute and strong-willed entrepreneur.[86] But in addition to his political mistake of backing the wrong side, he underestimated Yin's determination to fight inflation, and he failed to see the dramatic change in government financial and monetary policy after Yin became president of the BOT. Even decades later, Tang Chuanzong still attributed Tangrong's problem to the personal ambition of certain officials and the result of a power struggle among the top authorities.[87] In reality, his failure to adjust his strategy in time and to respond more positively to Yin's policy is the core reason for Tangrong's failure. The Tangrong case highlights the importance of effective coordination between the government and private enterprises.

However, the gap between the intention of government policy and the unanticipated consequences of this policy and its implications for the industrial structure should be emphasized. Yin's original goal was to stabilize the economy by reducing interest rates in the unorganized financial market. His other goal, never publicly announced, was to draw capital from the unorganized financial market to the public banks in order to raise funds for the Third Four-Year Plan (1961–64). The plan called for NT$6.3 billion of the over NT$50 billion required to be raised from the private financial market. Without lower interest rates, this goal could not have been realized.[88] Although Yin recognized the necessity for an unorganized financial market, he did not intend to force this market to improve the financial resources available for the private sector. However, an unexpected consequence was that his efforts lowered the cost to SMEs of borrowing money in this market. As we will see, this was highly significant for the future success of the SMEs.

Conclusion

The findings in this chapter suggest that the economic agencies in Taiwan were fragile. The role an institution played reflected the power of its director, and his power in turn depended on political support from the highest political leaders. On this basis, the chapter argues that we must understand Taiwan's economic bureaucracy from the perspective of bureaucratic politics. The strongman was symbolic of Taiwan's bureaucratic politics.

In terms of the consequences of the state's strategies and the interaction of the state and private actors on the formation of the industrial structure, state actions reinforced and safeguarded the position of the LEs in the domestic market. The dependence of economic growth on the private sector and the small size of private enterprises were more important than the regime's vigilance over local firms. This encouraged the state to focus on fostering and protecting a small number of firms. It did so through the provision of credits and other instruments. These measures enabled the privileged firms to engage in production for the domestic market and discouraged them from moving into the export markets. Activities that served the domestic market required a relatively large amount of capital because the domestic market involved not only manufacturing but also sales and marketing. Credits from the state-owned banks enabled the LEs to operate. The protectionist policy shielded the LEs from foreign competition and enabled them to enjoy monopolistic profits. The LEs were unwilling to engage in export activities because they did not want to face foreign competition in markets without government protection.

The government's export promotion policy had a significant impact on the formation of the industrial structure. The state contradicted its expressed goal when it discouraged the LEs from exporting, but the universalistic method of promoting exports accidentally led to the emergence of the SMEs in the export markets.

Moreover, the financial and monetary authorities' struggle to reduce the interest rates in the unorganized financial market not only served its explicit intention of safeguarding and regulating the market but also improved the financial resources available to the SMEs. This market was critical in the SMEs' shift to export production.

Table 6.1

U.S. Military and Economic Assistance to Taiwan, U.S. FY1950–67
(U.S.$ million)

Item	1950–55 Amount	%	1956–60 Amount	%	1961–67 Amount	%	1950–67 Amount	%
Economic	$627.8	47.1%	$500.5	32.0%	$457.5	42.6%	$1,585.8	39.9%
Gifts	607.8	96.8	378.4	75.6	205.8	44.9	1,192.0	75.2
Loans	20.0	3.2	122.1	24.4	251.7	55.1	393.8	24.8
Military	704.1	52.9	1,064.3	68.0	615.8	57.4	2,384.2	60.1
Gifts	704.1	100.0	1,064.3	100.0	614.9	99.9	2,383.3	99.96
Loans	–	–	–	–	0.9	0.1	0.9	0.04
TOTAL	1,331.9	100.0	1,564.8	100.0	1,073.3	100.0	3,970.0	100.0
Gifts	1,311.9	98.5	1,442.7	92.2	820.7	76.5	3,575.3	90.0
Loans	20.0	1.5	122.1	7.8	252.6	23.5	394.7	10.0

SOURCE: Wen Xinying, *Jingji qiji de beihou*, p. 91.

anxious to point to a "success story." It wanted Taiwan to "graduate," to serve as a model student. Indeed, the AID was right. Taiwan had graduated. Although many Taiwanese officials were surprised by the U.S. decision, the termination of the aid did not in fact greatly affect Taiwan's economy, as a prominent Taiwanese banker admitted in July 1964.[5] This was probably the reason for the prevailing attitude of pride and satisfaction that Taiwan was at last standing on its own economic feet.[6]

The termination of U.S. aid did, however, affect the state's capacity and autonomy. It had an important impact on state–private sector relations because the state had lost a vital resource. As we have seen, the possession of resources was a vital factor in the state's steering capacity. American aid was the state's primary resource, and it strengthened state autonomy vis-à-vis the private sector greatly. The cancellation of the aid inevitably undermined state capacity and autonomy by changing the subtle balance between the state and the private sector. Without the aid, the state had far fewer resources to distribute among private firms, and this weakened its ability to influence the private sector. This in turn reduced the private sector's reliance on the state (which in the long term actually ended up strengthening the private sector and encouraging growth). More discussion on this issue will follow in this chapter.

Furthermore, the termination greatly affected the economic bureaucracy. Aid-financed bodies, such as the ESB, CUSA, and CIECD (until 1965), were extremely powerful because of their control over the U.S. aid—all government departments approached them for money.[7] This was a fundamental reason for their power and influence. Inevitably, the cutoff weakened the power and authority of the CIECD substantially. The only financial resource of the CIECD after the phaseout was the surplus in the Counterpart Fund. After 1965, its authority and power rested solely on its personnel, particularly after Chiang Ching-kuo became head of the CIECD in 1969, rather than on its monetary resources. In addition to the new bureaucrats and new working style under ministers like K. T. Li, the ending of U.S. aid was another factor that undermined the importance of the CIECD relative to the MOEA and the MOF.

Index

State Survival Strategies

The shift in strategy from import substitution to exports and the new emphasis on the private sector were difficult decisions for Chiang Kai-shek to make since the changes posed three risks for the state: lifting restrictions on foreign exchange and quotas could worsen the balance of payments, tax reforms could reduce government revenue and increase inflation,[8] and developing the private sector might weaken the political and economic capacity of the state. Chiang's concerns about the military impact of the reforms was shared by others. The armed forces, and the SOEs and the LEs linked to the military, understandably opposed the freezing of defense expenditures. Furthermore, there was a difference of opinion between Chiang Kai-shek and his economic bureaucrats on the goals of the reforms. The bureaucrats viewed the issues more from an economic point of view, whereas Chiang's main concern was defense. Chiang's agreement to freeze military expenditures by no means meant that he had abandoned his goal of retaking the mainland by military means. For Chiang, developing the economy was merely a means of building up the military. Chiang continued to be preoccupied with defense. In June 1967, several years after the inauguration of the reforms, a National Security Agency was set up with Chiang as chair; its purpose was said to be to reform the state and build a strong force to secure Taiwan and retake the mainland. The agency was a response to the successful nuclear explosion in mainland China.[9] However, in spite of the different motives for developing the economy, as well as the resistance from vested interests, a consensus was reached that exports and more reliance on the private sector would solve Taiwan's problems.

The reforms eventually had their intended effect. Inflation, one of the top two economic problems until the late 1950s, was brought under control rather quickly. The increase in the retail price index was 3 percent in 1961, 3 percent in 1962, 6 percent in 1963, 3 percent in 1964, and –5 percent in 1965. The balance-of-payments problem, however, continued unabated until the early 1970s. The liberalization of trade in the late 1950s and the introduction of incentives to promote exports in the early 1960s were designed by the government to resolve this problem. These changes had a substantial impact on the ways the government dealt with the economy as a whole, as well as with the private sector in particular. Some of the administrative measures that had prevailed under the wartime economy had to be replaced by market mechanisms. As discussed in Chapter 5, the first demonstration of the state's new strategy was the attack on high interest rates in the private funds market in the early 1960s.

At the very beginning of the 1970s, there was reason for optimism. The problems that had previously threatened the government had disappeared. There was rapid economic growth, foreign trade was moving from deficits to surpluses, and inflation remained low: 3 percent in 1970 and 0 percent in 1971. Moreover, the internal political situation had stabilized. A crackdown on an attempt by a few prominent intellectuals to establish a party in 1960 quieted the opposition movement, and the KMT regime enjoyed a peaceful period during much of the 1960s. Internationally, Taiwan benefited economically and politically after it became a supply base for the U.S. troops fighting in Vietnam.

However, the good times did not last long. Some new problems emerged in the early 1970s. Politically, the international environment underwent a dramatic change. The Nixon administration planned to normalize U.S.-China relations by the end of the 1960s. Taiwan lost its UN seat after China was admitted in 1971. President Nixon then visited China in early 1972. More and more countries transferred diplomatic recognition from Taipei to Beijing. These diplomatic setbacks caused a political crisis on the island. For the first time, young elite intellectuals began to question the legitimacy of the KMT regime, which claimed to be the only legal government of all of China. They challenged the legitimacy of the "Long Parliament," which had not been dissolved since the move to the island. They also called attention to the plight of the rural islanders. Capital began to flow out of Taiwan. In the midst of the uncertainties about the island's future, foreign investment dropped, and exports fluctuated. The island was shrouded in pessimism.

Economically, two changes had serious consequences for Taiwan. First, the deterioration of U.S. trade conditions in 1968 and

1969 led to the collapse of the Bretton Woods system and the adoption of a floating exchange rate system by many countries. This change had a substantial impact on the exports that had acted as the engine of Taiwan's economic growth.[10] Beginning in late 1971, prices soared in the international market. The oil crisis of 1973 wreaked havoc on the economy. It worsened the price situation in the global market, increased inflationary pressures on Taiwan, and severely threatened exports due to the global recession it caused.[11]

The structure of Taiwan's export-oriented economy is shown in Fig. 6.1. In a cycle of importing-processing-exporting, a small quantity of production equipment, raw materials, and some capital and technology were imported, using a small amount of domestic capital and technology. These were used to establish firms to produce cheap light industrial products, which were then exported to the global market. The more Taiwan exported, the more foreign exchange it earned; the more foreign exchange it earned, the more equipment and raw materials it imported. In turn, more and larger processing plants were established, and more goods were exported. This cycle led to full employment and an increase of per capita GNP, savings, and capital supply, thereby reinforcing the cycle.[12] This was the economic landscape of Taiwan in the 1960s and 1970s.

This economic pattern made Taiwan highly dependent on the world market, however. Taiwan benefited greatly when the global economy was strong. But it was inevitably hurt by a global economic slowdown. Both exports and imports separately accounted for over 40 percent of GNP. Together, they took about 90 percent of GNP, sometimes even 100 percent.[13] As a consequence of the oil crisis, Taiwan's economy began to sputter after 1973.

In response, the state undertook a number of measures to ease the political crisis and economic difficulties. The reforms were orchestrated by Chiang Ching-kuo, who consolidated his position as his father's heir by assuming the premiership in 1972. In the political sphere, "Taiwanization" allowed more political participation by native Taiwanese. This was a significant move to resolve the political crisis and the increasing demands for political participation. As a result, a number of young Taiwanese elites were promoted to

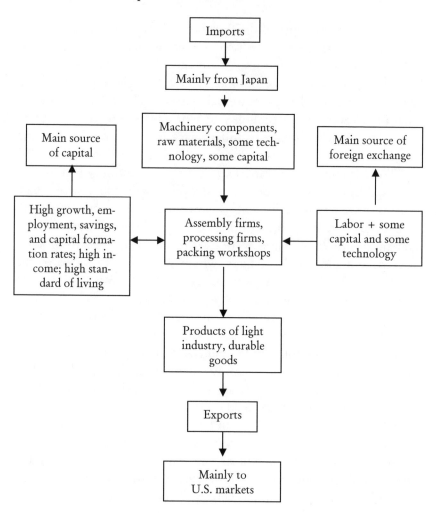

Fig. 6.1 Basic structure of Taiwan's economy (SOURCE: derived from Wang Zuorong, *Women ruhe chuangzaole jingji qiji?* p. 56)

higher KMT and government positions. Partial elections for the National Assembly began. In order to maintain order in the countryside, the exploitative rice policy was abandoned, and the rural sector received increased subsidies and protection.[14]

In the economic arena, financial, fiscal, monetary, and price measures were adopted to curb inflation.[15] The most significant change was that the government adopted a new strategy that emphasized heavy and chemical industries. As more developing countries joined the labor-intensive-product exporters in the world market, Taiwan was becoming less competitive. A transformation from labor-intensive industries to capital-, technology-, and skill-intensive industries was needed for Taiwan to remain competitive in the global market.

Symbolic of this change were the Ten Major Development Projects announced by Chiang Ching-kuo in November 1973 at the Fourth Plenum of the Tenth KMT Congress.[16] Seven of the ten projects were infrastructure projects in the areas of new highway, railway, airport, and harbor construction and nuclear energy development. The other three were steel, petrochemicals, and shipbuilding ventures. The ten projects were widely viewed as a signal that the government's economic strategy had shifted to heavy and chemical industries. Who or what was responsible for this policy process? Why was it done? What goals were hoped to be achieved and what were the results?

Unfortunately, the records on the policy discussions behind the ten projects are limited. From the information available, however, it is fair to say that the ten projects were economically as well as politically motivated. First, most of the ten projects were based on economic development considerations. Seven of the ten projects— the steel plant, the international airport, the petrochemical plant, the highway, Taizhong port, the electric railway, and the nuclear power plant—had previously been written into the Sixth Four-Year Plan (1974–76) by the economic planning agency. Some of the projects were already under construction or in operation. For example, the first naphtha-cracking plant of the China Petroleum Corporation (CPC) began operations in 1968. Construction of the second plant had begun in 1970. The first nuclear power plant was also on line. The other two, the shipbuilding yard and the Tropic of Cancer railway, were under study at the time of Chiang Ching-kuo's announcement. The only truly new project was the Suao port, which was added by Chiang Ching-kuo at the last minute, because he wanted to separate the military port from the commercial and fishing ports in Suao.[17]

Why did the economic planning agencies choose these projects? The motives varied from project to project. Military considerations were behind the steel plant, and the infrastructure projects were intended to benefit the entire economy. The petrochemical projects were a response to the changing economic reality. The rapid development of exports of downstream, labor-intensive manufactured goods, mainly plastics and textile products, in the second half of the 1960s had created a strong demand for intermediate inputs and led to the construction of the CPC's first naphtha-cracking plant. The development of metal-processing and machinery industries had increased the demand for steel goods. Because of these trends, the idea of "backward integration" had been proposed by the economic planning agencies and began to be accepted by the top leaders in the early 1970s.[18] Hence, most of the ten projects were based on changing economic realities.

However, the announcement of the ten projects was politically motivated. It came at a time of mounting political crises, economic challenges, and foreign setbacks. The hastiness of the policy process confirms the political nature of the announcement. According to Ye Wan-an, Fei Hua, the secretary-general of the CIECD (chosen by Chiang Ching-kuo to replace K. T. Li in 1969), asked his subordinates to compile a list from existing projects already in the Sixth Four-Year Plan. Fei picked seven projects and added the shipbuilding yard and the Tropic of Cancer railway. In order to bring the number up to ten, Fei also added the nuclear power plant.[19] In K. T. Li's opinion, the list was based on Minister of Economic Affairs Sun Yunxuan's six-project suggestion.[20] Both sources (Li and Ye) suggest that the policy network was limited to a few of Chiang Ching-kuo's closest aides. Hence, the new premier's announcement of the ten projects at the KMT conference in November 1973 came as a surprise to Finance Minister Li and many other high-ranking economic officials.[21] Perhaps Chiang wanted to use the ambitious ten projects to inspire morale and enhance confidence on the island at a time of political and economic difficulties and foreign setbacks. Economic considerations may not have been his first concern. The timing of the announcement suggests that the move was more a matter of needing a "policy" so that the state appeared to be in control, even though in fact there was no policy. It occurred because the boss needed it. In this respect, it is similar to SME policy in the 1970s, as we shall see in Chapter 8.

As one might expect, there were doubts about the projects. The government planning bodies as well as economists worried that the ten projects would cause inflation if they were to start simultaneously. The feasibility of some of the projects was questioned. A report by EPB researchers suggested, for example, that the Tropic of Cancer railway be postponed, and eventually it was tabled because of the oil crisis that erupted soon thereafter.[22] This case reminds us again that economic policy is not always consistent. However political the announcement may have been, the ten projects affected Taiwan's industrial structure by reinforcing the SOEs. In the name of "backward integration," the state intentionally strengthened the presence of the SOEs in upstream industries.

The ten projects highlight the necessity of exploring the economic bureaucracy during the 1960s and the first half of the 1970s. How did it work?

Changing the Economic Bureaucracy: The Decentralization of Institutions

During this period, drastic changes took place in the economic bureaucracy, both organizationally and in terms of personnel. These changes had an impact on government economic policy making. The CUSA was replaced by the CIECD and the EPB. The changes went in two conflicting directions. On one hand, in terms of the evolution of the economic bureaucracy, there was a decentralization as the functions and powers of the economic planning agency were reduced when the EPB replaced the CIECD and the roles of the constitutional government ministries increased. On the other hand, since Chiang Ching-kuo took charge of economic affairs himself, economic policy making was centralized.

Evolution of Institutions

The CIECD replaced the CUSA in 1963, and the EPB replaced the CIECD in 1973. The anticipated phasing out of U.S. aid was the major reason for replacing the CUSA with the CIECD. As early as 1960, the United States warned the Taiwan government about a forthcoming shift in emphasis from grants to loans. Before the U.S. aid stopped completely, Taiwan began looking for alternative sources. The World Bank and its two subsidiary bodies—the International Development Association (IDA) and the International Finance Corporation (IFC)—which provided funds to developing countries, were approached. But the World Bank did not provide funds to recipients of U.S. aid. In order to qualify for funding from the World Bank, the IFC, the IDA, or other international financial bodies as alternatives to the U.S. aid, the name CUSA had to be changed, and the CIECD was established in September 1963.

Originally, the CIECD was called the Council for International Cooperation. But Chen Cheng was dissatisfied with this title. He thought "cooperation" alone implied a passive body and hence favored the addition of the word "development." Hence, the newly established body became the Council for International Cooperation and Development. The CIECD inherited the functions of the CUSA and expanded them to some extent by incorporating groups from related ministries, such as the Industrial Development and Investment Center and the Center for Economic Research of the CUSA; the Industrial Development and Coordination Group and the Agricultural Development and Coordination Group of the MOEA; and the Transportation Coordination Group of the Ministry of Transportation. These consolidations concentrated economic planning in the CIECD. The CIECD thus had more authority than its predecessor; its capacity to plan and the quality of planning were improved largely due to improvements in the handling of statistics and the adoption of the metrological model. However, the CIECD did not function very well because its head was Yan Jiagan, who was not a bureaucratic strongman. The fact that the CIECD had fewer funds also undermined its functions.

This situation began to change when Chiang Ching-kuo took control in 1969. Although Yan Jiagan took Chen Cheng's positions as premier and as head of the CIECD, he was cautious by nature and had less seniority than Chen. The vacuum in political power over economic affairs created by Chen Cheng's death was filled by Chiang Ching-kuo, then deputy head of the Executive Yuan (the deputy premier), when he replaced Premier Yan Jiagan as the head of the CIECD in August 1969. The newspapers hailed this change with the headline: "To strengthen its administrative functions, [the CIECD] is chaired by the deputy premier." Despite the younger Chiang's formal subordination to the man he replaced as chair of the CIECD, he helped strengthen the CIECD's authority and increase its power. In contrast to the situation under Yan, few disagreements surfaced from the ministries at the CIECD meetings under Chiang. Once the head gave his consent, no one else dared say anything different. As a result, the assistants at the CIECD found that their work became easier.[23] This is consistent with the bureaucratic strongman thesis. Nevertheless, the autonomy of the CIECD was undermined once Chiang controlled it directly.

However, after almost five years under the charge of Chiang Ching-kuo, a reversal occurred in the role of the economic planning agency when the CIECD was replaced by the EPB in 1973.[24] The EPB was much weaker than the CIECD. Its only function was economic planning, as the CIECD's technology cooperation, international funds, and public relations sections were integrated with the Finance and Economic Affairs ministries. The ESB, CUSA, and CIECD had been headed by the premier or the deputy premier. But the head of the EPB was appointed by the premier, and its members were deputy heads of ministries, instead of the ministers. Unlike its predecessors, the EPB was not a supraministerial body. On paper, major economic policies were decided by the Five-Member Group under the Executive Yuan, which consisted of the heads of the Central Bank, the MOF, the MOEA, and the Central Statistics Bureau. In fact, however, the group only reported on economic matters at its weekly meetings, and it did not make policy. Major economic policies were made by Chiang

Ching-kuo himself.[25] The EPB played only a consulting role for the group, and thus it was not an important body.

The decentralization of Taiwan's economic bureaucracy was also reflected in the transfer of routine economic policy making to the economic and financial ministries, especially to the MOEA. Beginning in the early 1960s, bureaucrats from the economic planning agencies were reassigned to the constitutional ministries. Many bureaucrats from the U.S. aid–financed economic bodies, such as the CUSA and the CIECD, were placed in the MOEA and MOF. They brought with them the work style of these economic bodies as well as their assistants. This substantially changed these ministries. K. T. Li, deputy head of the CIECD, was appointed minister of economic affairs (1965–69) and then finance minister (1969–76).

The MOEA became increasingly important under "economic strongman" K. T. Li. Li, the most influential and powerful bureaucrat after Yin Zhongrong, brought both his style and a number of capable assistants with him from the CIECD. He substantially changed the MOEA and strengthened its role. Prior to that, the CUSA and CIECD had initiated policies, which the MOF and MOEA either passively followed or opposed. Li's initiative dramatically changed the style of the MOEA, and as a result, the MOEA started actively proposing policies and carrying out projects.[26] It took over many businesses previously run by the CUSA or CIECD, such as the export processing zones and the industrial parks, as well as responsibility for administering the Statute for the Encouragement of Investment.

The practice of appointing a strongman to head the MOEA persisted. The emergence of Sun Yunxuan, who became minister of the MOEA in 1969, as a major bureaucrat in the 1970s was important to the economic bureaucracy. His increased role was based on two factors. First, he was highly trusted by Chiang Ching-kuo, who wanted him to replace K. T. Li. Second, like Li, Sun also had a forceful personality. As we shall see in the next chapter, Sun was committed to the high-tech industry, and under Sun's leadership, the MOEA played an active role in its development.

The establishment of the Industrial Development Bureau (IDB) in 1970 contributed further to the active role of the MOEA in eco-

nomic policy making.[27] The IDB had three functions: industrial policy planning and formulation, policy consulting, and policy implementation. Many of these functions had previously been the
responsibility of the CIECD, for example, the planning and management of the industrial zones. In fact, most of the IDB's staff came
from the CIECD. Its first head, Wei Yongning, had previously been
the deputy head of the CIECD. The establishment of the IDB led to
the transfer of some authority from the CIECD to the MOEA, thus
weakening the CIECD. This was another signal of the strengthening of the routine government economic bureau-cracy. Sun often
backed plans and policies formulated by the IDB even if there was
opposition.[28] It also marked a change in the examination and approval process for some loans; for example, the IDB was responsible
for screening applications for the special loans for machinery
equipment exports undertaken by the Bank of China.[29] Given its
power and authority, the IDB became a major government body
dealing with the private sector. Its role further increased after the
weak EPB replaced the CIECD. But, as we will see in Chapter 7, its
power declined in the late 1970s and early 1980s.

Personnel Changes: End of the Generation of Economic Strongmen

Institutional change was not the only factor that influenced economic policy in Taiwan. Politicians and bureaucrats had an even
more important impact, as the institutions were decentralized. A
generational transformation of both political control of economic
policy and key staff was completed during this period. An ailing
Chen Cheng resigned as premier and head of the CIECD in November 1963, only two months after its establishment. Yan Jiagan
succeeded him as premier until 1973 and as head of the CIECD until 1969, when Chiang Ching-kuo became vice premier and director
of the CIECD. This marked the beginning of a new era in economic policy, as Chiang took full charge of economic policy making. His rise signaled the completion of the transfer of authority
over economic policy from Chiang Kai-shek's generation of politicians to the younger generation. Because of the divergent views of

the senior and the junior Chiang and differences in personality and ideology between Chen Cheng and Chiang Ching-kuo, this change had an important impact on economic policy.

The generational transformation also took place in the bureaucracy. Yin Zhongrong died in 1963 (overwork was the most frequently cited cause). This allowed the younger generation of bureaucrats to emerge. The vacuum resulting from Yin's death was filled by K. T. Li. Trained as a physicist, Li began his career as a bureaucrat in the IDC, when it was established in 1953. Like Yin, he was full of initiative, outspoken, and aggressive. He joined the team of top bureaucrats when he became secretary-general of the CUSA in 1958, where he coordinated the drafting of the Statute for the Encouragement of Investment. He was named secretary-general of the newly established CIECD in 1963 and two months later became its deputy director after Yan Jiagan was named premier and CIECD head. But it was Li who was actually in charge of Taiwan's economic policy.[30] From 1965 to 1969 he was concurrently the minister of economic affairs, and from 1969 to 1976 he was finance minister. He was the most important bureaucrat after Yin Zhongrong. Furthermore, Li was highly trusted by Chiang Kai-shek, who saw Li as the most talented bureaucrat after Yin and one on whom he could rely.[31]

However, after Chiang Ching-kuo assumed control of economic affairs in 1969, he and Li were often at odds. According to Li, Chiang did not trust bureaucrats. Chiang did, however, trust Sun Yunxuan, who became the minister of the MOEA in 1969, and Yu Guohua; this suggests that it was not bureaucrats per se but particular bureaucrats that were the foci of Chiang's suspicions. He had confidence in the new generation of strongmen such as Sun and Yu and relied heavily on them. Chiang differed with the CIECD on many economic issues, but he tended to agree with Sun.[32] In contrast, Chiang rejected many of Li's suggestions, such as his price policy and his proposal to privatize the three public commercial banks.[33] The difference in Chiang's attitudes toward Li and Sun shows that he intended to use junior bureaucrats to replace senior bureaucrats like Li and his colleagues on the CIECD. In 1973, in order to reduce the power of the planning commission and to win support at the Ministries of Economic Affairs and Finance, Chiang downgraded the commission by reshuffling its personnel and transferring much of its power to the constitutional ministries. Thus, Chiang's takeover of economic policy dramatically changed the map of the policy-making network, as a new group of bureaucrats, represented by Sun, emerged.

Two main reasons suggest themselves for Chiang Ching-kuo's distrust of K. T. Li. First, Chiang Ching-kuo lacked confidence because of his limited knowledge of economics. Many retired officials, in their memoirs as well as in interviews with me, referred to Chiang Kai-shek as "open-minded" in describing his easy acceptance of the opinions of the economic officials; the unspoken comparison was that his son was reluctant to listen to them. They recalled that Chiang Ching-kuo liked to make decisions based on his own judgment and past experience and felt that he trusted bureaucrats less than his father did.[34]

Part of the reason for this was that Chiang Ching-kuo had no background in economics. Although he had built a solid base in the party, military, and intelligence services, because of the growing importance of economic development, he had to establish credibility in economic affairs in order to secure legitimacy as his father's successor. His lack of knowledge caused him to fear a loss of power over economic policy making and made him want even more to retain discretionary power in this field—hence his suspiciousness of K. T. Li and his tight grasp on economic policy authority. More important, when Chiang Ching-kuo began to take charge of economic affairs, the outspoken Li had already cemented his reputation as the number-one bureaucrat in Taiwan. Li's seniority and standing presented a threat to Chiang, and his aggressiveness made Chiang uncomfortable.

A second reason for Chiang Ching-kuo's attitude toward K. T. Li was his tendency to stress the political implications of economic issues. Inflation, prices, and stability were Chiang's major concerns and influenced his support for particular economic policies. Chiang was especially obsessed with keeping prices low. In contrast, the bureaucrats in the CIECD approached policy from an economic perspective, and they would later suffer for their policy suggestions.[35] For example, during the world oil crises in 1973, Chiang Ching-kuo ignored the advice of CIECD bureaucrats to let prices rise.[36] Li later argued that the sharp differences between Chiang and the CIECD on the price issue was a major reason for Chiang's disbandment of the CIECD in 1973.

Chiang's ideas had a strong impact on economic policy. His ideology and dislike of business people had important consequences for government economic policy. Ten years of living in the Soviet Union had had a major impact on his ideology.[37] "No merchant is not unscrupulous" and "Nine out of ten merchants are unscrupulous" were the maxims with which Chiang approached business people.[38] Although his famous "fight against tigers" in Shanghai in 1948 cannot be attributed solely to his antibusiness ideology (building his future career in politics was the most important motive behind it), it demonstrated his feelings about business.[39] Pointing to the corrosive effects of the close collaboration between politicians and the *zaibatsu* in Japan, he insisted that Taiwan avoid this. After becoming premier, he expressed repeatedly that "the government of the Republic of China will never collude with any business group."[40]

Because of his fear of the control of key sectors by a business group, Chiang rejected K. T. Li's proposal to privatize the three publicly owned banks and to merge the *Economic Daily*, a newspaper belonging to one of the two major newspaper groups on Taiwan, and Formosa Plastics, the largest corporation on the island. Chiang insisted that the banks were a public resource, and it would not be in the country's best interest for the financial system to be dominated by a business group. He likewise thought that the media should not be controlled by a business group.[41]

Chiang also adamantly opposed businessmen taking positions in the government.[42] He had almost no friends who were in business, and after becoming premier, he suspended all contact with a close friend who was a businessman.[43] Chiang Ching-kuo's ideology and attitude were well known to both officials and business people in Taiwan and had an important impact on government-business relations. During his tenure in high office, government officials became very cautious in their dealings with the private sector.[44]

Bank–Private Sector Relations

The most important links between the state and the private sector were the publicly owned banks, which played a key role in carrying out government policy. In particular, these banks made a major contribution to the formation of the industrial structure through the provision of credit to the LEs. This section focuses on four issues: the restructuring of the banking system, the deposit and loan structure of the banks, bank-LE relations, and bank-SME relations.

Restructuring the Banking System

One way a government can wield economic influence is through interbank relations and the structure of the banking system. Taiwan's financial system experienced a significant change during the late 1950s and early 1960s as the financial system expanded in order to coordinate the shift in economic policy and to enable the banks to provide more credit to the private sector.[45] Three major mainland banks, the Central Bank, the Bank of Communications, and the Bank of China, resumed operations. The establishment of two private banks, the Commercial Bank of Overseas Chinese and Nippon Dai-Ichi Kangyo Bank, together with formation of the CDC, further altered Taiwan's banking system, which had hitherto been owned by the government.

Moreover, the mission of the public banks changed. The Bank of Communications had been an industrial bank before relocating to Taiwan, and after it reopened in 1960 it began providing medium- and long-term funds to industry. The rejuvenation of the Bank of Communications and the establishment of the CDC also signaled government attempts to improve the provision of industrial credit. Most of the CDC's capital came from foreign and private sources, whereas the Bank of Communication's capital came from domestic deposits. In this regard, the two banks were mutually complementary.

Reactivation of the Bank of China in 1960 dramatically changed the foreign exchange business. Until September 1959, the Bank of Taiwan's role as the only bank involved in the foreign exchange business had made it easy for the government to impose stringent restrictions on foreign exchange, which constituted an important part of the command economy. The BOT's monopoly ended in September 1959 when Nippon Dai-Ichi Kangyo Bank opened a branch in Taiwan to meet the needs of the expanding trade with Japan.[46] This marked the opening of Taiwan's foreign exchange market. The Bank of Communications was also authorized to engage in foreign exchange related to industrial development. The reactivation of the Bank of China reflected the government's policy emphasis on trade, because foreign exchange control was one of its main methods for controlling imports. These actions can be viewed as part of the overall change in government economic policy during the late 1950s and early 1960s.

The Central Bank reopened in 1961. The establishment of a central banking system to replace the provincial government's BOT was a goal of the nineteen-point reform program. Because the newly resumed banks were owned by the central government, there would have been administrative problems if the BOT's supervisory role over the other banks had continued.[47] The resumption of the central bank marked a return from temporary arrangements to normal government banking policy.[48]

The existing provincial government–owned banks also experienced some restructuring. Until 1961, government departments and the public sector had been the main borrowers from the BOT, with the private sector receiving only a small proportion of its loans. After the reactivation of the Central Bank, the BOT increased its provision of loans to private firms, in particular by expanding export-related credit services in the second half of 1961. The increase in the proportion of loans to the private sector accelerated even further when its local branches were ordered to provide loans to private firms.[49] The proportion of loans to the private sector, worth NT$25,354 million, reached 48 percent in 1975, and loans to the public sector dropped 42 percent. This was a fundamental change. In the restructuring, a division of labor was formed between the banks owned by the provincial government and those owned by the central government. The provincial banks concentrated on the private sector, and the central banks serviced mainly the public sector. The main consequence of this restructuring was that it facilitated access to the public banks by the private sector (mainly the LEs). This reflected, and in turn reinforced, the increasing importance of the private sector in the economy.

The expansion and restructuring of the banking system came about as government policy refocused on accelerating exports and promoting the private sector. This constituted part of the government's efforts to develop the economy. Nevertheless, as shown below, the major borrowers from the state-owned banks were not exporters. As we shall see, this had an impact on the formation of the industrial structure. The immediate aim of the expansion of the banking system was to free the private sector from the high interest rates of the informal financial market. But an additional motive was the government's attempt to control the private sector, and the entire economy, by tying the private sector to the state-owned banks.[50] This restructuring was thus part of the overall transformation of the political and economic systems to maintain state control under the new situation.[51]

Categorization of a bank as publicly or privately owned depends on the holder of the controlling interest. Of the fourteen banks listed in Table 4.1, only three, the Commercial Bank of Overseas Chinese, the CDC, and Nippon Dai-Ichi Kangyo Bank, qualified as privately owned. The eleven public banks belonged either to the central government or to the provincial government. There were some differences between the two types of public banks. Among the provincial banks, the three commercial banks (First Commercial Bank, Chang-hua, and Hua-nan) and the Co-operative Bank had been restructured in colonial times. Native Taiwanese shares constituted an important part of their capital, and they were closely associated with local capital. By contrast, the central government banks were associated primarily with capital from the mainland.

These banking arrangements were an attempt by the state to continue to control the banking sector, and the expansion and restructuring of the banking system in the early 1960s did not challenge state interests in the banking sector or threaten the state's monopoly of the banking system. The relationship between the central government's and the provincial government's banks, and between the public banks and the private banks, was hierarchical.[52] Because of their administrative power, the central government's banks enjoyed many more privileges than the provincial banks and the public banks more than the private banks.[53]

Bank Deposits and Loan Structures

An examination of the deposit and loan structures of the public banks elucidates the functions of the banks and the composition of their borrowers. Tables 6.2A and B show that the Central Trust of China and the Bank of Communications were the main recipients of deposits from publicly owned firms. Most government deposits and U.S.-aid Counterpart Funds were channeled into the Central Bank and the Bank of Taiwan. The holdings of the Land Bank of Taiwan and the Co-operative Bank consisted almost entirely of sums from rural depositors. It is noteworthy that almost all the deposits of the three commercial banks were from individuals and private firms. This confirms the closer relations between the commercial banks and the private sector.

Tables 6.3A and B provide information on loans categorized by sector and the source bank. It is clear that manufacturing, with 38.8 percent of all loans, was the largest sector to receive bank loans, far outstripping the second-ranked commerce. With the exception of the Co-operative Bank and the Land Bank, the manufacturing sector was the largest borrower from all banks. The three central government banks, the Bank of China, the Central Trust of China, and the Bank of Communications, lent most of their money to the manufacturing sector, as did the four provincial government banks, the BOT, the First Bank, Hua-nan, and Chang-hua.

Tables 6.4 and 6.5 clarify the distribution of loans between the private and the public sectors. As shown by Table 6.4, of the total of NT$21,180 million in loans at the end of 1964, NT$10,893 million went to the private sector—almost twice the amount that went to the public sector. Table 6.5 shows changes in the distribution of loans from 1952 to 1966. The proportion of loans to the private sector and others began to exceed those to the public sector in 1958. It then grew by a wide margin, reaching over three times that to the public sector in 1965 and 1966. This trend accelerated in the late 1960s.

Relations Between the Banks and Large Enterprises

In the 1950s, private enterprises were small in size. Beginning in the 1960s, however, a few privileged enterprises began to grow rapidly. These enterprises established a close relationship with the banks and became the major recipients of loans. Despite the limited information on this issue, a Central Bank report entitled "Analysis of Key Loans of All Banks Until the End of June 1973" reveals that by the end of June 1973 all bank loans totaled NT$141.3 billion. The 1,019 key-loan borrowers (loans over NT$10 million) accounted for NT$70.4 billion, or about 50 percent of all bank loans. Table 6.6 clearly shows that the proportion of key loans steadily remained above 50 percent from 1965 to June 1973. In other words, half of all bank loans went to several hundred large borrowers (the figure first exceeded 1,000 in June 1973). The obvious question is Who were these borrowers?

The distribution of key loans among the government departments, the public sector, and the private sector as of the end of June 1973 is presented in Table 6.7. About 70 percent of the key loans went to the private sector. Table 6.8 shows the sectoral distribution of the key loans within the private sector. Table 6.8 should be examined together with Table 6.9, which provides a breakdown of manufactured exports by sector. The top five export industries in 1971 were clothing and footwear, electrical machinery, miscellaneous manufactures, textiles, and wood products. This sequence remained unchanged in 1976. In fact, these five sectors accounted for roughly three-quarters of exports during most of the 1970s. But, as Table 6.8 shows, in 1973 the top five recipients of key loans were textiles, food processing, chemicals, other industries, and trade. Of these five sectors, since it is hard to differentiate domestic and external trade in the trade sector, we cannot discover

Table 6.2A
Deposit Structure of Deposit Sources by Bank, December 1964

Bank	Deposits (NT$ million)	As percentage of total					
		Total	Public sector	Private sector	Personal	Gov't. agencies	Counterpart Fund
Central Bank	$6,108	100.0%	-	-	15.2%	18.5%	66.3%
Bank of China	90	100.0	24.5%	42.4%	27.5	5.6	-
Bank of Communications	1,184	100.0	71.6	4.9	23.3	0.2	-
Central Trust of China	694	100.0	71.4	3.7	19.7	5.2	-
Bank of Taiwan	8,683	100.0	9.6	3.1	43.1	26.2	18.0
Land Bank	2,625	100.0	-	14.1	82.8	3.1	-
Co-operative Bank	3,440	100.0	0.1	5.1	93.2	1.6	-
First Bank	2,726	100.0	0.2	34.9	63.7	1.2	-
Hua-nan Bank	2,690	100.0	0.7	45.7	52.9	0.7	-
Chang-hua Bank	2,826	100.0	0.5	32.0	66.8	0.7	-
Commercial Bank of Overseas Chinese	61	100.0	-	58.8	41.2	-	-
TOTAL	30,727	100.0	6.4	13.1	50.3	11.9	18.3

SOURCE: Liu Jinqing, *Taiwan zhanbou jingji fenxi*, p. 291.
NOTE: The numbers shown in the first column are those given in the source; they total 31,127. The difference is unlikely to be statistically significant.

Table 6.2B
Deposit Structure of Banks by Deposit Source, December 1964

Bank	Total	Public sector	Private sector	Personal	Gov't. agencies	Counterpart Funds
Central Bank	19.9%	–	–	6.0%	31.0%	72.1%
Bank of China	0.3	1.1%	1.0%	0.1	0.2	–
Bank of Communications	3.7	40.8	1.4	1.7	0.1	–
Central Trust	1.3	14.1	0.3	0.5	0.6	–
Bank of Taiwan	28.3	41.9	6.6	24.2	62.5	27.9
Land Bank	8.5	–	9.2	14.1	2.2	–
Co-operative Bank	11.2	0.1	4.4	20.7	1.5	–
First Bank	8.9	0.3	23.7	11.2	0.9	–
Hua-nan Bank	8.4	1.0	29.4	8.9	0.5	–
Chang-hua Bank	9.2	0.7	22.5	12.3	0.5	–
Commercial Bank of Overseas Chinese	0.3	–	1.5	0.3	–	–
TOTAL	100.0	100.0	100.0	100.0	100.0	100.0
Deposits (NT$ million)	30,727.0	1,991.0	4,024.0	15,456.0	3,642.0	5,614.0

SOURCE: Liu Jinqing, *Taiwan zhanhou jingji fenxi*, p. 291.

Table 6.3A
Loan Structure of Banks by Sector, Yearend 1964

Bank	Amount of loans (NT$ million)	Percentage of bank loans by sector							
		Total	Agriculture & fisheries	Mining	Manufacturing	Transportation	Commerce	Other finance	Other
Central Bank	$180	100.0%	–	–	–	–	–	–	100.0%
Bank of China	778	100.0	–	–	58.2%	12.9%	3.1%	–	25.8
Bank of Communications	1,061	100.0	–	4.3%	80.3	12.0	–	–	3.4
Central Trust	534	100.0	–	–	89.0	10.7	–	–	0.3
Bank of Taiwan	6,871	100.0	1.9%	1.6	46.4	20.2	13.9	–	16.0
Land Bank	2,609	100.0	49.3	2.2	17.4	0.8	5.6	–	24.7
Co-operative Bank	3,594	100.0	20.6	0.9	15.3	1.0	37.8	13.8%	10.6
First Bank	1,742	100.0	8.6	2.6	40.9	2.5	33.0	–	12.4
Hua-nan Bank	1,832	100.0	2.5	3.7	41.3	6.8	30.9	–	14.8
Chang-hua Bank	1,843	100.0	5.3	4.1	36.2	2.7	40.3	–	11.4
Commercial Bank of Overseas Chinese	136	100.0	0.3	–	60.5	–	27.6	–	11.6
TOTAL	21,180	100.0	11.6	2.0	38.8	9.2	20.8	2.3	15.3

SOURCE: Liu Jinqing, *Taiwan zhanhou jingji fenxi*, p. 292.

Table 6.3B
Loan Structure of Banks by Bank, Yearend 1964

Bank	Total	Agriculture & fisheries	Mining	Manufacturing	Transportation	Commerce	Other finance	Others
Central Bank	0.9%	–	–	–	–	–	–	5.5%
Bank of China	3.7	–	–	5.5%	5.2%	0.6%	–	6.2
Bank of Communications	5.0	–	10.6%	10.4	6.5	–	–	1.1
Central Trust	2.5	–	–	5.8	2.9	–	–	–
Bank of Taiwan	32.4	5.3%	25.8	38.9	71.2	21.6	–	33.7
Land Bank	12.3	52.4	12.8	5.6	1.1	3.3	–	19.8
Co-operative Bank	17.0	30.2	7.5	6.7	1.9	30.8	100.0%	11.7
First Bank	8.2	6.1	10.5	8.7	2.2	13.1	–	6.6
Hua-nan Bank	8.7	1.9	15.3	9.2	6.5	12.8	–	8.4
Chang-hua Bank	8.7	4.0	17.5	8.2	2.5	16.9	–	6.5
Commercial Bank of Overseas Chinese	0.6	0.1	–	1.0	–	0.9	–	0.5
TOTAL	100.0	100.0	100.0	100.0	100.0	100.0	100.0	100.0
Deposits (NT$ million)	21,180	2,455	432	8,191	1,952	4,406	494	3,250

SOURCE: Liu Jinqing, *Taiwan zhanhou jingji fenxi*, p. 292.

Table 6.4
Bank Loans to the Public and Private Sectors, Yearend 1964
(NT$ million)

	Total		Public sector		Private sector		Personal		Gov't. agencies	
	Amount	%	Amount	%	Amount	%	Amount	%	Amount	%
Central Bank	$180	0.9%	–	–	–	–	–	–	180	34.2%
Bank of Taiwan	6,871	32.4	$3,673	64.5%	$2,657	24.4%	$341	8.4%	200	38.0
Other banks	14,129	66.7	2,019	35.5	8,236	75.6	3,728	91.6	146	27.8
TOTAL	21,180	100.0	5,692	100.0	10,893	100.0	4,069	100.0	526	100.0

SOURCE: Liu Jinqing, *Taiwan zhanhou jingji fenxi*, p. 296.

Table 6.5
Distribution of Loans and Discounts to All Banks, 1952–66
(NT$ million)

Year	Total	Gov't. agencies		Public sector		Private sector and others	
		Amount	%	Amount	%	Amount	%
1952	1,525	35	2.30%	1,490	97.70%	–	
1953	1,999	26	1.30	1,358	67.93	615	30.77%
1954	2,656	60	2.26	1,603	60.35	993	37.39
1955	3,739	83	2.22	1,983	53.04	1,673	44.74
1956	4,452	93	2.09	2,472	55.52	1,887	42.39
1957	5,607	149	2.66	2,816	50.22	2,642	47.12
1958	6,761	128	1.89	3,091	45.72	3,542	52.39
1959	8,103	102	1.26	3,183	39.28	4,818	59.46
1960	9,369	145	1.55	3,662	39.07	5,562	59.34
1961	12,790	203	1.59	4,904	38.34	7,683	60.07
1962	16,275	228	1.40	6,463	39.71	9,584	58.89
1963	17,408	278	1.60	5,298	30.43	11,832	67.97
1964	21,179	525	2.48	5,692	26.88	14,962	70.64
1965	26,091	994	3.81	5,922	22.70	19,175	73.49
1966	30,427	1,683	5.53	6,246	20.53	22,498	73.94

NOTE: All eleven banks listed in Tables 6.3A–B, as well as the Shanghai Commercial and Savings Bank, are covered in this table.

SOURCE: Derived from Lin Lin, "Banking Development of Taiwan," p. 417.

Table 6.6
Percentage of Key Loans Among All Loans, 1965–73

Year	Amount of key loans (NT$ million)	Number of borrowers	Amount of all loans (NT$ million)	Percentage of key loans among all loans
1965	$13,425	291	$25,935	51.9%
1966	17,284	388	30,605	56.5
1967	21,349	528	37,140	57.5
1968	25,788	648	50,466	51.0
1969	33,392	798	66,717	50.1
1970	38,861	640	75,538	51.4
1971	47,041	711	93,915	50.1
1972	59,152	841	111,565	53.0
1973 (to March)	61,413	918	121,009	50.7
1973 (to June)	70,423	1,019	141,262	50.0

NOTE: From the end of 1970 the standard amount of key loans increased from NT$5 million to NT$10 million. Minor discrepancies between the amounts and the percentages shown are due to rounding.
SOURCE: Zhongyang yinhang, "Ge yinhang zhongdian fangkuan fenxi baogao," p. 6.

Table 6.7
Distribution of Key Loans, End of June 1973

	Number of borrowers	Percentage	Amount of key loans (NT$ million)	Percentage
Gov't. departments	28	2.75%	$6,603	9.38%
Public sector	24	2.36	14,677	20.84
Private sector	967	94.90	49,142	69.78
TOTAL	1,019	100.00	70,422	100.00

SOURCE: Derived from Zhongyang yinhang, "Ge yinhang zhongdian fangkuan fenxi baogao," p. 8.
NOTE: Minor discrepancies between the amounts and the percentages shown are due to rounding.

Table 6.8
Sectoral Distribution of Key Loans Within the
Private Sector, End of June 1973

Sector	Amount (NT$ million)	Percentage
Textiles	$14,754	30.0%
Food processing	6,949	14.1
Chemicals	3,763	7.6
Other industries	3,485	7.1
Trade	2,848	5.8
Machinery	2,695	5.5
Electrical engineering	2,359	4.8
Steel	2,336	4.8
Shipping	2,291	4.7
Culture and tourism	1,934	3.9
Timber	1,515	3.1
Papermaking	1,208	2.5
Social associations	870	1.7
Construction	794	1.6
Cement	724	1.5
Mining	229	0.5
Fishery	225	0.5
Personal	163	0.3
TOTAL	49,142	100.0

SOURCE: Derived from Zhongyang yinhang, "Ge yinhang zhongdian fangkuan fenxi bao-gao," pp. 30–32.

the link between trade and exports. Food products amounted to only 0.7 percent of total exports in 1971, chemicals to only 2.3 percent. It is unclear what was included under "other industries." The only industry that contributed significantly to exports was textiles, which constituted around 14 percent of exports in the early and mid-1970s. In contrast, this sector received some 30 percent of the key loans in 1973. If one includes clothing as part of the textile industry, the percentage of textiles among all exports would be over 20 percent. It thus appears that the key loans contributed substantially to textile exports. This issue requires further explanation.

Although textiles were one of the major export industries in the

1960s and 1970s, not all textile manufacturers were major exporters. Many LEs originated in textile companies in the 1950s under the government policy of fostering and protecting industries. But they served mainly the domestic market. The one exception was the Yuandong (Far East) Company. In 1960, Yuandong became the first textile firm in Taiwan to export garments,[54] and it was the only large textile-based enterprise that continued to export thereafter. In other words, most of the LE recipients of the 30 percent of key loans provided to the textile industry did not export their products. This is confirmed in other statistics. Taiwan's 25 business groups produced over 50 percent (by total sales) of all woven cloth, and these groups sold most of this output to small and medium-sized non-business-group firms, which produced 88 percent of total sales of all finished garments and other apparel made in Taiwan, about 75 percent of which was exported.[55] Although the time period to which these statistics refer was not given, they still reflect the general situation. We can conclude from these numbers that the 30 percent of key loans going to large textile firms made little direct contribution to textile exports. Instead, they reinforced the domestic-oriented production of the LEs in the textile industry. They also strengthened the division of labor between the suppliers of intermediate inputs (the LEs) and the consumers of these products (the SMEs).

Who were the main borrowers in the private sector? At a time when a number of private enterprises were being transformed from small firms into large firms and business groups, their relations with the banks are a window onto state-LE relations. Among the key loans going to the private sector, NT$22,986 million, or about 46 percent of all loans, went to 115 borrowers whose borrowings exceeded NT$100 million each.[56] Among these 115 borrowers, there were seventeen whose borrowings exceeded NT$300 million apiece; the loans to them totaled NT$10,579 million, or 46.02 percent of all borrowings. Twelve firms borrowed between NT$200 million and NT$300 million each, for a total of NT$2,918 million or 12.70 percent of all key loans. Sixty-nine borrowed between NT$10 million and $200 million, for a total of NT$9,489 million or 41.28 percent of the total. The top 29 enterprises, whose borrowings exceeded NT$200 million each, borrowed 58.72 percent of all key loans to the private sector. This means that 27.47 percent of all loans by Taiwan banks to the private sector by the end of June 1973 went to 29 enterprises. Thus, there was a high concentration of bank loans to a few large private firms. Among the 30 top borrowers from the state-owned banks in 1971, thirteen were from the top twenty business groups listed in Table 6.10.

The names of the 29 enterprises and the persons in charge are listed in Table 6.10. According to an analysis by the Monetary Department of the MOF, the first seventeen enterprises listed in Table 6.10 were related business groups. Each had three to five business units.[57] Table 6.10 tells us two things. The first is that a few enterprises had grown substantially, from single firms into business groups. The second is that the state's close relations with certain companies in the 1950s and 1960s continued as they grew into business groups. This kind of relationship appeared to be the pillar of state–private sector relations.

More important, Table 6.10 shows the role of state-owned banks in maintaining the unique industrial structure. As we have seen, the emergence of LEs during the era of import-substitution industrialization was a result of the state fostering and protecting policy, which provided credits through state-owned banks and a variety of protection measures. Except for a few cases, such as Formosa Plastics and Yuandong, and shipping companies, which might provide services for export, most of the other 29 business groups listed in Table 6.10 served primarily the domestic market. It is clear that the loan policy of the state-owned banks still favored the LEs, which continued to serve mainly the domestic market. Two conclusions can be drawn from this situation. First, although Taiwan's state-owned banks were criticized for their reluctance to provide credit to the SMEs, their role in the development of LEs was positive—they created rents through financial restraint to induce private agents to "increase the supply of goods and services that might be underprovided in a pure market."[58] The second conclusion is derived from the first. "Financial restraint" maintained and strength-

Table 6.9

Composition of Manufactured Exports, Selected Years 1956–81
(as percentage of total manufacture exports)

Sector	1956	1961	1966	1971	1976	1981
Food, beverages, and tobacco	48.7%	13.5%	11.1%	0.7%	0.2%	0.2
Food	48.5	11.0	10.1	0.5	0.1	0.2
Beverages	0.2	0.2	0.1	0.0	0.0	0.0
Tobacco	0.0	2.3	0.9	0.2	0.1	0.0
Nondurable consumer goods	14.2	36.1	37.0	58.0	58.0	50.5
Textiles	9.4	28.1	19.9	14.6	14.0	10.1
Clothing and footwear	3.9	5.8	9.6	27.0	25.7	21.4
Furniture	0.0	0.0	0.1	0.5	1.3	2.0
Printing and publishing	0.0	0.0	0.2	0.1	0.1	0.1
Miscellaneous manufactures	0.9	2.2	7.2	15.8	16.9	16.9
Intermediate goods industries	26.3	36.3	29.6	14.1	12.3	13.1
Wood products	1.1	8.4	12.5	7.9	5.3	3.9
Paper and paper products	0.5	3.4	2.1	0.4	0.6	0.6
Leather and leather products	0.0	0.1	0.1	0.7	0.2	0.5
Rubber products	0.0	0.5	0.6	0.5	0.8	0.9
Chemicals	20.6	12.7	6.0	2.3	2.4	2.7
Petroleum and coal products	4.1	5.5	1.1	0.5	1.6	2.2
Nonmetallic mineral products	0.0	5.7	7.2	1.8	1.4	2.3

Metals and machinery	10.8	14.1	22.3	27.2	29.5	36.2
Metal products	2.8	1.3	3.0	2.5	3.4	5.0
Basic metals	7.7	10.0	6.6	3.3	1.7	2.4
Non-electrical machinery	0.3	0.9	4.0	4.1	4.7	5.1
Electrical machinery	0.0	1.7	8.1	15.9	17.0	19.6
Transport equipment	0.0	0.2	0.6	1.4	2.7	4.1
TOTAL	100.0	100.0	100.0	100.0	100.0	100.0

SOURCE: Chou, *Industrial Organization in a Dichotomous Economy*, p. 20.

Table 6.10
Top 29 Borrowers from State-Owned Banks, End of June 1973

Enterprise	Person in charge	Amount of loan(s) (NT$ million)
Yuandong Related	Xu Youxiang	$1,528
Yulong Related	Yan Qingling	1,433
Formosa Related	Wang Yongqing	1,198
Xinguang Related	Wu Huoshi	657
Zhongxing Textile	Bao Wenshi	644
Zhonghua Trade	Zhang Rentao	621
Daming Fibre	Xiao Bohuang	619
Weiquan Related	Huang Liehuo	501
Tainan President	Wu Xiuqi	479
Hexinxing Related	Cai Kekuan	472
Liuhe Textile	Zong Lutang	411
United Nylon Related	Lai Qingtian	394
Datong Related	Lin Tingsheng	345
Longchang Related	Wang Zhuqing	327
Fuxing Shipping	Yang Guanbei	325
Yili Shipping	Xu Wenhua	315
Taiwan Pineapple	Xie Chengyuan	310
Lianhua Industry	Miao Yuxiu	297
Liangyou Industry	Zhang Mingqian	276
Xinhua Related	Tao Zihou	274
Taiwan Cement	Gu Zhenfu	263
Donghe Textile	Zheng Wang	262
Qiafa Industry	Hong Bu	256
Sandong Related	Wang Changyu	245
Guochan Automobile	Zhang Tiangen	229
Huayang Related	Cai Wenhua	212
Dongyu Textile	Lin Qiaodong	204
Yishou Shipping	Dong Hancha	200
Kaili Plastics	Fan Heyan	200

SOURCE: Zhongyang Yinhang, "Ge yinhang zhongdian fangkuan fenxi baogao."

ened the LEs' domestic market–oriented activities. These rents encouraged the LEs to continue their inward, intermediate activities. In this fashion, the provision of credit from the state-owned banks helped maintain the dualistic and tripartite industrial organization. This evidence substantiates a main argument of this book—the

Table 6.11
Amount of Export Loans from All Banks by Industry,
End of September 1973

Industry	Amount (NT$ million)	Percentage
Textiles	$3,232	37.69%
Food	1,590	18.54
Plastics	584	6.81
Plywood	526	6.13
Electronics	399	4.65
Chemicals	258	3.00
Cement	137	1.60
Steel	89	1.04
Wool spinning	80	0.93
Rubber	79	0.92
Frozen seafood	61	0.71
Cable	49	0.57
Glass	37	0.43
Gourmet powder	2	0.02
Feather processing	0	0.00
Fertilizer	0	0.00
Aluminum	0	0.00
Machinery	0	0.00
Others	1,453	16.94
TOTAL	8,576	100.00

NOTE: Because of rounding, percentages do not total 100.00.
SOURCE: Derived from Li Guoding Archives: "Quanti yinhang waixiao daikuang yu'e."

state maintained and safeguarded the marketplace through the provision of credit.

But did the state do anything deliberately to promote exports? The answer is clearly yes. The state resolved the problem of limited export-related capital by creating new funds out of the normal loans of banks. In order to boost exports, various special loan funds were established during this period, and the General Rules on Loans for External Selling were promulgated in 1962. Low-interest loans were available for material purchases and working funds to make products for the international market. The Central Bank established its Discount Measures for Loans for External Selling in 1970, which provided funds to banks for loans to promote exports. The interest rate for these loans was as low as 6.5 percent. Other special loans, such as the Loans for Working Funds for Export-Oriented Enterprises, the Small Loans for Small and Medium Enterprises, and the Special Export Working Loans for Small and Medium Enterprises, were also established. Some banks also provided special loans for exports. For example, in accordance with the Procedural Measures for Export Loans issued jointly by the MOF, the MOEA, and the Central Bank, the Bank of China established a section for export finance in 1971, with the goal of providing long- and medium-term loans for exports of machinery, equipment, and other important industrial products. A total of NT$200 million was specifically set aside for this purpose. This was the first time that long- and medium-term loans had been designated for exports in Taiwan. From 1971 to 1977, a total of 112 such loans were made.[59] However, it is unclear if, and what percentage of, the export-related funds went to SMEs.

As shown in Table 6.11, the top seven industries that received export loans were textiles, food, plastics, plywood, electronics, chemicals, and cement. The top seven exports were textiles, metals, food, chemicals, lumber, basic metal industries, and non-metallic mineral products.

Relations Between the Banks and the SMEs

As a whole, the SMEs were not favored by the government, and they had little access to the publicly owned banks. This discrimination arose in part because the SMEs had unsound accounting systems, failed to provide sufficient collateral, had no guarantors, and lacked knowledge about capital planning.[60] Taiwan's banks were known for their conservatism and overemphasis on collateral. They trusted the LEs because of their long-term relationships. Loans to the SMEs meant the trouble of extra credit investigations. Hence, it is not surprising that the banks discouraged approaches from the SMEs. As shown in Chapter 8, the SMEs had to resolve their capital problems through the unorganized financial market and a trust structure within family and kinship networks that socialized funds.[61]

There were two major sources of financing for the SMEs. One was "private"; the other was a high-fund-turnover delayed payments system.[62] There are no data on the number of sources of funds for the SMEs during this period. But according to a survey made in the 1990s, the percentage of SME funds borrowed from banks (the so-called organized financial system) was 32.71 percent.[63] The percentage between 1961 and 1975 must have been lower since banks placed more restrictions on lending to the SMEs at that time. As discussed in the preceding chapter, given the importance of the unorganized financial market to the SMEs, they benefited from the government's successful efforts to lower interest rates in this market, although the rates were still rather high.

The State and the Dual Financial System

There is a close link between Taiwan's industrial structure and its dual financial system. As in many developing countries, Taiwan has an organized financial system, or formal financial system, and an unorganized financial system, or underground financial market. The main reason for the existence of this system is "financial repression."[64] In the case of Taiwan, the employees of the publicly owned banks were civil servants, who were restricted by rules and unwilling to take risks. This was one of the major reasons for the banks' extremely conservative approach to collateral. The strict government controls and the conservatism of the banks forced those seeking capital to turn to the unorganized financial market, where access was much easier. And because interest rates in the unorganized financial market were higher than those in the formal market, people who had cash preferred to deposit their money there. Therefore, the creditors of the unorganized financial market included not only individuals and private firms but also public firms and even government officials, as we saw in the Tangrong case.

As shown in the preceding and present chapters, the formal financial system served mainly the public sector and the LEs. Various studies confirm that the main source of financing for the SMEs was the unorganized financial market.[65] But what was the relationship between the dual financial structure and the dichotomous

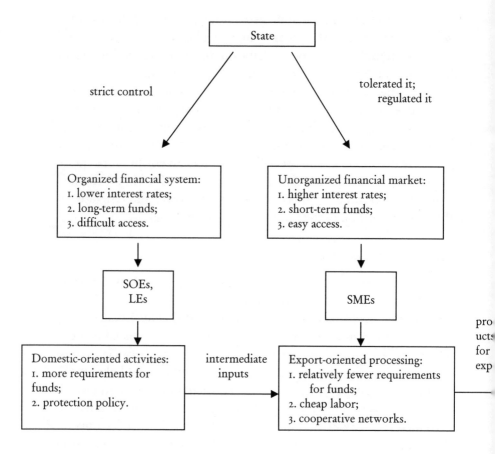

Fig. 6.2   The state, the dual financial structure, and the industrial structure

industrial structure (see Fig. 6.2)? Although most researchers note the existence of the two structures, Zhou Tiancheng is one of the few who has tried to find a link between them. He argues that the division of labor between the two parts of the financial system was such that the organized financial system supported mainly the domestic-oriented industries, and the unorganized financial system the export-oriented industries.[66] In this division of labor, the two financial markets were complementary.[67] If these assumptions can be proved statistically, they would answer a critical question about Taiwan's unique industrial structure—Was Taiwan's unique industrial structure supported by its dual financial structure? From Zhou's assumption, it follows that the financial structure enabled the LEs to engage in domestic market–oriented activities and the SMEs to engage in export-oriented production. Therefore, we must look at the role of the state in the formation and persistence of the dual financial structure.

The preceding analysis has shown that a major reason for the dual financial structure was government control of the formal financial system. What was the role of the state in this structure? We have already noted the primary reasons for government control over the financial system: the bitter lessons of the KMT's failure on the mainland, the desire to curb inflation, and the goal of steering the economy. However, the government's intentional actions resulted in the emergence of the unorganized financial market—which was not the government's intention. Furthermore, the government did two things critical to the persistence of the unorganized market. First, it tolerated it. Yin Zhongrong accepted the necessity for the unorganized financial market as a short-term response to demand.[68] Second, it regulated it. To curb inflation and raise funds for the Third Four-Year Plan, Yin used Tangrong to force the unorganized financial market to lower its interest rates. These efforts resulted in regulation of the unorganized financial market. In fact, the unorganized financial market had always been monitored by the central monetary authorities. Since the early 1950s they had conducted weekly curb market (unorganized financial market) surveys. When the curb market exchange rates shifted or the interest rates rose, or when the curb dealers experienced a string of defaults, the central bank took note. When such trends were corroborated by other indicators, changes in monetary policy were likely to follow.[69]

As we have seen, the state-owned banks directed the bulk of their loans to the domestic market–oriented LEs during the entire period under review here. This in turn reinforced the LEs' domestic market orientation. To improve the provision of credit for export-oriented firms, the state created new sources of funding outside the existing lending arrangements. This policy helped reinforce the industrial division of labor.

The Development of
the Tripartite Industrial Structure

Bifurcation of the LEs and SMEs

The period from 1961 to 1975 was a critical era in the evolution of Taiwan's private sector. First, the LEs and SMEs began to diverge, and a division of labor evolved. During the first decade of KMT rule on the island, the private sector underwent a period of growth. Except for the four privatized public enterprises, some mainlander and native Taiwanese textile enterprises, some newly established cement companies, and a few others in the steel and iron sectors, there were only a small number of large enterprises. These companies were protected by the government through rigid tariffs, import controls, and restrictions on new factories. As shown in Chapters 3 and 4, the privileged and protected firms shared a monopoly over the domestic market with the public sector. They had easy access to government-controlled resources, particularly loans and foreign exchange allocations. The rest of private industry was not under government protection. However, the situation changed substantially from 1961 to 1975 when the private sector diverged into two directions—a few large enterprises continued to grow and became business groups based on their domestic trade, whereas a large number of SMEs emerged and prospered through their activities in producing for the export market. This section examines the two different components of the private sector during this period.

The large enterprises were mainly in textiles, food, cement, papermaking, and plastics. Of the total of 54 major private enterprises listed in Table 6.12, 23 were textile-related, showing the importance of this industry in the 1960s. Food and cement also had a solid base in the 1960s. The leading industries were those fostered and protected by the government in the 1950s. This suggests that government protection was a key reason for the development of certain sectors. This was also true of individual enterprises. Almost all the enterprises targeted by the government in the 1950s are on the list of leading enterprises in the mid-1960s. Good relations with the

Table 6.12
Taiwan's Major Private Enterprises, 1964–66

	Listed		Unlisted	
Rank	Name	Capital (NT$ million)	Name	Capital (NT$ million)
1	Taiwan Cement	500	Xinguang Textile	66
2	China Manmade Fibre	270	Wanyuan Textile	60
3	Weiquan Food	225	Yixin Textile	60
4	Asian Cement	150	Yulong Auto	60
5	Taiwan Papermaking	150	Jiaxin Cement	56
6	Jinjin Gourmet	140	East Asian Textile	50
7	China Ferment	120	China Wool Spinning	50
8	Datong Steel	100	Zhanghua Textile	43
9	Taiwan Ironworks	100	Liuhe Textile	40
10	Formosa Plastics	100	Taiyuan Textile	40
11	Cathay Plastics	100	Xinhua Wool Spinning	40
12	Taiwan Industry	100	New Taiwan Textile	37
13	Dahua Industry	100	Fuhua Wool Spinning	36
14	Cathay Construction	100	Dadong Textile	35
15	Xinzhu Glass	90	Taiwan Qinyi	30
16	Taiwan Agriculture	83	Lin Plywood	30
17	Weixin Food	80	Taiwan Pineapple	27
18	Wanhua Industry	75	Tailing Textile	26
19	China Pharmacy	70	Taiwan Textile	26
20	Nangang Tire	68	Fulong Textile	25
21	Pacific Cable	60	Cathay Insurance	20
22	China Wool	40	Tainan Textile	15
23	Liangyou	40	Zhonghe Textile	15
24	Huayuan Hotel	40	Wangtian Textile	10
25	Shilin Paper	33	Datai Textile	7
26	Taiwan Fluorescent	32	Zhongfang Textile	6
27	Yishou Shipping	25		
28	Taiwan Match	6		

SOURCE: Derived from Tanikaba, *Taiwan de gongyehua*, p. 132.

government were apparently critical to the success of individual enterprises. Some enterprises benefited from relations established in the 1950s and continued to grow in the 1960s.

Table 6.13
Top Twenty Private Enterprise Groups, 1971

Rank	Name	Rank	Name
1	Formosa Plastics Group	11	Taiwan Pineapple Group
2	Lai Qingtian Group	12	Jiaxin Group
3	Yadong Group	13	Cathay Group
4	Xiao Brothers Group	14	Yongfengyu Group
5	Taiyuan Group	15	Dong's Shipping Group
6	Datong Group	16	Lai Senlin Group
7	Lin Rongchun Group	17	Donghe Group
8	Tainan Textile Group	18	Xu Jinde Group
9	Xinguang Group	19	Weiquan Group
10	Huaxia Group	20	He Chaoyu Group

SOURCE: Wang Kejing, *Taiwan minjian chanye sishi nian*, p. 62.

Based on accumulation during the 1950s and 1960s, these few enterprises expanded into enterprise groups. The names of the top twenty enterprise groups in 1971 are listed in Table 6.13. Seven of the top ten groups (Lai Qingtian, Yadong, Xiao Brothers, Taiyuan, Lin Rongchun, Tainan, and Xinguang) were textile-based. As in the mid-1950s, textiles were the most important sector in Taiwan. The most significant change was the fast rise of Formosa Plastics, which jumped from the tenth largest company in 1964–66 to the largest business group in 1971.

An enterprise group or business group refers in Taiwan to a cluster of enterprises based either on common or related ownership or on a business connection.[70] The Chinese term *guanxi qiye*, whose English equivalent is "related enterprises," is also used to refer to a business group. Nomazaki Ichirō defines *guanxi qiye* as a "cluster of enterprises owned and controlled by a group of persons tied by a network of various *guanxi*."[71] During the period under study, most enterprise groups were family enterprises. Except for a few vertically integrated companies engaged in materials, manufacturing, and distribution in the same sector, such as Formosa Plastics, most united enterprises crossed horizontally into various sectors. These enterprise groups played an important role in the economy. Their combined sales accounted for 34 percent of GNP

Table 6.14
Number of Enterprises and Employees
in the Manufacturing Sector, 1961

Size of staff	Number of enterprises	Percent- age	Number of employees	Percent- age
1–9	46,145	89.5%	141,121	31.1%
10–29	3,872	7.5	63,985	14.1
30–99	1,163	2.3	56,482	12.4
100–299	259	0.5	41,476	9.1
300–499	59	0.1	22,247	4.9
500–999	41	0.1	30,111	6.6
≥ 1,000	28	–	98,850	21.8
TOTAL	51,567	100.0	454,272	100.0

SOURCE: Derived from Taiwansheng gongshangye pucha zhixing xiaozu, "Di er ci gong-shangye pucha zongbaogao," pp. 124–27; Tanikaba, *Taiwan de gongyehua*, p. 143.

in 1973.[72] In a report dated October 19, 1973, the MOF listed seventeen related groups, each of which had three to five related business units.[73] This suggests that a few large enterprises were on their way to becoming business groups. Among the top twenty enterprise groups, only Jiaxin Group and Huaxia Group were mainlander-owned; the other eighteen were controlled by native Taiwanese capital. Taiwanese capital absolutely dominated industry.

Although the number of LEs continued to grow, the number of SMEs began to boom. As mentioned above, in the 1950s most Taiwanese businesses were extremely small. As shown in Table 6.14, about 90 percent of these enterprises employed from one to nine employees in 1961. The public sector remained virtually unchanged in the 1960s. Even though it expanded in the 1970s because of the Ten Major Development Projects, the increase in the number of publicly owned enterprises was negligible compared to the increase in the number of all enterprises.

The changes shown in Tables 6.15A and B affected mainly the private sector. Between 1961 and 1966, the number of businesses declined by 46 percent from 51,567 to 27,709, whereas the number of employees increased from 454,272 to 589,660, a jump of 135,388 or 30 percent. This increase indicates that the manufacturing sector

Table 6.15A
Economic Index of the Manufacturing Sector by Enterprise Scale, 1966

Size of staff	Number of enterprises	Number of employees (000)	Capital amount (NT$100 million)	Value of output (NT$100 million)	Total wages (NT$100 million)	Average number of employees per enterprise	Economic index per employee (NT$10,000)		
							Capital amount	Value of output	Wages
1–9	19,982 (72.1%)	75,621 (12.8%)	$40 (4.6%)	$121 (14.2%)	$6.9 (9.3%)	4 (0.3)	$5.3	$16.0	$0.9
10–19	3,726 (13.4)	50,275 (8.5)	23 (2.6)	43 (5.1)	4.6 (6.2)	13 (0.8)	4.6	8.6	0.9
20–49	2,476 (8.9)	74,805 (12.7)	43 (4.9)	75 (8.8)	7.3 (9.9)	30 (1.9)	5.7	10.0	1.0
50–99	754 (2.7)	51,176 (8.7)	39 (4.5)	54 (6.4)	5.7 (7.7)	68 (4.3)	7.6	10.6	1.1
100–499	640 (2.3)	132,764 (22.5)	181 (20.7)	169 (19.9)	14.9 (20.4)	207 (13.2)	13.6	12.7	1.1
≥ 500	131 (0.5)	205,019 (34.8)	548 (62.7)	388 (45.6)	34.7 (46.9)	1,565 (100)	26.7	18.9	1.7
TOTAL	27,709 (100%)	589,660 (100%)	874 (100%)	850 (100%)	74.1 (100%)	21	14.8	14.4	1.3

NOTE: Because of rounding, percentages may not total 100%.

SOURCES: Derived from Tanikaba, *Taiwan de gongyehua*, p. 133; Taiwansheng gongshangye pucha zhixin xiaozu, "Di san ci gongshangye pucha zongbaogao," p.751; Xingzheng-yuan, Tai-min diqu gongshangye pucha weiyuanhui, "Zhonghua minguo qishinian Tai-min diqu gongshangye pucha baogao," pp. 426–27.

Table 6.15B

Economic Index of the Manufacturing Sector by Enterprise Scale, 1976

Size of staff	Number of enterprises	Number of employees (000)	Capital amount (NT$100 million)	Value of output (NT$100 million)	Total wages (NT$100 million)	Average number of employees per enterprise	Economic index per employee (NT$10,000)		
							Capital amount	Value of output	Wages
1–9	47,358 (68.1%)	192,848 (10.1%)	$475 (4.5%)	$544 (6.6%)	$77 (7.9%)	4 (0.3)	$24.6	$28.2	4.0
10–19	8,922 (12.8)	119,527 (6.3)	266 (2.5)	311 (3.8)	48 (4.9)	13 (0.8)	22.3	26.0	4.0
20–49	6,953 (10.0)	213,300 (11.2)	584 (5.5)	667 (8.1)	92 (9.4)	31 (2.3)	27.4	31.3	4.3
50–99	2,988 (4.3)	209,702 (11.0)	691 (6.6)	717 (8.7)	97 (9.9)	70 (5.2)	33.0	34.2	4.6
100–499	2,851 (4.1)	576,084 (30.2)	2,383 (22.6)	2,391 (29.2)	284 (29.1)	202 (15.1)	41.4	41.5	4.9
≥ 500	445 (0.6)	596,120 (31.3)	6,128 (58.2)	3,565 (43.5)	379 (38.8)	1,340 (100)	102.8	59.8	6.4
TOTAL	69,517 (100%)	1,907,581 (100%)	10,527 (100%)	8,195 (100%)	977 (100%)	27	55.2	42.9	5.1

NOTE: Because of rounding, percentages may not total 100%.
SOURCES: See Table 6.15A.

expanded from 1961 to 1966; the rate of increase was even larger from 1966 to 1976. From 1966 to 1976, the number of enterprises jumped sharply from 27,709 to 69,517, a 150 percent increase. There was also an impressive rise in the number of employees, from 589,660 to 1,907,581, or over 220 percent. The average number of employees in each enterprise increased from 21 to 27. Significantly, the proportion of enterprises with fewer than twenty employees decreased from 85.2 percent to 80.9 percent. The proportion of enterprises with over 500 employees underwent practically no change, from 0.5 percent to 0.6 percent. However, the percentage of enterprises with between 20 and 499 employees increased from 13.9 percent to 18.4 percent. This change reflected the change in the value of output. The percentage of the total value of output accounted for by enterprises with under twenty employees decreased from 19.3 percent to 10.4 percent, and by those with over 500 employees from 45.6 percent to 43.5 percent. That for firms with 20–499 employees increased from 35.1 percent to 46 percent. The margin of increase was the largest for those enterprises with between 100 and 499 employees. In terms of value of output, it is clear that these enterprises were the backbone of the private sector. These statistics suggest that the SMEs expanded substantially after the second half of the 1960s.

Formation of a Division of Labor Between the LEs and the SMEs

As the private sector began to bifurcate in size, a division of industrial labor also started to form. Although there are few statistics on the division of industrial labor, we can derive a general picture
from the available information. Gary Hamilton, William Zeile, and Wan-Jin Kim's comparative studies of the correlation between the sales shares and sectoral characteristics of business groups in Japan, South Korea, and Taiwan provide some relevant information (see Table 6.16).[74] First, compared to their Japanese and South Korean counterparts, whose concentration is only loosely associated with production for intermediate use, Taiwan business groups dominate

Table 6.16
Correlation Between Sales Shares and Sectoral Characteristics
of Business Groups in Japan, Korea, and Taiwan

Sectoral characteristics	Japan	Korea	Taiwan
Intermediate demand ratio[a]	0.152	0.197	0.419 (0.496)
Labor share of value added[b]	−0.303	−0.487	−0.065 (−0.406)
Export share[c]	0.234	−0.005	−0.273 (−0.354)

NOTE: Data are based on 20 manufacturing sectors in Korea and Taiwan and 13 in Japan. For Japan, the figures refer to 16 major groups in FY 1982; for Korea, the top 50 *chaebol* in 1983; and for Taiwan, the 96 largest groups in 1983.

[a]Ratio of total intermediate demand to total (intermediate plus final) demand for the output of the sector.

[b]Total payments to labor input divided by total value added (net of indirect taxes) for the sector.

[c]Ratio of exports to total domestic products for the sector.

SOURCE: Hamilton et al., "The Network Structures of East Asian Economies," p. 117.

the intermediate goods sector, which has forward linkages with other sectors of the economy. Second, business groups in Taiwan are more concentrated in import-substitution sectors. According to data on the export propensity of ten business groups in 1980, their combined turnover was 16 percent of GNP, whereas their percentage of total exports was 11 percent. But two of these ten business groups (Formosa and Yuandong) accounted for 60 percent of their exports, and the other groups made only minor contributions to exports. Hence, these business groups were significantly inward-oriented. Hamilton's data reveal similar trends.[75] Of the top ten business groups in 1983, which together accounted for nearly 50 percent of total sales and assets of the top 96 groups, only two (Yu-long Motors and Datong Electric) manufactured final products. Datong produced for both the export and the domestic market, and Yulong produced automobiles exclusively for local use. Of the ten largest business groups, only one produced substantially for export; the other groups supplied services and intermediate goods for the domestic market.[76]

A more detailed discussion of the second aspect of the division of industrial labor between the LEs and the SMEs in Taiwan is presented in Chapter 8. However, a brief description here will aid in

understanding the problem. The SMEs were downstream producers that manufactured final goods for export. Over 50 percent of
the output of the SMEs in 1972, 1973, and 1975 was for export. Although the policy emphasis shifted to exports in the late 1950s and
the early 1960s, actual exports did not increase substantially until
the second half of the 1960s. The value of exports doubled from
NT$5,966 million in 1960 to NT$17,987 million in 1965. But between 1965 and 1976 exports increased sixteenfold, from NT$17,987
to NT$309,913.[77] Since the LEs were basically entrenched in domes-
tic activities, the increase in exports can be linked to the expansion
of the SMEs. In other words, the SMEs were the major contributors to the rapid expansion of exports.

The SMEs played a crucial role in Taiwan's export-led industrialization. They formed the overwhelming majority of enterprises in
terms of proportion of products among total exports, in the number
of workers employed, and in their driving role in backward integration. However, the statist account of Taiwan's development either
ignores or downplays the success of the SMEs. Nevertheless, this
success needs to be explained. Given the importance of the subject, I
defer a detailed discussion of the issue until Chapter 8.

With respect to the issue of the industrial division of labor, we
must also take into account the role of another player—the SOEs.
The public sector was responsible for most of Taiwan's exports in
the early 1950s. For example, it accounted for 77.7 percent of total
exports in 1952.[78] But the bulk of these exports were agricultural
products, mainly rice and sugar. However, the percentage of exports produced by the public decreased sharply thereafter, falling
to 6.7 percent in 1972 and to 3.2 percent in 1981. If rice, sugar, and
other agricultural products are excluded, the percentage of public
sector exports is much lower (only 2.5 percent in 1981).[79] The percentage of industrial goods among the SOEs' exports was negligible,
and the upstream SOEs were exclusively domestic producers.

Conclusion

The chapter shows that state actions during the 1960s and 1970s
maintained and reinforced the industrial structure. The provision
of industrial finance by state-owned banks played a vital role in en-

couraging the LEs to become entrenched in the domestic market. This in turn forced the SMEs into the export market. The unorganized financial market, which came under the regulation of the economic planning authorities in the early 1960s, constituted a primary source of credit for the SMEs, and the state did little to lend them direct assistance. Thus, the emergence of the SMEs in the export market was an unanticipated consequence of interactions between the state and the private sector.

The chapter also shows that many economic measures adopted by the state were based on political rather than economic concerns. This suggests that non-economic considerations have an impact on economic performance. Other goals and strategies also affect the marketplace and the choices available to private actors.

CHAPTER 7

Industrial Upgrading, 1976–1985: A New Commitment?

From 1976 to 1985, Taiwan's economy underwent a transformation from being labor-intensive to technology-intensive. The state encouraged this transformation by pursuing two, contradictory strategies: it strengthened its ties with large businesses by providing them more rents, and it deliberately promoted small businesses in the high-tech industries. The first supported the persistence of the dual market structure for traditional industries, whereas the second encouraged an integrated market for high-tech industries. What were the political and economic bases for these strategies?

This chapter argues that the strengthening of state relations with the LEs was driven mainly by political concerns, and the encouragement of SMEs in high-tech industries was economically motivated. This chapter begins by exploring the major challenges facing the state and ways the state dealt with them. It then analyzes the changes in the economic bureaucracy and in relations between the state and the private sector. Next, it discusses the role of the state in the development of the information industry and, finally, the role of SOEs in the industrial structure.

Major Challenges and the State's Response

Between 1976 and 1985, the state on Taiwan fought both political and economic battles. Politically, it was under severe pressure because of a legitimacy crisis. After its expulsion from the United

Nations in 1971 and a subsequent series of diplomatic setbacks, Taiwan became internationally isolated. This isolation threatened the authority of the KMT regime, which had claimed to be "the sole legal government of China." The establishment of relations between the United States and mainland China in 1979 exacerbated this crisis. The diplomatic crisis prompted calls for political reform, especially from the upper middle classes. Over two decades of economic development had created a sizable middle class. The agitation for reform grew as Taiwan's international position continued to deteriorate, and the political stability that the state had enjoyed in the 1950s and 1960s seemed to have dissipated.

On the economic front, the second oil crisis tested Taiwan's economy by substantially weakening its international competitiveness. Hardest hit was the petrochemical industry, which suffered fierce competition from cheaper U.S. products. As a result, inventories increased sharply, and most factories had to reduce production. Some even suspended operations. This situation exposed the weakness of the state's strategy, adopted in 1973, to promote heavy and chemical industries. Another economic factor was Taiwan's loss of its comparative advantage in labor costs as mainland China and low-wage countries in Southeast Asia became labor-intensive exporters and Taiwan's wage levels continued to rise. The deteriorating political and economic situations of the late 1970s also led to a stagnation in domestic investment.

What were the state's political strategies for dealing with the problems? Was the state able to continue practicing its strategy of "dominant engagement," which the KMT had used to distance itself from society when it faced a legitimacy crisis and was under increasing pressure to expand political participation? If not, how did it modify its political strategies to deal with liberalization? Did it begin to make a transition toward democratization? What were the consequences of these changes for the state's economic policy? The answers to these questions will help us understand the political transformation of Taiwan during this period.

The increasing international competition and the second oil crisis brought pressures for an upgrading of industry. A major task facing the government as well as the private sector was how to promote such an upgrade. The requirements for this task differed from those of previous development plans because of changes in the state and in state-society relations. Vested interests both within the state and within the private sector had been formed over the preceding two decades because of the government's provision of rents and because of businesses' rent-seeking activities. The necessary adjustments in the existing industrial structure surely would encounter resistance, and the capacity of the state to coordinate contending interests and formulate and implement policies for restructuring would be tested. Was the state able to work out a scenario for restructuring? If so, what were its capabilities? To answer these questions, we need to understand the role of the top leaders in economic policy making because of Chiang Ching-kuo's domination of both economic policy and the various economic bureaucracies. To do so, we must examine changes in the economic organs. Since the role of the private sector in policy formulation and implementation was becoming increasingly important, we must also look at industry's responses to the industrial restructuring proposals and to the government's scheme for an industrial upgrade, and how it exerted an influence on policy making. However, to answer these questions, we must first examine the preoccupations of the state during this period.

Liberalization: Expanding Participation and Taiwanization

During this period, Taiwan was liberalizing. To use Adam Przeworski's definition, liberalization is "an opening that results in the broadening of the social base of the regime without changing its structure."[1] In Taiwan, liberalization was a response from above both to the demand for political participation from society and to the legitimacy crisis caused by the external diplomatic shocks. The opposition movement that emerged after the diplomatic crisis used two issues to win support: the social problems stemming from the government's exploitative agricultural policy and lack of environmental planning; and the subethnic cleavages, or "the native Taiwanese pathos," as it was called, which reflected a strong sentiment that the "locals" on the island had been suppressed by the mainlanders. This challenge forced the state to take measures to pre-empt the opposition and consolidate its own power base so as to forestall an alliance between the opposition and the capitalists.

Liberalization was also a response to the diplomatic crisis and the KMT's loss of legitimacy. Given Taiwan's unique geopolitical position, U.S. diplomatic recognition had been a major source of legitimacy for the KMT regime, and the American shift to Beijing in 1979 shocked the KMT ruling class.[2] The regime now had to seek a new legitimacy from within society—to win support from the society by strengthening ties with it. The previous sources of legitimacy had been external—U.S. military support and diplomatic recognition; this shift can be characterized as an internalization of legitimacy.[3]

Two other points highlight the complexity and importance of Taiwan's political transformation. First, the demand for political participation coincided with a political succession in the KMT—the transfer of power from Chiang Kai-shek to Chiang Ching-kuo. Thus, the regime's drive for internal legitimization coincided with the new leader's search for personal legitimization. As we will see below, this timing had an impact on liberalization.

Second, the native Taiwanese played a role in the liberalization. During the first two decades of KMT rule in Taiwan, the KMT was exclusively a mainlanders' party, and the Taiwanese majority was excluded from politics. This began to change after Chiang Ching-kuo cemented his power by assuming the premiership in 1972. One of his major political reforms was to co-opt younger members of the Taiwanese elite into the higher ranks of the ruling party and the government. This conflicted with the existing political taboos. The resolution of this conflict was a test of the scheme to broaden the social base of the regime, which, in 1975, was governing 16 million people. Consequently, as in many other countries undergoing a political transformation, a controlled political liberalization was attempted with the goal of overcoming the legitimacy crisis. In Taiwan, liberalization, as orchestrated by Chiang Ching-kuo, consisted of an expansion of political participation and Taiwanization.

The KMT's project of allowing more participation appeared to be intended to control the openings of political space. The reforms included partial elections for the National Assembly, the Legislative Yuan, and the Control Yuan (the memberships of all three had been frozen since the KMT retreat to Taiwan). In 1972, many opposition figures won election to the National Assembly and the Legislative Yuan. In the 1977 local elections (the KMT had permitted elections for county-level offices and legislative bodies under the provincial level since the 1950s), more opposition and non-KMT figures won office as legislators, Taipei City councilors, and county magistrates.

Chiang Ching-kuo viewed opening the political process to the Taiwanese as a valuable card, and he chose to play it by carrying out a Taiwanization scheme. Inevitably, Chiang's efforts were challenged by the conservative mainlander elite and caused a split within the KMT. Ignoring the opposition within the KMT, Chiang began appointing young Taiwanese to important offices, increasing the number of Taiwanese in the cabinet, naming a Taiwanese as governor of the province, and, after he became KMT chairman in 1976, increasing the number of Taiwanese on the KMT's Central Standing Committee (CSC; the percentage of Taiwanese members increased from 14 percent in 1973 to 33 percent in 1979). Taiwanization was an important part of Chiang Ching-kuo's liberalization strategy.

The Taiwanization strategy simultaneously served two goals—it broadened the social base of the KMT regime, and it legitimized Chiang Ching-kuo as the new leader. In his efforts to succeed his father, Chiang tried to change his image. The former director of intelligence became a populist politician through Taiwanization. He visited remote areas and offshore islands wearing casual clothes instead of a suit, and he shook hands and chatted with fishermen, farmers, and the elderly. The KMT-controlled media often reminded the public how many ordinary friends Chiang Ching-kuo had made during his frequent visits to the countryside. In 1987 Chiang declared: "After living in Taiwan for almost forty years, I am also a Taiwanese."[4] Taiwanizing the regime and Taiwanizing its new leader were the major political strategies for resolving the regime's legitimacy crisis.

The consequences of these moves were far-reaching. Taiwanization fundamentally changed the state and state-society relations on the island. It also caused tensions in relations across the strait. Despite Chiang's adamant opposition to Taiwan independence, his Taiwanization scheme paradoxically paved the way for the emergence of the pro-independence movements. Lee Teng-hui, the first Taiwanese president (selected by Chiang Ching-kuo as his successor), who has been widely seen as promoting the island's independence, merely accelerated the pace of Taiwanization. Taiwanization showed that the state could not opt for ideology over reality. It solved the legitimacy crisis by altering the basis of the regime's legitimacy to its effective governance of Taiwan rather than its fictitious claim of sovereignty over mainland China.[5]

Controlled liberalization was the state's strategy for consolidating its rule. It both expanded the KMT's power base by absorbing native Taiwanese into the ruling coalition and encouraged the opposition by creating an opening for political participation. By expanding its power base, the KMT maintained control of the situation; by increasing participation, it alleviated political pressures and initiated a process that eventually led to democratization in the second half of the 1980s.[6]

In addition, the state also emphasized the private sector so as to deal with the crisis of transition. As is shown below, the state began to integrate leading capitalists into the policy process in the mid-1980s and to provide them more economic rents. State-LE relations shifted from domination to cooperation. The state also launched a series of policies favorable to the SMEs in the early 1970s. This change had both economic and political origins. The SMEs had demonstrated their economic might as major exporters over the preceding decade, and they had gained political significance because their grass-root connections could serve the regime's Taiwanization efforts and help resolve the legitimacy crisis. Indeed, their success could be cited as proof of the regime's legitimacy. The state could no longer ignore the SMEs and could even use them to restrict the business groups. As a result, a set of more systematic policies on the SMEs was developed. Chapter 8 focuses on this issue.

The changing political situation inevitably affected the ways the state dealt with economic affairs. Before the 1980s, the political situation had been under KMT control. This alleviated pressure on the state and enabled it to focus on economic transformation. But beginning in the 1980s, it had to devote more energy to dealing with the growing demands for political participation, which ultimately could undermine the basis of its rule. It had to compromise economic interests for political purposes by practicing a more flexible strategy toward major social forces. This tendency was reflected in many specific policies on prices and taxes. As shown below, it was also particularly evident in the regime's handling of the LEs.

Industrial Upgrading

Meanwhile, the state was preoccupied with economic issues. Because of the two oil crises, the soaring wage bill, and the increasing competition from the cheap labor economies, Taiwan's economy was facing serious difficulties. The most affected industry was petrochemicals. Plants responded by reducing production or even shutting down. More and more people, from government officials to economists and editorial writers, began to express doubts about the heavy and chemical industrialization strategy adopted in the early 1970s. These capital- and skill-intensive industries included steel, steel products, heavy machinery, and petrochemical intermediaries. Critics argued that, unlike the labor-intensive "light" industries, which had been responsible for most of Taiwan's export production, these resource-consuming and capital-intensive industries were inappropriate for resource-poor Taiwan. They suggested an industrial restructuring that would increase the value-added component of Taiwan's exports. Facing a serious economic recession and under strong pressure from business lobbyists, in the late 1970s the government adopted an economic policy of upgrading industry in order to maintain Taiwan's international competitiveness. As shown below, this new vision was incorporated into the ten-year plan drafted by the CEPD in 1979.

However, government efforts to change industrial priorities encountered serious resistance from vested interests within the government and the private sector. The final outcome represented a compromise. Even when technology-intensive and knowledge-based industries became the government's priority, the petrochemical industry managed to retain its key position. This reflected the complicated state–private sector relationship in Taiwan (discussed in detail below). It was difficult for the state to promote high-tech industries given the changing economic bureaucracy (both in terms of institutional structure and personnel) and the less than enthusiastic reaction from the private sector. We will see below how the state dealt with this challenge.

Chiang Ching-kuo's concerns differed from those of his economic bureaucrats. Whereas the civil servants tended to view economic issues from an economic point of view, he often applied political considerations to economic issues. Since Chiang Ching-kuo continued to dominate economic policy, his personal preferences and interests had a direct and substantial impact. He was a populist with strong socialist ideas, and he was concerned about the interests of ordinary people. These interests, as well as his worries about political stability in the early 1970s, often led Chiang to put political considerations before economic considerations. For example, higher prices were never an option. When, for example, the MOEA suggested that electricity prices for tourist hotels be lowered in order to promote tourism and that the price of diesel oil, which was subsidized for fishermen, be increased, thus creating a black market for diesel oil, Chiang Ching-kuo vetoed the plan. He argued that since rich tourists could well afford the costs of the hotels, electricity prices did not need to be lowered. In contrast, the low-income fishermen needed protection.[7]

Chiang's concerns were reflected in his strong interest in big projects that he thought would benefit ordinary people. But the inflation caused by the vast increases in spending required by these projects conflicted with his populist ideology. Chiang's solution was to forbid a rise in prices. This put the bureaucrats in a bind,[8] as shown in Chapter 6 in the case of the Ten Major Development Projects. In 1976, Chiang announced his Twelve Projects, which

were concerned with "software" construction, such as cultural facilities. He also consistently opposed tax increases. As minister of
finance in Chiang's cabinet, K. T. Li was torn between raising
money for the big projects and not increasing taxes.[9] Here again,
political concerns had an impact on government economic policy.
For example, when Chiang established "seeking growth with stability" as a principle in 1981, his premier, Sun Yunxuan, echoed
him, saying that "the government will give consideration to both
price stability and economic growth. If they cannot be achieved at
once, growth should be sacrificed for stability."[10] How can
Chiang's influence be measured and separated from the economic
concerns of the bureaucrats?

Taiwan's economic policy was determined not only by the top
political leader but also by external changes. As international competition increased both from economies at similar levels of development, such as South Korea, and from more recent rivals, such as
the "little tigers" of Southeast Asia and mainland China, global
competitiveness became an important item on the government
agenda. The government viewed this issue in three ways. First, the
experiences of the developed countries, especially Japan, were regarded as models and goals for Taiwan. For example, the Sixth
Four-Year Plan called for the promotion of heavy and chemical
industries as a response to the backward linkage of downstream industries. This new strategy was based on the experiences of the developed economies.

Second, Southeast Asia and mainland China were seen as potential rivals in the global market. As labor-intensive manufacturers
and exporters in the world market, these economies challenged
Taiwan's labor-intensive exports, which still constituted a considerable part of Taiwan's exports during the 1970s. This challenge came
just as Taiwan was experiencing labor shortages and substantial
wage increases (which doubled between 1976 and 1981) in the late
1970s. This issue was of much concern to local businessmen as
well.[11]

Third, and most important, beginning in the late 1960s, South
Korea was consistently viewed as Taiwan's greatest and most for-

midable rival. Korea had a similar view of Taiwan. As a major competitor at the same level of industrialization, Korea's performance had two contradictory implications for Taiwan. On one hand, Korea was a state Taiwan could study. A number of study delegations from Taiwan paid visits to South Korea each year. Taiwan's EPB sent a delegation, led by deputy head Sun Zhen, every year after the first oil crisis,[12] and a proposal submitted by a delegation impressed with the power and authority of Korea's EPB led to the establishment of the CEPD.

On the other hand, Taiwan worried about being overtaken by South Korea. The two economies were frequently compared—for instance, at the seventh economic meeting chaired by Chiang Ching-kuo.[13] Business was concerned that Korea would surpass Taiwan.[14] The Koreans' ambitious plans and fast progress in the heavy and chemical industries made the Taiwanese uneasy. However, the toughest competition between the two little tigers was in the field of the high-tech and information industries. This is discussed in further detail later in this chapter.

As shown above, the government's industrial strategy changed dramatically in the late 1970s. Although heavy industries and petrochemicals were chosen as key sectors in the early 1970s, the severe impact of the two oil crises forced a change in policy in the late 1970s. The newly restructured CEPD formulated a Ten-Year Plan for 1980–89 in which the emphasis shifted from heavy and chemical industries to high-value-added, technology-intensive, non-energy-consuming, and nonpolluting industries, such as information, electronics, robotics, and machinery. However, as we will see below, resistance from vested interests and a change in the government's economic leadership led to renewed governmental support for petrochemicals in the mid-1980s. In response, a new package of incentives was created to channel resources into strategic and high-tech sectors. Among other actions, Xinzhu Science Park was established; R&D was promoted through government-sponsored institutes; preferential credits were provided for the export of machinery and capital goods; the Statute for the Encouragement of Investment was revised to reduce taxes on strategic and high-tech industries and to remove heavy and chemical goods from the list of those sectors to be encouraged; and plans for the CPC's fifth naphtha-cracking plant and China Steel Corporation's second expansion were suspended. The issues surrounding implementation of this new policy involved the economic bureaucracy.

The Economic Bureaucracy

As part of the state, the economic bureaucracy changed significantly because of the developments in the international situation and state-society relations. These alterations had a substantial impact on government policy and on the way the state approached the private sector. The adjustments took place on two fronts: institutional and personnel.

Institutional Changes in the Economic Bureaucracy

On the institutional front, the formation of the CEPD was triggered by the establishment of South Korea's powerful Economic Planning Board in early 1977. The Taiwanese viewed the Korean move as motivated by a desire to catch up with Taiwan. Taiwan took the challenge seriously and sent a delegation to Korea to investigate. Impressed by Korea's EPB, the delegation concluded that Taiwan's EPB was too weak and suggested a restructuring and expansion. The CEPD, a higher-level and more powerful economic planning body, replaced the EPB in December 1977. The CEPD became a permanent government department in 1985 when the Legislative Yuan approved its rules of organization. The members of the EPB had been deputy ministers. The head of the CEPD was either a minister or the equivalent of a minister without a portfolio. The functions of the CEPD were expanded beyond those of the EPB, which had included formulating, screening, and coordinating economic plans and examining the budgets of the government and the public sector in order to improve coordination between budgeting and planning. In addition to these tasks, the CEPD was made responsible for drawing up intermediate- and long-term plans and key projects. Its powers included the devising of macroeconomic development plans, analysis of the current economic situation, and evaluation of large-scale public enterprise projects.

In general, the establishment of the CEPD was a result of internal changes in the economic bureaucracy in the direction of decentralization and professionalization. Although more powerful than its predecessor, the EPB, the CEPD cannot be compared to the CIECD, CUSA, or ESB. In contrast to those three bodies, the CEPD was not headed by the premier or vice president but by a minister. Nor did it enjoy the resources of the ESB, CUSA, and CIECD—namely, U.S. aid. Moreover, as had other government ministries, the economic bureaucracy as a whole had significantly improved in terms of the quality. As noted in previous chapters, one major reason the ESB, CUSA, and CIECD had been powerful was that other parts of the economic bureaucracy, particularly the MOEA and the MOF, were weak. This changed after the late 1960s, and the increasing competence of the other economic bodies reduced the importance of the CEPD.

The CEPD was also a response to the changing relationship between the state and the private sector. Society had become more pluralistic with the rise of a middle class, and there were more demands for democracy. The state no longer dominated society absolutely. The private sector was becoming stronger economically, and its influence on economic policy making was increasing. The government's decision to compile a list of strategic industries provoked a debate within the private sector. Some even argued that no industry should be designated strategic. As we will see in the next section, state–private sector relations were moving in the direction of systematization and institutionalization during this period. This situation required an institutionalized economic planning body. In short, the CEPD resulted from external pressures, internal developments in the economic bureaucracy, and changing state–private sector relations. The state structure had evolved dramatically over the previous three decades as the economic bureaucracy became more institutionalized and power shifted from the nonconstitutional economic planning agencies to the routine ministries.

Another significant change in the economic bureaucracy during this period was the establishment of the Department of Small and Medium Business (DSMB) in 1981. As shown above and in the analysis in the next chapter, in the 1970s the state began to focus on the SMEs after they had become economically important and politically significant. The establishment of the DSMB was a move to adapt to these new circumstances. The new body took over some of the tasks of the IDB and became the major government organ for communicating with private enterprises. To some extent, this change modified the bureaucratic map.

However, this change had a far greater impact than might be apparent from the regulations outlining the DSMB's powers. After only one decade of existence, the IDB, the highest-level agency to conduct detailed sectoral planning and implementation for industry, found its importance largely diminished.[15] Internally, low morale, inadequacies in its internal organization and personnel system, too much work, and loose discipline seriously undermined its efficiency. Externally, a confusing division of powers and functions between the IDB and other organs such as the CEPD and the DSMB and the high profile of these bodies weakened the IDB. For example, the plans and suggestions of the IDB were often criticized by the scholars-turned-officials in the CEPD. In response, the frustrated officials in the IDB became more passive in policy making. Consequently, the IDB gradually ceased to be the leading agency for industrial development, and its discretionary powers were reduced. In the late 1970s and early 1980s, other agencies took over the task of policy making for major industries such as automobiles, petrochemicals, information, and energy.[16] High-level officials lost confidence in the IDB and assigned important tasks to the DSMB. Business people stopped asking the IDB for help and turned to the minister of the MOEA or the ministers without portfolios. Worst of all, the IDB was excluded from discussions on important industrial policies. Its function was limited to implementing policies devised by other departments.[17] The rise of the DSMB and the decline of the IDB show that the function and role of government agencies vary because of their own internal organizational structure as well as because of changes in leadership.

Chiang Ching-kuo's Continued Dominance of Economic Affairs

On the personnel front, the final say on economic policy remained in the hands of Chiang Ching-kuo. Beginning in 1969, when he was named deputy premier and head of the CIECD, and continuing until his death in 1987, Chiang remained the dominant policy maker in economic affairs. His chief tools for maintaining his influence were his control of personnel assignments and his attendance at meetings.

Manipulating personnel. Chiang placed bureaucrats whom he trusted in key economic bodies. As we saw in the previous chapter, soon after he took control of economic policy, he replaced K. T. Li with Sun Yunxuan as the primary civil servant in economic affairs. To weaken the influence of veteran bureaucrats, Chiang disbanded the powerful CIECD and replaced it with the lower-level and less powerful EPB.

In addition to Sun Yunxuan, Chiang also trusted and relied on Yu Guohua. In postwar Taiwan there were two different streams of top economic officials: the Chiang family's presidential residence faction and the non–presidential faction bureaucrats, such as Yin Zhongrong, K. T. Li, and Sun Yunxuan, who dominated economic policy making and implementation. A few leading officials, such as Xu Boyuan and Yu Guohua, enjoyed the trust of both Chiangs and controlled financial matters. They were used to check other bureaucrats like Yin and Li. Xu Boyuan played a major role before he handed over the governorship of the central bank to Yu Guohua in 1969. Yu Guohua subsequently played an important role in financial affairs, based on his special relationship with the Chiang family. He was from the same county as the Chiang family and served as Chiang Kai-shek's personal secretary from 1931 to 1944. He later studied at Harvard and the London School of Economics and then worked for the World Bank and the International Monetary Fund. As a senior financial official after 1955, he was widely regarded as the "Chiang family banker."[18] Thus, it is not surprising that he was highly trusted by both the senior and the junior Chiang; Chiang Ching-kuo in particular relied on him for economic and financial advice.

According to Wang Zhaoming, K. T. Li's removal as minister of the MOEA and appointment as minister of finance in the 1969 cabinet reshuffling represented a compromise: Chiang Ching-kuo wanted to remove Li, but Premier Yan Jiagan protected him.[19] At the same time, Yu Guohua was named governor of the Central Bank as a check on Li. In the resulting division of labor, the MOF was responsible for the drafting of laws and rules, and the Central Bank was in charge of inspection. As the governor of the Central Bank, Yu was thus able to check the power of the MOF. Yu was the longest-serving governor of the Central Bank in postwar Taiwan and continued in that post until he was named premier in 1984. In addition, he was also named head of the CEPD in 1977.

Yu exercised his power in a subtle fashion. Chiang Ching-kuo's trust made him the most influential and powerful economic official. Chiang consulted Yu on major economic decisions, and under Yu the CEPD became known as the "little Executive Yuan." Most economic proposals were submitted first to the CEPD and, only with its approval, were sent to the Executive Yuan.[20] Even Premier Sun Yunxuan asked his subordinates to send new economic policy suggestions to Yu before sending them to him.[21] On the other hand, Yu did not play as active or aggressive a role as Yin Zhongrong and K. T. Li because of his personal style and his background. Yu had been well known as a conservative and austere banker who resisted pressure from special-interest groups, and he had little contact with business. Basically a financial rather than an economic official, he tended to view economic issues from a financial and fiscal point of view. He saw himself as the governor of the Central Bank first and then as the head of the CEPD. Yu took no initiatives and made few contributions. His restraint largely undermined the functions of the CEPD, which was supposed to focus on economic policy making.[22] Because he concurrently held the two positions, the Central Bank's financial policy became the basis for the CEPD's economic planning.[23] This led to calls for Yu's resignation as the head of the CEPD in 1981 and 1982.

Steering economic meetings. Chiang Ching-kuo's second method for dominating economic policy was through direct involvement in policy making by means of economic steering meetings. Beginning in June 1978, Chiang Ching-kuo began chairing a series of economic meetings attended by all key economic officials. These included the ministers of economic affairs, finance, and transportation, the governor of the Central Bank, the head of the CEPD, the secretary-general of the KMT Central Committee, and the secretary-general of the Executive Yuan. At the meetings, the responsible officials would present reports on the general economic situation. Other officials would then report on specific questions. Almost all economic issues, from general matters such as prices, trade, exchange rates, rice production, foreign investment, and international competitiveness to individual projects, like railways, ports, and even tunnels, were discussed at these meetings. Sometimes very specific issues were discussed. For example, an overseas Chinese business-man's investment in a chain bridge to a temple was a topic of discussion at the fifth meeting. Chiang Ching-kuo gave instructions on every issue.[24] Three points are worth noting about these meetings. First, they were the highest-level economic meetings. They involved the president, the premier, and all leading economic and financial officials. Second, they were decision-making occasions. Third, the meetings proceeded in a *dirigiste* fashion. There were few real discussions; Chiang Ching-kuo always dominated the meetings.

For Chiang, the meetings served two goals: they kept him informed about the economic situation, and they allowed him to dominate policy making. The very range of issues brought up at the meetings enabled Chiang to keeps tabs on the economic situation. The fact that Chiang as president bypassed the premier to convene meetings of cabinet members on economic issues was unusual in itself. Premier Sun Yunxuan rarely voiced an opinion at the meetings. The officials reported directly to Chiang and received instructions from him, instead of from the premier who was also sitting among them. As we shall see below, Chiang also dominated economic policy by convening business circles.

Chiang's dominance injected politics into economic policy. From his political point of view, Chiang stressed the importance of maintaining a balance between development and stability, and his instructions on prices, agriculture, the money supply, and other matters were oriented toward preserving social order rather than following the market.

Despite Chiang's personal dominance of economic policy, beginning in the early 1970s there was a trend toward decentralization of the economic bureaucracy in terms of institutions and personnel. One major sign of this was the end of the economic strongmen. K. T. Li's resignation as minister of finance in 1976 marked the end of an era in which a leading bureaucrat was surrounded by a team of loyal underlings. The differences between Chiang Ching-kuo and Li over economic ideas and policies had gradually widened. The event that triggered Li's resignation was a dispute over the salt tax. Li suggested abolishing the tax but maintaining the price in order to reflect real prices. Chiang insisted on reducing prices if the tax were to be abolished. Otherwise, he claimed, it was "cheating." A bitter debate ensued. In the end, Chiang told Li that seven things—fuel, rice, oil, salt, soy sauce, vinegar, and tea—were daily necessities. Therefore, their prices could not rise.[25]

Yin Zhongrong had been the first economic strongman; Li was the second, and the last. They had participated in all of Taiwan's major economic reforms during the late 1950s and early 1960s. Li's departure signaled that Taiwan had moved to a new stage in which economic policy began to be decentralized in terms of both institutions and personnel. Even though Chiang intended to replace Li with Sun Yunxuan, Sun was far less senior and less influential. Furthermore, shortly thereafter, in 1978, he was named premier and left the MOEA. Given this situation and Yu Guohua's conservatism, the state's ability to deal directly with the private sector was largely undermined and henceforth the state would rely more on institutional conduits to influence the private sector.

Bureaucratic Change and the
Personal Role of the Strongman

A salient and persistent phenomenon despite the transformation of the economic bureaucracy was the role of the veteran bureaucrat. This is well represented by K. T. Li's personal role in the development of the high-tech industry. Although he left the center of economic policy making, Li was still able to play a leadership role in promoting this industry. This case merits close attention because it is the last example of a strongman at work in Taiwan's development. Interestingly, Zhao Yaodong, appointed minister of economic affairs in 1981, had all the hallmarks of a potential strongman, but he never evolved into that role, evidence perhaps of how far the institutionalization of the bureaucracy had proceeded. Following his resignation as minister of finance, Li was named minister without portfolio, and he continued to play an active role in economic affairs. In fact, Li soon found a new stage. Chiang appointed him chairman of the newly established Research Group of Applied Technology. Li believed that, with his academic training and experience as a bureaucrat, he would be able to join technology and industry.[26] But with no staff and no budget, the group was not an institutional body.

Despite the many challenges, however, Li was ultimately able to play an effective role by moving beyond institutions. With the approval of Chiang Ching-kuo, Li convened the first National Science Conference in January 1978. In May, Chiang Ching-kuo was elected president, and Sun was appointed premier. With his background as an engineer, Sun stressed the importance of science and technology. With Sun's support and encouragement, Li drafted a Development Plan for Science and Technology based on the conclusions of the conference. The plan served as the basic framework for Taiwan's high-tech industry. Li also used his substantial personal influence to promote an upgrading of industry. Among other things, he played a substantial role in the development of the information industry, as we will see below; engaged in efforts to recruit engineering personnel and to expand engineering-related postgraduate programs in leading universities;[27] successfully lobbied for the inclusion of a provision in the revised Statute for the Encouragement of Investment in 1981 that required industries receiving benefits under the statute to spend a standard amount of money on R&D;[28] and helped attract venture capital for high-tech investment.[29] Li also used his influence to get the private sector involved. For example, he raised money from the private sector to establish an Institute of the Information

Industry and invited private-sector investment to establish the Taiwan Semiconductor Corporation (TSMC). His efforts earned him the title "father of Taiwan's high-tech industry."

Li's leadership role reflects the unique role of the economic bureaucracy during the industrial transformation. Decentralization and institutionalization of the economic bureaucracy redefined the roles and functions of economic institutions. The institutional divisions of labor were ambiguous, and there was an administrative vacuum. Some senior and influential bureaucrats such as K. T. Li, who was not at the center of policy making during their transition, filled this vacuum and played a leadership role. Li's active role compensated for the weaknesses of the economic institutions during this period. When the transformation was completed in the early 1990s, the stage for personal bureaucrats was narrowed and the importance of institutions increased. Thus, there were fewer opportunities for "bureaucratic personalism." This explains why K. T. Li was the last economic strongman in Taiwan's history.

The Strongman and the Success of Industrial Policy

As pointed out in Chapter 1, the strategic intelligence argument in the statist account of Taiwan's industrialization encounters efficacy problems at both the theoretical and the practical level. At the theoretical level, the account assumes the state's steering capacity to carry out industrial policy. The prerequisite for this capacity is the existence of a coherent and monolithic economic bureaucracy whose constituent agencies work well together. As I have argued, however, this assumption is apolitical. Given the endemic differences and conflicts among the different government agencies, coordination is critical if industrial policy is to be successful. But the selective industrial policy argument ignores the significance of coordination.

At the practical level, this account is challenged by the failures of some targeted industries, for instance, the automobile industry. It does not explain why some industries succeeded and others failed. Some successful industries were strategic industries, but others were not. And some strategic industries failed. Strikingly, the success of the downstream industries was outside the framework of state intervention. The state's capacity to steer the activities of the SMEs was weak. Seemingly, the reasons for the success of certain industries are more complex than the strategic intelligence account can address. Sectoral industrial policy is thus inadequate as an explanation of industrial development in Taiwan.

We therefore need a more sophisticated explanation for the industrial success of Taiwan. Masahiko Aoki and his colleagues suggest that coordination failure is more fundamental than market failure to economic development.[30] This book agrees that coordination is critical to industrial success. However, the scope of coordination in the definition of Aoki et al. is too narrow because it refers only to the market. They fail to consider the role of the state in the economic development of a developing society. I argue that coordination is crucial not only in the market sphere but also within the government. It is a determinant at the level of both policy formulation and policy implementation. A successful industrial policy is the result of good coordination, which can solve differences and conflicts among the concerned government agencies. As we have seen, institutions in Taiwan were not well integrated. As the case of the automobile industry makes clear, failure was a result of poor coordination and the inability to resolve internal differences and conflicts. Therefore, the key is the mechanism that solves coordination problems within the government and partly solves coordination problems between the state and the private sector (private institutions also play a part in this).

Does coordination depend on institutions or on individuals? The empirical studies presented in this book point to the latter. As we will see below in the case of the semiconductor industry, before the early 1980s institutions in Taiwan were fragile and weak. They were not in a position to coordinate different government agencies or between the state and the private sector. This situation created an opening for a strongman. Authority was attached to individuals rather than to institutions. I argue that the success of Taiwan's industrial policy depended to a great extent on the leadership of individuals because they were the only ones able to solve the coordination problem.

Three factors enabled the strongmen to play this role. First, they obtained political support from the highest leaders. This crucial political capital gave the strongmen legitimacy and enabled them to overcome obstacles. Second, the strongmen had personal charisma, which facilitates problem solving. Third, the strongmen had access to resources and instruments, including both funds and human assets. For example, Yin Zhongrong could draw on U.S. aid, and both Yin and K. T. Li assembled a group of capable aides. Even when they lacked funds and/or human resources, however, the strongmen could resolve conflicts through the top leaders' political support and their own influence, connections, and personal charisma. K. T. Li's role in promoting the semiconductor industry is a perfect example. As we have seen, Li used a wide array of policy instruments to realize his policy goals, such as the Statute for the Encouragement of Investment, to solve problems relating to capital, human resources, and other aspects of this sector.

Four preconditions are required for the success of an industrial policy. The first is political support from the top leaders. Political support, usually given to a strongman, is critical for resolving coordination problems. In the case of Taiwan's auto industry, the lack of political support led to unresolved conflicts between the CEPD and the MOEA and thus was instrumental in the failure of the industry.[31] A second condition is the existence of a strongman; the absence of a strongman who could solve the coordination problem was the major reason for the failure of the auto industry policy. These first two conditions are obviously interrelated. A third condition is the expectation that investment in an industry carries few risks. This was particularly important in Taiwan because the private sector was reluctant to invest in an industry until it became profitable, as seen in the cases of steel, petrochemicals, and semiconductors. The SOEs thus played a leading role as pioneers and models in establishing these industries. The final condition is a policy on the operation of market forces. Policy can either restrict or facilitate market competition. In many cases, the state in Taiwan did not allow industries to be monopolized by a few operators. Instead, it deliberately allowed as many LEs as possible entry. This was the case for petrochemicals and semiconductors. Such a policy has both political and economic ramifications. It aims to avoid monopolies and political rivalries and to encourage competition. The accomplishments of industries like petrochemicals and semiconductors show that the success depends on a policy design that facilitates market competition.

State–Private Sector
Relations in Transformation

State–private sector relations underwent a transformation during this period because of changes in the state, society, and state-society relations beginning in the early 1970s. The external legitimacy crisis forced the state to seek an internal source of legitimacy. The middle class–based opposition movement and the various social movements forced the state to strengthen its links with the Taiwanese elite by expanding their political participation. Cooperation and negotiation replaced coercion and manipulation. Along with expanding participation and Taiwanization, the strengthening of state–private sector relations was an important tactic for overcoming the political crisis.

One reason for the change in relations with the private sector was pressure from increasingly powerful capitalists, who pursued rent-seeking activities and tried to use their might to influence state policy. Noteworthy were the attempts by petrochemical capital to move to upstream industries and by financial capital to enter the banking sector and the successful lobbying by intermediate LEs to persuade the state to side with them in their disputes with the downstream SMEs. The state's response to these demands was significant—it blocked the former because it would have affected the SOEs' monopolies and state control of the banking sector and cooperated on the latter since it did not harm state interests. The government rejected the application of Taiwan's largest business group, the Formosa Plastics Group, to establish a naphtha-cracking plant. Calls from the private sector to open banking to the private sector increased, but efforts to lift the government's ban were unsuccessful. Evidence shows that the rent-seeking activities of business groups increased in the late 1970s and early 1980s.

Another reason was the growing influence of local factions beginning in the 1980s. The KMT had begun to seek support from local factions in grass-roots elections in the early 1950s. As an émigré regime with a weak social basis, the KMT nurtured at least two factions for office in each district in order to exercise power at the local level. Due to the pivotal role of factions in the local elections, the KMT became very dependent on them.[32] The state manipulated a party-directed spoils system to offer them regional economic rents.[33] After three decades of development, the local factions had become a significant political and economic force. They had begun creating cross-district alliances, and, more important, they were becoming economically powerful. Using their political influence, they took control of local financial systems and monopolized local public works projects and other profitable businesses. In effect, they became business groups.

The rise of opposition candidates contending for local electoral offices forced the KMT regime to rely even more on local factions to win local elections. This in turn reinforced the factions' rent-seeking activities. As opposition activity increased, so did the KMT's dependence on the local factions; this in turn made these factions even more powerful and encouraged their rent-seeking activities. This trend is clearly seen in two sets of statistics. The percentage of legislators from local factions or supported by local factions rose from 13.89 percent in 1972, when Chiang Ching-kuo began to carry out his Taiwanization scheme, to 18.92 percent in 1975, 30 percent in 1980, 47.89 percent in 1983, and 49.32 percent in 1986.[34] And the number of KMT legislators with local factional backgrounds grew from 16.27 percent in 1972 to 20 percent in 1975, 31.58 percent in 1980, 48.39 percent in 1983, and 58.45 percent in 1986.[35] Relations between the KMT and the local factions were obviously increasing. As liberalization proceeded, the importance of the local factions to the KMT increased. With the establishment of the first opposition party, the Democratic Progressive Party (DPP), in 1986 and the beginning of democratization in 1987 (signaled by the lifting of martial law), this trend continued.

A third factor in the transformation of state–private sector relations was the rise of a younger generation within the KMT, particularly in the Department of Organization, the division responsible for elections, intraparty affairs, and Taiwanese recruits. Because these younger cadres rose as Chiang Ching-kuo took power, they were generally close to Chiang. Compared to the older generation of mainlander elites, the new generation viewed capitalists and the Taiwanese differently—they were not opposed to the capitalists, and they had more connections with the Taiwanese. One such key figure was General Wang Shen, who headed the powerful Department of Political Affairs. A longtime protégé of Chiang Ching-kuo, he became the number-two figure in the KMT in the early 1980s. In general, the younger group took a much softer line than their predecessors.[36] Their rise coincided with a deterioration in Chiang Ching-kuo's health that began in 1983. Their positions and their ambitions drove them to seek allies outside the KMT.

As powers both inside and outside the state sought to advance their own interests, existing state–private sector relations had to change. Basically, the KMT regime was struggling between restricting and relying on the LEs. On the one hand, faced with the increasingly pluralistic society, especially an active political opposition, the KMT needed the support of the LEs. In exchange for their support, the state was more willing to give them economic rents. On the other hand, to avoid losing its control over the economy, the state also needed to control strategic industries—the upstream sectors—and the banking system. When the LEs attempted to expand their rent-seeking activities into these areas, the state had to stop them. As the state struggled with these two conflicting objectives, it found its options constricted. The change in its own internal structure was undermining its ability to tackle the situation. This situation had an impact on state–private sector relations, particularly in the areas of economic rents and policy making.

State-LE Relations and Economic Rents

To strengthen its ties with the LEs, the state relied increasingly on economic rents. This was due not only to the increasingly pluralistic nature of society and the growth of political opposition but also to greater rent-seeking activities by the LEs. The private sector as a whole had become powerful enough to pressure the state to provide more rents. A typical case is the petrochemical industry. As we shall see, private investment in the petrochemical industry began under the state's nurturing and protection program in the late 1950s. The boom in export-oriented downstream manufacturing of synthetic fibers and plastics created a strong backward integration effect and led to the expansion of intermediate and upstream industries. In the late 1970s and early 1980s, petrochemicals became a pivotal sector in Taiwan. In terms of value-added, the petrochemical industry accounted for 10.8 percent of the manufacturing sector and 3.2 percent of GDP in 1970; the corresponding figures for 1985 were 15.07 percent and 5.67 percent.[37] The petrochemical industry was also the most vertically integrated sector of upstream SOEs, intermediate LEs, and downstream SMEs in Taiwan.

As noted in Chapter 6, the petrochemical industry was designated a key sector by Chiang Ching-kuo's newly inaugurated cabinet in 1973. The regime's emphasis on heavy and chemical industries reflected concerns about national security because of changes in the international environment. The two oil crises, however, cast doubts on the feasibility of developing the oil-hungry and polluting petrochemical industry in oil-importing Taiwan. Accepting suggestions from scholars, including Bela Balassa, a leading free-market economist who was consulted by the Taiwan government, the Sun Yunxuan cabinet modified the industrial strategy and decided in 1981 to suspend further expansion of the intermediate-stream sectors of the petrochemical industry. The upstream SOEs were allowed to set up new plants offshore but not in Taiwan. As part of the policy revisions, the CPC's planned fifth cracking plant was indefinitely postponed.[38]

Unsurprisingly, vested interests in both the public and the private sectors of this well-developed and powerful industry vigorously opposed this decision. Simultaneously, a dispute between the intermediate-stream LEs and the downstream SMEs erupted over the prices of intermediate petrochemicals. Because of the 1979 oil crisis, the CPC had to raise the price of upstream ethylene goods, and the cost of intermediate products soon exceeded the price of U.S. imports. The intermediate manufacturers passed the increases along to the downstream users, who turned plastics, man-made fibers, and synthetic rubber into final products. When they threatened to turn to cheaper imports in order to remain competitive in the international market, both the intermediate LEs and the downstream SMEs pressured the state to resolve the dispute. The manufacturing associations in the synthetic fibers, plastics, and petrochemical sectors joined in submitting petitions to the state. The state ultimately had to arbitrate, but it was torn between maintaining SOE profits or SME competitiveness in the world market. It decided to sacrifice the SOEs' profits by reducing the prices of the CPC's upstream products to international levels and by allowing some imports of petrochemical goods. CPC prices for ethylene products were on average 23 percent higher than U.S. prices before 1982, the year the agreement on production and sales was reached, but 4 percent lower after 1982.[39] The intermediate-stream LEs did not reduce the prices, however, and they became the only beneficiaries of these arrangements. The CPC lost NT$2 billion per year.[40] Obviously, the state's efforts to maintain the SMEs' international competitiveness by lowering the CPC's price and thus reducing the expenses of the SMEs was unsuccessful.

Why did the state permit the intermediate LEs to benefit? One reason was political: the state provided the LEs economic rents in exchange for support. The business groups in the intermediate petrochemical sectors had close relations with the state. They were powerful not only in the petrochemical industry but also in the entire economy. In comparison, the downstream SMEs were fragmented and thus had less political leverage. In the early 1980s, when the state faced political challenges, support from the LEs was more crucial than ever. The dispute offered the state a good opportunity to give the LEs rents in exchange for support. Subsequent developments make this point clearer. The move solved the problems caused by the oil crisis, and thus it should have been temporary. But in fact it became a permanent arrangement and remained unchanged as late as 1989. A second reason was financial. From the late 1970s on, the KMT began to invest in the intermediate sectors of the petrochemical industry and acquired minority holdings in eight companies. The combined share of these companies in the sector's total output was slightly less than 10 percent.[41]

The victory of the petrochemical LEs was even greater after Yu Guohua replaced Sun as premier in 1984. The petrochemical industry regained the strategic designation it had lost four years earlier, in part because of strong lobbying by the powerful private sector in the industry. Wang Yongqing (C. C. Wang), the outspoken founder of Formosa Plastics Group, which had become the largest business group, was the most influential tycoon in Taiwan. The private sector was joined by the SOEs in lobbying for the reinstatement of petrochemicals. After decades of expansion in the upstream sector, the public sector had developed its own interests (Evans found similar developments in the Brazilian petrochemical industry). Another factor was disagreement within the state regarding development strategy. Wang Zhenhuan argues that the reversal of the targeted position of the petrochemical industry owed much to the support of certain bureaucrats.[42] Sun and Yu had different views about Taiwan's development. Given Yu's closer ties with the SOEs, it makes sense that Yu reversed Sun's decision and restored the petrochemical industry's position as a favored industry. The private sector thus had supporters within the state, and powerful vested interests pressured the state to reverse its policy.

Private Sector–State Alliances and Economic Rents

The private sector also tried to breach the state's restrictions by forming alliances. The efforts of newly emerging capital in the financial sector to end restrictions on private sector borrowing from the banks went beyond collective actions, such as appeals and petitions, and entailed attempts to find allies within the state. The purpose of these challenges was to allow credit companies to become banks.

The main challenge came from the Cai family. The Cai family had established Cathay Life Insurance in 1962 and Cathay Credit in the 1970s. Its holdings increased rapidly, and by the early 1980s it had become Taiwan's richest family. One member of the family was elected to the legislature in 1983. He brought together twelve other legislators, all from business, most of whom had a background in local financial institutions, to form the "Thirteen Brothers." This group became a powerful force within the Legislative Yuan pushing for a revision of the Bank Act to allow credit companies to become involved in bank-related business. As representatives of the Legislative Yuan and financial institutions, two members of the Cai family and another business tycoon were invited by the MOF to join the team responsible for revising the Bank Act.[43] The revised Bank Act had a clause allowing credit companies to become involved in bank-related business. But the revisions encountered fierce objections in the Legislative Yuan from senior legislators fearful of the Thirteen Brothers, and the act did not pass. The draft was sent to the Central Standing Committee of the KMT for arbitration in January 1984, and the clause was deleted. The revised Bank Act eventually passed the Legislative Yuan the following year.

This challenge from the private sector and local factions to the state ended in failure, mostly because of the objections of senior legislators. But there were two additional reasons as well. First, it involved a coalition involved in the KMT succession struggle. The Thirteen Brothers, leaders of local factions and some key figures within the KMT government, formed a clique in the early 1980s. The clique included General Wang Shen, the KMT secretary-general, and the minister of finance. The power of this alliance caused widespread concern when Chiang Ching-kuo's health began to deteriorate in 1983. It was feared it would take power if Chiang were to die.[44] Behind the Legislative Yuan's and the KMT Central Standing Committee's resistance to the efforts of these capitalists to amend the Bank Act were concerns about KMT rule.

When Chiang recovered his health in 1985, he sided with those resisting the Thirteen Brothers and broke up the alliance. The credit companies were heavily involved in real estate and stocks; under the protection of the alliance, their activities had been financed by borrowing from the government-owned banks. The credit companies were deeply resented on the island, and a scandal in the Tenth Credit Corporation, a business controlled by the Cai family, ignited island-wide anger against the Cais and offered an opportunity for Chiang to act against the alliance.

The successful rent-seeking activities of the petrochemical industry and the failed challenge from financial capital illustrate the state's different tactics for dealing with pressures from capitalists. It used rents to encourage supporters, but it applied punishments to penalize challengers.

Capitalists and Policy Making

The third significant change during this period was that the state co-opted leading capitalists into the policy process as part of its attempt to strengthen ties with traditional supporters. Before this, the private sector could influence policy making only through personal contacts with bureaucrats and politicians and by petitioning through the manufacturing associations. The private sector could *influence* policy, but it was not involved in the *making* of policy.[45] This situation changed considerably at the beginning of the 1980s.

This change was reflected in the participation of businessmen in the attempted revision of the Bank Act. Although we lack knowledge of the details of the policy process leading to the MOF's version of the Bank Act, it is clear that inclusion of the clause allowing credit companies to run bank-related businesses owed much to these businessmen-advisers. This was indicative of a new trend in state–private sector relations. However, in this case, it was the capitalists who took the initiative, and the state that remained passive. In other cases, the state took the initiative and invited leading capitalists to join the policy network.

On Chiang Ching-kuo's instructions, the Industrial Consultative Commission was formed in March 1985.[46] The aim of the commission was to make "feasible and practical suggestions and proposals that are helpful to the nation's economy through long-term exchange of opinions."[47] This body, made up of officials, scholars, and business people, provided a forum for capitalists,[48] and became an institutional conduit between the state and the private sector.

Another group established in May of that same year, the temporary Economic Reform Commission, was charged with reforming the existing system for investments by taking stock of outdated regulations, rules, and laws. Business people, including two influential tycoons, Gu Zhenfu and Wang Yongqing, constituted 15 percent of the commission. Many resolutions were passed at its meetings. The most far-reaching outcome was that a consensus reached in the commission—namely, "liberalization, internationalization, and institutionalization"—would guide the government's economic goals for the next decade. Faced with increasing pressure from the United States over Taiwan's huge trade surplus, Taiwan was asked to reduce controls. The deteriorating investment climate due to the social movements and other problems resulted in a decrease in investment—the percentage of fixed investment in GDP decreased from 30 percent in 1980 to 18.1 percent in 1986. The consensus at the meeting was echoed by calls from academics, the media, and the private sector to reduce controls and improve the investment environment.

The regime's contradictory policy of both restricting and relying on the LEs was reflected in Chiang Ching-kuo's own actions. Chiang smashed the alliance between his protégés and the capitalists. Yet he could not ignore the influence of the capitalists. At the series of meetings he chaired, Chiang instructed his officials to pay more attention to the opinions of the private sector. In addition to the Industrial Consultative Commission, Chiang invited the leading capitalists in every industry to attend a series of four meetings in July and August 1978. Under Chiang's chairmanship, the purpose of the meetings was to solicit views and opinions from the private sector about the economic situation and to determine how the state could help resolve the problems faced by the private sector. Issues raised at the meetings ran the gamut from the general economic situation to specific sectoral problems.[49] These meetings took place just as the economy was facing a serious slump as a result of international competition and soaring wages. Both the state and the private sector needed to overcome these difficulties, and this motivated the state to strengthen its contacts with the private sector.

It is clear that during this transitional period in state–private sector relations, the state was becoming more flexible vis-à-vis the LEs by making concessions in rents and incorporating some of the LEs into the policy network. The state's embeddedness in society was no longer based solely on coercion and manipulation and was moving toward cooperation and negotiation. Linda Weiss and John M. Hobson have argued that the exercise of power *through* society is superior to the exercise of power *over* society and that the former is responsible for the effective role of the state in East Asian economic development (as in Japan),[50] but the Taiwan experience of coercion and manipulation prior to the mid-1970s does not support their argument. It was only after the late 1970s that Taiwan began to follow the East Asian pattern of state–private sector relations analyzed by Weiss and Hobson. Facing growing political, economic, and social pressures, the Taiwan state sought to maintain control by granting concessions and incorporating local social forces into the ruling coalition. Like its opening of political space for the Taiwanese elite, the incorporation of capitalists into policy making was part of the state's overall strategy for responding to the transition. The adjustments made by the KMT regime are what Gramsci called a "passive revolution."[51] These changes laid a foundation for the overwhelming changes that would take place at the next stage, when the president and the premier of the pro-business regime publicly announced that the task of the government was to help the capitalists make money.

Nonetheless, the state was still able to play a leadership role. The next section focuses on the semiconductor industry to examine the state's impact on the transformation of industry.

Promoting the Information Industry

The success of the information industry represents a new height in Taiwan's economic "miracle." The information industry now forms the largest sector of Taiwan's export market, and Taiwan has become one of the world's major suppliers of information products. This case provides the latest example of the evolution of state–private sector relations and highlights the state's pivotal role in economic transformation. The overhaul of the information industry in Taiwan was characterized by two phenomena. First, it was a state-led process. Second, it was the SMEs, instead of the LEs, that dominated this sector. During a period of transformation when the state structure and state–private sector relations were undergoing substantial change and the private sector had become increasingly powerful, the state was still able to promote an industrial upgrade. How was the state able to play a leadership role? At a time when Japanese and South Korean semiconductor manufacturers were closing their offshore factories or becoming debt-ridden due to the economic crisis in 1998, manufacturers in Taiwan were continuing to expand rapidly. Observers predicted that in 1999 Taiwan's investment in semiconductors would reach U.S.$4.5 billion, three times that of South Korea. It was anticipated that Taiwan's semiconductor industry would surpass that of Japan in 2002.[52] In order to explain the implications of this growth for state–private sector relations, this section focuses on three issues: the state's sponsoring of the information industry, the implementation of the project to sponsor the semiconductor industry, and the role of the private sector in the development of the semiconductor industry.

Sponsoring of the Information Industry

The overhaul of the information industry in Taiwan began in the mid-1970s at the urging of individual officials rather than institutions. At that time, the CEPD, a newly restructured and centralized planning body, emphasized technology-intensive, non-polluting, non-energy-guzzling industries. Second, and more important, two key officials, Sun Yuanxuan and K. T. Li, took an interest in semiconductors.

Inspired by South Korean efforts to develop industrial technology at all costs, Sun Yunxuan proposed to set up the Industrial Technology Research Institute (ITRI), which was established in 1973 despite fierce opposition in the Legislative Yuan. Sun regarded semiconductors as a key industry. Backed by Chiang Ching-kuo, Sun resisted mounting opposition from within the government and in the society and created the integrated circuit (IC) project with NT$400 million in funding.[53] To ensure the project's success, he put the ITRI under the MOEA so he could protect it. Sun was also active, together with K. T. Li, in recruiting new personnel. He invited a number of overseas Chinese engineers to head the project.

Among them was Pan Wenyuan, an electrical engineer who had worked for RCA. Pan devised the blueprint for the industry and was the key person in charge of persuading overseas Chinese engineers working at Bell Labs, IBM, and various universities to form a Technical Advisory Committee (TAC) for the project in the United States.

K. T. Li also played an important role in this project. With his background in physics, Li had always been a strong proponent of high-tech development. As minister of finance, he supported Sun's efforts by providing funds and by recruiting personnel through his wide connections. As we have seen, after resigning as minister of finance, he was named minister without portfolio and put in charge of technology development. Li committed himself to promoting the development of the high-tech industry. Sun's direct involvement in the project ended after he became premier in 1979. Li was left as the only remaining strongman. He provided leadership in two respects. First, he recruited personnel and invited foreign advisers, led by Pat Haggerty, former board chairman of Texas Instruments. He also recruited Morris Chang, CEO of General Instruments and previously the head of chip production at Texas Instruments, to be the head of the ITRI and chairman of the joint state-private venture United Microelectronics (UMC) and later to be president of Taiwan Semiconductor (TSMC). Chang brought in state-of-the-art technical expertise, initiated the idea of a joint venture, and sold the idea to Phillips. Under his leadership, TSMC grew rapidly. Second, K. T. Li was critical in providing financing to TSMC. He persuaded the government Development Fund to invest $100 million in the venture, and he invited Phillips to take a 27.5 share of the corporation and domestic companies 24.2 percent, with the government retaining 48.3 percent.[54] Li's coordination in both these areas was pivotal to the development of the semiconductor industry.

Thus, there was neither state-led nor market-led development in the semiconductor industry. Neither the state nor the institutions played a role in solving the coordination problems. Rather, it was an individual, a man no longer at the center of economic policy making, who took on this task. What enabled him to accomplish this?

First, he enjoyed the political support of Chiang Ching-kuo and Sun Yunxuan. At the initial stage, Sun had also played a leadership role. Also, representing Chiang, the then-secretary-general of the Executive Yuan, Walter Fei, a senior bureaucrat who shared Sun's and Li's vision that technology was essential to Taiwan's continued development, was actively involved in coordinating the project. His high profile signaled Chiang's backing, and he was able to counter mounting opposition to the project.[55] After Sun was named premier in 1979, he provided Li all the support needed. As an engineer, Sun shared Li's view about the importance of technology in economic development. Sun also respected Li. According to Li, Chiang's attitude toward him changed completely after he resigned as minister of finance,[56] and Chiang began to implement Li's suggestions. He assigned Li to supervise the development of science and technology. Apparently once Li no longer posed a threat to him, Chiang began to trust him. Chiang's political support was a prerequisite for the development of the industry.

Second, Li's outspokenness and strong style had earned him a lot of respect. This charisma enabled him to invite foreign experts, recruit personnel, and attract domestic investment. He was also able to persuade Yu Guohua to support his project. As a banker, Yu knew little about technology and showed little interest in it. After Yu succeeded Sun as premier in 1984, support for the semiconductor and other high-tech projects decreased. However, in 1986 Li was able to persuade Yu to agree to set up the TSMC. Li's role in the semiconductor industry shows that a strongman with political support and charisma could play an important role in solving coordination problems that could not be resolved by institutions.

Implementation of the Project

Various government agencies and society expressed vocal opposition to the efforts to develop the semiconductor industry. The dissenting voices thought the project was too expensive and doubted Taiwan's ability to develop semiconductors. "Canada and England have tried and failed—how can we succeed?"[57] opponents asked.[58] Many lawmakers in the Legislative Yuan opposed Sun's proposal to set up the ITRI for fear that an institute would be autonomous from the government. The debate lasted for over a year, and the legislature finally rejected the proposal. The dispute even caused a split in the largest parliamentary faction.[59] But after steady lobbying, the proposal passed in 1973.

In addition to the part played by key officials, acceptance of the proposal owed much to overseas Chinese engineers and foreign advisers, and the independent research institutes and joint ventures initiated and funded by the government. Although funded by the government, the ITRI was organized as a corporation to ensure its independence and its freedom from bureaucratic proceedings. The ITRI became a major base for R&D. However, the most important institute for IC development was the Electronics Research Service Organization (ERSO). The ERSO was created in 1974 within the ITRI and was responsible for most of the local R&D. Until the early 1980s, the ERSO was funded entirely by the government. The significance of the ERSO in IC development was reflected in the continuous spin-offs of its staff, who left to establish their own companies. This resulted in a dispersion of IC technology and an expansion of the IC sector. This spread of knowledge differed greatly from that found in South Korea, where technology was transferred from research institutes directly to the large private conglomerates.[60]

Overseas Chinese engineers played a key role in Taiwan's IC development. Most of them worked for leading American high-tech companies, some of them as upper-level managers. They contributed state-of-the-art technology and expert advice on IC development to the government; some even returned to Taiwan to take up posts in the industry. The contributions of Pan Wenyuan and Morris Chang have already been noted. The TAC was organized in the United States, and its members met regularly to decide which U.S. companies would be invited to submit bids for a technology transfer agreement (the nod went to RCA). These overseas Chinese engineers received a great deal of attention from the government. When Pan was first invited to Taiwan to study ways to upgrade the industry, he met with Sun, Walter Fei, the minister of communications, and Chiang Ching-kuo. The decision to develop semiconductors was made by Sun and Fei at a breakfast meeting with Pan on a Sunday morning in February 1974.[61] Some foreign advisers, for example, Pat Haggerty, also played a constructive role in the semiconductor project. The Science and Technology Advisory Group (STAG), which was created in 1979 under the Executive Yuan, included, in addition to Haggerty, Fred Seitz (a key figure in semiconductors from Texas Instruments), Bob Evans (from IBM), and Mackay (given name unknown; from Bell Labs). Evans even steered the semiconductor industry in a more ambitious and competitive direction.[62]

The Private Sector and Semiconductors

In general, the private sector showed little interest in the semiconductor project until it proved itself to be profitable and promising. Initially the private sector viewed investment in the high-tech sector as too risky. When creating the UMC, the MOEA approached some leading electronics companies, such as Datong, Sampo, and Tiko, and tried, unsuccessfully, to interest them in investing. Eventually, the government had to "use its influence" to obtain contributions from them. One company still refused.[63] Consequently, the UMC was established as a joint state-private venture (the state holding 44 percent and the private sector 55 percent). But the real share of the private sector was only 30 percent. Because of the high risk, the private sector asked the ERSO to claim some of its shares.[64] Again, when the TSMC was established in 1987, Formosa Plastics Group bought some shares under pressure from the government. But Wang Yongqing sold them as soon as he could. Eight years later, after semiconductors had become a profitable industry, Formosa Plastics had to spend about U.S.$600 million to establish its own high-tech company.[65] As these examples show, the private sector in Taiwan could be conservative and lacking in vision.

Beginning in the mid-1980s, some private firms like Acer began to show increased interest in the high-tech industry. But the leading business groups did not follow them until the 1990s. The reluctance of the private sector forced the state to undertake entrepreneurial tasks on its own. Ironically, the state's activism was a

Table 7.1
Characteristics of Business Groups in Taiwan, South Korea, and Japan

Characteristic	Taiwan	South Korea	Japan
Number of groups	96	50	16
Total sales (in billions)	NT$634	54,663 *wŏn*	¥217,033
Equivalent U.S.$ (in billions)	U.S.$16.48	U.S.$68.32	U.S.$871.26
Number of firms	745	552	1,001
Firms/business group	7.8	11.0	62.6
Workers/firms	444	1,440	2,838
Percentage of total workforce	4.7%	5.5%	9.5%

NOTE: Data for Taiwan and Korea refer to 1983; for Japan, to 1982. Each country's largest groups are included. Japan's sixteen groups include the six major enterprise groups and the ten largest industrial groups.
SOURCE: Hamilton et al., "Enterprise Groups in East Asia," table 1; cited in Wade, *Governing the Market*, p. 68.

consequence of the private sector's refusal to play a role. Evans found a similar phenomenon in Brazil; there the initiative came from the state, and the early development of the computer industry was led by the state.[66]

Why did the private sector show so little entrepreneurial spirit vis-à-vis the high-tech industry? Why did the private firms view investing in semiconductors as extremely risky? First, the private sector lacked entrepreneurship, particularly the core requirement of being willing to undertake risk.[67] Even Wang Yongqing, who has been lauded as the "God of Management" in Taiwan, was short-sighted in this respect. There have been few explanations for this phenomenon, and it deserves further study. I postulate that the relatively small size of Taiwan's private firms is the primary reason. As shown in Table 7.1, Taiwan's business groups were much smaller than their South Korean and Japanese counterparts in terms of sales and workers. Their smallness undermined their ability and willingness to take risks. In contrast, the large scale of the South Korean conglomerates allowed them to risk investing vast amounts of money in semiconductors.[68]

The private sector's passivity and reluctance left the task of developing the high-tech industry to the state, and until the mid-1980s, all semiconductor projects in Taiwan were state-led. The state assumed this role because it viewed semiconductors as key to the industrial upgrading deemed critical for Taiwan's future development and because the private sector alone was unable to develop this industry due to its small scale and the lack of cooperation. The state had an advantage in terms of human resources, money, and coordination.[69] As a result, the state acted as sponsor as well as entrepreneur. Because the project formed the core of its industrial upgrading strategy, the state allocated funds and recruited the necessary personnel. The state-funded ITRI and ERSO undertook R&D. Until the late 1980s, all long-term projects of the ITRI were initiated by the state, not by the private sector. In the face of a lack of interest from the private sector, the state acted as an entrepreneur and became the major investor in UMC and induced the private sector to follow suit. The state's entrepreneurship remained crucial, given the absence of private investment. In this case, the problem was not a coordination failure but a market failure.[70] Although over the long term the government acted to resolve the coordination problems, in the initial stage it stood in for the market in the absence of the private sector.

However, the fate of the semiconductor project still hinged on the efforts of key officials. The state's role was characterized by its personal rather than institutional leadership. As noted above, some top bureaucrats with science or engineering backgrounds were the most important players in the semiconductor project. Using their power and influence, they made decisions, coordinated activities, and even provided protection. The weak institutional entities played only a negligible role. Furthermore, in order to avoid the bureaucracy, the key officials created independent research institutes free of government control. This project is a useful example of the role of the state in economic transformation. During this time the economic bureaucracy was undergoing decentralization and institutionalization, and economic institutions were redefining their roles and functions. The division of labor among institutions was unclear. Some senior and influential bureaucrats filled the resulting administrative vacuum and took on a leadership role. This was a special arena for bureaucrats who had left the center of policy making during the transformation. The active role of the strongmen compensated for the weaknesses of the economic institutions. However, when the institutionalization of the economic bureaucracy was completed in the late 1980s, institutions began to play their assigned role, thus ending the era of the strongmen.

The case of the semiconductor industry also shows that the state had to strengthen its social contacts in order to develop an industry. To upgrade industry, the state had to seek the cooperation of the private sector. This is why the state "invited" leading business groups to invest in the semiconductor industry. It is also the reason why officials forged links with overseas Chinese engineers and foreign advisers. In launching the project, imported personnel drew up the blueprints for the industry and headed the project. They compensated for the absence of a domestic private sector and provided key assistance to the state. Although the leading domestic business groups were initially reluctant, they were eventually "persuaded" by the government to take 30 to 40 percent of the shares of TSMC and UMC. Furthermore, the long-term development and expansion of the industry involved the private sector. Without the cooperation of the private sector, the state could hardly have realized its goals. In other words, in its efforts to promote the high-tech industry, the state needed the assistance and collaboration of the private sector.

Not only was the development of Taiwan's semiconductor industry state-led (or to be more precise, strongman-led), but also, unlike its Japanese and Korean counterparts, it was dominated by small companies rather than by conglomerates. As we have seen, the LEs were not interested in the semiconductor industry, and the method of technology transfer favored smaller rather than larger firms. Another factor was the cultural preference for being one's own boss rather than an employee; as we will see in Chapter 8, this played an important role in the development of the SMEs.

A final reason is government policy. The state had no intention of running the semiconductor industry. Although the project was orchestrated by the state, it did not want it to remain a state operation because of concerns about the efficiency of public enterprises. Even in the creation of the UMC, the state preferred a joint state-private venture. But the state also did not want to leave the semiconductor industry entirely to the LEs. It wanted the sector open to everyone, including the domestic private sector as well as overseas Chinese engineers and foreign corporations.

State incentives encouraged the creation of small- and medium-sized high-tech firms. In order to encourage private investment, the state adopted several measures. First, in 1980 it created the Xinzhu Science Park, which became the main base for Taiwan's high-tech industry. The firms within the park were entitled to a wide range of incentives, from tax cuts to low-interest loans to other government investment.[71] Second, the government provided financial incentives to high-tech firms, for example, by introducing the American practice of venture capital. A major strategy was to invite Chinese graduates of American universities to return to Taiwan to head these firms. Most of the firms in the science park were small enterprises created by Chinese who had been trained or had worked in the United States and who had returned to Taiwan because of patriotism and the attractions of the government's ambitious project. The government encouraged the emergence of these small firms by offering technical and financial assistance, in the hope that they would create a new niche for goods from Taiwan in the global market before the Japanese got there.[72]

As a result, rather than the vertically integrated conglomerates that dominate the high-tech industry in Japan and South Korea (e.g., Mitsubishi, Samsung, Daewoo, and Hyundai), there are numerous small design houses and manufacturing firms in Taiwan. Acer, a computer giant in Taiwan that entered the semiconductor field, began as a manufacturer of computers. With its distinctive industrial structure, Taiwan's semiconductor industry has competed successfully in the global market and has maintained its position as the world's third largest after the United States and Japan.

In the high-tech sector, we see a different marketplace from that found in the traditional industries. Rather than a dualistic or tripartite structure, the high-tech sector is well integrated, in no small part due to the significant change in the state's policy toward the private sector. The state ceased to be a policeman committed to safeguarding the division of labor among the SOEs, the LEs, and the SMEs. Unlike the marketplace for traditional industries, which was an unintended consequence of state actions, this new market-place was an intended outcome. What did remain unchanged, however, was that the state still did not purposely foster large enterprises in the high-tech industry. Rather than offering them special privileges, the state encouraged the LEs to invest in the IC sector. In the meantime, the state deliberately encouraged investment by individuals and small firms by offering various incentives. The emphasis was on recruiting young Chinese who had been educated or employed abroad. The state's changing role in the formation of the marketplace was a result of changes in the state's view of industrial development—the state was increasingly committed to integrated sectoral development. The motive behind this strategy was the belief of key officials like K. T. Li that it would give full play to Taiwan's comparative advantages because these young entrepreneurs knew state-of-the-art technology and many of them had connections with leading American companies. Largely for political reasons, the state practiced a policy of fostering small firms. This contrasted sharply with its previous policy toward the SMEs.

SOEs and the Industrial Structure

Definition of SOEs

In 1987, Taiwan's huge public sector accounted for 20.8 percent of domestic gross capital formation. As we saw in Chapter 3, this public sector originated in confiscated Japanese assets, assets transported from the mainland, and assets established in the postwar period. Despite the extremely complex ownership of the public sector,[73] the state-owned enterprises can be roughly divided into those operated by the military (run by the Vocational Assistance Commission for Retired Servicemen); the KMT (run by a special party body); and the government (run by various levels of government). The military and party firms were involved in intermediate and downstream industries, finance, construction, services, and facilities. They were independent of the economic planning agencies.

The public sector performed five important functions for the state: it controlled the economy and secured the state's power; it

Table 7.2
Linkages Between Upstream, Intermediate, and Downstream
Sectors in the Petrochemical Industry

Sector	Production	Input	Output
I	Naphtha cracker		Petrochemical materials
II	Chemical materials	Feedstock	Raw materials — for plastics —synthetic fibers —synthetic rubbers
III	Downstream	Output from II	Plastic products Synthetic fibers and textiles Rubber products

SOURCE: Wan-wen Chu, "Import Substitution and Export-Led Growth," p. 783.

provided revenues; it prevented the penetration of foreign capital and safeguarded economic independence; it could be used to reward political followers and bureaucrats; and it was an ideological symbol.[74] A number of studies have called attention to the significance of the public sector in the economy.[75]

For the purposes of this book, it is the role of the SOEs in the industrial structure that is important. I am referring to those upstream enterprises established in the 1960s and 1970s and run by the MOEA, such as the CPC and China Steel Corporation. Their significance is that they controlled the upstream sectors and played a key role in the formation and persistence of the industrial structure. In the petrochemical industry, there was a complete vertical linkage of upstream and downstream industries (see Table 7.2). The primary sector (Sector I in Table 7.2) was dominated by the SOEs, and the secondary sector by the LEs. The downstream sectors were run by the SMEs and manufactured Taiwan's major export products. The following section uses the petrochemical industry to examine the role of SOEs in the industrial structure and the relationship between state–private sector interactions and the development of the petrochemical sector.

SOEs and the Development of the Petrochemical Industry

This historical summary of the petrochemical industry in Taiwan is based on Wan-wen Chu's careful and thorough case study.[76] In the 1950s, the IDC promoted some chemical-related industrial projects, for instance, plastics, cement, glass, and fertilizer. Many of them, for example, Formosa Plastics, which produced PVCs, became LEs in the following decades. However, Formosa Plastics used calcium carbide not petroleum in its production processes, and hence technically it was not part of the petrochemical industry. Taiwan's petrochemical industry really began only in 1968. The petrochemical industry was favored by the government in the early 1960s and was listed as a key project in the Fourth Four-Year Plan (1965–68). During this period, CPC was considering the possibility of establishing a naphtha-cracking plant. However, it was unsuccessful because it could not find intermediate firms to absorb the upstream petrochemical materials it produced. No private enterprise showed any interest in investing in the intermediate sectors. The economic planning agency's principle was that CPC was responsible only for upstream production, and it left the intermediate industries to the private sector. There were two reasons for this policy: the government was committed to fostering the private sector, and it had fears about the marketing weaknesses of the SOEs. Hence, it assumed that the SOEs would be unable to set up linkages between the intermediate and the downstream sectors.

Although local enterprises showed no interest in investing in the intermediate industries, an American company, the National Distillers and Chemical Corporation (NDCC), was optimistic about Taiwan's future development and established a plant to absorb the output of the CPC's first naphtha-cracking plant. However, it could absorb only three-fifths of the production. Despite the potential for excess capacity, the CPC went ahead and established its naphtha-cracking plant. The government became involved because it thought the petrochemical industry was strategic for Taiwan's industrial development, since there already existed a solid downstream base. Meanwhile, in order to absorb the other two-fifths of the production, the MOEA and the CPC invited four private firms that were already producing PVCs, including Formosa Plastics, to set up a joint venture. These four firms had previously used the acetylene process to produce PVCs. Subsequently, they adopted the oxychlorination process and used vinyl chloride monomers (VCMs); this marked their entry into the petrochemical sector. The CPC did not earn a profit from the first plant, but the NDCC operation entered the black in 1968.

The MOEA and CPC began to plan a second naphtha-cracking plant in 1971. After their experience with the first plant, they did not expect an enthusiastic reaction from the private sector, and they planned to set up intermediate-stream SOEs to absorb the output of the second plant. But the reaction of the private sector was more positive than expected. The first naphtha-cracking plant had revealed the government's commitment to promoting the petrochemical industry. Moreover, the intermediate industries were expected to be profitable, and the government's plan to develop the petrochemical industry was seen as feasible. Consequently, eight plants joined the intermediate industries (one public, two public-private joint ventures, and five private). The CPC transferred many projects that it had originally planned to run by itself to the private enterprises after they showed strong interest.

The inclusion of the petrochemical industry in the Ten Major Development Projects, coupled with the government's commitment to develop a petrochemical industry as reflected in the building of the first two cracking plants, and the successful experience of those private firms already in the intermediate sectors, showed that the risk was within acceptable limits and these industries could be profitable. Meanwhile, the first oil crisis caused the prices of petrochemical products to soar. Because of all these factors, the attitude of the private sector toward the petrochemical industry was reversed. Consequently, when the CPC began studying a third cracking plant, it received 54 applications to set up intermediate-stream plants. It had no choice but to reject some of them. Formosa Plastics Corporation even applied to set up a cracking plant, but its application was rejected by the MOEA. Minister Sun Yunxuan gave two reasons for the rejection. First, oil refining was a source of government revenue, and it was required for defense materials; hence it should be run by the state. Second, the government had to prevent unfair competition. Basic raw materials could not be monopolized by the private sector, because this would threaten the downstream SMEs. The irony is that although the third cracking plant was completed in 1976, it could not begin operations until 1978 because many enterprises withdrew their plans when both the international petrochemical industry and Taiwan's domestic economy fell into a depression. Even so, the number of enterprises investing in intermediate projects increased steadily. As we saw earlier in this chapter, the growing private sector soon began to challenge the SOEs. Thereafter, the state's industrial policy subtly switched from encouraging and fostering the private sector to restricting it.

The Role of SOEs in the Industrial Structure

By undertaking upstream projects, the SOEs acted as pioneers and models in creating industries that the state viewed as critical to the entire economy. In these projects, the state acted not only as an organizer, designer, and coordinator but also as an entrepreneur. The presence of SOEs was a necessary condition for the birth of these capital- and technology-intensive industries. The private sector was unwilling to take the risk until the SOEs resolved the externalities, the state promoted the industries, and the industries demonstrated the prospects for profit. At the initial stage, the state and the SOEs had an overwhelming advantage in terms of information and technology, and they were in a position to resolve the informational asymmetry, which should have been the task of private institutions.[77] For instance, in the case of the petrochemical industry, SOEs not only provided engineers and managers but also, together with related government departments like the MOEA and the IDB, supplied information and knowledge to private enterprises. Wanwen Chu argued that without the SOEs, there would have been no petrochemical industry.[78] The CPC's cracking plants were policy- rather than profit-driven. Since the purpose of the first cracking plant was to help develop the industry, profits were not among its goals. The CPC made up for the losses of the first plant with profits from its other operations. In the semiconductor industry the ITRI and the ERSO played a role similar to that of the CPC. They undertook R&D and provided engineers for the private sector. Without them, Taiwan's semiconductor industry would not exist in its present form.

The SOEs played this role for two reasons. First, these were industries targeted for development as strategic industries. The CPC's cracking plants were intended to create intermediate sectors so as to establish a complete vertical industrial linkage. The task of the ITRI and ERSO was to promote a new industry that could not have been developed solely by the private sector. Second, these industries provided economic rents that could be used to gain political support. This was especially true in the petrochemical industry. Most of the LEs in the intermediate industries were leading business groups that were traditional supporters of the KMT. In exchange for their support, the KMT used the SOEs to provide rents. In addition, in some cases, the sacrifices on the part of the SOEs helped the KMT financially. In the petrochemical case, KMT capital was among the beneficiaries when the CPC forfeited its own profits to compensate the intermediate operators.

Moreover, the SOEs created strong forward linkages by inducing and nurturing the intermediate LEs. The economic planning agency was committed to fostering private firms in the intermediate sectors and thus established a boundary for the SOEs—they were to stay in the upstream sectors. This policy was based on efficiency considerations. MOEA officials believed that private enterprises would outperform the SOEs in the intermediate sectors because they could link to the downstream sectors. Even though the government had to establish intermediate firms to absorb the upstream products when there was no private interest, this changed as soon as the private sector showed interest.

As it had during the era of import substitution in the 1950s, the state fostered and protected the intermediate LEs. It did this by restricting imports of petrochemicals and by forcing the downstream firms to purchase intermediate products from domestic producers through tariff controls and pricing policies.[79] These measures ensured the absorption of the output of the intermediate producers.

Meanwhile, the government encouraged competition among the intermediate LEs. It did this by setting relatively low entry barriers through the distribution of the intermediate projects. It allowed as many firms as possible. This strategy enhanced the LEs' competitiveness.[80]

Backward linkage does not mean that the sequence went from the downstream sectors to the intermediate stream sector to the upstream sectors. In fact, a large number of downstream SME producers first became export producers; the state then set up the upstream SOEs, which created a forward linkage and led to the establishment of the intermediate-stream LEs, thus completing the industrial structure. Wan-wen Chu finds that in the case of the petrochemical industry, "the sequence of events is clear, that is, sector III developed first, sector I next, and sector II last" (see Table 7.2).[81] Therefore, the SOEs were critical to the formation of a division of labor. This was the case in the petrochemical industry and in other industries as well.

The SOEs also blocked the upward expansion of private enterprises. When the economic planning agency decided to develop the petrochemical and steel industries, it had no intention of placing these projects in the hands of the private sector. Although the state originally planned to leave the steel project in the hands of the private sector, it did not intend to let it be run by individual private firms. Instead, it invited a number of firms to invest in the project in order to prevent a single firm from having a monopoly. As we have seen, the reasons for this included revenue and defense consideration, as well as the desire to prevent unfair competition. After the private enterprises had grown and had enough muscle to challenge the SOEs, the state used the SOEs to block their efforts to move up. This shows that the state's intention was to maintain the SOEs' control over the upstream industries. There were increasing conflicts between the SOEs and the LEs as the latter attempted to break the SOEs' monopolies. In the intermediate sectors, the state allowed as many entrants as possible not only to stimulate competition but also to guard against monopolies. Although this was criticized as a policy failure because it led to poor integration of the upstream and intermediate sectors in Taiwan's petrochemical industry, in fact this was an intentional part of state strategy. Although the state agreed to let the Integrated Steel Plant be run by the private sector, it wanted it to be operated by a number of firms instead of one single firm. This contrasts with South Korea's "one item, one firm" principle for promoting the petrochemical industry.[82]

This suggests that the state not only restricted the LEs by policy, law, and regulations, as shown in the previous chapters, but also used the upstream SOEs to constrain the LEs. Thus, the state's capacity in Taiwan to regulate the marketplace derived both from resources, instruments, and institutions and from the upstream SOEs. The state was able to design and police the industrial structure through the upstream SOEs. However, it is worth noting that this did not occur in the semiconductor and computer industries because, beginning in the late 1970s, the state grew more committed to integrated industrial development.

Conclusion

Due to the internal and external political and economic challenges that arose from the mid-1970s to the mid-1980s, the state had to alter its strategy of being disengaged from society and adopt a more open policy. Politically, the state tried to reinforce its rule by expanding political participation, especially by co-opting native Taiwanese into the ruling party, rather than by strengthening its political grip. It is striking that the state rewarded supporters with economic rents even as it punished challengers. The extension of state assistance to the SMEs was not based solely on economic considerations. Rather, it was a move based on political considerations as well. Taiwanization was an option the leadership and the regime had to accept. Chiang Ching-kuo's efforts to Taiwanize both himself and the regime reflected the inevitability of this trend. In the face of political challenges, the state not only subordinated its economic policies to its political concerns, but also changed its economic policies when its political concerns changed.

During this period, the economic bureaucracy was undergoing decentralization and institutionalization. This transformation had an impact on the economic policy process and on relations with the private sector. But since the economic institutions were not fully functional, veteran bureaucrats stepped in to fill the vacuum and played key roles in promoting the high-tech industry.

This chapter has shown the inadequacy of the selective industrial policy account of Taiwan's success and argues that the existence of the strongman was a critical determinant in the accomplishments of Taiwan's industrial policy. The strongman's ability to solve coordination problems was critical to policy formulation and implementation. Equally crucial to the success of Taiwan's industrial policy were the state's ability to minimize risk and its design of policies.

The SOEs' role in the industrial structure was crucial. They were pioneers and models in industries critical to the growth of Taiwan's economy. They blocked the LEs' upward expansion and also provided economic rents to the LEs in exchange for political support. In addition to the resources, policy instruments, and institutions cited as sources of the East Asian states' capacity to intervene in the economy, the SOEs in Taiwan were an effective state tool for designing and policing the marketplace.

The state changed its policy toward the SMEs in new industries, such as semiconductors and computers, by deliberately promoting them as main players. Rather than pick "winners," the state was committed to creating a marketplace in which winners could emerge. In its efforts to promote the semiconductor industry, the state allowed entry to all potential incomers. This change indicates that the state was committed to promoting integrated sectoral development. This change affected the formation of the marketplace for these new industries—the dual market structure found in traditional industries did not appear in these new industries. Unlike the dual market structure, which was largely an accidental consequence of state action, this integrated marketplace was an intended result of state design.

CHAPTER 8

State, Market, and SME Success

The SMEs have been the backbone of Taiwan's impressive success as an exporter, which in turn has been the engine of Taiwan's industrialization. From 1981 to 1985, for example, the SMEs accounted for over 60 percent of the value of exports (see Table 8.1). If we compare Taiwan to South Korea and Japan, the significance of the SMEs in the economy is even more striking. In Japan and South Korea, the conglomerates contributed the greater part of GNP and provided most of the final products for export. In 1983 in South Korea, for example, 70 percent of exports were generated by the top ten business groups.[1] Given the importance of the SMEs in the Taiwanese economy, the analytical challenge is to find an explanation for their success. The pivotal questions are What enabled the SMEs to flourish? How much of their success can be attributed to state policy? Is there a significant link between the state and the SMEs? If so, is the link direct and explicit: for example, by virtue of an effective SME public policy, by the provision of credit, and so forth? Or is it indirect and implicit—the unintended consequences of state strategies that did not have the SMEs or economic goals as their foremost concern? The success of the SMEs also challenges statist analyses, in which the SMEs' accomplishments are ignored, or at least downplayed.

This chapter attempts to answer these questions. At the heart of the argument is the contention that the principal effect of state action was to exclude the big firms—the LEs and SOEs—from the export markets. The SMEs stepped into the resulting vacuum. In this sense, the state's actions created the necessary condition for the successes of the SMEs as exporters, but, and this is the nub of the argument, state action is not a sufficient explanation for the SMEs' success. Although freed from competition from their larger domestic rivals, they still faced formidable international competition in the export markets. The argument presented here is that the SMEs mobilized an array of "societal goods" to offset their disadvantages and that the industrial production system they consequently formed was the source of their success.

The chapter begins by summarizing the role of the SMEs in Taiwan's economy. It then discusses the state's public policy toward SMEs and explores how the state's political strategies and public policies relate to the success of the SMEs. Finally, it analyzes how production modes, labor costs, cultural traits, cooperative networks, and international connections contributed to the extraordinary performance of the SMEs.

The Role of the SMEs

The SMEs have been vital to Taiwan's economy in terms of the total number of businesses, workers, the value of production, and exports. Tables 8.1 through 8.2 provide an indication of their importance. The SMEs accounted for the overwhelming majority of Taiwan's enterprises, over 98 percent of the total number of enterprises (even though their numbers declined from 99.6 percent of the total in 1961 to 98.5 percent in 1985). They accounted for 44.9 percent of the entire value of production in 1976 and 47.6 percent in 1984. They employed 61 percent of all workers in 1976. And they contributed roughly two-thirds of the value of exports from 1981 to 1985 (see Table 8.1). [2] In short, the SMEs were so important to the economy that it is impossible to understand Taiwan's economic "miracle" unless we can explain their success.

How can we explain the success of the SMEs? Statism fails to do this because, by and large, it ignores the SMEs. On the other hand, authors who stress the role of society are perhaps too quick to dismiss the role of the state in the success of the SMEs. [3] For a more balanced view, we need to re-examine what the state has done for the SMEs.

Table 8.1
Amount of Exports by SMEs and Their Percentage
Shares of All Exports, 1981–85

Year	Manufacturers		Traders		Total	
	Amount (U.S.$ million)	Percentage	Amount ($U.S. million)	Percentage	Amount ($U.S. million)	Percentage
1981	$10,559	71.8%	$4,832	61.1%	$15,391	68.1%
1982	10,613	73.5	4,858	62.5	15,471	69.7
1983	10,926	66.9	5,001	56.9	15,927	63.4
1984	12,379	62.5	5,666	53.2	18,045	59.2
1985	12,897	64.6	5,903	54.9	18,800	61.2

NOTES: The percentages are the proportion of exports contributed by SMEs to the entire amount of exports each year. The amount of total exports in 1981 was U.S.$22,611 million; in 1982, U.S.$22,204 million; in 1983, U.S.$25,122 million; in 1984, U.S.$30,456 million; and in 1985, U.S.$30,717 million.

The amount of exports by SMEs was equal to what was left after subtracting the exports of manufacturing firms with more than NT$40 million in capital and subtracting the exports of trading firms whose business earnings were above NT$40 million.

SOURCE: Jingjibu, Zhongxiao qiyechu, *Zhongxiao qiye tongji*, p. 234.

State Policy Toward the SMEs

SME Policy Before the Mid-1970s

Until the mid-1970s, there was no SME policy in Taiwan. The small and fragmented size of the SME sector limited its political influence; consequently, it was virtually ignored by the state. The state made no deliberate, systematic efforts to promote the SMEs, and economic measures directed at the SMEs were uneven and sporadic. In short, the SMEs received little assistance from the government, and the relationship between the state and the SMEs was the most ambiguous part of state-business relations in Taiwan.

In the 1950s, almost all private firms were small. The only large firms were the SOEs. During the period of import substitution industrialization, the state based its decisions to foster certain sectors and private enterprises on their ability to save or earn foreign exchange or the amount of political support they could offer or

Table 8.2
Percentage of Domestic Sales and Exports
of Products by SMEs, 1972–85

Year	Domestic sales	Exports	Business income
1972	44.3%	55.7%	100.0%
1973	46.6	53.4	100.0
1974	57.0	43.0	100.0
1975	47.0	53.9	100.0
1976	42.8	57.2	100.0
1977	46.5	53.5	100.0
1978	43.3	56.7	100.0
1979	41.0	59.0	100.0
1980	33.3	66.7	100.0
1981	25.2	74.8	100.0
1982	24.1	75.9	100.0
1983	26.7	73.3	100.0
1984	28.2	71.8	100.0
1985	28.9	71.1	100.0

NOTE: Figures may not total to 100.0 percent because of rounding.
SOURCE: Zhou Tiancheng, "Quanli bianchui de zhongxiao qiye," p. 115.

muster. Under the benevolent protection of the state, a number of private enterprises developed into major firms. This practice led to close connections between the government and these favored firms, most of which developed into leading business groups in subsequent decades. When policy shifted decisively toward emphasizing the export market, rather than privileging or deliberately fostering a few large enterprises, as was done in South Korea after 1963, the state lowered entry barriers across the board. As Karl Fields has noted: "In Taiwan, the incentive structure for all exporters—big or small, manufacturer or specialized trader—was virtually the same."[4]

The government, however, did not expect the SMEs to become exporters, and it did nothing to encourage them. Moreover, because of their organizational shortcomings, the SMEs were not positioned to take advantage of the incentives aimed at promoting industrial development. For example, the 1960 Statute for the Encouragement of Investment, a major export-promotion act, limited incentives for SMEs. First, the statute was applicable only to limited-liability companies, and most SMEs were unincorporated family businesses. Even as late as 1985, about 70 percent of the SMEs were sole proprietorships.[5] As a result, the overwhelming majority of the SMEs did not quality for the incentives. Second, except in certain technology-intensive industries such as machinery, electrical tools, electronics, and organic chemicals, the statute, mainly through tax exemptions and tax cuts, attempted to encourage expansion of the scale of production to increase economies of scale; for this purpose, it required a minimum level of productivity. This also excluded many of the remaining SMEs.[6] Furthermore, the Stocks Act and the Bank Act also included many clauses unfavorable to the SMEs.[7]

To exacerbate matters, even when the incentives, such as the export tax rebates, were applicable to the SMEs, the operators of the SMEs were often unaware of their existence. In a seminar conducted by the government to inform business people about government economic policies, one official was surprised to find that many exporters did not know about the incentives but were still able to export.[8] We can draw two conclusions from this: the implementation of state policy was not necessarily effective, and the SMEs were more than able to export without the state's assistance.

Since state "guidance" of the SMEs is commonly supposed to be an important part of the government's SME policy, it deserves a closer look. Before the 1970s, there was little systematic government guidance of the SMEs. The Rules of Guidance for SMEs were first promulgated in 1967. Until 1964, there was no government agency devoted to helping the SMEs. In that year, a working group on small businesses was set up under the CIECD to provide assistance and advice to export-oriented SMEs. However, it had few clients. When the IDB was established in 1970, in cooperation with other related economic and financial agencies, it set up the United Service Center, based in the MOEA. The center's assistance was limited to manufacturing and processing SMEs, and it focused on funds, technology, and sales. Since the SMEs were not a major concern of the state, the personal views of the officials played a major role in the implementation of SME-related measures. For example, the Department of Small Business Guidance, which was created in 1966 on the initiative of officials within the CIECD, was disbanded in 1973 when the CIECD was replaced by the EPB.

The state's indifference toward the SMEs was also reflected in industrial finance. Although access to banks had always been a difficult problem for the SMEs, the state undertook no substantial measures to improve it. It was not until 1974 that the Fund for Credit Guarantees was set up to insure SMEs loans from banks and not until 1976 that banks specifically for SMEs began to be established (for more on the provision of industrial finance to the SME sector, see below).

SME Policy After the Mid-1970s

The state began to devise an SME policy in the mid-1970s in response to the legitimacy crisis and the economic difficulties caused by the oil crises. As we saw in the preceding chapter, to meet these crises, the KMT regime expanded political participation and engaged in Taiwanization. Chiang Ching-kuo also sought to Taiwanize himself to legitimate his succession.

The change in relations with the private sector was an important part of the state's strategy for overcoming the political and economic crises. As one element in this strategy, the state modified its policy on SMEs and began paying attention to them. Politically, this served the strategy of Taiwanization. We have no data on the geographical origins of SME owners, but there is no doubt that, because of their local connections, they were overwhelmingly Taiwanese. In addition, the SMEs, both in urban and in rural areas, were very much grass-roots entities. Therefore, winning their support was crucial for resolving the regime's legitimacy crisis.

There were also economic considerations behind the new SME policy. Over the previous decade, the SMEs had proven their economic significance as export champions. The rapid economic growth that accompanied export-driven industrialization enabled the government to stake a new claim on legitimacy at a time of internal political skepticism and external diplomatic crises. Equally important as the vanguard of the export drive (whatever the state's contribution to their success), the SMEs were a critical source of foreign exchange—a geopolitically sensitive issue for the internationally beleaguered Taiwan. International competitiveness was another consideration. From the 1970s on, Taiwan's labor-intensive exports encountered growing competition from low-wage countries. By helping the SMEs, the state hoped to maintain Taiwan's international competitiveness. This became a "joint project," to borrow Peter Evans's term,[9] of the state and the SMEs.

In terms of both economic growth and political stability, the SMEs had become significant to the state. They could no longer be ignored in public policy. The implications of this shift were profound and wide-ranging.

As a number of private enterprises developed into business groups in the early 1970s, the LEs became increasingly influential. As we have seen, the state both increased rents to the LEs to win their political support and thwarted their attempts at upward expansion. It soon became apparent to political leaders that the SMEs could counterbalance the influence of the LEs. Thus, overcoming the legitimacy crisis and economic difficulties was not the only reason Chiang Ching-kuo repeatedly emphasized the importance of formulating an SME policy. On various occasions in the late 1970s, Chiang called for government officials and public banks to provide assistance to the SMEs.[10] In 1973 Sun Yunxuan said that the main reason for preventing the business groups from obtaining a monopoly over the upstream petrochemical industries was to protect the interests of the downstream SMEs. Formosa Plastics, for example, might supply its own downstream firms first if there were a shortage of materials; this would, Sun explained, constitute unfair competition.[11]

Consequently, the state dramatically changed its policy on SMEs and began to encourage them. If the industrial structure and the SMEs were the unanticipated consequences of state political strategies and public policy, the KMT began to safeguard the industrial structure once it realized that this structure could serve its own interests. Against this background, a more systematic and coherent public policy toward the SMEs began to evolve, particularly in the areas of financing and institutional support.

The state's first move was to establish the Credit Guarantee Fund for Small and Medium Businesses in 1974, because of the public banks' unwillingness to provide loans to the SMEs. The fund was a corporate body charged with providing credit guarantees to promising SMEs that lacked collateral and with helping them receive loans from banks. By reducing the banks' risks, the fund would, it was thought, make them more willing to loan to the SMEs. The fund's assets were provided by the government-owned banks. Initially, the fund backed each loan with a 50–70 percent credit guarantee. Beginning in 1979, this was increased to 80–90 percent. In other words, the risk to the banks was only 10–20 percent. The fund provided guarantees to four categories of business: production units, general businesses, small commercial businesses, and start-ups by young entrepreneurs.

The fund had an effect. Until the end of June 1979, there were 23,957 guaranteed loans, for a total of NT$11,577,426. From 1974 to 1990, 63,738 SMEs were aided by the fund, and NT$665 billion in loans were guaranteed. To the end of June 1979, machinery, textiles, chemicals, electronics, and plastics were the top five sectors that benefited from the fund. These sectors were also Taiwan's major exporters. In 1989, the top five sectors were machinery and metals (16.8 percent), general trading (15.6 percent), electrical machinery and electronics (9.7 percent), imports and exports (9.0 percent), and textiles and garments (8.3 percent).[12] The significance of the fund should not be overstated, however. First, the fund was not widely known among SMEs. A survey of over 3,000 SMEs in 1990 found that 28 percent of them had never heard of the fund, whereas 48 percent had heard of it but had never taken advantage of it.[13] Second, the banks did not fully recognize the authority and reliability of the fund. For 42 percent of the loans the banks had asked the fund to provide full collateral, and in 32 percent of the cases they had asked for the difference between the collateral offered by the borrower and the full collateral.[14] This is indicative of the extreme conservatism of Taiwan's banks, but the banks' discounting of the fund's credit guarantees shows that they did not take the fund seriously. Third, some of the rules governing uses of the fund, for instance, the percentage of guarantees and the fees for guarantees, limited it from taking a more active role.

The state's second move was to create banks specifically for the SMEs. Beginning in 1976, all eight of the cooperative savings companies began to be restructured into banks for small and medium businesses. One of the eight, the Taiwan Bank for Small-Medium Business, was owned by the provincial government; the other seven were privately owned regional savings companies. Ironically, it was not the MOF's original intent to restructure these old-fashioned, poor-quality savings cooperatives into banks for SMEs. The ministry had hoped these cooperatives would become banks serving a particular region (a county or a city), somewhat like most American banks, because these savings cooperatives were not qualified to be banks. However, this plan was strongly opposed by the shareholders of the cooperatives because some of them had already expanded beyond their local regions. The president of one cooperative was the speaker of the provincial legislature, and he had strong political connections. He successfully pressured the Executive Yuan to overturn the MOF's plan and to agree that all local savings cooperatives be restructured into banks for SMEs along the example of the publicly owned Taiwan Bank for Small-Medium Business.[15] According to the revised Bank Act, these banks "are to provide SMEs with medium and long-term credits and help them improve their plant, financial structure, and management."[16] The MOF mandated that 70 percent of the total amount loaned by these banks be given to the SMEs.

Bank loans to SMEs are shown in Table 8.3. From 1981 to 1984, the banks for SMEs did fulfill the requirement of making over 70 percent of their loans to SMEs. Only a small percentage of the loans made by the state-owned banks went to SMEs; the three commercial banks owned by the provincial government, the Cooperative Bank of Taiwan, and the private Commercial Bank of Overseas Chinese directed half to two-thirds of their loans to the SMEs. The state-owned banks had fewer relations with the SMEs than the non-state-owned banks. However, in terms of aggregate totals, the SME banks accounted for only about 25 percent of the amount loaned, and the other banks combined for about 75 percent. In other words, most loans to SMEs came from ordinary

Table 8.3
Banks' Total Accumulated Loans to SMEs, 1981–84
(NT$)

Bank	1981 Loans to SMEs	1981 Percentage of all loans	1982 Loans to SMEs	1982 Percentage of all loans	1983 Loans to SMEs	1983 Percentage of all loans	1984 Loans to SMEs	1984 Percentage of all loans
Bank of Communications	$1,213,570	2.30%	$1,729,023	2.62%	$2,563,655	3.23%	$3,355,659	3.96%
China Farmers Bank	2,868,711	8.28	2,985,505	8.25	4,334,139	9.85	5,752,916	9.76
China Central Trust	466,759	2.82	586,050	2.81	497,651	2.51	333,369	1.68
China Bank of Imports and Exports	247,975	3.23	342,440	7.05	217,164	2.68	231,922	2.74
Bank of Taiwan	16,308,114	12.85	18,726,928	12.31	20,524,211	12.13	21,330,566	11.92
Taipei City Bank	4,895,559	9.46	5,440,799	10.10	5,561,671	9.74	6,428,835	9.78
Gaoxiong City Bank	—	—	716,371	22.36	1,256,468	20.53	1,211,629	20.50
Taiwan Land Bank	5,098,118	7.05	7,282,043	5.67	7,934,492	5.48	7,272,663	4.42
Taiwan Cooperative Bank	35,221,467	42.11	44,209,570	42.28	63,372,420	44.05	78,249,791	44.05
First Commercial Bank	45,992,921	59.52	56,968,318	64.03	65,631,389	65.53	76,350,621	66.33
Chang-hua Bank	44,947,957	64.19	48,747,191	65.83	58,446,849	67.77	63,660,886	67.53
Hua-nan Bank	40,702,628	61.29	47,315,740	63.38	58,392,090	64.80	65,427,838	65.52
China Bank of International Commerce	3,505,160	7.71	3,631,729	7.22	3,207,351	7.04	2,915,044	7.61

Shanghai Commercial & Savings Bank	436,647	14.63	712,086	23.36	568,680	15.32	1,641,735	35.49
Overseas Chinese Bank	4,313,313	40.94	4,949,205	41.71	6,490,836	47.87	5,572,627	40.31
Shihua United Bank	2,165,634	12.78	3,505,087	22.02	3,700,148	22.52	3,220,117	15.06
Taiwan Bank for SMEs	29,037,424	77.86	38,987,625	78.76	59,230,844	81.28	72,905,166	83.03
Taipei Regional Bank for SMEs	8,285,523	78.62	9,957,357	75.06	12,649,813	75.01	15,131,668	73.80
Xinzhu Regional Bank for SMEs	3,531,882	73.02	4,951,858	73.25	5,913,585	73.66	7,797,201	75.28
Taizhong Regional Bank for SMEs	6,137,300	89.40	8,526,746	88.67	10,499,366	87.74	12,430,516	81.76
Tainan Regional Bank for SMEs	2,741,799	73.49	3,230,645	73.05	3,967,465	73.50	4,933,810	73.50
Gaoxiong Regional Bank for SMEs	2,618,469	74.23	3,122,156	79.38	3,380,693	73.81	4,424,479	75.26
Taidong Regional Bank for SMEs	711,634	81.11	428,456	50.89	637,129	70.02	910,409	70.08
Hualian Regional Bank for SMEs	252,870	37.62	621,159	76.11	731,660	73.17	897,196	73.94
TOTAL	262,701,434	32.60	317,674,087	32.50	399,709,900	34.76	462,386,663	35.54
Foreign banks	3,684,206	4.12	3,494,734	3.99	3,086,592	3.53	3,006,396	3.45

SOURCE: Chung-hua Institution for Economic Research, *Zhongxiao qiye rongzi zhi yanjiu*, p. 63.

banks rather than from SME banks. This suggests that the role of the SME banks in funding industry should not be overestimated.

The third measure taken by the state to strengthen its SME policy was the establishment of the Department of Small and Medium Business (DSMB) under the MOEA in 1982 as its top administrative body for the SMEs. This move signaled that SME policy was becoming institutionalized and SME guidance more positive and systematic. The DSMB provided collective guidance to sectors rather than to individual firms. Even though the DSMB did not function well because of its organizational shortcomings and a lack of staff (see Chapter 7),[17] it was more active in the early years of its existence. Government policy toward the SMEs became more systematic and positive after the mid-1970s only in comparison with previous years. By international standards, even in recent years, SME policy was far from consistent and systematic and the organs meant to guide SMEs suffered from insufficient funding, power, and staffing.[18]

Another step in the state's effort to provide institutional support to the SMEs was the establishment of the United Service Center. The center was founded in 1982 with funds donated by seven banks owned by the provincial government to provide assistance and advice to SMEs involved in strategic industries as well as other promising enterprises. Since unsound accounting procedures and poor financial management were common problems for SMEs, the center focused on providing training in these areas. It also helped them obtain loans. The center maintained close contacts with the DSMB, the MOEA, the Credit Guarantee Fund, and the Taiwan Bank for Small-Medium Business. The center's performance was not impressive, however. First, the center's suggestions were only "recommendations," and the banks did not necessarily accept its guidance. Moreover, the SMEs distrusted advice from the center. The center consulted on 98 cases in 1983, 48 in 1984, and 46 in 1985.[19] It is fair to say that its role was limited and declining.

Since financing had always been a major problem for the SMEs, the effect of the state's efforts to aid the SMEs can be tested by the provision of industrial finance. Generally, from 1983 to 1990, loans

Table 8.4
Percentage of Loans to SMEs by Banks, 1983–90
(%)

Year	Ordinary domestic banks	SME-specialized banks	Total domestic banks	Foreign banks
1983	29.30%	88.75%	34.76%	3.53%
1984	29.92	88.58	35.54	3.54
1985	31.19	84.66	36.00	3.82
1986	32.10	82.73	37.17	4.37
1987	35.42	79.16	40.19	11.23
1988	37.83	76.95	41.95	16.19
1989	36.61	74.37	40.74	18.68
1990	36.80	75.46	41.46	20.77

SOURCE: Chung-hua Institution for Economic Research, *Zhongxiao qiye rongzi zhi yanjiu*, p. 144.

from ordinary domestic banks to SMEs never exceeded 38 percent of their total amount of loans (see Table 8.4). When loans from the SME banks are added in, the percentage is still below 42 percent. The equivalent figure for Japanese banks is 50 percent. Considering the higher proportion of SMEs in Taiwan than in Japan, the proportion of bank loans to SMEs can be regarded as fairly low. Seemingly, the Taiwanese SMEs had more difficulty gaining access to bank loans than their Japanese counterparts.

Clearly, the state did implement a wide range of measures to improve its SME policy beginning in the mid-1970s, and its policy began to be more systematic and coherent. However, although the state adopted a systematic SME policy in the mid-1970s, figures from 1976 show that the SMEs had already achieved a level of success *before* there was an SME policy. The SMEs' share of the value of production was 44.9 percent in 1976, and from 1981 to 1985, the SMEs' share of exports varied between 59.2 percent and 69.7 percent (see Table 8.1). To what extent, then, was the SMEs' outstanding performance attributable to state policy? The SMEs did have financial and coordination problems, but how far did state policy resolve these problems? The analyses presented in this book remind us that we should be cautious in judging the effects of a policy. In general, in terms of both guidance and industrial finance, the assistance and support the state extended to the SMEs was minimal. The flourishing of the SMEs can hardly be attributed to state assistance. The political implications of the policy outweighed its practical consequences. In other words, it was more symbolic than effective.

The state begin to devise an SME policy in the mid-1970s when it recognized the SMEs' political and economic significance in a dramatically changed situation, and it played the SME card to deal with the emerging political and economic challenges. The SMEs' exports solved a serious problem and a source of worry for the state for decades: foreign exchange. Taiwan's international balance of payments registered in the black in 1970, and its foreign exchange reserves increased steadily thereafter, all because of the rapid increase in exports.[20] By and large, the state included the SMEs in public policy from the mid-1970s because the state sorely needed the SMEs, rather than vice versa. The significance of the SMEs in the state's increasing vigilance over the business groups underscored their weight in the state's political goals.

State Political Strategies, Public Policy, the Marketplace, and the SMEs

Although the extraordinary performance of the SMEs can hardly be attributed to state policy, we cannot draw the conclusion, contrary to the claims of Gary Hamilton, that the state was not involved at all in the success of the SMEs.[21] Rather, I would argue that state action significantly, but indirectly, contributed to the success of the SMEs. The indirect consequences of state action— particularly with respect to the making of the market and policing entry to SME-dominated markets—were critical prerequisites for the success of the SMEs.

Unlike conventional scholarship on the success of SMEs, this book argues that one critical determinant in the success of SMEs was Taiwan's unique industrial structure or marketplace. This structure enabled societal goods to be mobilized. It can be hypothesized that societal goods exist and operate in an environment that either constrains or mobilizes them. This environment is the marketplace. In Taiwan, the marketplace was a result of state public policy and the interplay of the state and private actors.

The state's political strategies determined its public policy. As we have seen, until the mid-1970s the KMT practiced strategies of dominance in order to keep society at a distance. These strategies ensured its independence and prevented it from being captured by social forces. The Taiwan state differed significantly from those in South Korea and Latin America in terms of its relations with society and with foreign capital. In many Latin American countries, alliances were forged between the state and either the working class or the capitalists involved in import substitution and foreign capital. These alliances were political as well as economic and determined the pattern of economic development. In South Korea, industrialization was dominated by the conglomerates. In Latin America, the triple alliance of the state, local capital, and foreign capital was responsible for a second round of import substitution industrialization,[22] which contrasts sharply with East Asia's shift to export-oriented industrialization after an initial round of import substitution. The state in South Korea fostered a few large conglomerates and formed an alliance with them after the 1961 military coup for the purpose of economic development.[23] However, before the 1970s, the state in Taiwan never relied on any particular social force and never formed alliances with any of them as part of its efforts to achieve its development goals. Since the governments in South Korea and Latin America were politically or economically weak, they had to rely on alliances with social forces. In comparison, the state in Taiwan was economically and politically independent and thus was able to dominate the social forces. These strategies enabled and encouraged the KMT regime to practice a policy of protecting yet restricting the activities of the LEs and neither encouraging nor restricting the SMEs. The core of state–private sector relations was state coercion and manipulation of the private sector.

The policy of protecting the LEs can be seen in a variety of government initiatives and in the provision of credit through state banks, which enabled the LEs to engage in import substitution activities that required large sums of capital. The state's restriction policy prevented the LEs from entering the upstream sectors and controlled their size through legislation and regulation. The result was that a number of privileged private enterprises emerged and, with the SOEs, jointly monopolized the well-protected domestic market. Their safe domestic markets made them unwilling to move into the risky export market when the state shifted to an export-oriented industrialization strategy. In this sense, Taiwan's SMEs were luckier than their counterparts in South Korea, where space to act was limited because the vertically integrated conglomerates discriminated against their less-integrated competitors.

The policy of neither encouraging nor restricting the SMEs meant that the state neither promoted the SMEs nor set entry barriers against manufacturing for export. More specifically, although access to export promotion and to credit from state banks was denied the SMEs, entry into downstream manufacturing was easy. This policy enabled the SMEs to engage in exporting because of the absence of the LEs, the low entry barriers, and the lower capital requirements compared with import substitution activities. Unlike the LEs, which burgeoned under state protection and fostering, the SMEs emerged because the state did not set entry barriers in the export-oriented sectors. Access to the downstream sectors was open to everyone, and "open entry" encouraged the rise of the SMEs. This neo-classical, laissez-faire policy was a result of the state's political strategies, however, and did not reflect adherence to free-market doctrines.

There was another consequence to the lack of state barriers. The state's policy toward the LEs was based on picking winners and fostering supporters. But the state did not extend this policy to the SMEs. Instead, policy was universalistic rather than particularistic. The SMEs faced an open competition in the marketplace. Consequently, unlike the LEs, which were picked and protected by the state, the SME winners emerged from a cutthroat competition that eliminated the losers. Thus surviving SMES were strongly competitive, vital, and tenacious.

The state played a role in the persistence of the industrial structure. The original design had been an unintended by-product of the state's political strategies, but once it became apparent to the state that this new economic configuration could serve its political and economic purposes, it deliberately preserved and policed it. In brief, the state—

continued to support the LEs by providing them with credit and other types of economic rents;

implemented a policy on the SMEs;

used the SOEs to block the LEs' upward expansion and prevent them from becoming vertically integrated conglomerates;

restricted the size of the LEs through laws and regulations;

settled disputes between the LE providers of intermediate products and downstream SME producers.

Of particular importance was the state's decision to restrict the size of the LEs through laws and regulations. The Company Act limited the size of business operations and regulated re-investment by restraining inter-firm equity flows. These restrictions, which discouraged industrial integration, were profound and far-reaching. They were indicative of the institutionalization of the state's efforts to contain large businesses. When the regime shifted to a pro-big business strategy in the late 1980s and early 1990s, the rules limiting big business remained unchanged. Even in 1999, Morris Chang, the president of Taiwan Semiconductor and the "godfather" of Taiwan's integrated circuit industry, complained that the existing rules encouraged companies to break up.[24] The state's efforts to restrict big business were a decisive element in the persistence of a marketplace favorable to the SMEs, even though this was not the intent of these arrangements. They provided the SMEs immunity from competition from the LEs and SOEs, while ensuring they had access to the intermediate products of the LEs.

As we have seen, this led to the dual market structure. The SOEs and LEs were geared to domestic production and consumption and had little connection with international markets. This was not a free market—indeed, it was close to being a "governed market"—and it was well protected by the state through monopolies, subsidies, and other nonmarket phenomena. The SMEs were free to operate in the export market. Competition, comparative advantage, free trade, were the rules of the game. Rather than being governed, this market was close to the neo-classical account of the optimal free market. These two markets depended on each other for their continued existence. The first market provided products to the second market; the second market consumed the inputs of the first and sold its products abroad. The state intervened in the first market and practiced a laissez-faire policy toward the second. The second market cannot be explained by either the "selective industrial policy" or the "governed market" argument.

This does not mean that the state had no influence in the second market. Rather, the state influenced it by steering the first market and adjusting its macroeconomic policies. For example, the SMEs benefited from government macroeconomic policies aimed at boosting exports, such as the depreciation of the currency in the late 1950s and export tax rebates, although many SMEs were ineligible for other incentives. Land reform and state efforts to improve education and the infrastructure and to squeeze the agricultural sector to keep industrial wages low also helped create a favorable environment for the SMEs. However, these conditions were insufficient by themselves to enable the SMEs to become successful exporters.

As has been noted, the way the state promoted exports was universalistic. It neither fostered selected enterprises to create major exporters, as was done during the import substitution period, nor did it channel resources to a few conglomerates to make them export giants, as the South Korean state did. Rather, the Taiwan state created an overall environment that encouraged firms to engage in exporting. Although, because of their size, most SMEs were denied access to a number of specific incentives designed to promote exports, they benefited from the general measures introduced by the government to boost exports, such as unification of the exchange rates, tax exemptions, tax rebates for exports, simplification of administrative procedures, and liberalization of regulation. Compared with the tight controls the state exercised over import substitution, it created an unusual "economic democracy" to promote exports. The SMEs were the beneficiaries of this democracy. The state's tolerance of the unorganized financial market was also important, since this was the major source of credit for the SMEs.

The state's dispersed industrialization policy was also important. In contrast to South Korea, where industrialization took place only in a few large cities, Taiwan's industrialization was scattered throughout the island. This decentralization was a consequence of state policy. In the 1960s and the 1970s, 38 industrial estates were established; nearly two-thirds of these were located away from the major cities and their suburbs. Behind this policy was not simply the existence of a relatively evenly developed infrastructure, as Samuel Ho suggests.[25] There was also a desire to maintain a regional developmental balance.[26] However, and more important, the policy of dispersing industrial estates was more a political policy than an economic one. The motive was to balance the interests of the local political factions rather than to design a carefully considered industrial plan.[27] This consideration was a logical consequence of the state's political strategies. However, whatever the motivation, the principal economic effect was not direct; rather, a strong demonstration effect stimulated the growth of SMEs throughout the island. By June 1968, only 711 factories had been built in the estates, occupying only 40 percent of all planned industrial land; 4,416 factories had been built outside the estates.[28]

Societal Goods, International Connections, and the Success of the SMEs

As we have seen, the SMEs emerged in a unique marketplace from which the SOEs and LEs were excluded. This was a necessary condition for the success of the SMEs in the export markets. It was not, however, a sufficient condition. Like SMEs in other countries, they faced formidable challenges, ranging from management to technology to marketing. The most serious was the shortage of capital. Success in the export markets depended on overcoming these problems. The SMEs solved these problems, I will argue, by minimizing their disadvantages and maximizing their advantages. To substantiate this model, this book draws on a body of research on SMEs conducted by local observers. These empirical studies have been little used, but they enable us to understand more fully the success of the SMEs. Five factors contributed to the

success of the SMEs: flexible production, low labor costs, cooperative networks, cultural traits, and the resolution of management
problems.

Flexible Production

Taiwan's SMEs enjoyed certain advantages in terms of their production structure, notably a flexibility that allowed them to shift
production to meet changes in the market. As an alternative to
mass production, flexible production has led to prosperity in many
industries in developed countries.[29] Gary Gereffi has shown that
Taiwan's economic growth parallels the rise of the mass-marketing
retail revolution, in which "big buyers," such as Gap, Nike, Ree-
bok, the Price Club, the Limited, and Wal-Mart, that do not own
their own production facilities turn to global sourcing.[30] Although
Taiwan's SMEs do not exhibit the characteristic forms of flexible
production that Michael Piore and Charles Sabel find in the more
developed areas, still they engage in flexible production. In contrast
to flexible producers in the developed countries, Taiwan's SMEs
produced low-priced goods. But like their counterparts in the developed countries, Taiwan's SMEs relied on cooperation. This is in
line with the two core characteristics of flexible production: flexibility and specialization. As flexible producers capable of accom-
modating change and specializing in certain products and components, the SMEs found niches in international markets and became
a link in global commodity chains. In essence, the SMEs' competitiveness and efficiency rested on their flexible production structure.
This structure became a kind of comparative advantage for the
SMEs and to some extent helped them to overcome their disadvantages. As we shall see, the advantages of flexible production were
underpinned by cooperative networks among the SMEs.

However, flexible production alone could not resolve such disadvantages as the scale of operations, organization, management,
capital, technology, and marketing. These problems afflict SMEs
everywhere. Nevertheless, compared to their counterparts in other
countries, Taiwan's SMEs can boast of greater successes. How can
this success be explained?

Labor Costs

Low wages were another important element in the SMEs' success as producers of labor-intensive, light products. Until the 1980s, Taiwan's wage level was low compared to that in the more developed countries (see Table 8.5). This gave Taiwan an advantage globally as an exporter of labor-intensive products. And the SMEs paid even lower wages than did the large enterprises.

Wages were low in Taiwan because a weak, internally fragmented, and disciplined work force had been formed by political controls established in the early years of export-oriented industrialization and by enterprise-level controls.[31] More specifically, the lower wages in the SMEs (see Table 8.6) can be attributed to the subcontracting network. G. S. Shieh argues that "subcontracting consent" between the contractors and home workers was responsible for the low wages.[32] The opportunity for workers to be their own "boss," the spin-off mechanism, may have placated workers and ensured their acquiescence.[33] However, we should be cautious about attributing the growth of the SMEs to low wages. Before the mid-1970s, the lower wages paid by SMEs in Taiwan were a comparative advantage relative to more advanced economies such as Japan and the United States, since only a few underdeveloped countries were involved in labor-intensive exports. Once Taiwan's wage levels soared and cheaper labor competitors became exporters of labor-intensive products, this advantage disappeared, and experience, managerial expertise, technological know-how, and international connections built up over the previous decades replaced low

Table 8.5
Monthly Income of Manufacturing Workers by Country, 1966

Country	Monthly income (U.S.$)
United States	$449.36
Japan	112.52
Taiwan	38.16
South Korea	20.30

SOURCE: Liang Guoshu, "Taiwan de duiwai maoyi yu jiuye," p. 230, table 16.

Table 8.6
Wages per Worker Based on Firm Scale, 1976 and 1986
(NT$1,000)

Scale of firms	Number of employees		Amount of wages	
	1976	1986	1976	1986
Average	27	24	$51 (79.7%)	$158 (69.6%)
Fragmentary operators (1–29)	7	7	40 (62.5)	130 (57.3)
Small firms (30–99)	53	52	45 (70.3)	150 (66.1)
Medium firms (100–499)	202	192	50 (78.1)	178 (78.4)
Large firms (≥ 500)	1,339	1,348	64 (100.0)	227 (100.0)

NOTE: Wages of large firms = 100.0%.
SOURCE: derived from Liu Jinqing et al., *Taiwan zhi jingji*, p.151.

wages as comparative advantages and the sources of the SMEs' competitiveness.

Flexible production and low labor costs were certainly pivotal elements in the success of Taiwan's SMEs. Since these two characteristics can be found in many countries, however, they are not a sufficient explanation for the conspicuous achievements of the SMEs.

Cooperative Networks

Flexible production and low labor costs have to be examined in a broader context. Evidence suggests that the success of Taiwan's SMEs was deeply and widely rooted in social and economic organizations and cultural characteristics. These factors are the "societal goods" that shaped the SMEs' environment—an internal and external structure in which production, financing, and sales networks took shape. These goods were the sources of three features of Taiwan's SMEs—dispersion, adaptability, and tenacity[34]—and the basis of the SMEs' vitality and competitiveness.

Cooperation among the SMEs was also important. It is noteworthy that cooperation between large firms and SMEs based on production needs was fairly weak. Chen Mingzhang is one of few observers who has tried to explain this. He cites three reasons: cultural traits, problems at the level of the firms, and government failures. The cultural traits are the strong preference for being one's own boss, the lack of a team mentality, and distrust of other people. With respect to the firms themselves, Chen Mingzhang, perhaps tautologically, notes an unwillingness to cooperate and a lack of ethics and norms of cooperation. He also cites the government's failure to promote collaboration and to provide laws and rules to structure cooperation, as well as the public banks' failure to encourage it.[35] Ultimately, however, Chen Mingzhang's account is unconvincing. The reasons cited by Chen should also hinder cooperation throughout Taiwanese business, yet there was a strong and extensive cooperative network among the SMEs. The real reason for the lack of cooperation between the LEs and SMEs should, I argue, be sought in the division of labor among the upstream SOEs, intermediate-stream LEs, and downstream SMEs.

In South Korea, industrialization was dominated by large business groups. Although the relative roles of large business groups and SMEs in the Japanese economy are disputed,[36] large business groups in Japan undeniably played a far greater role than their Taiwanese counterparts. The vertical integration of both Japanese and South Korean conglomerates leaves limited room for SMEs. In South Korea, for example, the vertically integrated *chaebol*s discriminate against their less-integrated competitors. As a result, room for the SMEs was limited. The SMEs had no choice but to become integrated into the conglomerate-led center-satellite system, in which a large company has numerous SMEs as dependent minor partners. In contrast, the unique industrial structure of Taiwan provided no room for vertically integrated conglomerates.

The division of labor in Taiwan determined that the upstream SOEs supplied goods to the intermediate-stream LEs, which in turn supplied goods to the downstream SMEs. The relationship among the three was one of suppliers and consumers rather than one of cooperative partners. This type of relationship did not require cooperation between the different streams. This vertical separation of production delimited a domain for each player. Within this industrial chain, the downstream SMEs were inde-

pendent of the upstream SOEs and the intermediate LEs as consumers of the intermediate products provided mainly by the LEs.
This independence allowed the SMEs to take advantage of the relationship between themselves and the intermediate input suppliers.
For example, an SME usually could choose among several suppliers
and hence had leverage in price negotiations. A survey of the knitting industry revealed that 76 percent of knitwear export manufacturers bought yarn from between six and twenty suppliers; only 18
percent dealt with fewer than five suppliers. This situation reinforced the SMEs' bargaining position, and they could avoid paying
more than the market price.[37] This is the real reason that cooperation between large firms and SMEs was weak in Taiwan. As a result, the SMEs were more dependent on cooperation with one another than on cooperation with the SOEs and the LEs. Embedded
in cooperative networks, family connections, and international
markets, the SMEs as a whole were able to act as independent
players in the economy without depending on the SOEs and the
LEs. In short, collaboration among firms in Taiwan does not take
the form of a center-satellite system but of a cooperative network.
The SMEs are linked in an "elastic cooperation of enterprises," that
is, a flexible aggregate of numerous enterprises that cooperate with
respect to technology, management, funds, and marketing.[38] The
core of this structure is a network in which a subcontractor sup-
plies components to more than one contractor, rather than to only
one company as a satellite firm does within a center-satellite system.
Research on textiles, shoemaking, machinery, and the information
industries confirms the importance of parallel production and sales
cooperation among SMEs.[39]

This cooperative network is a source of the strength and vitality
of Taiwan's SMEs. The network has two bases, which took shape
over the decades of industrialization: the unbreakable connections
among the upstream, midstream, and downstream industries and
the meticulous division of labor among firms. Each SME is embedded in this network. The cooperation among the SMEs was based
on a high level of specialization. Not only are parts or components
manufactured by particular producers, but assembling, packaging,
and even the handling of documents from foreign buyers and visits

by them, customs clearance, and tax rebates are undertaken by specialized SMEs, trading companies, and customs clearance firms. "A call, a meal, a letter of credit, or an order form may become the basis for mutual subcontracting and cooperation."[40]

This cooperative network is reinforced by a number of elements. First, kinship is critical. The kinship network includes not only family members, relatives, and people with the same surname but also friends, people from the same villages, and former schoolmates. It is a powerful relationship. Most SMEs are family businesses. Kinship is a significant factor in gaining access to funds, technological assistance, and marketing information, solving management problems, and setting up new firms. Kinship reinforces the coordination function otherwise provided by the market. Second, industries run by SMEs are bunched geographically. This cluster phenomenon both reduces transaction costs and enhances the operations of the SMEs in the same cluster because they can learn from and compete with one another. Third, every contractor and subcontractor has multiple relationships. Each contractor works with a number of subcontractors; each subcontractor receives orders from more than one contractor. Both sides benefit from such multiple relationships in terms of production scale, production costs, and business risks.

In the process, the weaknesses and disadvantages of each individual firm are offset by this network. The combination of numerous SMEs generates an amplifying effect in which the "tenacious constitution" of the SME collective linked from bottom to top, from family workshops to large firms, compensates for the "weak constitution" of an individual company.[41] The cooperative network affords the SMEs considerable benefits in terms of managerial know-how, technology, financing, and marketing, areas universally held to be the main problems facing SMEs. The network contributes to the comparative advantage of Taiwan's SMEs.

Cultural Traits

The cooperative network sustaining a myriad of SMEs and small and medium-sized trading companies (SMTs) is complemented by the "it is better to be the head of a chicken than the tail of an ox" mentality. The contribution of this cultural trait of valuing being one's own boss to the prevalence of SMEs in Taiwan is widely recognized and confirmed by participants in case studies. It is characterized by Shieh as "spinning off bosses."[42] Workers in SMEs are prone to set up their own manufacturing workshops once they accumulate sufficient experience.[43] This mentality is widespread and deep-rooted in Taiwan. The situation differs from the lifetime employment and employee loyalty found in Japan. It is also different from the situation in South Korea, where workers are better organized and trade unions have more leverage with the government. Diligence is another cultural trait widely acknowledged as contributing to the success of Taiwan's SMEs. The "'workization' of life— subjecting life to work" is a common practice among SME operators.[44] Family values and families' close relationships are also seen as key elements in the success of Taiwan's SMEs.[45]

Resolution of Management Problems

SMEs face operating problems in terms of capital, management, technology, and marketing. A number of mechanisms developed in Taiwan to overcome these problems.

Capital. Observers agree that SMEs in Taiwan relied mainly on unorganized financial sources[46] because they lacked access to banks for funds. Here, social connections and cultural traits play a significant role. The funds needed to set up a workshop or firm were usually given or lent by family members, relatives, or friends.[47] Ke Zhiming's case study of the garment industry reveals, for example, that the majority of funds came from these sources.[48] There were, however, other sources. The most important was the personal savings of the owners themselves, followed by money and capital markets. Reinvestment by family members and friends constituted a third source.[49] Significantly, capital shortages were overcome to a considerable extent by the cooperative network. Subcontractors within a network shared fixed capital costs, thus decreasing the costs to an individual firm. Each firm needed to invest only in a simple workshop, equipment to make specific products or components, or wages for a few workers. The rest of the investment was absorbed by the other subcontractors in the network. This "static proportioning of funds" was immensely helpful to the SMEs, especially small-scale firms and family workshops without access to the financial system and capital markets. Also, there was a mutual-financing relationship between contractors and subcontractors based on the principle of production and a relationship of mutual trust and profit-maximizing among the cooperating SMEs. All firms benefited from this financial cooperation. This "dynamic proportion of funds"—the term is Chen Jiexuan's—functioned as a transformer that created long-standing and stable cooperative relationships among the SMEs.[50] Empirical evidence is provided by a survey of the knitting industry: 43 percent of the respondents confirmed that, when necessary, knitwear export manufacturers financed their subcontractors.[51]

An important lacuna in our understanding of the financing of SME export activities concerns the extremely high cost of capital on the informal capital market. This market, as we have seen, was a major source of SME capital. Yet its interest rates were extremely high—the figure in 1971 was 21.6 percent (see Table 5.5). How were the SMEs able to compete in such an environment? The answer lies in the industrial production system developed by the SMEs; they avoided having to rely on capital whenever possible. First, since the products manufactured by the SMEs for export were labor-intensive, they generally required less capital. Second, the cooperative network played an important role in solving the SMEs' financial problems—by sharing fixed capital and through the widespread practice of mutual financing between contractors and subcontractors.[52] Third, to a great extent, the practice of using letters of credit as a means of payment reduced the amount of capital required for export production. Fourth, family members, relatives, and friends helped in resolving capital problems.

There were a number of other ways of relieving capital shortages as well. For example, Chung-hsing Hsieh's empirical study shows that contractors sometimes sold old machines to subcontractors at depreciated prices. Or a contractor might finance a subcontractor's purchase of new machinery.[53]

Management and technology. SMEs are typically weak in terms of management and technology. Different practices were developed in Taiwan to overcome this weakness. In the larger firms, management hinged mainly on a few core members of a management team based on trust and ability. In most SMEs that were family businesses, kinship played a major role in management. In both cases, culture (trust) and social relations (kinship) helped to solve management problems. In addition, the cooperative networks also played a part in overcoming the management problems. Contractors could provide subcontractors with assistance if they saw the need.

The labor-intensive nature of SME products largely offset the technological weakness. The required technology was simple and cheap, if not free. The division of labor within the cooperative network also helped. The finished product was the work of numerous SMEs. Most of the SMEs, in particular family workshops, were processors of export products that demanded relatively low skills and technology. The SMEs were able to develop skills through years of on-the-job training, and this gave them a comparative advantage. Consequently, in order to reduce costs, the contractors, mainly medium and sometimes large firms, subcontracted the production of products or components to parallel or smaller-scale SMEs rather than manufacturing them themselves. This division of labor and cooperation overcame the limitations of the larger parent companies or contractor firms and increased efficiency by utilizing the subcontractor SMEs fully. Based on a division of labor and cooperation, an unbreakable, interdependent relationship was forged between contractors and subcontractors. In many cases, the contracting firms provided technological assistance to the subcontracting SMEs.

Marketing. Whereas solutions to the problems of management, technology, and capital shortages were rooted in the internal social structure of firms, economic connections among the SMEs, and cultural characteristics, marketing problems were resolved by drawing upon both domestic resources and external connections. Again, although entry to downstream production remained open to the SMEs, the domestic market, which was jointly monopolized by the SOEs and the LEs, was closed. This meant that the SMEs had no choice but to export their products. This raises a crucial question: What made it possible for the SMEs to become involved in exports? Competition in the international market was stiff. As noted above, the unwillingness of the LEs to engage in exports implied an assessment that they were unable to compete in the world market. But the SMEs were in fact much less competitive than the LEs. How, then, did they manage to sell goods in a world market with which they were unfamiliar and to which they had no access? Initially, Japanese trading companies helped the SMEs sell their products abroad, mainly in the United States. With their traditional connections in Taiwan (in the 1950s most SME owners were native Taiwanese who had been born during the colonial period and spoke Japanese), as well as their connections with the world markets, the Japanese trading companies were well positioned to play such a role. Although the estimated percentage of exports handled by foreign companies decreased sharply in the 1980s, in the mid-1970s it was thought that these companies were responsible for between half and two-thirds of all exports. The percentage would have been much higher in earlier years. The dominance of Japanese companies was confirmed in my own interviews, and even in the mid-1970s it remained a source of concern for the government. It should be stressed here that the Japanese trading companies helped to pull Taiwan's SMEs into the world market. Being pushed from the monopolized domestic market would not necessarily have forced the SMEs into the world market.

The timing of the rise of Taiwan's SMEs is also significant—as noted above, it corresponded with the emergence of large, international brand merchandisers that did not have their own factories. This provided an opportunity for Taiwan's SMEs to participate in global commodity chains.[54] The Japanese companies acted as the SMEs' bridge to the global commodity chains. When the SMEs were pushed from the monopolized domestic market, the Japanese trading companies pulled them into the global market. This push-plus-pull thus became the driving force behind the emergence of Taiwan's SMEs. This is supported by Wu Huilin and Zhou Tiancheng's argument that the SMEs could focus on production because the Japanese trading companies took care of marketing.[55]

Statistics about early exports are inaccurate, especially for the breakdown of the proportions of exports steered through foreign trading companies, local trading companies, and the SMEs themselves. Some argue that for years Taiwan's export market was controlled mainly by foreign trading companies, especially the large Japanese trading companies. Wu Huilin and Zhou Tiancheng support the official estimate of 50 percent.[56] In 1976, 10 percent of Taiwan's exports were handled directly by the manufacturers; of the remaining 90 percent, 10 percent went through publicly owned trading companies, 15 percent through private trading companies, and over 65 percent through foreign trading companies. These figures are close to the official estimates cited above. Nevertheless, they may underestimate the importance of domestic trading companies.

Taiwan's foreign trading sector was dominated by SMTs. This differs sharply from the situation in Japan and South Korea, where general trading companies (GTCs) (in South Korea fostered by the state) dominated international trade. Efforts by some officials to create large trading companies (LTCs) in Taiwan were unsuccessful due to opposition within the government.[57] Taiwan thus ended up with many small trading companies. The number of SMTs reached 20,000 in 1976[58] and 36,000 in 1983. In contrast, Japan, which had 16.7 times more trade than Taiwan, had 6,600 trade companies in 1972.[59] It is also far more than the 2,100 trading companies in South Korea, where trading activity nearly equaled that of Taiwan in 1976. In 1981, 77 percent of Taiwan's trading companies employed fewer than ten employees. The five largest trading companies exported only 0.81 percent of all exports, whereas the top five Korean trading companies exported 29 percent of that country's total exports.[60] Research on the textile, shoemaking, machinery, and information sectors suggests that it was the SMTs and export-oriented SMEs, not the large trading companies, that dominated Taiwan's export trade.[61] The prevalence of SMTs was closely linked to the SMEs' cooperative network. SMTs and SMEs were

Table 8.7

Distribution of Manufacturing Establishments by Firm Size in Terms of Products
for Export, Methods of Export, and Ratio of Exports, 1985

| Firm size | Products for export? | | | Ways of exporting | | Ratio of exports |
	No	Yes	Directly	Through domestic trading companies	Through foreign trading companies	
1–4	86.2%	13.8%	19.1%	80.4%	0.5%	16.0%
5–9	64.0	36.0	23.4	76.2	0.4	31.0
10–19	47.9	52.1	31.6	67.8	0.6	34.5
20–29	38.4	61.6	42.8	56.3	0.9	37.3
30–39	32.5	67.5	49.2	50.2	0.6	41.3
40–49	28.1	71.9	54.6	45.0	0.4	40.5
50–99	22.3	77.7	63.0	36.1	0.9	42.6
100–199	15.0	85.0	73.8	25.1	1.1	44.7
200–499	12.6	87.4	82.7	16.0	1.3	n.a.
≥ 500	10.1	89.9	89.9	8.8	1.6	n.a.

SOURCE: Jingjibu, "Gongchang touzi yu caozuo diaocha baogao," p. 185.

interdependent, and cooperation between them created an "absorbing network of foreign trade," which allowed them to remain in the international market.[62]

An official survey affords some corroboration of the export role of the SMTs—particularly in the 1980s. As shown in Table 8.7, the market generally operated by direct exports and exports through domestic trading companies. In 1985, 42.5 percent of the export-oriented firms exported their products directly, and 56 percent of them used domestic trading companies. Only 0.7 percent of the firms exported through foreign trading companies. Table 8.7 clearly indicates that the larger the firm, the greater the tendency to manage its own exports; conversely, the smaller the firm, the greater the reliance on domestic trading companies. This fits the picture of close cooperation between SMEs and SMTs in the export process. In addition, Table 8.7 also shows that the larger the firm, the more they were involved in exporting. However, most of the firms with fewer than ten employees were small subcontracting workshops that provided components or products to contractors but did not themselves produce products for export.

Table 8.7 highlights the importance of direct exports by SMEs. Again, the significant question is How did they do it? Did they market themselves, or did they have direct links with foreign buyers? Some evidence suggests that many SMEs obtained contracts directly from foreign buyers. This means that they exported directly, using neither domestic nor foreign trading companies. Years of cooperation between these SMEs and their buyers, as well as the accumulation of experience, enabled the SMEs to win the trust of buyers in terms of technology, management, quality control, delivery, and price. The SMEs' earlier unilateral dependency on buyers was gradually replaced by a mutual dependency between the SMEs and international buyers.[63] Such cooperative relationships were more likely to be established with the larger SMEs that operated under better conditions. The fact that the larger firms did more of their own exporting confirms this point. Table 8.7 suggests that firms with 50–99 employees handled almost two-thirds of their own exports; the percentage of direct exports by larger firms was even higher. Apparently this type of exporting had become increasingly important since the beginning of the 1980s. The role of foreign trading companies, which had been so important in the 1950s and 1960s, declined as domestic trading companies and export-oriented firms found ways to export Taiwan's products.

Generally, the factors contributing to the success of the SMEs can be summed up as follows. The marketplace that resulted from state action was critical to the performance of the SMEs in export markets because it created the necessary space by excluding the SOEs and the LEs. But the marketplace was not in itself a sufficient condition for the extraordinary achievement of the SMEs. Despite the absence of domestic rivals, the SMEs still faced considerable international competition and a wide range of disadvantages, in particular capital shortages. They could not operate as exporters unless mechanisms were created to resolve these problems. The market did, however, facilitate the mobilization of an array of societal goods: cooperative networks, kinship ties, cultural traits, an informal financial system, a flexible production system, industrial clustering, and international connections. The mobilization of these goods permitted the development of an entrepreneurial system geared to minimizing the SMEs' disadvantages and maximizing their advantages—above all, with respect to capital. The system includes the following elements:

Product choice—labor-intensive products that do not require capital concentration;

Product choice with respect to technology choice—simple and easy, and free or cheap technology;

Production methodology—the "Dell" approach (purchase of parts, production, and assembly postponed until an order is received), which reduces inventory and warehouse costs;

A cooperative network—to spread risks; reduce information management, and transaction costs; share fixed costs; allow for mutual financial assistance;

Geographic concentration—to reduce transaction costs;

Exporting by relying on foreign and domestic trading companies (international division of labor)—to save marketing costs;

Direct exporting (cooperating with foreign buyers)—to reduce marketing costs.

This system evolved in response to capital shortages. In essence, it is a "capital-substituting" industrial production system in which at all stages, from product choice to technology choice, production methodology, management, and marketing, the goal is to reduce capital costs. The system is designed to compensate for the lack of funding. It mobilized kinship ties, drew upon local values of diligence and independence, and then wedded these to cheap labor, flexible production, an informal financial system, a cooperative network, and industrial clustering. The emergence of this system coincided with the development of international commodity chains, which integrated Taiwan into the system as a supplier of labor-intensive products. The imperative that drove the system— the concern to reduce capital requirements—was often tantamount to an urgent need to reduce costs and pursue efficiency. It is not a pure market system but a hybrid in which market-bred solutions to problems of coordination are supported by kinship ties. By mobilizing societal goods, the SMEs allocated resources efficiently and maximized their utility. As a whole, the system drew on, created, and maintained a comparative advantage. Despite all the parallels between the SMEs and the free market account of developmental success, the neo-classical explanation for Taiwan's economic miracle is incomplete because it attributes the island's industrial success to the government's macroeconomic policy, such as the free trade regime, high interest rates, conservative budgeting, and stable real effective exchange rates. To point to the existence of the peculiar industrial structure that benefited the SMEs, as some have done, is also inadequate to explain the SMEs' export success.

Conclusion

The case of the SMEs challenges the statist account that attributes Taiwan's economic performance to the state's strategic industrial policy. Nor does it support the selective industrial policy and governed market arguments. The outstanding performance of the SMEs was attributable mainly to a production system that mobilized a complex of societal goods to solve the SMEs' problems. My interpretation of the success of the SMEs is a marketplace-based explanation.

My account also differs from the society-centered approach, which attributes the success of the SMEs exclusively to societal goods. My argument is that the industrial structure was a critical precondition for the rise of the SMEs as exporters because they did not have to compete with large firms and that the marketplace facilitated the development of an industrial production system which mobilized societal goods. But this industrial structure had political origins—the state's political strategies and public policy contributed to the shaping of the marketplace. Basically, the success of the SMEs was an unanticipated consequence of state action. Until the state needed their support, however, it did little to help them explicitly. However, market conditions did not on their own overcome the SMEs' operating problems. These problems were solved by societal goods and the production system. This book's explanation for the success of the SMEs is multifactoral—the SMEs emerged and grew because of a wide array of conditions. State actions created a critical marketplace for the SMEs, and societal goods and the production system that was formed in this market enabled the SMEs to become successful exporters.

Conclusion

The book has focused on the political dimension of Taiwan's development, particularly as it affected the economic bureaucracy, industrial policy, and SME-led export-oriented industrialization. It has argued that the economic bureaucracy is better understood as a world of bureaucratic politics rather than as a set of discrete monolithic institutions; and that the Taiwanese state enjoyed a "steering capacity" only because individuals exercising leadership mobilized networks to initiate, design, and implement policy. The "strongman" rather than a bureaucratic agency was responsible for the success of the industrial policy. Although the industrial policy undoubtedly played a role, it was not the principal factor in Taiwan's successful economic development. Here the plaudits must go to the multitude of small- and medium-sized enterprises, which learned how to exploit the economic opportunities afforded to them by a highly unusual industrial structure. This was the critical precondition for their success. The structure was neither a result of industrial policy nor an intended design of it. Rather, it was an inadvertent consequence of the state's political strategies. In the process, the SMEs evolved into what is here termed "a capital-substituting production system," characterized by the mobilization of a complex of "societal goods" to support the entrepreneurial activities of the SMEs and above all to offset capital shortages and the high costs of industrial capital.

The "statist" account of Taiwan's development argues that Taiwan's industrial success can be attributed to the state. For this to be the case, the state must have a great steering capacity and coherent and consistent economic policies, as well as the right institutional mix to implement and sustain them. According to proponents of the statist view, the economic bureaucracy's autonomy, which derived from the authoritarian political system, and its institutional arrangements enabled the state to concentrate on economic development and to conduct a selective industrial policy that led to the economic successes of Taiwan.[1]

As we have seen, there was no such institutional mix in Taiwan. Case studies show that Taiwan's economic bureaucracy was neither monolithic nor harmonious, and its steering capacity was questionable. My investigation of the period from the 1950s to the mid-1980s confirms this finding. The economic bureaucracy was not integrated, and it had little autonomy. It was full of internal conflicts and divisions. The economic planning agencies, which played a greater role than the government ministries, had limited institutional continuity. The performance of these agencies was determined by their directors rather than by the institutions themselves. Seemingly, statism's institution-based account of Taiwan's economic bureaucracy is inaccurate.

This book proposes instead an explanation based on bureaucratic politics and a three-layer analytical framework. The highest layer consisted of the political leadership, which was paramount. Men such as Chiang Kai-shek, Chen Cheng, and Chiang Ching-kuo exercised authority without interference. In the final analysis, they were above the state and the party. They could and did establish and dissolve bureaucratic institutions as they wished. The effectiveness and even continued existence of an agency depended fundamentally on the support of the political leaders. For example, CUSA owed its success to support by Chiang Kai-shek and Chen Cheng. Similarly, the dissolution of the CIECD and its replacement by the EPB were personal decisions by Chiang Ching-kuo. Parliament did not act as a significant check on the president. The legislators, most of whom were KMT members, had come from the mainland in 1949, and they had benefited from the freezing of elections to the National Assembly, which, in the process, lost most of its autonomy.

The next layer was the upper echelon of the state bureaucracy. Leading figures—state ministers, heads of economic agencies, and so forth—were designated by the president after discussions with the premier, who himself was a member of the top political leadership and also a presidential appointee of the president. Formally, the parliament approved these appointments, but certainly up until the late 1970s, it could do little more than approve the selection. From this layer of ostensibly equal ministers and agency heads emerged the strongmen—pivotal figures who could command their agencies and above all had the support of the top leaders. Inevitably, these senior officials had to compete upwards for support from the political leaders, especially when two strongmen were at loggerheads over contentious policy issues. However, it would be a mistake to view the political leaders as particularly vulnerable to such competition since the principal determinants of the relationship between the highest leaders and the bureaucratic strongmen were loyalty, trust, and other informal norms and practices. Without political support, it was impossible to become a strongman.

Having secured the support of the political leaders, the strongmen had to negotiate the third layer of bureaucratic politics—agencies, constitutional ministries, and the extra-constitutional economic planning agencies. In addition to the support of political leaders and their own personal charisma, the resources and instruments available in this third layer provided the strongmen another set of tools to exercise their power. The constitutional ministries and extra-constitutional planning agencies had little autonomy. Their roles and functions were attached to the persons who headed them. Until the early 1970s the economic planning agencies were more active than the formal government ministries, but they were short-lived and existed at the discretion of the political leaders. Under such conditions, rule by individuals colored the economic bureaucracy. Before the late 1970s, power and authority were attached to the strongmen rather than to the institutions.

The argument here is based on the nature of bureaucratic politics in the KMT regime. The internal conflicts and cleavages in the economic institutions highlight the importance of coordination. The weakness of the constitutional ministries and the fragility and discontinuity of the economic planning agencies determined that institutions alone were unable to solve coordination problems. The highly personalized nature of bureaucratic politics created a stage for individual officials. A few strongmen thus played a crucial leadership role in economic policy making. Using the political support of the highest leaders, their personal charisma, and the resources and instruments available to them, they were able to solve coordination problems in the formulation and implementation of industrial policy. Whatever steering capacity the state may have had was dependent on the strongmen.

Of course, rule by a strongman was not the only element necessary to the success of industrial policy. A no-risk guarantee to the firms and a policy design that policed the market and showed state commitment to the industry were also required. Thus at least two of the prerequisites of the statist argument—institutional mix and steering capacity—were questionable in the case of Taiwan. Insofar as there was an effective steering capacity, it was found not at the level of the state but at the level of the individual strongmen. Thus we can anticipate that industrial policy in toto was unlikely to be successful (in the absence of a mechanism for coordinating the activities of the strongmen) or, at best, to be patchy and inconsistent: that is to say, successful in sectors where the strongmen were present, but unsuccessful elsewhere. In fact, there were both successes and failures.

It has been suggested that theories about selective policy adequately account for this unevenness. Proponents of the so-called selective industrial policy, such as Robert Wade, argue that this policy enabled the government to guide, or to govern, market processes and outcomes to a greater extent than would have been the case with either free-market or simulated free-market policies.[2] There were some success stories—the semiconductor industry, for example, was a spectacular instance of strategic design. Perhaps here the state did manage to govern the market; yet, it could equally well be argued that the semiconductor industry is an example of the efficacy of the strongman. Moreover, not all industries targeted in a strategic design were successful. The automobile industry is a case in point. Arguably, however, this was a consequence of the inability of the responsible minister of economic affairs to play the role of a strongman fully. The most significant counterevidence was the dramatic success of industries that were never part of a strategic design. The outstanding performance of the downstream industries in the conspicuous absence of state intervention is a clear example.

The major weakness of the selective industrial policy argument is that it ignores the issue of coordination. Coordination is critical to the formulation and implementation of industrial policy, given the widespread internal conflicts and divisions in the economic bureaucracy and the ephemerality of the economic planning agencies. The selective industrial policy argument is premised on a monolithic and coherent bureaucracy. In fact, Taiwan's bureaucracy was anything but this. Rather, the strongman coordinated the efforts of the agencies and created state capacity; he, not the bureaucracy, was the critical determinant of the success of the industrial policy. The policy for the automobile industry failed because of a lack of coordination between different economic agencies, a failure born of the absence of a strongman. In contrast, the success of the semiconductor industry was due to strongman K. T. Li's ability to solve the coordination problems. Even though Li did not hold a powerful position and had no resources, he was able to play a leadership role because of political support from the highest leaders and his personal charisma. Institutions played only a small role in the development of semiconductors. This is not an isolated case; the same is true of textiles and plastics.

There are also instances of conspicuous industrial successes in the absence of a political strongman. These tend, however, to confirm rather than to refute the importance of individual leadership in the promotion of industrial development. Petrochemicals is one example, and steel is another. The fostering of the steel industry was debated in the late 1950s and opposed on grounds of its strategic significance to the economy as a whole. At the time, defense expenditures were the first and foremost priority. The sponsoring of the petrochemical industry did not appear on the developmental agenda until the mid-1960s. Significantly, neither petrochemicals nor steel was central to Taiwan's economic policy until the twin legitimacy challenges of the early 1970s, when they were selected by the super- or, more accurately, supra-strongman Chiang Ching-kuo. Both industries were beneficiaries of Chiang Ching-kuo's Ten Project Plan in 1973, his attempt to associate himself with a grand design appropriate to the heir apparent to Chiang Kai-shek. These industries served his own interests as well as those of the regime.

The comments of Ryutaro Komiya on the industries supported by the Japanese state are applicable here. What, he asks, were the characteristics of the industries chosen for support?

First, they had to be the industries, symbolic of industrial might, that had already been pursued by countries more advanced than Japan (modern states in the Meiji period to the early post-WWII years, advanced nations in the period of rapid growth, and technologically leading nations from the 1970s on). The industries themselves were seen as ones that Japan could develop with a greater or lesser amount of effort (meaning protection and promotion). Second, these industries had to have a certain size, so that the theme of their development could garner people's attention, that is, they had to have "news value" both domestically and internationally. Industries that met these two criteria gained the attention of policymakers as candidates worthy of protection and promotion policies.[3]

We can add that, in the cases of both petrochemicals and steel, the economic rationale for supporting these industries was strong. In short, good politics was also good economics.

As we have seen, the state subordinated economic policies to political concerns, and economic policies changed when political concerns changed. The book argues that Taiwan under the KMT was not a developmental state. The highest politicians were preoccupied with security, military goals, and their own power. The majority of government expenditures went for defense. The financial bureaucrats, who controlled important instruments and had the support of the top leaders, were concerned with revenues and the balance of payments. They served as a check on the economic bureaucrats. Only a few economic bureaucrats were concerned with economic development. Providing economic rents in exchange for political support often overrode economic concerns and compromised the regime's economic goals.

Indeed, the issue of economic and political rationales is the main challenge to conventional treatments of Taiwan's economic policy.

Economic policy is routinely viewed as an economic issue and is explained in terms of economics. However, in the real world economic and political goals do not always match, and political goals often have a higher priority on a regime's agenda than economic goals. When the two are contradictory, economic goals are usually compromised for the sake of the political goals, not vice versa. Economic policy is thus not always rational in economic terms and cannot be explained merely by economics. Only when political and economic goals coincide does the economic rationale come to the fore.

Taiwan's dual market structure for traditional industries was a result of the conflict between political and economic goals, and the integrated industrialization of the new industries can be attributed to a match between the two. In reality, the two rationales seldom coincide, and thus economic rationales are insufficient to account for economic policy. This book therefore argues that economic policy cannot be reduced to economics and that the political dimensions of policy must be taken into account.

Nor does the developmental state thesis explain the success of the SMEs—a fundamental characteristic of Taiwan's development. Driven by the discipline of competition in world markets, the SMEs were, by virtue of their backward linkages to intermediate and upstream producers, the tugboats—rather than the locomotives—of Taiwan's economy. The statistics given in Chapter 8 illuminate the importance of the SMEs to Taiwan's economy, but their significance is even greater than the data suggest. As we have seen, Taiwan's unique tripartite industrial structure and the horizontal division of markets pushed the SMEs into downstream production and the export market. Given the small scale of Taiwan's domestic market,[4] the dynamics of industrialization had to be rooted in exporting rather than in the domestic market. Taiwan is a typical example of a "buyer-driven" economy. This differs from a "production-driven" economy in which larger firms in the networks create a demand for smaller firms outside the networks.[5] In contrast, in "buyer-driven" networks, big businesses function as upstream suppliers of intermediate goods and services in response to demand generated by SMEs. The manufacturing activities of

SMEs are, in turn, a response to the demands of buyers in markets external to the producing networks.[6] Thus, in Taiwan, LEs are not organizing nodes in commodity chains.

As a result, Taiwan's industrialization was characterized by strong backward integration. The backward linkages developed in the early 1960s and began with the export-oriented downstream SMEs. Goods destined mainly for export markets—textiles (final goods), plastic products, metal processing, and machinery—created a great demand for intermediate products. To respond to this demand, upstream SOEs began to be established in the late 1960s that generated a forward linkage and led to the establishment of intermediate LEs. The robust demand for intermediate goods on the part of SMEs supported the development of the intermediate LEs and the upstream SOEs that supplied these goods. The backward linkage effect was strongest in the petrochemical industry and important in the steel sector as well. Some industries—shipbuilding, for example—might seem unaffected by these backward linkages, but in fact they are indirectly linked as well. The shipbuilding industry developed in the 1970s to meet the rapidly increasing need to import crude oil and ores and to export products. Obviously, this was a result of the expansion of the downstream industries and exports. Of course, this was not the only mechanism in Taiwan's industrialization, but it was clearly a very critical and powerful mechanism.

The relationship between downstream industries and exports requires further clarification. Most of Taiwan's exports were downstream products, but not all downstream industries were export-oriented. Exports played only a minor part in the LEs' overall activities; their downstream activities were domestic-oriented. Many LEs began during the import substitution era of the 1950s in downstream industries, such as textiles, food, plastics, appliances, and so forth. However, their products were only for the domestic market. Only LEs were able to engage in such activities because the costs of entering the domestic market were high due to their capital-intensive nature, particularly for distribution. The provision of credits by the state-owned banks enabled the LEs to run these industries. The government limited entry to the LEs. As a re-

sult, a few LEs monopolized these activities, and the SMEs per-
force had to find other markets. What the SMEs could afford to
enter and what they were allowed to enter were those export-
oriented downstream activities that the LEs were not willing to enter. "Could afford to" is somewhat misleading since the ability of
the SMEs to export depended ultimately on their ability to gener-
ate a mode of production that required as few capital inputs as possible—what I have called the "capital-substituting industrial production system."

The SMEs' emergence in export-oriented downstream industries
completely changed the landscape of Taiwan's economy, since the
island's economy was no longer confined to a small domestic market and was supported by international markets. The growth of
the SME sector meant the expansion of markets abroad, and therefore the economy expanded as the SMEs' exports increased. The
continuing expansion of the economy depended on the SMEs' exports, and the SMEs' export-oriented manufacturing was vital to
the entire economy.

Accordingly, given the significant role of the SMEs' output in the
economy, the manufacturing sector occupied a conspicuously important position. From 1981 to 1985, the percentage of manufacturing in GDP was roughly 36 percent, far higher than the 14 percent
share of finance, insurance, and business services (the second leading
sector) and the 13 percent of commerce (ranked third). Considering
the backward linkages in the manufacturing and the service sectors,
it is fair to conclude that the economy was largely driven by the
downstream SMEs' exports. The rapid expansion of SMEs' exports
broke through the limits of the domestic market and maximized
both market and production. The SMEs' strong and sustaining demand supported the development of the upstream SOEs and the
intermediate-stream LEs. Without the SMEs, there would have been
few if any exports from Taiwan, and without the exports, there
would have been no "economic miracle." In this economy, the SOEs
and LEs are huge tankers pulled by the SME tugboats. Indeed, the
entire economy is pushed by the numerous SME tugboats.

The analytical challenge is to explain the extraordinary performance of the SMEs. The key questions are What enabled the

SMEs to flourish? and How much did the state contribute to their success?

This book argues that the success of the SMEs was predicated on Taiwan's unique industrial structure. State action and the interplay between state and private sector actors resulted in an industrial structure that made it possible for the SMEs to flourish in the export markets. We have explored how this industrial structure came into being and how much the state contributed to its emergence. In brief, the industrial structure had deeply political roots, which derived from the state's strategy for maintaining power. The processes of dominant engagement and strategic disengagement determined the state's public policy. In particular, the preferred political strategy encouraged and enabled the state to practice two different types of public policy: it protected and restricted the LEs but neither encouraged nor restricted the SMEs. The state protected the LEs because it needed them to perform certain economic functions and it needed their political support to prevent the emergence of political challengers. It did not restrict the SMEs because they did not present a threat to the regime. This policy resulted in a strict division of labor among the upstream SOEs, the intermediate-stream LEs, and the downstream SMEs. The unanticipated consequence of this industrial structure obliged the SMEs to engage in exporting since they were denied access to the domestic markets. But they were afforded a near monopoly of the export markets.

The state policed the industrial organization to preserve the division of labor that it had secured. It did this through a variety of instruments, such as a universalistic rather than a particularistic export promotion policy, state maintenance and regulation of the unorganized financial market, which was the major source of capital for the SMEs, reinforcement of the LEs' inward activities through "financial constraints" and the distribution of other economic rents, strengthening of the SOEs' upstream monopoly, and, not least, restrictions on firm size and legal and regulatory discouragement of expansion, which might create dangerous political rivals. The consequences for the SMEs were highly significant: immunity from competition from the SOEs and LEs without loss of access to intermediate products and a marketplace that facilitated societal goods.

The industrial structure was not designed to provide a market-place in which the SMEs might flourish, but this was indeed its effect. The role of the state in defining the industrial structure was critical but not always intended—much of it was the unanticipated consequence of the state's political strategies. The state was not only the unwitting architect of this unique industrial structure but also the witting and watchful policeman that safeguarded the industrial division of labor.

Taiwan's Industrialization: Between State and Market

The explanation given in this book for the success of the SMEs is a marketplace-based account. The book makes a distinction between the success of industrial policy and the success of industries, because although Taiwan is known for its successful industrial policy, not all its industrial success can be attributed to its industrial policy. In short, industrial success is not reducible to successful industrial policy. We need to distinguish between two different marketplaces. The first market consisted of the upstream and intermediate-stream industries in which the SOEs and LEs operated. The second market was the downstream industries dominated by the SMEs. The state governed the first market while leaving the second to market forces. Industrial policy refers to state actions to influence the development of industries. In Taiwan, such state actions existed only in the first market. Therefore, the industrial policy explanation of the Taiwan miracle applies only to the first market. It is irrelevant to the second market since the state let the SMEs have free run in the downstream sectors. These industries were not strategically designed, and the market was not governed. Thus, the success of these industries cannot be attributed to the state's strategic design; rather, it was mainly the result of a capital-substituting industrial production system and societal goods.

The clear-cut cleavage between the two markets until the mid-1970s is a striking feature of Taiwan's political economy. Thereafter the political strategies of the state changed, as a new basis for regime legitimacy was sought in response to U.S. recognition of the PRC. The new strategies were Taiwanization and a concerted effort to link the state to the success of the SMEs. The promotion of the semiconductor and computer industries was the first clear example of a willingness both to target the SMEs and to allow the LEs to engage in new economic activities. The state was less and less the policeman of upstream economic activities and more and more the champion of integrated industrial development. A significant consequence of this change was that the two-market division found in traditional industries did not appear in the marketplace for the new industries or high-tech industries. This new marketplace was an integrated market and, unlike the dual market structure, was a result of intentional state design. The changing role of the state in the formation of the marketplace was a result of state views of industrial development—the state increasingly committed itself to integrated sectoral development. It was also a consequence of the change in political concerns in response to the changing nature of the state, state structure, state-society relations, and international circumstances. However, this does not imply that a new institutionalized steering capacity had come into existence. The success of industrial promotion in both the semiconductor and the computer industries was the work of two remarkable men. The leadership of strongmen still remained decisive.

The findings of this book draw scholarly attention to fundamental facts about Taiwan's development and allow a reinterpretation of its experience. My explanation supports two claims of the statist account of Taiwan's experience: the state was politically dominant, and it was economically *dirigiste*. However, this explanation refutes two basic assumptions of the statist account: the economic bureaucracy had autonomy and steering capacity, and the selective industrial policy was responsible for the industrial success. To the contrary, state autonomy was limited, and its steering capacity was questionable. Political dominance and economic *dirigisme* cannot be equated with autonomy and steering capacity. The state's political dominance did not translate into an autonomous economic bureaucracy. *Dirigisme* did not necessarily convert to steering capacity. Autonomy and capacity are irrelevant in explaining the role of the state in Taiwan's economic development.

In the case of Taiwan, the selective industrial policy argument is inadequate, and the governed market thesis is one-sided.

Statism errs in ignoring the influence of politics on economic development. It depoliticizes the state's economic behavior, the economic bureaucracy, and the policy process, and it neglects the economic consequences of the state's policitcal actions. Another problem of the statist account is its disregarding of the issue of leadership in economic development. In contrast, this book has demonstrated the importance of politics and leadership to the economy. Political action, essentially leadership, could create successful industries. Any explanation of the success of the industrial policy has to be multivariate because of the complexity and multiplicity of conditions required for its success. As a replacement for the oversimplified strategic account, the book argues that there are four prerequisites for the success of industrial policy: political support, leadership by a strongman, no-risk guarantees, and policy design. These conditions depend not only on economics but also on politics.

The book has also demonstrated the indirect importance of politics in shaping the marketplace. Taiwan's unique marketplace was a consequence of state political strategies to deal with both society and the economy. What we can learn from the Taiwanese experience is the importance of politics in economic policy; politics must be placed at the center of our analysis of economic policy. Politics is inherently a part of economic activity and contributes to economic development both directly and indirectly. Given the role of politics in economic development, Taiwan's economic success cannot be explained as "state-led industrialization." Instead, it is better understood as a "politically inspired industrial success."

It follows that although the free market assumed by the neoclassical thesis did not exist in Taiwan, my explanation for the success of the SMEs partly supports this notion. The market in which the SMEs operated was close to a free market dominated by market forces. In a sense, the success of the SMEs was based on their comparative advantage and a maximization of that comparative advantage. Both efficient resource allocations and capital accumulations were realized through market forces.[7] The coordination problem was solved by market mechanisms supported by societal goods. However, in contrast to the neo-classical thesis, this book argues that the fundamental determinant for the formation of the market was neither market forces nor the government's macro-policy of acting in accordance with market rules. Rather, it was the state's public policy, which derived from its political concerns, and the state's inaction, which was a result not of free-market concerns but of political considerations.

My explanation for the success of the SMEs confirms the basic argument of the neo-classical thesis that a market which facilitates the operation of market forces is essential to economic growth. Nevertheless, it refutes the neo-classical claim that this market should and can form by itself; in contrast, my explanation shows that this market did not and could not form on its own. To a great extent, it was shaped by state action and by the interplay between the state and private actors. From the Taiwan experience, it can be concluded that state action can result in a market that stimulates the operation of market forces. The state's contribution to economic growth depends on its commitment to the emergence and persistence of such a market rather than to a distortion of it, as the developmental state thesis claims.

The Taiwan Case and Comparative Political Economy

Comparative political economy can find much of interest in the Taiwan case because of its implications for the issue of the impact of rent seeking on economic growth. From the point of view of economics, rent seeking distorts the allocation of resources. Rent seeking inevitably creates winners and losers. Someone must ultimately pay the price of the rents. In many cases, the losers are the weaker elements in the society. A typical case is Robert Bates's finding that in tropical Africa farmers paid the price for the state's provision of economic rents to its allies.[8] As a consequence, the farmers were crushed, and agricultural production decreased. In Taiwan the SMEs paid for the economic rents created for the LEs. As we have seen, however, this did not lead to the collapse of the SMEs.

Japan offers a similar example. Like Taiwan, Japan also had a protected domestic economy, part of which was remarkably unproductive, and an unprotected and competitive economy in the export markets. The government provided economic rents to agriculture, the retail sector, construction, and some heavy industries. The domestic economy's poor allocation of resources is underpinned by lax enforcement of regulations and the laws on competition. This situation resulted from a coalition of the ruling Liberal Democratic Party, the bureaucrats, and the conglomerates—the "iron triangle." Rent seeking created inefficiencies and gave rise to increased costs. The producers of export goods paid the price in high wages, high prices for inputs, and expensive land. How, then, could these firms be efficient and competitive? How do we explain the difference in outcomes between tropical Africa and Taiwan and Japan?

Complete answers to these questions will require more study, but some tentative answers are possible. In tropical Africa, the rent payers were farmers producing mainly for the domestic market. In Taiwan and Japan, the rent payers were for the most part manufacturers producing mainly for international markets. The system in tropical Africa was a closed one; those in Taiwan and Japan were open. Although someone must pay for economic rents, the ways the price is paid can vary. The tropical African farmers were the final bearers of the costs of the economic rents provided by the state to the large enterprises, and as a result, they were crushed. However, a producer of final goods in an industrial economy that is part of the world market can pass part of the cost of the rents to the world market. The costs of domestic rents can be shared internationally, at least in part. In other words, the global division of labor helped to spread the firms' costs. This reduced the burden on the SMEs in Taiwan.

Moreover, as actors in an industrial economy, the SMEs could take advantage of societal goods to offset the disadvantages they otherwise faced in terms of capital shortages and other goods. As a result, at least until the late 1980s, the SMEs were able to pay the costs caused by the economic rents. However, in the late 1980s wages soared, environmental movements became more active, and land prices increased. The SMEs could no longer bear these burdens. In response, they relocated to Southeast Asia and mainland China in order to maintain their competitiveness in world markets. For much the same reasons, export-oriented Japanese firms could afford the cost of the economic rents until the early 1980s, when they, too, began to transfer their manufacturing activities to lower-cost regions to escape the skyrocketing costs in the domestic market.

The Taiwanese experience allows us to make several comments of general significance to comparative political economy. First, free markets and the intent of the state to be market conforming are less significant for economic development than is the particular configuration of the market that emerges from the interaction of the state and private actors and the kind of opportunities that this affords economic actors. The importance of the market lies in its capacity to facilitate the functioning of societal goods, which in turn enables private actors to exercise entrepreneurship.

Second, the political goals of the state have consequences for the marketplace. It is too narrow to view the role of the state in economic development merely in terms of its economic goals. Nor can the role of the state in economic development be reduced to policy. Furthermore, it is inadequate to assume that those in power will seek to ensure that good politics will also be good economics and vice versa. Empirical facts from the Taiwanese case do not support this. The influence of the state on the economic process is far more than that which can be addressed in terms of "intervention"—the magnitude of state behavior can only be conveyed by "action."

Third, the impact of state action on economic development is not always intentional, and actual economic performance is not always a result of state intentions. The state's goals and economic outcomes are not always congruent. Some efforts may end in failure, and some projects may succeed beyond expectations. It is thus misleading to attribute economic success to state intentions.

Fourth, the marketplace is an outcome of the interplay between the state and private actors. The scope of this relationship is far more than a matter of "cooperation" or "coordination," both of which refer to direct and formal links between the two. Indirect and invisible interactions between the state and private actors can also affect the course of economic development.

Finally, institutions are not reducible to rules and organizational structures. Institutions must be "humanized" and "politicized." In fact, individuals may play an even more significant role than institutions. Thus, the issue of leadership should be a critical focus in analyses of the role of the state in economic development and of public policy. This conclusion is particularly important for societies in which the institutions are not yet well developed.

Reference Matter

Notes

Chapter 1

1. In this book, "SMEs" includes only manufacturing firms.
2. World Bank, *The East Asian Miracle*.
3. Wade, *Governing the Market*, p. 13.
4. Jingjibu, Zhongxiao qiyechu, *Zhongxiao qiye tongji*, p. 234.
5. Gereffi, "Organization of Buyer-Driven Global Commodity Chains," pp. 96–99.
6. Hamilton, "Organization and Market Process," p. 82.
7. Rhee, *The State and Industry in South Korea*, p. 204.
8. Wade, *Governing the Market*, p. 192.
9. See, e.g., Evans, "Transferable Lessons?"
10. Pempel, "The Developmental Regime," p. 144.
11. Wang Zhaoming, *Wang Zhaoming huiyi lu*, p. 76; personal interview notes.
12. There are two explanations for Chiang Ching-kuo's action. The first is that he felt that the CIECD was so powerful that it represented a threat to him (Ye Wan-an, "Taiwan jingji sheji jigou," p. 60). The second is that Chiang was at odds with the people from the CIECD over various economic issues (Kang Ludao, *Li Guoding*, pp. 211–12; personal interview with K. T. Li, 1998). I would argue that Chiang's intention was to strengthen his control over economic policy by winning the support of the ministries and weakening the powerful economic planning agency.
13. Wang Zhaoming, *Wang Zhaoming huiyi lu*, pp. 51–53.
14. The higher-salaried talents recruited by the economic planning agencies increased the pivotal role of these agencies, but it is insufficient to assume that these agencies enjoyed unusual organizational autonomy; see Cheng, Haggard, and Kang, "Institutions and Growth."

15. For example, from 1978 on, Chiang Ching-kuo chaired a series of economic meetings attended by all key economic officials. From the minutes of these meetings, it is obvious that Chiang bypassed the premier and dominated the meetings. He gave instructions on every issue. See "Zongtong zhuchi caijing huiyi jilu."

16. Personal interview with K. T. Li, January 1998.

17. Pempel, "Developmental Regime," p. 144.

18. Arnold, "Bureaucratic Politics."

19. Noble, "Contending Forces."

20. Wang Zhenhuan, *Shei tongzhi Taiwan?*, chap. 3; Qu Wanwen, "Chanye zhengce de shifan xiaoguo"; Hsueh, Hsu, and Perkins, *Industrialization and the State.*

21. Bates and Krueger, "Generalizations Arising from the Country Studies."

22. Bates, *Markets and States.*

23. Lasswell, *Politics: Who Gets What, When, How.*

24. Buchanan, *Liberty, Market and State.*

25. Allison, *Essence of Decision.*

26. The most representative critiques are Art, "Bureaucratic Politics and American Foreign Policy"; and Krasner, "Are Bureaucracies Important?"

27. For an idea-driven model as an alternative to Allison's interest-driven Model III, see Rhodes, "Do Bureaucratic Politics Matter?"

28. Kim et al., *Catalyst of Change*; Kim, *The Civil Service System.*

29. Sipress and Mufson, "Powell Takes the Middle Ground"; McGeary, "Odd Man Out."

30. Wade, *Governing the Market*; Cheng, "Political Regimes."

31. Woo-Cumings, "National Security."

32. Cheng, "Political Regimes," pp. 146–47.

33. From 1950 to 1970, between 50 and 80 percent of government expenditures were devoted to defense and diplomacy (Caizhengbu, *Jinrong tongji* [1967], pp. 36–37; idem, *Jinrong tongji nianbao*, pp. 116–17).

34. Zhu Yunhan, "Guazhan jingji"; and Yun-han Chu, "Realignment of Business-Government Relations"; Gold, *State and Society*; Winckler, "Industrialization and Participation"; Wade, *Governing the Market*; Amsden, "State and Taiwan's Economic Development."

35. Evans, *Dependent Development*; Cardoso and Faletto, *Dependency and Development.* "Second ISI" refers to a decline in imports of intermediate and capital goods and a simultaneous increase in domestic production of these goods.

36. Fields, *Embedded Enterprises*; Jung-en Woo, *Race to the Swift*, chap. 6.

37. Jung-en Woo, *Race to the Swift*; Amsden, *Asia's Next Giant*; Jung, "Business-Government Relations."

38. See Hamilton, Orru, and Biggart, "Enterprise Groups," table 1.

39. Ye Wan-an, "Yixie zhongda jingji zhengce (2)," p. 18.

40. Lin Zhongxiong and Peng Baixian, "Zhongxiao qiye jinrong," p. 428; Liu Taiying, "Taiwan zhongxiao qiye touzi huanjing," p. 450.

41. See "Zongtong zhuchi caijing huiyi jilu"; and "Zongtong zhuchi minying gongye zuotanhui jilu."

42. Wade, *Governing the Market*, pp. 179–80.

43. Evans, *Embedded Autonomy*, pp. 77–81.

44. Ibid., p. 79.

45. Wade, *Governing the Market*, pp. 176–77.

46. Qu Wanwen, "Chanye zhengce de shifan xiaoguo"; Wan-wen Chu, "Import Substitution And Export-Led Growth."

47. Hong, *Industrial Policy in East Asia*, chap. 3; Shen Rongqing, "Taiwan jiti dianlu"; Meaney, "State Policy."

48. Wan-wen Chu, "Import Substitution and Export-Led Growth"; Qu Wanwen, "Chanye zhengce de shifan xiaoguo."

49. Zhou Tiancheng, "Taiwan jinrong guanzhi"; Zhou Tiancheng, "Taiwan waixiangxing zhongxiao qiye."

50. Aoki et al., *The Role of Government in East Asian Economic Development*.

51. The neo-classical view of comparative advantage has been challenged. For example, Park, the governor of the Korean Central Bank, denounced "comparative advantage" by saying "Don't listen to 'comparative advantage' advice. Whenever we wanted to do anything the advocates of comparative advantage said 'We don't have comparative advantage.' In fact, we did everything we wanted, but whatever we did, we did well" (quoted in Wade, "East Asia's Economic Success," p. 270).

52. Aoki et al., *The Role of Government in East Asian Economic Development*.

53. World Bank, *The East Asian Miracle*; Amsden, *Asia's Next Giant*.

54. Amsden, *Asia's Next Giant*; Lee, "The Government, Financial System and Large Private Enterprises."

55. Kirby, *Germany and Republican China*, p. 80. According to Chang Chia-ao, general manager of the Bank of China from 1923 to 1935 (in an interview), "[KMT leaders] wanted everything to be influenced by the government. It was felt that if the party-government did not have influence in business (industry, banking, commerce), it would lose its influence in the country. The one-party system was an incentive to push for government control of large enterprises for political purposes" (H. D. Fong,

"Industrial Capital in China," p. 73; quoted in Kirby, *Germany and Republican China*, p. 287n13).

56. Coble, *Shanghai Capitalists*.

57. Shea, "Taiwan: Development and Structural Change"; Shea and Yang, "Taiwan's Financial System"; Liu Shouxiang, "Shuangyuan jinrong tixi"; Xu Jiadong and Guo Pingxin, "Woguo de yinhang zijin."

58. Zysman, *Governments, Markets, and Growth*, p. 76.

59. Ibid., pp. 56–57.

60. Hayami and Aoki, *The Institutional Foundations of East Asian Economic Development*.

61. Lundberg, "Fiscal and Monetary Policies," p. 280.

62. Wade, *Governing the Market*, p. 159.

63. Zhou Tiancheng, "Taiwan waixiangxing zhongxiao qiye"; idem, "Taiwan jinrong guanzhi."

Chapter 2

1. On December 23, 1949, the U.S. secretary of state stated his department's view: "Formosa, politically, geographically, and strategically is part of China." On January 5, 1950, President Truman formally spelled out U.S. policy: "The United States has no predatory designs on Formosa or on any other Chinese territory. The United States has no desire to obtain special rights or privileges, or to establish military bases on Formosa at this time. Nor does it have any intention of utilizing its armed forces to interfere in the present situation. The United States will not pursue a course which leads to involvement in the civil conflict in China. . . . Similarly, the United States will not provide military aid or advice to Chinese Forces on Formosa" (see Kerr, *Formosa Betrayed*, pp. 386–87).

2. Taylor, *The Generalissimo's Son*, p. 181.

3. Yun-han Chu, "The Realignment of Business-Government Relations," p. 115.

4. Ibid., p. 143.

5. Ibid.

6. Wang Zhenhuan, *Shei tongzhi Taiwan?* p. 59.

7. For more on patron-client relations, see Eisenstadt and Roniger, "The Study of Patron-Client Relations"; Eisenstadt and Roniger, *Patrons, Clients, and Friends*; and Powell, "Peasant Society and Clientelist Politics."

8. Gold, *State and Society*, p. 52.

9. As used in this book, the term "public sector" refers to both state-owned and local government–owned sectors. The first refers to firms

owned by the central government; the second to firms owned by the various levels of local government, mainly the provincial government.

10. Clark, *Taiwan's Development*.

11. Wade, *Governing the Market*, p. 177.

12. Before 1958, the exchange rate for the New Taiwan Dollar (NT$) was NT$24.78 to the U.S. dollar; between 1958 and 1979, the rate was NT$40; and between 1985 and 1997 it was NT$26–27.

13. Liu Jinqing, *Taiwan zhanhou jingji*, p. 24.

14. Zheng Youkui et al., *Ziyuan weiyuanhui*, p. 214. Chen Yi, then Taiwan provincial governor, preferred state socialism. He wanted to establish a public economy in Taiwan based on public-owned production, transportation, trade, and finance. He hoped to realize the Principle of the People's Livelihood advocated by Sun Yatsen; see Wu Ruoyu, *Zhanhou Taiwan gongying shiye*, p. 41. This in part explains the controversy between the provincial government and the NRC over the disposition of the confiscated Japanese firms.

15. Liu Jinqing, *Taiwan zhanhou jingji*, p. 25.

16. Wu Ruoyu, *Zhanhou Taiwan gongying shiye*, pp. 43–52.

17. Liu Jinqing, *Taiwan zhanhou jingji*, p. 28.

18. Zi Gu, "Taiwan jingji yu Riben," p. 123.

19. Li Guoding and Chen Muzai, *Woguo jingji fazhan*, p. 8.

20. Ye Wan-an, "Taiwan gongye fazhan zhengce," p. 2.

21. Yin Zhongrong, *Wo dui Taiwan jingji de kanfa*, 2: 36.

22. Liu Sufen, "Tangrong tie gongchang"; Liu Jingtian and Cai Weide, "Exing tonghuo pengzhang"; Makinen and Woodward, "Taiwanese Hyperinflation."

23. Jacoby, *U.S. Aid*, p. 118.

24. Yin Zhongrong, *Wo dui Taiwan jingji de kanfa*.

25. Staff problems in the economy-related departments included lack of professional training, lack of economic knowledge, and lack of foreign-language ability, especially English. Poor command of English remained a major obstacle in the 1950s and 1960s because of the overriding importance of U.S. aid to government economic affairs. One official who served successively in the IDC, CUSA, CIECD, MOEA, and MOF recalled that after he left the CIECD and went to the MOEA in 1965, he found his colleagues in the MOEA unable to provide satisfactory data or opinions about economic issues. Therefore, he had to return to the CIECD to ask for help from his former colleagues (interview).

26. Jacoby, *U.S. Aid*, p. 122; Schenk, "Taiwan fanke."

27. Interview.

28. Wen Xinying, *Jingji qiji de beihou*, p. 224.

29. Jacoby, *U.S. Aid*, p. 60.

30. Li Junxing, *Jing'anhui*, pp. 110–11. My interviews with retired officials also confirmed this point.

31. Interview notes.

32. Kang Ludao, *Li Guoding*, pp. 75–77.

33. Li Guoding, *Taiwan jingji kuaisu chengzhang*, p. 99.

34. Personal interview.

35. All the retired economic officials who had worked in the ESB, IDC, CUSA, and CIECD that I interviewed confirmed this point.

36. Zhu Yunhan ("Guazhan jingji," p. 147) argues that Chiang Kai-shek left financial power to the presidential residence faction as a means of checking the Chen Cheng faction. Xu Boyuan and Yu Guohua were regarded as members of the presidential residence faction. However, the relationship between the two factions was not always so clear-cut. When Yin Zhongrong concurrently held the positions of head of the BOT and the FETCC in the late 1950s and early 1960s, the border between the factions was blurred.

37. Wang Zhaoming, *Wang Zhaoming huiyi lu*; personal interview with Wang.

38. The reform program at first was strongly opposed by the Ministry of Finance because it called for tax reductions. After K. T. Li discussed the program with Minister of Finance Yan Jiagan, Yan accepted it, over the opposition of his MOF colleagues. Yan's support was regarded as critical (interview with K. T. Li).

39. Wang Zhaoming, *Wang Zhaoming huiyi lu*; personal interview with Wang.

40. Wen Xinying, *Jingji qiji de beihou*, pp. 218–26.

41. Jacoby, *U.S. Aid*, p. 57.

42. Ibid., p. 132.

43. Rankin, *China Assignment*, p. 262.

44. Jacoby, *U.S. Aid*, p. 134.

45. Personal interview notes.

46. Ye Wan-an, "Taiwan jingji sheji jigou (1)," p. 21.

47. Wen Xinying, *Jingji qiji de beihou*, p. 225; Ye Wan-an, "Taiwan jingji sheji jigou (1)," p. 3.

48. Ye Wan-an, "Yixie zhongda jingji zhengce (3)," pp. 1–2.

49. Interview with K. T. Li.

50. Li Guoding and Chen Muzai, *Woguo jingji fazhan*, p. 137; Kang Ludao, *Li Guoding*, p. 143.

51. The terms "command economy" and "controlled economy" are often used interchangeably to describe the planned economy on Taiwan be-

fore the late 1950s. Central planning and a state-run economy were its core characteristics.

52. Hsu, "Ideological Reflections," p. 312.

53. Ibid., pp. 316–18.

54. Kirby, *Germany and Republican China.*

55. Wu Ruoyu, *Zhanhou Taiwan gongying shiye,* p. 28.

56. Kirby, *Germany and Republican China,* p. 97.

57. Zheng Youkui et al., *Ziyuan weiyuanhui,* pp. 22–23.

58. Xing Muhuan, *Taiwan jingji celun,* pp. 238–39.

59. On the history of sources of the policies of Nationalist bureaucrats, see Kirby, *Germany and Republican China.* For a detailed and clear analysis of the debate among the bureaucrats over policy ideology in the early 1950s, see Fan Qinping and Liu Sufen, "The Formulation of Economic Policy," pp. 14–19.

60. Hall, *The Political Power of Economic Ideas.*

61. Yin Zhongrong, *Wo dui Taiwan jingji de kanfa,* Preface.

62. Yin Zhongrong, "Taiwan gongye zhengce shini," p. 9.

63. Chen Ciyu and Mo Jiping, *Jiang Shuojie,* pp. 79–80.

64. Ibid., pp. 88–89; Xing Muhuan, *Taiwan jingji celun,* pp. 238–39.

65. A sign of this change came during an unprecedented visit to Xing Muhuan, when Yin stated that Jiang and Liu had some "good opinions." This was also the occasion when Yin counseled Xing to be patient; see Xing Muhuan, *Taiwan jingji celun,* p. 241.

66. Fan Qinping and Liu Sufen, "The Formulation of Economic Policy."

67. Xing Muhuan, *Taiwan jingji celun,* p. 241.

68. Hall, *The Political Power of Economic Ideas,* pp. 383–86.

69. Kang Ludao, *Li Guoding,* p. 86.

70. Ye Wan-an, "Yixie zhongda jingji zhengce (2)."

71. Ibid.

72. Ibid., p. 3.

73. Wang Zhaoming, *Wang Zhaoming huiyi lu,* p. 94.

74. Kirby, "Technocratic Organization and Technological Development."

75. Giddens, *Consequences of Modernity,* p. 114.

76. Luhmann, "Familiarity, Confidence, Trust," p. 102.

77. Fukuyama, *Trust.*

78. Pye, *The Dynamics of Chinese Politics,* pp. 68–70.

79. Fukuyama, *Trust.*

80. Pye, *The Dynamics of Chinese Politics,* p. 70.

81. Winckler and Greenhalgh, "Elite Political Struggle," p. 156.

82. Sun, quoted in ibid., pp. 157–58.

83. Pye, *The Dynamics of Chinese Politics*, p. 259.

84. Yang Aili, *Sun Yunxuan zhuan*, pp. 175–76.

85. Zhang Jun, *Chuangzao caijing qiji*.

86. There are several reasons why Chiang chose Lee as his successor: Lee's Taiwanese identity (in accordance with the process of Taiwanization); his Cornell Ph.D. degree (which made him more acceptable to the United States); the fact that since Lee's son had died, he did not have a successor in his family; and Lee's own cautious and humble performance (according to Lee himself, he dared not lean back in his chair and perched on the edge of the seat whenever he met with Chiang). However, as noted below, his position as an agricultural economist with no factional connections was the most crucial factor.

87. Chen Mingtong, *Paixi zhengzhi*, p. 169.

88. Jiang Nan, *Jiang Jingguo*, pp. 416–20; Zhang Jun, *Chuangzao caijing qiji*, pp. 199–204.

89. See, e.g., Kim Hyung-ki et al., *Catalysts of Change*; and Kim Hyung-ki, *The Civil Service System*.

90. Kim Hyung-ki, *The Civil Service System*.

Chapter 3

1. For an introduction to the history of Japanese rule on Taiwan, see Gold, *State and Society*, chap. 3.

2. Zhou Xianwen, *Riju shida*, p. 62.

3. Ibid., pp. 64–65.

4. Ibid., p. 62.

5. Wang Shan, "Taiwan gongyehua," p. 75.

6. Zhang Zonghan, *Guangfu qian Taiwan*; Liu Jinqing, *Taiwan zhanhou jingji*, pp. 13–14.

7. Liu Jinqing, *Taiwan zhanhou jingji*, p. 250.

8. Tu Zhaoyan, *Riben diguozhuyi*, pp. 331–33; Zhou Xianwen, *Riju shidai*, pp. 82–83.

9. Zhou Xianwen, *Riju shidai*, p. 83.

10. Ibid., pp. 75–76.

11. Ibid., p. 76.

12. Tu Zhaoyan, *Riben diguozhuyi*, pp. 373–74.

13. Gu Xianrong's collaboration with the Japanese troops when they entered Taiwan in 1895 has long been controversial. Gu's assistance helped the Japanese establish their colonial rule despite local enmity. In return, the Gu family was allowed to run some monopolistic businesses, such as salt, on the island and was rewarded with large tracts of land. The family

thus quickly emerged as one of the top five families in Taiwan. For his actions, Gu is considered a traitor by the Chinese, and his descendants have long been troubled by this accusation. See Shen Zijia et al., *Gu Zhenfu zhuan*, pp. 1–10.

14. Because of a relatively larger proportion of landlords and its nationalist orientation, the Lin Xiantang clan had fewer connections with Japanese capital than the other top families; see Tu Zhaoyen, *Riben diguozhuyi*, pp. 421–22. In fact, Lin headed fifteen petition movements between 1921 and 1934 to set up a parliament in Taiwan. Because of this, his family's businesses suffered from interference by the colonial government. See Wu Sanlian, *Wu Sanlian huiyi lu*, pp. 46–50.

15. Tu Zhaoyen, *Riben diguozhuyi*, p. 402.

16. Ibid., pp. 447–48.

17. Zhang Zonghan, *Guangfu qian Taiwan*, p. 254.

18. Tu Zhaoyen, *Riben diguozhuyi*, p. 448.

19. Jung-en Woo, *Race to the Swift*, pp. 30–42.

20. Researchers agree that the KMT regime's top concern was to mitigate tensions with the farmers by giving them land in order to strengthen its rule on the island. However, the top-to-bottom agrarian reform was not intended to destroy the local landlord class. See, e.g., Liu Jinqing, *Taiwan Zhanhou jingji*, pp. 71–91; and Chen Cheng, *Taiwan tudi gaige*.

21. Chen Cheng, *Taiwan tudi gaige*, p. 69; Liu Jinqing, *Taiwan zhanhou jingji*, pp. 80–81.

22. Liu Jinqing, *Taiwan zhanhou jingji*, pp. 80–81. I use Chen Cheng's and Liu Jinqing's similar figures for the amount of the land confiscated from landowners and its value. Pan Zhijia, *Minying gongye*, p. 49, gives slightly different figures.

23. Liao Zhenghong et al., *Guangfu hou*, pp. 29–33.

24. *Taiwan yinhang jikan* 2, no. 4, p. 217.

25. Liu Jinqing, *Taiwan zhanhou jingji*, pp. 197–202.

26. Ibid., pp. 81–82.

27. *Yearbook of the Republic of China, 1953*, p. 173.

28. Liu Jinqing, *Taiwan zhanhou jingji*, pp. 71–86.

29. Pan Zhijia, *Minying gongye*, p. 49.

30. Wang Hongren, *Zhanhou Taiwan siren duzhan ziben zhi fazhan*, p. 35.

31. Liu Jinqing, *Taiwan zhanhou jingji*, p. 230.

32. Tang Xiyou, "Taiwan zhi zaozhi gongye," p. 133; Pan Zhijia, *Minying gongye*, p. 52.

33. Wang Hongren, *Zhanhou Taiwan siren duzhan ziben zhi fazhan*, p. 36.

34. Zhonghua zhengxinsuo, *Taiwan diqu qiye jituan yanjiu*, pp. 638–39.

35. The subsequent performance of firms stemming from the privatization of the state-owned corporations further indicates the significance of the emergence of local private capital. A list of the ranking corporate groups shows that all four privatized companies were among the top 100 company groups in 1985. Taiwan Cement Corporation was the 13th largest, the Yongfeng Group (from Taiwan Paper and Pulp Corporation) ranked 17th, the Xu Jinde Group (from Taiwan Industrial and Mining Corporation) was 29th, and the Taiwan Pineapple Group (from Taiwan Agricultural and Forestry Corporation) was 90th (Wang Hongren, *Zhanhou Taiwan siren duzhan ziben zhi fazhan*, pp. 22–25; Liu Jinqing, *Taiwan zhanhou jingji*, p. 80).

36. Taylor, *The Generalissimo's Son.*

37. Liu Jinqing, *Taiwan zhanhou jingji*, pp. 71–86; Wang Hongren, *Zhanhou Taiwan siren duzhan ziben zhi fazhan*, p. 22.

38. Duan Chenpu, *Taiwan zhanhou jingji*, p. 201.

39. Liu Jinqing, *Taiwan zhanhou jingji*, p. 206.

40. Lin Bangchong, "Taiwan mianfangzhi gongye," p. 77.

41. Wang Shan, "Taiwan gongyehua," p. 75.

42. Lin Bangchong, "Taiwan mianfangzhi gongye," p. 77; Liu Jinqing, *Taiwan zhanhou jingji*, p. 207.

43. Liu Jinqing (*Taiwan zhanhou jingji*, pp. 220–21) describes it as "bureaucrat capital."

44. The China Textile Construction Corporation was established in 1945 under the MOEA. It was originally intended to take over and run the former Japanese-owned textile mills and within two years to resell them to the private sector. It ran a total of 83 mills. After restructuring in Taiwan, it operated under the same name. See Zhu Peilian, *Shu Yunzhang xiansheng*, pp. 91–92, 102.

45. Arnold, "Bureaucratic Politics."

46. Liu Jinqing, *Taiwan zhanhou jingji*, p. 220.

47. Ibid., p. 209.

48. Ibid.

49. One interesting item in Table 3.7 is the category of "managers." Although the proportion of managers among all workers is fairly low (below 0.6 percent), the total of 8,600 Taiwanese managers is considerable. Compared to their 1,900 Japanese counterparts, the Taiwanese "managers" are noteworthy. However, we should not overestimate the significance of this figure. As indicated above, almost all large-scale and important firms were owned by the Japanese; the Taiwanese-owned firms were small in scale, poorly equipped, and largely concentrated in mining and

tea and sugar processing. In Table 3.7 "managers" refers for the most part to those working in the Taiwanese-owned firms.

50. Chen Mingtong, *Paixi zhengzhi*, p. 72.

51. There were five major factions within the KMT government. Immediately after Taiwan reverted to China, they began to contend for better posts in the government. The governor, Chen Yi, belonged to the Political Study Faction. There were also three factions within local political forces. The distribution of posts in the provincial government resulted in struggles among these factions.

52. Chen Mingtong, *Paixi zhengzhi*, p. 71.

53. Chan, "Developing Strength from Weakness."

54. Zhu Peilian, *Shu Yunzhang xiansheng*, p. 141.

Chapter 4

1. Wang Zuorong, *Taiwan jingji fazhan*, pp. 34–35.

2. Li Guoding and Chen Muzai, *Woguo jingji fazhan*, p. 69.

3. Ibid. 4. Jacoby, *U.S. Aid*, p. 51.

5. Ibid., p. 53. 6. Ibid., p. 153.

7. Li Guoding and Chen Muzai, *Woguo jingji fazhan*, p. 24.

8. Liu Jinqing, *Taiwan zhanhou jingji*, p. 308.

9. Ibid.

10. Jacoby, *U.S. Aid*, p. 38.

11. Wen Xinying, *Jingji qiji de bijou*, p. 110.

12. Liu Jinqing, *Taiwan zhanhou jingji*, pp. 352–53.

13. Wen Xinying, *Jingji qiji de beihou*, p. 137.

14. Jacoby, *U.S. Aid*, p. 48.

15. Ibid., pp. 48–49.

16. Wen Xinying, *Jingji qiji de beihou*, p. 244.

17. Ibid., p. 247.

18. Johnson, *MITI*.

19. Coble, *Shanghai Capitalists*.

20. Taylor, *The Generalissimo's Son*, p. 212.

21. Ye Wan-an, "Taiwan jingji sheji jigou," pp. 9–10.

22. Guo Tai, *Wang Yongqin fendou shi*, p. 25.

23. Ibid., p. 28.

24. Kang Ludao, *Li Guoding*, p. 99.

25. Wang Zhaoming, *Wang Zhaoming huiyi lu*, pp. 52–53.

26. Jingji anding weiyuanhui, "Jiaxin shuini."

27. Ibid., Appendix 8.

28. Ibid. 29. Ibid.

30. Ibid. 31. Ibid., Appendix 7.

32. Ibid., Appendix 8.

33. In fact, Shu did not like the job because of disagreements among the major shareholders of Jiaxin (Zhu Peilian, *Shu Yunzhang xiansheng*, pp. 170–71). After Jiaxin began operations, he felt he had contributed enough to the building of the plant and resigned as chairman of the board (ibid., p. 239).

34. Wang Zhaoming, *Wang Zhaoming huiyi lu*, pp. 95–97.

35. Wu Zunxian, *Rensheng qishi*, p. 49.

36. According to Wu Zunxian (ibid., pp. 51–52), when Universal was planning to purchase machinery from Kobe Steel Works, its Taipei representative refused to quote a price because he did not think the Taiwan government would approve an application for a new cement plant; the representative reported being shocked and angry about losing the contract when he learned that Universal Cement had received approval.

37. Li Qinggong, *Tainan bang yi shiji*, pp. 46–47.

38. Wu Xiuqi, a key figure in Tainan Textile, confirmed that Wu Sanlian "was highly praised within and outside the government. With his network and help from other relatives and friends, Tainan Textile received approval to be set up. Otherwise, it would have been more difficult than climbing to heaven to receive approval as one of the two lucky winners among over ten applicants that had abundant funds and strong support" (Gao Zongzhi, "Tainan bang," p. 220).

39. According to the Company Law, a company's president was its legal representative. At a meeting between Yin Zhongrong and the Jiaxin group led by general manager Zhang Minyu (Shu had resigned as president), Yin pointed to the procedural flaw when Jiaxin wrote to the ESB in the name of its general manager instead of its president (Jingji anding weiyuanhui, "Jiaxin shuini").

40. Aoki et al., *The Role of Government in East Asian Economic Development*.

Chapter 5

1. Ye Wan-an, "Yixie zhongda jingji zhengce (2)."

2. Yin Zhongrong, "Dui dangqian waihui," pp. 131–32; Kang Ludao, *Li Guoding*, p. 124.

3. Ching-yuan Lin, *Industrialization in Taiwan*, pp. 74–75.

4. Xia Qiyue, "Lun waihui maoyi," p. 6.

5. Ching-yuan Lin, *Industrialization in Taiwan*.

6. Ho, *Economic Development of Taiwan*, p. 195.

7. See, e.g., Haggard and Pan, "The Transition to Export-Led Growth"; Kang Ludao, *Li Guoding*; Wang Zhaoming, *Wang Zhaoming huiyi lu*; Ye

Wan-an, "Taiwan jingji sheji jigou"; and idem, "Yixie zhongda jingji zhengce (1, 2, 3)."

8. Chu Yanzheng, "Taiwan diqu guojia, waizi," p. 61.

9. Ibid.

10. Li Guoding Archives, "Chen Cheng shang zongtong qiancheng."

11. Personal interview with K. T. Li, January 1998.

12. Chen Yuxi, *Taiwan de yifuxing fazhan*; Gold, *State and Society*, p. 52.

13. Yin Zhongrong was very outspoken and aggressive, which often embarrassed Premier Yu at cabinet meetings. Yu took this very much to heart, and he ordered Yin to sign his name to the statement that "his powers were suspended due to legal reasons" before he resigned from his position because of the corruption case (Shen Yunlong, ed., *Yin Zhongrong xiansheng*, pp. 413–14). Premier Yu was one of Chiang Kai-shek's men because, as governor of the Central Bank, he had transferred large sums of gold from Shanghai to Taiwan just before the KMT government fled to the island. This explains why Premier Yu dared to use the Yangzi case to remove Yin even though Yin was Chen's protégé.

14. Wang Zhaoming, *Wang Zhaoming huiyi lu*, pp. 52–53.

15. Personal interview with Wang Zhaoming; Ye Wan-an, "Yixie zhongda jingji zhengce (2)," p. 18.

16. Subsequent developments confirm Chiang's trust in Xu Boyuan. He succeeded Yu Hongjun as the governor of the Central Bank of China in 1960 and was reappointed chairman of the FETCC in 1963 after Yin's death.

17. Chen Cheng said: "He [Yin] was certainly talented, very talented. But he acted as if only he was right and everyone else was wrong" (personal interview with Wang Zhaoming).

18. Zhang Jun, *Chuangzao caijing qiji*, pp. 202–4.

19. Personal interview with Ye Wan-an.

20. Arnold, "Bureaucratic Politics"; Yun-han Chu, "The Realignment of Business-Government Relations."

21. Shen Zijia et al., *Gu Zhenfu zhuan*, p. 27.

22. Wang Zhaoming, *Wang Zhaoming huiyi lu*, pp. 54–55; Kang Ludao, *Li Guoding*, p. 100.

23. Wang Zuorong, *Women ruhe chuangzao liao jingji qiji*, p. 56.

24. Kang Ludao, *Li Guoding*, p. 143.

25. Ibid., pp. 143–48.

26. Ye Wan-an, "Yixie zhongda jingji zhengce (1)," p. 18.

27. Jung-en Woo, *Race to the Swift*; Amsden, *Asia's Next Giant*.

28. Jacoby, *U.S. Aid*, pp. 34–35.

29. *Zhengxin xinwen*, May 4, 1959.

30. Ibid., Mar. 7, 1959.

31. Jinghehui disichu, "Zhonghua kaifa," pp. 10–11.

32. Liu Jinqing, *Taiwan zhanhou jingji*, p. 317.

33. Ibid.

34. Jinghehui disichu, "Zhonghua kaifa," pp. 4, 32.

35. Liu Jinqing, *Taiwan zhanhou jingji*, p. 297.

36. The clients of the CDC were limited to private companies (Jinghehui disichu, "Zhonghua kaifa," p. 18). In other words, small-sized factories were excluded from access to the CDC's lines of credit.

37. Liu Jinqing, *Taiwan zhanhou jingji*, p. 317.

38. According to Liu Jinqing (ibid., p. 284), state-business financial capital includes both state and business investments. "Chinese financial capital" is primitive capital in conjunction with bank capital; that is, ahead of the development of industrial capital. The goal of the latter is capital accumulation.

39. Fan Qinping and Liu Sufen, "Minguo sishi nian Tangrong yu minjian daikuan," p. 26.

40. Fan Qinping and Liu Sufen, "Qiye jingying yu lixing juece," p. 114.

41. There were many reasons for the government's action. First, Tangrong had over 4,000 employees. Including their families, more than 30,000 people would have been adversely affected; the likely result would have been social turbulence. Second, Tangrong was closely associated with the military. Many of its goods were military-related, and it was a large buyer of military waste goods. Therefore, the government did not want to see such an enterprise go bankrupt. Third, many higher-ranking government officials had put money into Tangrong because of its high rate of return. In order to protect their investment, the government had to save Tangrong. Fourth, the public banks had already lent money to Tangrong, and the government's actions would protect the interests of the public banks (Liu Jinqing, *Taiwan zhanhou jingji*, pp. 309–10).

42. Xu Xueji, *Minying Tangrong gongsi*, p. 221.

43. Ibid., pp. 99–100. 44. Ibid., p. 18.

45. Ibid. 46. Ibid., pp. 48–49.

47. Ibid., pp. 202–3. 48. Ibid., p. 117.

49. Ibid., pp. 21–46, 269–14. 50. Ibid., p. 26.

51. Ibid., pp. 100, 108, 133. 52. Ibid.

53. Ibid., p. 204. 54. Ibid., p. 12.

55. This fear also surfaced when a Japanese steel and an American steel company wanted to co-operate with Tangrong. The plan was rejected by Yin Zhongrong, who feared that the defense industry would be controlled by foreign capital (see ibid., p. 16).

56. Ibid., pp. 16, 196.

57. Liu Sufen, "Tangrong tie gongchang," pp. 222–23.

58. Tang Chuanzong hinted that Yin trimmed his sails in the end (Xu Xueji, *Minying Tangrong gongsi*, p. 26).

59. Ibid., p. 204.

60. Liu Sufen, "Tangrong tie gongchang," p. 216.

61. Fan Qinping and Liu Sufen, "Minguo sishi nian Tangrong yu minjian daikuan," p. 11.

62. Xu Xueji, *Minying Tangrong gongsi*, p. 177.

63. Ibid., p. 18.

64. On the evolution of interest rate policy and its relations with economic development in the 1950s, see the excellent analysis in Fan Qinping et al., "Lilü zhengce," pp. 153–82.

65. Yin Zhongrong, "Jinrong xianzhuang yu taiyin duice," p. 103.

66. Yin Zhongrong, "Taiwan de jinrong," p. 28.

67. This estimate was made by the China Credit Information Institute based on a 1959 survey. Yin cited these figures in his article "Idle Capital and the Rate of the Black Market," which was published in all major newspapers in Taipei on August 27, 1960 (Yin Zhongrong, "Lun youzi," p. 21).

68. Yin Zhongrong, "Jinrong xianzhuang yu Taiyin duice," p. 103.

69. Yin Zhongrong, "Lun youzi," pp. 22–23.

70. Jianchayuan, *Jianchayuan gongbao*, p. 2838.

71. Fan Qinping et al., "Lilü zhengce," p. 163.

72. As mentioned above, there were various reasons why the government forced Tangrong to seek help from the government. Liu Jinqing (*Taiwan zhanhou jingji*, p. 309) argues that the real reason was that the government wanted to protect the interests of the BOT and high-ranking government officials who were the creditors of Tangrong. However, this is difficult to prove.

73. Tangrong tie gongchang diaochatuan, "Tangrong tie gongchang."

74. Fan Qinping et al., "Lilü zhengce," p. 174.

75. Tangrong tie gongchang diaochatuan, "Tangrong tie gongchang."

76. Yin Zhongrong, "Taiwan de jinrong," p. 32.

77. Yin Zhongrong, "Qunian de jinrong," p. 116.

78. *Zhengxin xinwen*, Jan. 1, 1961.

79. Yin Zhongrong, "Woguo jinrong," p. 150.

80. Ching-yuan Lin, *Industrialization in Taiwan*, p. 81.

81. Ibid.

82. Ibid., pp. 81–82.

83. Li Guoding and Chen Muzai, *Woguo jingji fazhan celue zonglun*, p. 423.

84. Yin Zhongrong, "Taiwan tonghuo pengzhang," p. 193.

85. Evans, *Embedded Autonomy*.

86. Xu Xueji, *Minying Tangrong gongsi*.

87. Ibid., pp. 21–26.

88. *Zhengxin xinwen*, Nov. 22, 1960.

Chapter 6

1. Jacoby, *U.S. Aid*, p. 228.　　　2. Ibid., p. 229.

3. Ibid., p. 230.　　　　　　　　4. Ibid., p. 229.

5. Kuo-wei Chang, *Economic Development*, p. 11.

6. Jacoby, *U.S. Aid*, p. 230.

7. Personal interview with Wang Zhaoming.

8. Xiao Quanzheng, *Taiwan diqu de xin zhongshang zhuyi*, p. 70.

9. Wang Zuorong, *Women ruhe chuangzao le jingji qiji?* p. 71.

10. Lin Zhongxiong, *Taiwan jingji fazhan sishi nian*, p. 83.

11. Wang Zuorong, *Women ruhe chuangzao le jingji qiji?* pp. 75–77.

12. Ibid., p. 65.

13. Ibid., p. 77.

14. Xiao Quanzheng, *Taiwan diqu de xin zhongshang zhuyi*, pp. 125–26.

15. Wang Zuorong, *Women ruhe chuangzao le jingji qiji?* pp. 78–80.

16. The ten projects were a steel plant, a shipbuilding yard, a petrochemical plant, a highway, Taizhong port, Suao port, an electric railway, a railway at the Tropic of Cancer, Taoyuan international airport, and a nuclear power plant.

17. Ye Wan-an, "Yixie zhongda jingji zhengce (2)," p. 12.

18. Ibid., pp. 11–12.

19. Ibid., p. 14.

20. Kang Ludao, *Li Guoding*, p. 214.

21. Ibid.

22. Ye Wan-an, "Yixie zhongda jingji zhengce (3)," pp. 14–15.

23. Personal interview with Ye Wan-an.

24. Chiang Ching-kuo disbanded the CIECD because he felt that the CIECD was too powerful (Ye Wan-an, "Taiwan jingji sheji jigou," p. 6) and because he was at odds with the people from the CIECD over various economic issues (see Kang Ludao, *Li Guoding*, pp. 211–12; personal interview with K. T. Li). But Chiang trusted then–MOEA Minister Sun Yunxuan. In fact, Chiang's move served two goals—winning support from the ministries and weakening the economic planning agency. Both goals helped his efforts to dominate economic policy.

25. Kang Ludao, *Li Guoding*, p. 212.
26. Wang Zhaoming, *Wang Zhaoming huiyi lu*, p. 76.
27. The process of the establishment of the IDB reflects the interest differences among the economic departments. The idea of establishing an Industrial Development Bureau under the MOEA was initiated by K. T. Li while he was the minister of the MOEA. But his proposal was opposed by the then-secretary-general of the CIECD, Tao Shengyang. Tao insisted that industrial development remain the purview of the CIECD. The proposal was therefore tabled because of Tao's objections. However, when Tao replaced Li as minister of the MOEA in 1969, he changed his mind and insisted on establishing the IDB. See Liu Fenghan et al., *Wei Yongning xiansheng*, pp. 113–14.
28. Ibid., p. 118.
29. Zhongguo guoji shangye yinhang, "Zhongguo guoji shangye yinhang."
30. Wang Zhaoming, *Wang Zhaoming huiyi lu*, p. 60.
31. Kang Ludao, *Li Guoding*, pp. 151–53.
32. Ye Wan-an, "Yixie zhongda jingji zhengce (1)."
33. Ibid.
34. Kang Ludao, *Li Guoding*; personal interview with Li; Wang Zhaoming, *Wang Zhaoming huiyi lu*.
35. Kang Ludao, *Li Guoding*, p. 211.
36. Ibid.
37. Chiang Ching-kuo lived in the Soviet Union from 1926 to 1937. This period was crucial to the formation of his personal ideology. For more details, see Jiang Nan, *Jiang Jingguo*.
38. Su Ziqin, *Quan yu qian*, p. 38.
39. The entire country suffered from runaway inflation in 1948. Chiang blamed the Kong and Song clans for the economic disaster. Sent by his father, Chiang Ching-kuo went to Shanghai, the heart of China's business and finance, in late 1948 to fight the Kong and Song clans, who controlled Shanghai's economic and financial activities. His ambitious "fight against tigers" ultimately failed because of resistance from the two powerful families.
40. Su Ziqin, *Quan yu qian*, pp. 39–41.
41. Ye Wan-an, "Yixie zhongda jingji zhengce (2)," pp. 5–6.
42. Su Ziqin, *Quan yu qian*, pp. 41–42.
43. Ibid., p. 40.
44. Ibid.
45. Liu Jinqing, *Taiwan zhanhou jingji*, p. 303.
46. Yan Junbao, *Taiwan diqu yinhang*, p. 107.

47. Wu Ruoyu, *Zhanhou Taiwan gongying shiye*, p. 118.

48. Ibid.

49. Wang Yuan, *Taiwan yinhang sanshi nian*, p. 34.

50. Liu Jinqing, *Taiwan zhanhou jingji*, p. 303.

51. Wu Ruoyu, *Zhanhou Taiwan gongying shiye*, pp. 120–21.

52. Liu Jinqing, *Taiwan zhanhou jingji*, p. 289.

53. Ibid.

54. Xu Youxiang, *Zouguo bashi suiyue*, p. 121.

55. Hamilton et al., "The Network Structures of East Asian Economies," p. 123.

56. Zhongyang yinhang, "Ge yinhang zhongdian fangkuan fenxi baogao," p. 34.

57. Ibid., p. 1.

58. Hellmann et al., "Financial Restraint," pp. 163–64.

59. Zhongguo guoji shangye yinhang, "Zhongguo guoji shangye yinhang."

60. Dessus et al., *Chinese Taipei*, p. 81; Yin Naiping, *Zhongxiao qiye rongzi wenti*, p. 2.

61. Chen Jieying, "Taiwan zhongxiao qiye zijin yunzuo."

62. Ibid.

63. Cai Hongming, "Taiwan fu dalu touzi," p. 31.

64. Shaw, *Financial Deepening*; McKinnon, *Money and Capital in Economic Development*; Jiang Shuojie, "Huilü lilü yu jingji fazhan"; Hellmann et al., "Financial Restraint."

65. See, e.g., Peng Baixian and Zheng Suqing, "Taiwan zhi jinrong tixi"; Chen Yonghua, "Taiwan jinrong shichang"; Zhou Tiancheng, "Taiwan jinrong guanzhi"; and idem, "Taiwan waixiangxing zhongxiao qiye."

66. Zhou Tiancheng, "Taiwan jinrong guanzhi," p. 236.

67. Ibid., p. 229.

68. Yin Zhongrong, "Lun youzi."

69. Riegg, "The Role of Fiscal and Monetary Policies," p. 253; quoted in Wade, *Governing the Market*, p. 161.

70. Zhonghua zhengxinsuo, *Taiwan diqu jituan qiye yanjiu*, preface.

71. Numazaki, "The Role of Personal Networks."

72. Tanikaba, *Taiwan de gongyehua*, p. 137.

73. Zhongyang yinhang, "Ge yinhang zhongdian fangkuan fenxi baogao."

74. Hamilton et al., "The Network Structures of East Asian Economies."

75. Hamilton, "Organization and Market Process," p. 250, table 2.

76. Ibid., p. 249.

77. CEPD, *Taiwan Statistical Data Book* (1997), p. 188.

78. Li Guoding, *Taiwan jingji kuaisu chengzhang de jingyan*, 1978.

79. Chou, *Industrial Organization in a Dichotomous Economy*, p. 129.

Chapter 7

1. Przeworski, *Democracy and the Market*, p. 66.

2. The event provided momentum for the KMT's call for national unity. The diplomatic shift by the United States was viewed as a betrayal of Taiwan and incited anger throughout the island. The KMT seized the unexpectedly patriotic furor to legitimize itself. But the effect was only temporary.

3. Wang Zhenhuan (*Shei tongzhi Taiwan?* p. 58) calls this "downward legitimization."

4. Wakabayashi Masahiro, *Zhuanxingqi de Taiwan*, p. 101.

5. Tien, "Transformation of an Authoritarian Party State," p. 40.

6. In other countries as well, integrating new groups into the authoritarian institutions has been a common way to broaden the social base of the regime; see Przeworski, *Democracy and the Market,* p. 57.

7. Wang Zhaoming, *Wang Zhaoming huiyi lu*, pp. 189–90.

8. Ibid., pp. 190–91; Kang Ludao, *Li Guoding*, pp. 211–18.

9. Kang Ludao, *Li Guoding*, pp. 216–17.

10. Wang Zuorong, *Women ruhe chuangzao le jingji qiji*, p. 22.

11. For example, the main topic of discussion at a breakfast meeting of business people was competition in the textile and food sectors from mainland China. This meeting of business people was a series of meetings attended by almost all the leading businessmen in Taiwan. This forum had 34 members. It began in June 1974 and was held once a month. The position of chairman rotated among the members. According to the rules of the meetings, the purpose of the meetings was to discuss issues of concern to the industrial and commercial sectors, to express their views to the government, and to enhance international exchanges. Officials from the MOEA, MOF, and the central bank, such K. T. Li and Yu Guohua, were invited as guests to some meetings. To distinguish itself from other business organizations, however, the group operated in a rather secretive manner. It was in fact an exclusive club for tycoons. The subjects discussed at the meetings were wide ranging. The businessmen admitted that competition was a real threat and countermeasures needed to be worked out. K. T. Li pointed out that the island needed to prepare for a future economic battle with mainland China in the world economic market. He suggested that the government set up a group to study this problem ("Gongshangjie zaocanhui huiyi," 3rd meeting). At the seventh economic

meeting chaired by the president, Chiang Ching-kuo ordered that the Executive Yuan assign an agency to study mainland China's economy, the future challenges it posed, and the ways Taiwan should respond ("Zongtong zhuchi caijing huiyi," 7th meeting).

12. Personal interview with Sun Zhen.

13. "Zongtong zhuchi caijing huiyi," 7th meeting.

14. "Gongshangjie zaocanhui huiyi," 3rd meeting.

15. Because of a failure to note this, Robert Wade's description of the role and functions of the IDB is a bit too eulogistic; see his *Governing the Market*, pp. 201–8.

16. *Jingji ribao*, Dec. 8, 1981.

17. Ibid.

18. *Far Eastern Economic Review*, June 7, 1984.

19. Wang Zhaoming, *Wang Zhaoming huiyi lu*, pp. 93–95.

20. *Jingji ribao*, Dec. 6, 1981.

21. Wang Zhaoming, *Wang Zhaoming huiyi lu*, pp. 187–88.

22. *Gongshang shibao*, Apr. 11, 1982; *Jingji ribao*, Apr. 11, 1982; *Lianhebao*, Feb. 25, 1982.

23. *Lianhebao*, Feb. 25, 1982.

24. "Zongtong zhuchi caijing huiyi."

25. Kang Ludao, *Li Guoding*, p. 218.

26. Ibid., p. 220.

27. Ibid., pp. 227–28.

28. Gold, *State and Society*, p. 103.

29. Personal interview with K. T. Li.

30. Aoki et al., *The Role of Government in East Asian Economic Development*.

31. Arnold, "Bureaucratic Politics."

32. Huang Defu, "Xuanju, difang paixi"; Zhu Yunhan, "Guazhan jingji."

33. Winckler, "National, Regional and Local Politics"; Hu and Chu, "Electoral Competition and Political Democratization."

34. Wang Zhenhuan, *Shei tongzhi Taiwan?* p. 153.

35. Ibid., p. 154.

36. Cheng and Haggard, *Political Change*, pp. 12–13.

37. Wan-wen Chu, "Import Substitution and Export-Led Growth."

38. Wang Zhenhuan, *Shei tongzhi Taiwan?* p. 103.

39. There are different views about the purpose behind these arrangements. Wang Zhenhuan argues (*Shei tongzhi Taiwan?* pp. 103–4) that maintaining SME competitiveness in the world market was a major concern of the government. However, based on the fact that the CPC pro-

vided the intermediate-stream sector its products at international prices but did not ask the latter to lower its prices to the downstream users, Wan-wen Chu ("Import Substitution and Export-Led Growth," p. 788) deduces that the government's policy purpose was to maximize the value-added of Taiwan's exports rather than to maintain the international competitiveness of exports. I tend to accept the former argument because Chu's inference is not supported by evidence (Chu, "Import Substitution and Export-Led Growth," p. 786).

40. Duan, *Taiwan zhanhou jingji*, p. 191.

41. Wan-wen Chu, "Import Substitution and Export-Led Growth," pp. 790, 793, and note 29.

42. Wang Zhenhuan, *Shei tongzhi Taiwan?* pp. 105–6.

43. Ibid., p. 115.

44. Cheng and Haggard, *Political Change*, p. 14.

45. Wang Zhenhuan, *Shei tongzhi Taiwan?* p. 106.

46. Ibid., pp. 72–73.

47. Ibid., p. 73.

48. Ibid.

49. "Zongtong zhuchi minying gongye."

50. Weiss and Hobson, *States and Economic Development*, chap. 6.

51. Gramsci, *Selections from the Prison Notebooks*; Sassoon, "Passive Revolution and the Politics of Reform"; Wang Zhenhuan, *Shei tongzhi Taiwan?* pp. 71–72.

52. *Wall Street Journal*, Feb. 17, 1999.

53. Yang Aili, *Sun Yunxuan zhuan*, pp. 129–30.

54. Kang Ludao, *Li Guoding*, pp. 240–41.

55. Yang Aili, *Sun Yunxuan zhuan*, p. 130.

56. Kang Ludao, *Li Guoding*, p. 218.

57. In another version, Canada and France were cited as examples; see Meaney, "State Policy."

58. Yang Aili, *Sun Yunxuan zhuan*, p. 128.

59. Ibid., p. 128.

60. Kang Ludao, *Li Guoding*, pp. 234–35.

61. Pan Wenyuan, "Zhihua zhengwei."

62. Meaney, "State Policy."

63. Ibid.

64. Shen Rongqing, "Taiwan jiti dianlu," note 6.

65. Ibid., note 14.

66. Evans, "State, Capital, and the Transformation of Dependence."

67. Hirschman, *Strategy of Economic Development*.

68. Wu Yingchun, "Hanguo bandaoti."

69. Shen Rongqing, "Taiwan jiti dianlu," p. 57.

70. Aoki et al., *The Role of Government in East Asian Economic Development*, chap. 1.

71. Kang Ludao, *Li Guoding*, p. 232.

72. Gold, *State and Society*, p. 104.

73. Chen Shimeng et al., *Jiegou dangguo ziben zhuyi*.

74. Wu Ruoyu, *Zhanhou Taiwan gongying shiye*, pp. 7–8.

75. Wade, *Governing the Market*, pp. 175–82; Wu Ruoyu, *Zhanhou Taiwan gongying shiye*.

76. Wan-wen Chu, "Import Substitution and Export-Led Growth"; Qu Wanwen, "Chanye zhengce de shifan xiaoguo."

77. Stiglitz and Weiss, "Credit Rationing in Markets."

78. Wan-wen Chu, "Import Substitution and Export-Led Growth."

79. Wang Zhenhuan, *Shei tongzhi Taiwan?* p. 101.

80. Qu Wanwen, "Chanye zhengce de shifan xiaoguo," pp. 130–31.

81. Wan-wen Chu, "Import Substitution and Export-Led Growth," p. 786.

82. Kim and Ma, "The Role of Government in Acquiring Technological Capability," pp. 111–12.

Chapter 8

1. Rhee, *The State and Industry in South Korea*, p. 204.

2. Zhou Tiancheng, "Quanli bianchui de zhongxiao qiye," p. 115.

3. Hamilton, "Organization and Market Process."

4. Fields, "Trading Companies," p. 1087.

5. Lin Zhongxiong and Peng Baixian, "Zhongxiao qiye jinrong," p. 428.

6. Liu Taiying, "Taiwan zhongxiao qiye touzi huanjing," p. 450.

7. Lin Chen-you, "Taiwan zhongxiao qiye de falü fagui huanjing."

8. Ye Wan-an, "Taiwan jingji sheji jigou," p. 13.

9. Evans, *Embedded Autonomy*.

10. "Zongtong zhuchi caijing huiyi jilu"; "Zongtong zhuchi minying gongye zuotanhui jilu."

11. Yang Aili, *Sun Yunxuan zhuan*, p. 140.

12. Chung-hua Institution for Economic Research, *Zhongxiao qiye rongzi*, p. 86.

13. Ibid., p. 159.

14. Ibid., p. 160.

15. Zhao Jichang, *Caijing shengya wushi nian*, pp. 204–5.

16. Bank Act, Article 96.

17. Zhao Jichang, "Taiwan zhongxiao qiye zhi fudao," pp. 90–91.

18. Ibid., p. 91.

19. Chung-hua Institution for Economic Research, *Zhongxiao qiye rongzi*, pp. 94–97.

20. CEPD, *Taiwan Statistical Data Book, 1997*, p. 187, table 11–3.

21. Hamilton, "Organization and Market Process."

22. Evans, *Dependent Development*; Cardoso and Faletto, *Dependency and Development*.

23. Fields, *Embedded Enterprises*; Jung-en Woo, *Race to the Swift*, chap. 6.

24. *China Times* (electronic edition), Mar. 19, 1999.

25. Ho, "Economic Development and Rural Industry," p. 984.

26. Chen Shengyi, *Gongyequ de kaifa*, pp. 59–60; Liu Mincheng and Zuo Hongchou, *Gaishan touzi huanjing*, p. 23.

27. Cheng, "Political Regimes," p. 160.

28. Liu Mincheng and Zuo Hongchou, *Gaishan touzi huanjing*, p. 25.

29. Piore and Sabel, *The Second Industrial Divide*; Friedman, *The Misunderstood Miracle*.

30. Gereffi, "The Organization of Buyer-Driven Global Commodity Chains."

31. Deyo, "State and Labor," pp. 184–85.

32. Xie Guoxiong, "Yinxing gongchang."

33. Shieh, *"Boss" Island*, pp. 214–15.

34. Li Guoding, "Taiwan zhongxiao qiye."

35. Chen Mingzhang, ed., *Taiwan zhongxiao qiye fazhan*, pp. 391–95.

36. See, e.g., Friedman, *Misunderstood Miracle*.

37. Hsieh, "Industrial Development and Managerial Adjustment," p. 101.

38. Chen Jiexuan, *Xieli wangluo*, p. 23.

39. Ibid., pp. 25–26.

40. Zhou Tiancheng, "Taiwan waixiangxing zhongxiao qiye," p. 123.

41. Chen Jiexuan, *Xieli wangluo*, p. 35.

42. Shieh, *"Boss" Island*.

43. This cultural trait is unanimously claimed by both SME operators and local researchers as "very much Chinese." There is a risk, however, of falling into the trap of "cultural exclusivism" by asserting some habits or values as a certain country's unique characteristics. Wanting to be one's own boss is, of course, not a uniquely Chinese characteristic. In fact, the desire can be found throughout the world (for a study of this trait among Italians, see Orru, "The Institutional Logic of Small-Firm Economies," pp. 352–54). Exclusivist thinking can be both alarming and amusing—two examples will suffice: a Korean assertively claiming that eating rice is a "distinctively Korean habit"; a Japanese marveling at finding that a "foreigner [a Chinese in this case] is able to handle chopsticks so skillfully!"

44. Chen Jiexuan, *Xieli wangluo*, chaps. 10 and 11.

45. We should, however, remain cautious about the role of culture in economic development. Although culture is rooted in people's minds and in society, its role is to a great extent determined by other factors. The role of culture is either constrained or facilitated by the political system, social conditions, economic organizations, and the marketplace. For example, the desire to be one's own boss, however strong it may be, cannot always be realized. Other conditions that are both practical and tangible must be in place if this aspiration is to be achieved. Culture is a significant factor but not a determinant in economic development.

46. Peng Baixian and Zheng Suqing, "Taiwan minjian jinrong de zijin guandao"; Chen Yonghua, "Taiwan jinrong shichang"; Huang Shisheng, "Taiwan diqu huobi shichang"; Zhou Tiancheng, *Taiwan chanye zuzhi*, chap. 3; Chung-hua Institution for Economic Research, *Zhongxiao qiye rongzi*.

47. Chen Jiexuan, *Xieli wangluo*, pp. 78–79.

48. Ke Zhiming, *Taiwan dushi xiaoxing zhizaoye*.

49. Chen Jiexuan, *Xieli wangluo*, pp. 80–82.

50. Ibid., p. 106.

51. Hsieh, "Industrial Development and Managerial Adjustment," p. 81.

52. Chen Jiexuan, *Xieli wangluo*; Hsieh, "Industrial Development and Managerial Adjustment."

53. Hsieh, "Industrial Development and Managerial Adjustment," pp. 80–81.

54. For details about global commodity chains, see Gereffi, "Organization of Buyer-Driven Commodity Chains."

55. Wu Huilin and Zhou Tiancheng, "Shi jie Taiwan zhongxiao qiye zhi mi."

56. Ibid.

57. Fields, "Trading Companies."

58. Lin Lin, "Banking Development of Taiwan."

59. Ibid.

60. Chen Mingzhang, ed., *Taiwan zhongxiao qiye fazhan*, p. 385.

61. Chen Jiexuan, *Xieli wangluo*, p. 125.

62. Ibid., pp. 126–40.

63. Ibid., pp. 129–34.

Chapter 9

1. Wade, *Governing the Market*; Amsden, *Asia's Next Giant*; Haggard, *Pathways from the Periphery*; Deyo, ed., *The Political Economy of the New Asian Industrialism*; Evans, *Embedded Autonomy*.

2. Wade, *Governing the Market*.

3. Komiya, "Introduction," p. 8.

4. As early as the late 1950s, the domestic market in Taiwan, with a population of less than 10 million, was already saturated.

5. Gereffi, "The Organization of Buyer-Driven Global Commodity Chains," pp. 96–99.

6. Hamilton, "Organization and Market Process."

7. According to Wade (*Governing the Market*, p. 29), capital accumulation was more significant than efficient resource allocation in East Asian economic growth.

8. Bates, *Markets and States*.

Bibliography

Aberbach, Joel D.; David Dollar; and Kenneth L. Sokoloff, eds. *The Role of the State in Taiwan's Development*. Armonk, NY: M. E. Sharpe, 1994.

Alam, M. Shahid. *Governments and Markets in Economic Development Strategies: Lessons from Korea, Taiwan, and Japan*. New York: Praeger, 1989.

Allison, Graham. *Essence of Decision: Explaining the Cuban Missile Crisis*. Boston: Little, Brown, 1971.

Almond, Gabriel A. "The Return to the State?" *American Political Science Review* 82, no. 3 (Sept. 1988): 853–74.

Amsden, Alice H. *Asia's Next Giant: South Korea and Late Industrialization*. New York: Oxford University Press, 1989.

———. *The Rise of "the Rest": Challenges to the West from Late-Industrializing Economies*. New York: Oxford University Press, 2001.

———. "State and Taiwan's Economic Development." In Evans et al., eds., *Bringing the State Back In* (q.v.).

———. "Taiwan's Economic History." *Modern China* 5, no. 3 (1979): 341–79.

Aoki, Masahiko; Hyung-Ki Kim; and Masahiro Okuno-Fujiwara, eds. *The Role of Government in East Asian Economic Development: Comparative Institutional Analysis*. Oxford: Clarendon Press, 1996.

Appelbaum, Richard P., and Jeffrey Henderson. *State and Development in the Asian Pacific Rim*. Newbury Park, CA: Sage, 1992.

Arnold, Walter. "Bureaucratic Politics, State Capacity, and Taiwan's Automobile Industrial Policy." *Modern China* 15, no. 2 (Apr. 1989): 178–214.

Art, Robert J. "Bureaucratic Politics and American Foreign Policy: A Critique." *Policy Sciences* 4, no. 4 (Dec. 1973): 467–90.

"As Global Chip Industry Reinvents Itself Again, Taiwan Stands to Gain." *Wall Street Journal*, Feb. 17, 1999.

Azarya, Victor. "Recording State-Society Relations: Incorporation and Disengagement." In Rothchild and Chazan, *The Precarious Balance* (q.v.).

Azarya, Victor, and Naomi Chazan. "Disengagement from the State in Africa: Reflection on the Experience of Ghana and Guinea." *Comparative Studies in Society and History* 29 (1987): 106–31.

Bachrach, Peter, and Morton S. Baratz. *Power and Poverty: Theory and Practice.* New York: Oxford University Press, 1970.

Balassa, Bela. "The Lessons of East Asian Development: An Overview." *Economic Development and Cultural Change* 36, no. 3 (Supplement 1988).

———. *The Newly Industrializing Countries in the World Economy.* New York: Pergamon Press, 1989.

Balassa, Bela, et al. *Development Strategies in Semi-Industrial Economies.* Baltimore: Johns Hopkins University Press, 1982.

"Banking on Yu." *Far Eastern Economic Review (FEER)*, June 7, 1984.

Bardhan, P. "Symposium on the State and Economic Development." *Journal of Economic Perspectives* 4, no. 3 (1990): 3–8.

Barrett, Richard E., and Martin King Whyte. "Dependency Theory and Taiwan: Analysis of a Deviant." *American Journal of Sociology* 87, no. 5 (Mar. 1982): 1064–89.

Bates, Robert. *Beyond the Miracle of the Market: The Political Economy of Agrarian Development in Kenya.* Cambridge: Cambridge University Press, 1989.

———. "Contra Contractarianism: Some Reflections on the New Institutionalism." *Politics and Society* 16, nos. 2–3 (Sept. 1988): 387–401.

———. *Markets and States in Tropical Africa: The Political Basis of Agricultural Policies.* Berkeley: University of California Press, 1981.

Bates, Robert, and Anne O. Krueger. "Generalizations Arising from the Country Studies." In idem, *Political and Economic Interactions* (q.v.), pp. 444–72.

Bates, Robert, and Anne O. Krueger, eds. *Political and Economic Interactions in Economic Policy Reform: Evidence from Eight Countries.* Cambridge, MA: Basil Blackwell, 1993.

Bendor, Jonathan, and Thomas H. Hammond. "Rethinking Allison's Models." *American Political Science Review* 86, no. 2 (June): 301–22.

Berger, Peter L., and H. H. Michael Hsiao, eds. *In Search of an East Asian Development Model.* New Brunswick, NJ: Transaction Publishers, 1999.

Boyd, Richard. "Government-Industry Relations in Japan: Access, Communications, and Competitive Collaboration." In Wilks and Wright, eds., *Comparative Government-Industry Relations* (q.v.).

Boyd, Richard, and Aeiichi Nagamori. "Industrial Policy-Making in Practice: Electoral, Diplomatic and Other Adjustments to Crisis in the Japanese Shipbuilding Industry." In Wilks and Wright, eds., *Promotion and Regulation of Industry in Japan* (q.v.).

Bratton, Michael. "Peasant-State Relations in Postcolonial Africa: Patterns of Engagement and Disengagement." In Joel S. Migdal, Atul Kohlu, and Vivienne Shue, eds., *State Power and Social Forces: Domination and Transformation in the Third World*. Cambridge: Cambridge University Press, 1994.

Bromley, Daniel W. *Economic Interests and Institutions: The Conceptual Foundations of Public Policy*. New York: Basil Blackwell, 1989.

Buchanan, James. *Essays on Political Economy*. Honolulu: University of Hawaii Press, 1986.

———. *Liberty, Market and State: Political Economy in the 1980s*. Sussex, Eng.: Wheatsheaf Books, 1986.

———. "Rent Seeking and Profit Seeking." In James M. Buchanan, Robert D. Tollison, and Gordon Tullock, eds., *Toward a Theory of the Rent-Seeking Society*. College Station: Texas A&M University Press, 1980.

Cai Hongming. "Taiwan fu dalu touzi zhi zongti jingji yu chanye jiegou yinsu zhi tantao" (A study of the macroeconomy and the industrial structure of Taiwan's investment in mainland China). *Taiwan yinhang jikan* (Bank of Taiwan Quarterly) 43, no. 2 (1992): 1–48.

Caizhengbu (Ministry of Finance). *Zhonghua minguo jinrong tongji (1967)* (Financial statistics of the ROC [1967]). Taipei: Caizhengbu.

———. *Zhonghua minguo jinrong tongji nianbao* (Annual report on the financial statistics of the ROC). Taipei: Caizhengbu, 1986.

Cardoso, Fernando, and Enzo Faletto. *Dependency and Development in Latin America*. Berkeley: University of California Press, 1979.

CEPD (Council for Economic Planning and Development). *Taiwan Statistical Data Book*. Various editions. Taipei: CEPD.

Chan, Steve. "Developing Strength from Weakness: The State in Taiwan." In Clark and Lemco, eds., *State and Development* (q.v.).

Chang, C. C. "The Impact of the Phasing Out of U.S. Economic Aid on China's Economy." *Economic Review of the Bank of China*, July–Aug. 1964.

Chang, Kuo-wei, ed. *Economic Development in Taiwan*. Taipei: Zhengzhong, 1967.

Chang, Mau-kuei. "Middle Class and Social and Political Movements in Taiwan: Questions and Some Preliminary Observations." In Hsin-Huang Michael Hsiao, ed., *Discovery of the Middle Classes in East Asia*, pp. 121–76. Taipei: Institute of Ethnology, Academia Sinica, 1993.

Chazan, Naomi. "Patterns of State-Society Incorporation and Disengagement in Africa." In Rothchild and Chazan, eds., *The Precarious Balance* (q.v.).

Chen Cheng. *Taiwan tudi gaige jiyao* (Summary of Taiwan's land reform). Taipei: Zhonghua, 1961.

Chen Ciyu and Mo Jiping. *Jiang Shuojie xiansheng fangwen jilu* (The reminiscences of Dr. S. C. Tsiang). Taipei: Institute of Modern History, Academia Sinica, 1992.

Chen, Edward K. Y. *Hyper-Growth in Asian Economics: A Comparative Study of Hong Kong, Japan, Korea, Singapore and Taiwan.* London: Macmillan, 1979.

Chen Jiexuan. *Huobi wangluo yu shenghuo jiegou: difang jinrong, zhongxiao qiye yu Taiwan shisu shehui zhi zhuanhua* (Monetary network and life structure: local finance, SMEs, and social transformation in Taiwan). Taipei: Lianjing, 1995.

——. *Xieli wangluo yu shenghuo jiegou: Taiwan zhongxiao qiye de shehui jingji fenxi* (Cooperative networks and life structure: a socioeconomic analysis of Taiwan's SMEs). Taipei: Lianjing, 1994.

Chen Jieying. "Taiwan zhongxiao qiye zijin yunzuo de tese jiqi shehuixing xinggou tiaojian" (The characteristics of the use of funds of small and medium firms and the social circumstances forming them). *Zhongyang yanjiuyuan, Minzu yanjiusuo jikan* (Journal of the Institute of Ethnology of the Academia Sinica) 75 (1993).

Chen Mingtong. *Paixi zhengzhi yu Taiwan zhengzhi bianqian* (Factional politics and the evolution of politics in Taiwan). Taipei: Yuedan, 1995.

Chen Mingzhang. "Da qiye yu zhongxiao qiye hezuo jingying zhidao" (Method of cooperation between large and medium and small businesses). In idem, ed., *Taiwan zhongxiao qiye* (q.v.).

——. "Taiwan zhongxiao qiye de fudao zhengce" (The policy of guidance to the SMEs in Taiwan). In idem, ed., *Taiwan zhongxiao qiye.*

Chen Mingzhang, ed. *Taiwan zhongxiao qiye fazhan lunwenji* (Collection of essays on the development of SMEs in Taiwan). Taipei: Lianjing, 1994.

Chen Shengyi. *Gongyequ de kaifa* (The establishment of industrial estates). Taipei: Lianjing, 1982.

Chen Shimeng et al. *Jiegou dangguo ziben zhuyi: lun Taiwan guanying shiye zhi minyinghua* (Disintegrating KMT-state capitalism: a close look at privatizing Taiwan's state- and party-owned enterprises). Taipei: Taibei chengshe (Taipei Society), 1991.

Chen Yonghua. "Taiwan jinrong shichang zhi fazhan yu jiantao" (Analysis of the evolution of Taiwan's financial markets). *Taiwan yinhang jikan* (Bank of Taiwan Quarterly) 35, no. 3 (1984).

Chen Yuxi. *Taiwan de yifuxing fazhan —yifuxing fazhan jiqi shehui zheng-zhi houguo: Taiwan gean yanjiu* (Dependent development and its socio-political consequences: a case study of Taiwan). Taipei: Renjian, 1992.

Cheng, Tun-jen. "Democratizing the Quasi-Leninist Regime in Taiwan." *World Politics* 41, no. 4 (July 1989): 471–99.

———. "Political Regimes and Development Strategies: South Korea and Taiwan." In Gereffi and Wyman, eds., *Manufacturing Miracles* (q.v.).

Cheng, Tun-jen, and Stephan Haggard, eds. *Political Change in Taiwan.* Boulder, CO: Lynne Rienner, 1992.

Cheng, Tun-jen; Stephan Haggard; and David Kang. "Institutions and Growth in Korea and Taiwan: The Bureaucracy." *Journal of Development Studies* 34, no. 6 (Aug. 1998): 87–111.

Chiu, Stephen W. K., and Liu Tai-lok. "The Role of the State in Economic Development." In Thompson, ed., *Economic Dynamism in the Asia-Pacific* (q.v.).

Chou, Tien-chen. *Industrial Organization in a Dichotomous Economy: The Case of Taiwan.* Brookfield, VT: Avebury, 1995. See also Zhou Tian-cheng.

Chu, Wan-wen. "Import Substitution and Export-Led Growth: A Study of Taiwan's Petrochemical Industry." *World Development* 22, no. 5 (1994): 781–94. See also Qu Wanwen.

Chu Yanzheng. "Taiwan diqu guojia, waizi yu bendi siren ziben jian guanxi zhi zhengjing fenxi: 1949–1987" (Political economic analysis of the state, and foreign and local capital in the Taiwan area: 1949–1987). M.A. thesis, National Taiwan University, 1993.

Chu, Yun-han. "The Realignment of Business-Government Relations and Regime Transition in Taiwan." In MacIntyre, ed., *Business and Government in Industrialising Asia* (q.v.), pp. 113–41. See also Zhu Yunhan.

———. "State Structure and Economic Adjustment of the East Asian Newly Industrializing Countries." *International Organization* 43, no. 4 (Autumn 1989): 647–72.

Chung-hua Institution for Economics Research. *Zhongxiao qiye rongzi zhi yanjiu* (Study of the provision of industrial finance to SMEs). Taipei: Chung-hua Institution for Economics Research, 1992.

Clark, Cal. *Taiwan's Development: Implications for Contending Political Economy Paradigms.* New York: Greenwood Press, 1989.

Clark, Cal, and Jonathan Lemco, eds. *State and Development.* Leiden: E. J. Brill, 1988.

Coble, Parks M. *The Shanghai Capitalists and the Nationalist Government, 1927–1937.* Cambridge: Council on East Asian Studies, Harvard University, 1980.

Colburn, Forrest D. "Statism, Rationality, and State Centrism." *Comparative Politics* 20, no. 4 (July 1988).

Dai Xijun and Zhang Jiaming. "Taiwan zhongxiao qiye fazhan zhi yanjiu" (A study of the development of the SMEs in Taiwan). In Chen Mingzhang, ed., *Taiwan zhongxiao qiye* (q.v.).

Dessus, Sebastien; Shea Jia-Dong; and Shi Mau-Shan. *Chinese Taipei: The Origins of the Economic "Miracle."* Paris: Development Centre, OECD, 1995.

Deyo, Frederic. "State and Labor: Modes of Political Exclusion in East Asian Development." In idem, ed., *The Political Economy of the New Asian Industrialism* (q.v.).

Deyo, Frederic, ed. *The Political Economy of the New Asian Industrialism.* Ithaca: Cornell University Press, 1987.

Doner, Richard F. "Approaches to the Politics of Economic Growth in Southeast Asia." *Journal of Asian Studies* 50, no. 4 (Nov. 1991): 818–49.

———. "Limits of State Strength: Toward an Institutionalist View of Economic Development." *World Politics* 44, no. 3 (Apr. 1992): 398–431.

Dong Anqi. "Taiwan jingji sheji jigou de bianqian yu zhengfu de juese" (The change in the economic planning bodies and the role of government in Taiwan). Unpublished paper. Taipei: Institute of Economics, Academia Sinica, 1996.

Du Xiuzhen. *Taiwan diqu zhongxiao qiye fazhan yu fudao tujing zhi yanjiu* (A study of the development of SMEs and the method of guidance in the Taiwan area). Taipei: Shengchao, 1978.

Duan Chengpu. *Taiwan zhanhou jingji* (Taiwan's postwar economy). Taipei: Renjian, 1994.

Eisenstadt, S. N., and Louis Roniger. *Patrons, Clients, and Friends: Interpersonal Relations and the Structure of Trust in Society.* Cambridge: Cambridge University Press, 1984.

———. "The Study of Patron-Client Relations and Recent Developments in Sociological Theory." In *Political Clientelism, Patronage and Development*, ed. S. N. Eisenstadt and Rene Lemarchand. Beverly Hills, CA: Sage, 1980.

Encarnation, Dennis J., and Louis T. Wells, Jr. "Sovereignty en Garde: Negotiating with Foreign Investors." *International Organization* 39, no. 1 (Winter 1985): 47–78.

Evans, Peter. "Class, State, and Dependence in East Asia: Lessons for Latin Americanists." In Deyo, *The Political Economy of the New Asian Industrialism* (q.v.), pp. 203–26.

———. *Dependent Development: The Alliance of Multinational, State, and Local Capital in Brazil.* Princeton: Princeton University Press, 1979.

――――. *Embedded Autonomy: States and Industrial Transformation.* Princeton: Princeton University Press, 1995.

――――. "State, Capital, and the Transformation of Dependence: The Brazilian Computer Case." *World Development* 14, no. 7 (1986): 791–808.

――――. "Transferable Lessons? Re-examining the Institutional Prerequisites of East Asian Economic Policies." *Journal of Development Studies* 34, no. 6 (Aug. 1998): 66–86.

Evans, Peter; Dietrich Rueschemeyer; and Theda Skocpol, eds. *Bringing the State Back In.* Cambridge: Cambridge University Press, 1985.

Fan Qinping and Liu Sufen. "The Formulation of Economic Policy in Taiwan: The Case of Interest Rate Policy Between 1954–1961." Discussion paper. Taipei: Institute of Economics, Academia Sinica, 1996.

――――. "Minguo sishi niandai Tangrong yu minjian daikuan: jinrong zhongjie he jingji fazhan guanxi chutan" (Tangrong and the private financial market: financial intermediaries and economic development). Discussion paper. Taipei: Zhongyang yanjiuyuan, Jingji yanjiusuo, 1994.

――――. "Qiye jingying yu lixing juece: 1960 nian Tangrong shibai anli" (Enterprise operations and rational decision: the case of the failure of Tangrong, 1960). *Si yu yan* 33, no. 4 (1995): 107–42.

Fan Qinping, Liu Sufen, and Zhan Weiling. "Lilü zhengce yu Taiwan zaoqi jingji fazhan" (Interest rate policy and Taiwan's early economic development). *Si yu yan* 35, no. 4 (1997): 153–82.

Fei, John C. H. "The Taiwan Economy in the Seventies." In Leng, ed., *Chiang Ching-kuo's Leadership in the Development of the Republic of China on Taiwan* (q.v.).

Fei, John C. H.; Gustav Ranis; and Shirley W. Y. Kuo. *Growth with Equity: The Taiwan Case.* Ithaca: Cornell University Press, 1979.

Fields, Karl. *Embedded Enterprises: Business Groups and the State in Korea and Taiwan.* Ithaca: Cornell University Press, 1994.

――――. "Trading Companies in South Korea and Taiwan." *Asian Survey* 29, no. 11 (Nov. 1989).

Friedman, David. *The Misunderstood Miracle: Industrial Development and Political Change in Japan.* Ithaca: Cornell University Press, 1988.

Fukuyama, Francis. *Trust: The Social Virtues and the Creation of Prosperity.* New York: Free Press, 1995.

Galenson, Walter, ed. *Economic Growth and Structural Change in Taiwan: The Postwar Experience of the Republic of China.* Ithaca: Cornell University Press, 1979.

――――. *Foreign Trade and Investment: Development in the Newly Industrializing Asian Economies.* Madison: University of Wisconsin Press, 1985.

Gao Konglian. "Taiwan zhongxiao qiye hezuo jingying kexingxing zhi yanjiu" (The feasibility of cooperative operations of Taiwan's SMEs). *Taiwan yinhang jikan* (Bank of Taiwan Quarterly) 34, no. 3 (1983).

Gao Zongzhi. "Tainan bang" (The Tainan group). In idem, *Weiji zhong de qiye jituan* (Business groups in crisis). Taipei: Jiaodian, 1985.

Gates, Hill. "Small Fortunes: Class and Society in Taiwan." In Denis Simon and Michael Y. M. Kao, eds., *Taiwan: Beyond the Economic Miracle.* Armonk, NY: M. E. Sharpe, 1992.

Gereffi, Gary. "The Organization of Buyer-Driven Global Commodity Chains: How U.S. Retailers Shape Overseas Production Networks." In idem and Korzeniewics, eds., *Commodity Chains and Global Capitalism* (q.v.).

Gereffi, Gary, and Miguel Korzeniewicz, eds. *Commodity Chains and Global Capitalism.* Westport, CT: Greenwood Press, 1993.

Gereffi, Gary, and Donald L. Wyman, eds. *Manufacturing Miracles: Paths of Industrialization in Latin America and East Asia.* Princeton: Princeton University Press, 1990.

Gerschenkron, Alexander. *Economic Backwardness in Historical Perspective.* Cambridge: Harvard University Press, Belknap Press, 1962.

Giddens, Anthony. *The Consequences of Modernity.* Stanford: Stanford University Press, 1990.

———. *The Nation-State and Violence.* Berkeley: University of California Press, 1987.

Gold, Thomas B. *State and Society in the Taiwan Miracle.* Armonk, NY: M. E. Sharpe, 1986.

"Gongshangjie zaocanhui huiyi jilu (1–19), yijiuqisi nian liuyue siri zhi yijiuqiwu nian shieryue shiliuri" (Minutes of the breakfast meetings of businesspeople, nos. 1–19, from June 4, 1974 to Dec. 16, 1975). *Li Guoding dang'an* (Li Guoding archives). Taipei: Zhongyang yanjiuyuan, Jindaishi yanjiusuo.

Gramsci, Antonio. *Selections from the Prison Notebooks.* London: Lawrence and Wishart, 1971.

Grant, Wyn, ed. *The Political Economy of Corporatism.* New York: St. Martin's Press, 1985.

Grindle, Merilee S. "The New Political Economy: Positive Economics and Negative Politics." In Meier, ed., *Politics and Policy Making in Developing Countries* (q.v.).

Guo Tai. *Wang Yongqing fendou shi* (Wang Yongqing's history of struggle). Taipei: Yuanliu, 1985.

Guo Xuyin, ed. *Guomindang paixi douzheng shi* (The history of factional fights within the KMT). Shanghai: Shanghai renmin, 1992.

Haggard, Stephan. "Business, Politics and Policy in Northeast and Southeast Asia." In MacIntyre, ed., *Business and Government in Industrialising Asia* (q.v.), pp. 268–301.

———. "The Newly Industrializing Countries in the International System." *World Politics* 38, no. 2 (Jan. 1986): 343–70.

———. *Pathways from the Periphery: The Politics of Growth in the Newly Industrializing Countries.* Ithaca: Cornell University Press, 1990.

———. "The Politics of Industrialization in the Republic of Korea and Taiwan." In Hughes, ed., *Achieving Industrialization in East Asia* (q.v.), pp. 260–82.

Haggard, Stephan, and Robert R. Kaufman, eds. *The Politics of Economic Adjustment: International Constraints, Distributive Conflicts, and the State.* Princeton: Princeton University Press, 1992.

Haggard, Stephan, and Chung-in Moon. "Institutions and Economic Policy: Theory and a Korean Case Study." *World Politics* 44 (Apr. 1992): 210–37.

Haggard, Stephan, and Chien-kuo Pan. "The Transition to Export-Led Growth in Taiwan." In Aberbach et al., eds., *The Role of the State in Taiwan's Development* (q.v.), pp. 47–89.

Hall, Peter A. *Governing the Economy: The Politics of State Intervention in Britain and France.* New York: Oxford University Press, 1986.

Hall, Peter A., ed. *The Political Power of Economic Ideas: Keynesianism Across Nations.* Princeton: Princeton University Press, 1989.

Hamilton, Gary G. "Organization and Market Process in Taiwan's Capitalist Economy." In Orru et al., *The Economic Organization of East Asian Capitalism* (q.v.).

Hamilton, G[ary]. G., M. Orru, and N. W. Biggart. "Enterprise Groups in East Asia." *Shōken keizai* (Financial Economic Review) 161 (1987): 78–106.

Hamilton, Gary G.; William Zeile; and Wan-Jin Kim. "The Network Structures of East Asian Economies." In Stewart R. Clegg and S. Gordon Redding, eds., *Capitalism in Contrasting Cultures*, pp. 105–29. Berlin and New York: Walter de Gruyter, 1990.

Hawes, Gary, and Hong Liu. "Explaining the Dynamic of the Southeast Asian Political Economy: State, Society, and the Search for Economic Growth." *World Politics* 45, no. 4 (July 1993): 629–60.

Hayami, Yujiro. "Toward an East Asian Model of Economic Development." In idem and Aoki, eds., *The Institutional Foundations of East Asian Economic Development* (q.v.), pp. 3–35.

Hayami, Yujiro, and Masahiko Aoki, eds. *The Institutional Foundations of East Asian Economic Development.* London: Macmillan, 1998.

Hellmann, Thomas; Kevin Murdock; and Joseph Stiglitz. "Financial Restraint: Toward A New Paradigm." In Aoki et al., eds., *The Role of Government in East Asian Economic Development* (q.v.), pp. 163–207.

Henderson, Jeffrey. "The Role of the State in the Economic Orthodoxy: On the Making of the East Asian Miracle." *Economic and Social Volume* 2 (May 1993): 200–217.

———. "The Role of the State in the Economic Transformation of East Asia." In Chris Dixon and David Drakakis-Smith, eds., *Economic and Social Development in Pacific Asia*. London and New York: Routledge, 1993.

———. "Situating the State in the East Asian Development Process." In Applebaum and Henderson, *States and Development in the Asian Pacific Rim* (q.v.).

Hirschman, Albert O. *The Strategy of Economic Development*. New Haven: Yale University Press, 1958.

Ho, Samuel P. S. "Economic Development and Rural Industry in South Korea and Taiwan." *World Development* 10, no. 11 (1982): 973–90.

———. *Economic Development of Taiwan, 1860–1970*. New Haven: Yale University Press, 1978.

———. "Small-Scale Enterprises in Korea and Taiwan." Staff Working Paper no. 384. Washington, DC: World Bank, 1980.

Hong, Sung Gul. *The Political Economy of Industrial Policy in East Asia: The Semiconductor Industry in Taiwan and South Korea*. Cheltenham, UK, and Northampton, MA: Edward Elgar, 1997.

Hsiao, H. H. Michael. "Formation and Transformation of Taiwan's State-Business Relations: A Critical Analysis." *Bulletin of the Institute of Ethnology of the Academia Sinica* 74 (1993): 1–32.

———. "The Rise of Social Movements and Civil Protests." In Cheng and Haggard, eds., *Political Change in Taiwan* (q.v.), pp. 57–72.

Hsieh, Chung-hsing. "Industrial Development and Managerial Adjustment: The Export-Oriented Knitting Industry of Taiwan, 1960–1990." Unpublished paper, 1993.

Hsing, You-tien. *Making Capitalism in China: The Taiwan Connection*. New York: Oxford University Press, 1998.

Hsu, Chen-kuo. "Ideological Reflections and the Inception of Economic Development in Taiwan." In Aberbach et al., eds., *The Role of the State in Taiwan's Development* (q.v.).

Hsueh, Li-min; Chen-kuo Hsu; and Dwight H. Perkins, eds. *Industrialization and the State: The Changing Role of the Taiwan Government in the Economy, 1945–1998*. Cambridge, MA: Harvard Institute for International Development and Chung-hua Institution for Economic Research, 2001.

Hu, Fu, and Yun-han Chu. "Electoral Competition and Political Democratization." In Cheng and Haggard, eds., *Political Change in Taiwan* (q.v.).

Huang Defu. "Xuanju, difang paixi yu zhengzhi zhuanxing" (Election, local factions, and political transformation). *Zhongshan shehui kexue jikan* (Zhongshan Quarterly of Social Sciences) 5, no. 1 (1990): 84–91.

Huang Dongzhi. "Taiwan zhi fangzhi gongye" (Taiwan's textile industry). In Taiwan yinhang, Jingji yanjiushi, ed., *Taiwan zhi fangzhi gongye* (Taiwan's textile industry). Taiwan yanjiu congkan, no. 41. Taipei: Taiwan yinhang, Jingji yanjiushi, 1956.

————. "Taiwan zhi mianfang gongye" (Taiwan's cotton industry). In Taiwan yinhang, Jingji yanjiushi, ed., *Taiwan zhi fangzhi gongye* (Taiwan's cotton industry). Taiwan yanjiu congkan, no. 41. Taipei: Taiwan yinhang, Jingji yanjiushi, 1956.

Huang Shisheng. "Taiwan diqu huobi shichang zhi yanjiu" (Study of the money market in the Taiwan area). *Taiwan yinhang jikan* (Bank of Taiwan Quarterly) 35, no. 2 (1984).

Huang Yongren. "Zhongxiao qiye jinrong tixi de jiantao yu zhanwang" (Examination and prospects for the financial system of Taiwan's SMEs). In Chen Mingzhang, ed., *Taiwan zhongxiao qiye* (q.v.).

Hughes, Helen, ed. *Achieving Industrialization in East Asia.* Cambridge: Cambridge University Press, 1988.

Ikenberry, G. John. "The Irony of State Strength: Comparative Responses to the Oil Shocks in the 1970s." *International Organization* 40, no. 1 (Winter 1986): 105–37.

Islam, Iyanatul. "Between the State and the Market: The Case of Eclectic Neoclassical Political Economy." In MacIntyre, ed., *Business and Government in Industrialising Asia* (q.v.).

Jacoby, Neil H. *U.S. Aid to Taiwan: A Study of Foreign Aid, Self-help, and Development.* New York: Praeger, 1966.

Jianchayuan (Control Yuan [ROC]). *Jianchayuan gongbao* (Bulletin of the Control Yuan) 384: 2838–39.

Jiang Nan. *Jiang Jingguo zhuan* (Biography of Chiang Ching-Kuo). Taipei: Li Ao, 1993.

Jiang Shuojie. "Huilu, lilü yu jingji fazhan" (Exchange rate, interest rate, and economic development). Discussion Paper. Taipei: Zhongyang yanjiuyuan, Sept. 1976.

Jinghehui disichu (CIECD). "Zhonghua kaifa xintuo gufen youxian gongsi chazhang baogao" (Audit report on the CDC). Taipei, 1968.

Jingji anding weiyuanhui (Economic Stabilization Board). "Jiaxin shuini jiqi shebei daikuan" (The loan of equipment to Jiaxin cement). Appendixes 1–8. ESB 30060062000. Taipei, n.d.

"Jingjianhui zhuwei yi yu zhuanzhi" (The head of the CEPD must be full time). *Jingji ribao* (Economic Daily), Dec. 6, 1981.

Jingjibu (Ministry of Economic Affairs). "Gongchang touzi yu caozuo diaocha baogao" (Survey report on investment and operation of factories). Taipei, 1986.

Jingjibu. Zhongxiao qiyechu (Department of Small Business, Ministry of Economic Affairs). *Zhongxiao qiye tongji* (Census of small and medium-sized enterprises). Taipei, n.d.

"Jingji bu jingqi zhong dui Yu zongcai de qiwang" (What is expected of Governor Yu amid the economic recession). *Gongshang shibao*, Apr. 1, 1982.

Jingshehui. Jingji yanjiuchu. "Woguo shiyou huaxue gongye zhi xianzhuang yu wenti zhi tantao" (The current situation and problems in our country's petrochemical industries). *Ziyou Zhongguo zhi gongye* (Industry of Free China) 46, no. 5 (1976): 5–13.

Johnson, Chalmers. *MITI and the Japanese Miracle: The Growth of Industrial Policy, 1925–1975.* Stanford: Stanford University Press, 1982.

———. "Political Institutions and Economic Performance: The Government-Business Relationship in Japan, South Korea, and Taiwan." In Deyo, ed., *The Political Economy of the New Asian Industrialism* (q.v.), pp. 136–64.

Jordan, Amos A., Jr. *Foreign Aid and the Defense of Southeast Asia.* New York: Frederick A. Praeger, 1962.

Jung, Ku-hyun. "Business-Government Relations in the Growth of Korean Business Groups." *Korean Social Science Journal* 14 (Apr. 1988).

Kang Ludao. *Li Guoding koushu lishi: huashuo Taiwan jingyan* (The oral history of K. T. Li: Talking about the Taiwanese experience). Taipei: Zhuoyue wenhua, 1993.

Katzenstein, Peter J. *Corporatism and Change: Austria, Switzerland, and the Politics of Industry.* Ithaca: Cornell University Press, 1984.

———. *Small States in World Markets: Industrial Policy in Europe.* Ithaca: Cornell University Press, 1985.

Ke Zhiming. *Taiwan dushi xiaoxing zhizaoye de chuangye, jingying yu shengchan zuzhi: yi Wufenpu chengyi zhizaoye wei anli de fenxi* (Market, social network, and the production organization of small-scale industry in Taiwan: the garment industries in Wufenpu). Taipei: Zhongyang yanjiuyuan, Minzuxue yanjiusuo, 1993.

Kerr, George H. *Formosa Betrayed.* Boston: Houghton Mifflin, 1965.

Kim, Hyung-Ki. *The Civil Service System and Economic Development: The Japanese Experience.* Washington, DC: World Bank, 1996.

Kim, Hyung-Ki, and Jun Ma. "The Role of Government in Acquiring Technological Capability: The Case of the Petrochemical Industry in

East Asia." In Aoki et al., eds., *The Role of Government in East Asian Economic Development* (q.v.), pp. 101–33.

Kim, Hyung-ki, et al., eds. *The Japanese Civil Service and Economic Development: Catalysts of Change.* New York: Oxford University Press, 1995.

Kirby, William C. *Germany and Republican China.* Stanford: Stanford University Press, 1984.

―――. "Technocratic Organization and Technological Development in China: The Nationalist Experience and Legacy, 1928–1953." In *Science and Technology in Post-Mao China*, ed. Denis Fred Simon and Merle Goldman, pp. 23–43. Cambridge: Council on East Asian Studies, Harvard University, 1989.

Kitschelt, Herbert. "Industrial Governance Structure, Innovation Strategies, and the Case of Japan: Sectoral or Cross-national Comparative Analysis?" *International Organization* 45, no. 4 (Autumn 1991): 453–93.

Komiya, Ryutaro. "Introduction." In Ryutaro Komiya, Masahiro Okuno, and Kotaro Suzumura, eds., *Industrial Policy of Japan.* Tokyo: Academic Press, 1988.

Koo, Hagen. "The Interplay of State, Social Class, and World System in East Asian Development: The Cases of South Korea and Taiwan." In Deyo, ed., *Political Economy of the New Asian Industrialism* (q.v.), pp. 165–81.

Krasner, Stephen D. "Approaches to the State: Alternative Conceptions and Historical Dynamics." *Comparative Politics* 16, no. 2 (Jan. 1984): 223–46.

―――. "Are Bureaucracies Important? (Or Allison Wonderland)." *Foreign Policy*, no. 7 (Summer 1972): 159–79.

―――. "Sovereignty: An Institutional Perspective." *Comparative Political Studies* 21, no. 1 (Apr. 1988).

Krueger, Anne O. *Economic Policies at Cross-purposes: The United States and Developing Countries.* Washington, DC: Brookings Institution, 1993.

―――. "Government Failures in Development." *Journal of Economic Perspectives* 4, no. 3 (Summer 1990): 9–23.

―――. *Political Economy of Policy Reform in Developing Countries.* Cambridge, MA: MIT Press, 1993.

―――. "The Political Economy of the Rent-Seeking Society." *American Economic Review* 64, no. 3 (June 1974): 291–303.

Kuo, Shirley W. Y., and John C. H. Fei. "Causes and Roles of Export Expansion in the Republic of China." In Galenson, ed., *Foreign Trade and Investment* (q.v.).

Lai Yingzhao. *Taiwan jinrong bantu zhi huigu yu qianzhan* (Retrospect and forecast for Taiwan's financial and banking system). Taipei: Lianjing, 1998.

Laothamatas, Anek. *Business Associations and the New Political Economy of Thailand.* Boulder, CO: Westview Press, 1992.

Lasswell, Harold D. *Politics: Who Gets What, When, How.* Cleveland and New York: World Publishing, 1958.

Lee, Chung H. "The Government, Financial System, and Large Private Enterprises in the Economic Development of South Korea." *World Development* 20, no. 2 (1992).

Lee, Chung H., and Seiji Naya. "Trade in East Asian Development with Comparative Reference to the Southeast Asian Experience." *Economic Development and Cultural Change* 36, no. 3 supplement (Apr. 1988): S123–52.

Leff, N. "Optimal Investment Choice for Developing Countries: Rational Theory and Rational Decision-making." *Journal of Development Economics* 18, no. 2/3 (1985): 335–60.

Leng, Shao-chuan, ed. *Chiang Ching-kuo's Leadership in the Development of the Republic of China on Taiwan.* Lanham, MD: University Press of America, 1993.

Levi, Margaret. *Of Rule and Revenue.* Berkeley: University of California Press, 1988.

Li Guoding. *Taiwan jingji kuaisu chengzhang de jingyan* (The experience of Taiwan's rapid economic growth). Taipei: Zhengzhong, 1978.

———. "Taiwan minying gongye de chengzhang: dui Meiguo guoji hezuo zongshu yuandongqu gongye fazhan huiyi baogao" (Development of the private sector in Taiwan: report on reflections on American cooperation and industrialization in the East Asian region). *Guoji jingji ziliao yuekan* (International economics monthly) 3, no. 6 (Dec. 1959).

———. "Taiwan zhongxiao qiye zhi huigu yu qianzhan" (Retrospect and prospects for Taiwan's SMEs). In *Zhongxiao qiye wenxuan* (Selection of documents on SMEs). Taipei: Department of Small Business, Ministry of Economic Affairs, 1989.

Li Guoding and Chen Muzai. *Woguo jingji fazhan celue zonglun* (Taiwan's economic development strategy). 2 vols. Taipei: Lianjing, 1987.

Li Guoding Archives. "Chen Cheng shang zongtong qiancheng"(A letter to the president from Chen Cheng). In *Jiasu jingji fazhan yu nuli fangxiang (II)* (Accelerating economic development and the direction of future efforts, II). Taipei: Zhongyang yanjiuyuan, Jindaishi yanjiusuo, Dang'anguan, 1960.

———. "Jiasu jingji fazhan jihua zhi shuoming"(Clarification on the plan to accelerate economic development). In *Jiasu jingji fazhan yu nuli fang-*

xiang (II) (Accelerating economic development and the direction of future efforts, II). Taipei: Zhongyang yanjiuyuan, Jindaishi yanjiusuo, Dang'anguan, 1960.

———. "Quanti yinhang waixiao daikuan yu'e" (Amount of export loans from all banks). Archive number 133-14.

Li Junxing. "Jing'anhui yu Taiwan gongye fazhan" (The Economic Stabilization Board and Taiwan's industrial development). M.A. thesis. Taipei: Zhongguo wenhua daxue, 1995.

Li Qinggong. *Tainan bang yi shiji* (A century of the Tainan group). Gaoxiong: Paise wenhua, 1994.

Li Yongsan and Chen Shangcheng. "Taiwan jinrong fazhan zhi huigu yu qianzhan" (Retrospect and prospects for financial development in Taiwan). In *Taiwan jinrong fazhan huiyi* (Conference on financial development in Taiwan). Taipei: Zhongyang yanjiuyuan, Jingji yanjiusuo, 1984.

Liang Guoshu. "Taiwan de duiwai maoyi yu jiuye" (Foreign trade and employment in Taiwan). In Sun Zhen, ed., *Taiwan duiwai maoyi lunwen ji* (Collection of essays on Taiwan's foreign trade). Taipei: Lianjing, 1975.

Liao Zhenghong, Huang Junjie, and Xiao Xinhuang. *Guangfu hou Taiwan nongye zhengce de yanbian* (The evolution of Taiwan's agricultural policy since its reversion to China). Taipei: Zhongyang yanjiuyuan, Minzuxue yanjiusuo, 1986.

Lim, Linda Y. C. "Singapore's Success: The Myth of the Free Market Economy." *Asian Survey* 2, no. 6 (June 1983).

Lin Bangchong. "Taiwan mianfangzhi gongye fazhan zhi yanjiu" (Research on Taiwan's cotton textile industry). *Taiwan yanjiu congkan* (Series on Taiwan Research), no. 117. Taipei: Taiwan yinhang, Jingji yanjiushi, 1969.

Lin Chen-you. "Taiwan zhongxiao qiye de falü fagui huanjing" (The law and regulatory environment for Taiwan's SMEs). *Gongye yinhang jikan* (Industrial Bank Quarterly) 11, no. 1 (July 1987): 2–10.

Lin, Ching-yuan. *Industrialization in Taiwan, 1946–72: Trade and Import-Substitution Policies for Developing Countries.* New York: Praeger, 1973.

Lin, H. T. "US Aid and Taiwan's Economic Development." In *Conference on Economic Development of Taiwan.* Taipei: China Council on Sino-American Cooperation in the Humanities and Social Sciences, Academia Sinica, 1967.

Lin, Kenneth S., and Tsong-min Wu. "Taiwan's Big Inflation." In *The Second Conference on Modern Chinese Economic History.* Taipei: Institute of Economics, Academia Sinica, 1989.

Lin, Lin. "Banking Development of Taiwan." In *Conference on Economic Development of Taiwan*, pp. 397–419. Taipei: China Council on Sino-American Cooperation in the Humanities and Social Sciences, Academia Sinica, 1967.

Lin, Man-hong. "Interpretive Trends in Taiwan's Scholarship on Chinese Business History, 1600 to the Present." *Chinese Studies in History* 31, nos. 3–4 (Spring–Summer 1998): 65–94.

Lin Zhongxiong. *Taiwan jingji fazhan sishi nian* (Forty years of Taiwan's economic development). Taipei: Zili wanbao, 1987.

Lin Zhongxiong and Peng Baixian. "Zhongxiao qiye jinrong yu yiban jinrong zhi bijiao" (A comparison of the provision of SME finance and general finance). In Chen Mingzhang, ed., *Taiwan zhongxiao qiye*, (q.v.).

Lin Zhongzheng. "Weiquan zhuyi xia ruoshi tuanti xianghu boxue de xunhuan" (The mutual exploitative cycle of underprivileged groups under authoritarianism). In Xiao Xinhuang, ed., *Jiepou Taiwan jingji: weiquan tizhi xia de longduan yu boxue* (Dissecting Taiwan's economy: monopoly and exploitation under the authoritarian regime). Taipei: Qianwei, 1992.

Little, I. M. D. "The Experiences and Causes of Rapid Labor-Intensive Development in Korea, Taiwan Province, Hong Kong and Singapore and the Possibility of Emulation." In Eddy Lee, ed., *Export-Led Industrialisation and Development*. Bangkok: Asian Employment Programme, 1981.

Liu Fenghan et al. *Wei Yongning xiansheng fangtan lu* (The reminiscences of Mr. Wei Yongning). Taipei: Guoshi guan, 1994.

Liu Jingtian and Cai Weide. "Guangfu chuqi Taiwan diqu de exing tonghuo pengzhang" (Taiwan's runaway inflation in the early days after retrocession). *Jingji lunwen congkan* (Series of papers on economics) 1, no. 2 (1989): 233–62.

Liu Jinqing. *Taiwan zhanhou jingji fenxi* (An analysis of the postwar economy in Taiwan). Taipei: Renjian, 1995.

Liu Jinqing, Tu Zhaoyan, and Sumiya Mikio. *Taiwan zhi jingji: dianxing NIES zhi chengjiu yu wenti* (Taiwan's economy: a typical NIE's achievements and problems). Taipei: Renjian, 1995.

Liu Jinqing and Wakabayasi Masahiro. *Zhongri huizhen Taiwan: zhuanxing qi de zhengzhi* (Consultation on Taiwan: the politics of transformation). Taipei: Guxiang, 1988.

Liu Mincheng and Zuo Hongchou. *Gaishan touzi huanjing* (Improving the investment environment). Taipei: Lianjing, 1983.

Liu Shouxiang. "Shuangyuan jinrong tixi xia zhi jinrong zhongjie guocheng" (The financial intermediary under the dual financial system). In *Taiwan jinrong fazhan huiyi* (Conference on Taiwan's financial development). Taipei: Zhongyang yanjiuyuan, Jingji yanjiusuo, 1984.

Liu Sufen. "Minguo sishi niandai zhengfu jingji zhengce yu minying qiye: Tangrong tie gongchang gaiwei gongying zhi zhengce beijing" (Government economic policy and the private sector in the 1950s: the policy background of Tangrong Iron Works' shift to a public firm). In *Gaoxiong lishi yu wenhua lunji* (Collection of essays on Gaoxiong history and culture), vol. 2. Gaoxiong: Chen Zhonghe cishan jijinhui, 1995.

Liu Taiying. "Taiwan zhongxiao qiye touzi huanjing zhi yanjiu" (The investment environment for SMEs in Taiwan). In Chen Mingzhang, ed., *Taiwan zhongxiao qiye* (q.v.).

Luhmann, Niklas. "Familiarity, Confidence, Trust: Problems and Perspectives." In Diego Gambetta, ed., *Trust: Making and Breaking of Cooperative Relations*. Oxford: Basil Blackwell, 1988.

———. *Trust and Power*. New York: John Wiley and Sons, 1979.

Lundberg, Erik. "Fiscal and Monetary Policies." In Galenson, ed., *Economic Growth and Structural Change in Taiwan* (q.v.), pp. 263–307.

MacIntyre, Andrew. *Business and Politics in Indonesia*. St. Leonards: Allen & Unwin, 1990.

———. "Business, Government and Development: Northeast and Southeast Asian Comparisons." In idem, ed., *Business and Government in Industrialising Asia* (q.v.).

MacIntyre, Andrew, ed. *Business and Government in Industrializing Asia*. Ithaca: Cornell, 1994.

Makinen, Gail E., and G. Thomas Woodward. "The Taiwanese Hyperinflation and Stabilization of 1945–1952." *Journal of Money, Credit and Banking* 21, no. 1 (1989): 90–105.

March, James G., and Hojan P. Olsen. "The New Institutionalism: Organizational Factors in Political Life." *American Political Science Review* 78, no. 3 (Sept. 1984): 734–49.

Mathews, Trevor, and John Ravenhill. "Strategic Trade Policy: The Northeast Asian Experience." In MacIntyre, ed., *Business and Government in Industrializing Asia* (q.v.), pp. 29–78.

Matsuyama, Kiminori. "Economic Development as Coordination Problems." In Aoki et al., eds., *The Role of Government in East Asian Economic Development* (q.v.).

McGeary, Johanna. "Odd Man Out." *Time*, Sept. 10, 2001, pp. 24–32.

McKinnon, R. I. *Money and Capital in Economic Development*. Washington, DC: Brookings Institution, 1973.

McLeod, Ross H., and Ross Garnaut, eds. *East Asia in Crisis: From Being a Miracle to Needing One?* London and New York: Routledge, 1998.

Meaney, Constance Squires. "State Policy and the Development of Taiwan's Semiconductor Industry." In Aberbach et al., eds., *The Role of the State in Taiwan's Development* (q.v.), pp. 170–92.

Meier, Gerald M., ed. *Politics and Policy Making in Developing Countries: Perspectives on the New Political Economy.* San Francisco: ICS Press, 1991.

Mingzhi chubanshe, ed. *Taiwan jianshe* (Taiwan construction). Taipei: 1950.

Moon Chung-in. "The Demise of a Developmentalist State? Neoconservative Reform and Political Consequences in South Korea." *Journal of Developing Societies* 4 (1988): 67–84.

Nabli, Mustapha K. "The New Institutional Economics and Its Applicability to Development." *World Development* 17, no. 9 (1989): 1333–47.

"Nengzhe duolao buru nengzhe duo er fenlao" (More able people sharing work is better than one able man doing more). *Lianhebao* (United Daily), Feb. 25, 1982.

Niskanen, William A., Jr. *Bureaucracy and Representative Government.* Chicago: Aldine, Atherton Press, 1971.

Noble, Gregory W. "Contending Forces in Taiwan's Economic Policymaking: The Case of Hua Tung Heavy Trucks." *Asian Survey*, no. 6 (June 1987): 683–704.

North, Douglass C. *Structure and Change in Economic History.* New York: W. W. Norton, 1981.

Numazaki, Ichiro. "Networks of Taiwanese Big Business." *Modern China* 12, no. 3 (Oct. 1986): 487–534.

———. "The Role of Personal Networks in the Making of Taiwan's *Guanxiqiye* (Related Enterprises)." In Gary Hamilton, ed., *Business Networks and Economic Development in East and Southeast Asia.* Hong Kong: Centre of Asian Studies, University of Hong Kong, 1991.

O'Donnell, Guillermo. *Modernization and Bureaucratic-Authoritarianism: Studies in South American Politics.* Berkeley: Institute of International Studies, University of California, 1973.

———. "State and Alliances in Argentina, 1956–1976." *Journal of Development Studies* 15, no. 1 (Oct. 1978): 3–33.

O'Donnell, Guillermo; Philippe C. Schmitter; and Laurence Whitehead. *Transitions From Authoritarian Rule.* Baltimore: Johns Hopkins University Press, 1986.

Okimoto, Daniel I. *Between MITI and the Market: Japanese Industrial Policy for High Technology.* Stanford: Stanford University Press, 1989.

Onis, Ziya. "The Logic of the Developmental State." *Comparative Politics* 24, no. 1 (Oct. 1991): 109–26.

Orru, Marco. "The Institutional Logic of Small-Firm Economies in Italy and Taiwan." In idem et al., eds., *The Economic Organization of East Asian Capitalism* (q.v.).

Orru, Marco, Nicole W. Biggart, and Gary Hamilton. *The Economic Organization of East Asian Capitalism.* Thousand Oaks, CA: Sage, 1997.

Pack, Howard. "Fostering the Capital-Goods Sector in LDCs." *World Development* 9, no. 3 (1981): 227–50.

Pan Wenyuan. "Zhihua zhengwei dui woguo keji fazhan zhi gongxian" (Fei Hua's contribution to our country's science and technology development). *Yousheng* (Xinzhu: Jiaotong daxue), 1984.

Pan Yuye. "Taiwan zhongxiao qiye wenti zhi tantao" (Problems of Taiwan's SMEs). In Chen Mingzhang, ed., *Taiwan zhongxiao qiye* (q.v.).

Pan Zhijia. *Minying gongye de fazhan* (The development of the private sector). Taipei: Lianjing, 1983.

Pang, Chien-kuo. *The State and Economic Transformation: The Taiwan Case.* New York and London: Garland, 1992.

Park, Y. C. "Korea: Development and Structural Change of the Financial System." In Patrick and Park, eds., *The Financial Development of Japan, Korea, and Taiwan* (q.v.).

Park, Y. C., and D. W. Kim. "Korea: Development and Structural Change of the Banking System." In Patrick and Park, eds., *The Financial Development of Japan, Korea, and Taiwan* (q.v.).

Patrick, H. T., and Y. C. Park, eds. *The Financial Development of Japan, Korea, and Taiwan: Growth, Repression, and Liberalization.* New York: Oxford University Press, 1994.

Pempel, T. J. "The Developmental Regime in a Changing World Economy." In Woo-Cumings, ed., *The Developmental State* (q.v.).

Peng Baixian and Zheng Suqing. "Taiwan minjian jinrong de zijin guandao" (The source of funds for private finance in Taiwan). *Taiwan yinhang jikan* (Bank of Taiwan Quarterly), no. 3 (1985): 165–205.

———. "Taiwan zhi jinrong tixi shuangyuanxing yu gongye fazhan" (The dual financial system and industrial development in Taiwan). In *Taiwan gongye fazhan huiyi* (Conference on Taiwan's industrial development). Taipei: Zhongyang yanjiuyuan, Jingji yuanjiusuo, 1983.

Piore, Michael J., and Charles F. Sabel. *The Second Industrial Divide: Possibilities for Prosperity.* New York: Basic Books, 1984.

Poggi, Gianfranco. *The Development of the Modern State.* Stanford: Stanford University Press, 1978.

Powell, John Duncan. "Peasant Society and Clientelist Politics." *American Political Science Review* 64, no. 2 (1970): 411–25.

Przeworski, Adam. *Capitalism and Social Democracy.* Cambridge: Cambridge University Press, 1985.

————. *Democracy and the Market: Political and Economic Reforms in Eastern Europe and Latin America*. Cambridge: Cambridge University Press, 1991.

Pye, Lucian W. *The Dynamics of Chinese Politics*. Cambridge, MA: Oelgeschlager, Gunn & Hain, 1981.

————. *The Mandarin and the Cadre: China's Political Cultures*. Ann Arbor: Center for Chinese Studies, University of Michigan, 1988.

————. *The Spirit of Chinese Politics*. Cambridge, MA: MIT Press, 1968.

Qu Wanwen. "Chanye zhengce de shifan xiaoguo: Taiwan shihuaye de chansheng" (Demonstration effects and industrial policy: the birth of Taiwan's petrochemical industry). *Taiwan shehui yanjiu jikan* (Taiwan: A Radical Quarterly in Social Studies) 27 (Sept. 1993). See also Chu, Wan-wen.

Ranis, Gustav, and Chi Schive. "Direct Foreign Investment in Taiwan Development." In Galenson, ed., *Foreign Trade and Investment* (q.v.).

Rankin, Karl L. *China Assignment*. Seattle: University of Washington Press, 1964.

Rhee, Jong-Chan. *The State and Industry in South Korea: The Limits of the Authoritarian State*. London and New York: Routledge, 1994.

Rhodes, Edward. "Do Bureaucratic Politics Matter? Some Disconfirming Findings from the Case of the U.S. Navy." *World Politics* 47 (Oct. 1994): 1–41.

Riegg, Nicholas. "The Role of Fiscal and Monetary Policies in Taiwan's Economic Development." Ph.D. diss., University of Connecticut, 1978.

Robinson, E. A. G., ed. *Economic Consequences of the Size of Nations*. London: Macmillan, 1960.

Rothchild, Donald, and Naomi Chazan, eds. *The Precarious Balance: State and Society in Africa*. Boulder, CO: Westview Press, 1988.

Rowen, Henry S., ed. *Behind East Asian Growth: The Political and Social Foundations of Prosperity*. London and New York: Routledge, 1998.

Sachs, Jeffrey D., ed. *Developing Country Debt and the World Economy*. Chicago: University of Chicago Press, 1989.

Sassoon, Anne. "Passive Revolution and the Politics of Reform." In idem, ed., *Approaches to Gramsci*. London: Writers and Readers, 1982.

Sato, Kazuo, ed. *Industry and Business in Japan*. White Plains, NY: M. E. Sharpe, 1980.

Schenk, Hubert G. "Taiwan fanke" (Visitors to Taiwan). *Ziyou Zhongguo zhi gongye* (Free China Industry) 3, no. 4 (1955): 5–9.

Seligman, Adam B. *The Problem of Trust*. Princeton: Princeton University Press, 1997.

Shaw, Edward S. *Financial Deepening in Economic Development*. New York: Oxford University Press, 1973.

Shea, Jia-Dong. "Taiwan: Development and Structural Change of the Financial System." In Patrick and Park, eds., *Financial Development of Japan, Korea, and Taiwan*.

Shea, Jia-dong, and Ya-hwei Yang. "Taiwan's Financial System and the Allocation of Investment Funds." In Aberbach et al., eds., *The Role of the State in Taiwan's Development* (q.v.).

Shen Rongqing. "Taiwan jiti dianlu chanye xingcheng de lujing xuanze" (The choice of the route for the formation of Taiwan's IC industry). *Taiwan yinhang jikan* (Bank of Taiwan Quarterly) 48, no. 3 (Sept. 1997).

Shen Xida. "Taiwan zhongxiao qiye zhi chanxiao wenti" (Production and marketing of Taiwan's SMEs). *Taiwan yinhang jikan* (Bank of Taiwan Quarterly) 34, no. 3 (1983).

Shen Yunlong, ed. *Yin Zhongrong xiansheng nianpu chugao* (A draft chronicle of Yin Zhongrong's life). Taipei: Zhuanji wenxue, 1988.

Shen Zijia, Zhang Jueming, and Zheng Meilun. *Gu Zhenfu zhuan* (Biography of Gu Zhenfu). Taipei: Shuhua, 1994.

Shieh, G. S. *"Boss" Island: The Subcontracting Network and Micro-Entrepreneurship in Taiwan's Development*. New York: Peter Lang, 1992.

Sipress, Alan, and Steven Mufson. "Powell Takes the Middle Ground." *Washington Post*, Aug. 26, 2001, p. A01.

Skocpol, Theda. "Introduction: Bringing the State Back In." In Evans et al., eds., *Bringing the State Back In* (q.v.).

———. *States and Social Revolutions*. Cambridge: Cambridge University Press, 1979.

Smith, Heather. "Industry Policy in East Asia." *Asian-Pacific Economic Literature* 9, no. 1 (May 1995).

Stepan, Alfred. *The State and Society: Peru in Comparative Perspective*. Princeton: Princeton University Press, 1978.

Stiglitz, J. E. "Markets, Market Failures, and Development." *American Economic Review* 79, no. 2 (May 1989): 197–203.

Stiglitz, J. E., and A. Weiss. "Credit Rationing in Markets with Imperfect Information." *American Economic Review* 71, no. 3 (1981): 393–410.

Su Ziqin. *Quan yu qian: toushi Taiwan zhengshang guanxi* (Power and money: looking at government-business relations in Taiwan). Taipei: Xin xin wenhua, 1992.

"Taiwan bandaoti gongye jishu yijing chaoyue Riben he Nanhan" (Taiwan's semiconductor technology has already surpassed that of Japan and South Korea). *Ouzhou shibao* (Europe times), Feb. 20–24, 1999.

Taiwansheng gongshangye pucha zhixing xiaozu. "Di er ci gongshangye pucha zongbaogao" (General report on the second industrial survey in Taiwan province). Taipei, 1962.

——. "Di san ci gongshangye pucha zongbaogao" (General report on the third industrial survey in Taiwan province). Taipei, 1968.

——. "Taiwansheng gongshangye pucha zongbaogao" (General report on the industrial survey in Taiwan province). Taipei, 1956.

Taiwansheng zhengfu xuanchuan weiyuanhui. *Taiwan xianzhuang cankao ziliao* (References on the current situation in Taiwan). Taipei, 1946.

Taiwan yinhang. Jingji yanjiushi. "Taiwan diqu gongkuang qiye zijin diaocha baogao" (Report of the survey on the funds of industrial firms in the Taiwan area). Taipei: Taiwan yinhang, Jingji yanjiushi, 1976.

Taiwan yinhang. Jingji yanjiushi, ed. *Taiwan gongye fazhan celue yu maoyi xingtai zhi zhuanbian* (Transformation of strategies for industrial development and trading patterns in Taiwan). Taipei: Taiwan yinhang, Jingji yanjiushi, 1984.

——. *Taiwan yinhang jikan* (Bank of Taiwan quarterly). Various issues.

——. *Taiwan zhi gongye lunji* 2 (Taiwan's industry, vol. 2). Taiwan yinhang yanjiu congkan, no. 66. Taipei: Taiwan yinhang, Jingji yanjiushi, n.d.

Tang Xiyou. "Taiwan zhi zaozhi gongye" (Taiwan's papermaking industry). *Taiwan yinhang jikan* (Bank of Taiwan quarterly) 2, no. 3 (1975).

Tangrong tie gongchang diaochatuan. "Tangrong tie gongchang touzi diaocha baogaoshu" (Investigation report on the Tangrong Iron Corporation). Taipei, 1961.

Tanikaba Takao, ed. *Taiwan de gongyehua: chukou jiagong jidi de xingcheng* (The industrialization of Taiwan: the formation of the export-processing base). Taipei: Renjian, 1993.

Taylor, Jay. *The Generalissimo's Son: Chiang Ching-kuo and the Revolutions in China and Taiwan.* Cambridge: Harvard University Press, 2000.

Thompson, Grahame, ed. *Economic Dynamism in the Asia-Pacific: The Growth of Integration and Competitiveness.* London and New York: Routledge, 1998.

Tien, Hung-mao. *Government and Politics in Kuomintang China, 1927-37.* Stanford: Stanford University Press, 1972.

——. "Taiwan in Transition: Prospects for Sociopolitical Change." *China Quarterly*, no. 64 (Dec. 1975): 615-44.

——. "Transformation of an Authoritarian Party State: Taiwan's Development Experience." In Cheng and Haggard, *Political Change in Taiwan* (q.v.).

Tu Zhaoyan. *Riben diguozhuyi xia de Taiwan* (Taiwan under Japanese rule). Taipei: Renjian, 1993.

Turner, Louis, and Neil McMullen. *The Newly Industrializing Countries, Trade and Adjustment.* London: Royal Institute of International Affairs, 1982.

Ueno, Hiroya. "The Conception and Evaluation of Japanese Industrial Policy." In Sato, *Industry and Business in Japan* (q.v.).

U.S. Mutual Security Mission to China. *Economic Progress of Free China, 1951–1958.* Westport, CT: Greenwood Press, 1958.

Wade, Robert. "East Asia's Economic Success: Conflicting Perspectives, Partial Insights, Shaky Evidence." *World Politics* 44, no. 2 (Jan. 1992): 270–320.

———. *Governing the Market: Economic Theory and the Role of Government in East Asian Industrialization.* Princeton: Princeton University Press, 1990.

———. "Managing Trade: Taiwan and South Korea as Challenges to Economics and Political Science." *Comparative Politics* 25, no. 2 (Jan. 1993): 147–67.

———. "The Visible Hand: The State and East Asia's Economic Development." *Current History* 92, no. 578 (Dec. 1993): 431–40.

Wakabayashi Masahiro. *Zhuanxingqi de Taiwan: tuo neizhan hua de zhengzhi* (Taiwan in transition: politics out of civil war). Taipei: Guxiang, 1989.

Wang Hongren. "Zhanhou Taiwan siren duzhan ziben zhi fazhan" (The evolution of private monopoly capital in postwar Taiwan). M.A. thesis, National Taiwan University, 1988.

Wang Kejing. *Taiwan minjian chanye sishi nian* (Forty years of Taiwan's private sector). Taipei: Zili wanbao, 1987.

Wang, N. T., et al., eds. *Taiwan's Enterprises in Global Perspective.* Armonk, NY: M. E. Sharpe, 1992.

Wang Shan. "Taiwan gongyehua zhi tezheng" (The characteristics of Taiwan's industrialization). In *Riben tongzhi xia Taiwan jingji zhi tezheng* (The characteristics of Taiwan's economy under Japanese rule). Taiwan yanjiu congkan (Series of Taiwan Research), no. 53. Taipei: Taiwan yinhang, Jingji yanjiushi, 1957.

Wang Yuan, ed. *Taiwan yinhang sanshi nian* (Thirty years of the Bank of Taiwan). Taipei: Taiwan yinhang, 1976.

Wang Zhaoming. *Wang Zhaoming huiyi lu* (The memoirs of Wang Zhaoming). Taipei: Shibao wenhua, 1995.

Wang Zhenhuan. *Shei tongzhi Taiwan?* (Who rules Taiwan?). Taipei: Juliu tushu, 1996.

————. *Ziben, laogong yu guojia jiqi: Taiwan de zhengzhi yu shehui zhuan-xing* (Capital, labor, and the state: the political and economic transformation of Taiwan). Taipei: Tangshan, 1993.

Wang Zuorong. *Caijing wencun san bian* (Essays on the economy, III). Taipei: Shibao wenhua, 1988.

————. *Caijing wencun xu bian* (Essays on the Economy, II). Taipei: Shibao wenhua, 1989.

————. *Taiwan jingji fazhan lunwen xuanji* (Taiwan's economic development). Taipei: Shibao wenhua, 1981.

————. *Women ruhe chuangzao le jingji qiji?* (How did we make an economic miracle?). Taipei: Shibao wenhua, 1989.

Waterbury, John. *Exposed to Innumerable Delusions: Public Enterprise and State Power in Egypt, India, Mexico, and Turkey.* New York: Cambridge University Press, 1993.

Weber, Max. *Economy and Society.* Ed. Guenther Roth and Claus Wittich. New York: Bedminster Press, 1968.

Weiss, Linda, and John M. Hobson. *States and Economic Development: A Comparative Historical Analysis.* Cambridge, Eng.: Polity Press, 1995.

Wen Xinying. *Jingji qiji de beihou: Taiwan meiyuan jingyan de zhengjing fenxi* (Behind the economic miracle: a political economy analysis of the U.S. aid experience in Taiwan). Taipei: Zili wanbao wenhua, 1990.

White, Gordon, ed. *Developmental States in East Asia.* London: Macmillan, 1988.

Whitley, Richard. *Business Systems in East Asia: Firms, Markets and Societies.* Newbury Park, CA: Sage, 1992.

Wilks, Stephen, and Maurice Wright. "Conclusion: Comparing Government-Industry Relations: States, Sectors, and Networks." In Wilks and Wright, eds., *Comparative Government-Industry Relations* (q.v.), pp. 274–313.

Wilks, Stephen, and Maurice Wright, eds. *Comparative Government-Industry Relations: Western Europe, United States, and Japan.* New York: Oxford University Press, 1987.

————. *The Promotion and Regulation of Industry in Japan.* London: Macmillan, 1991.

Williamson, Oliver E. *The Economic Institution of Capitalism.* New York: Free Press, 1985.

Winckler, Edwin. "Industrialization and Participation on Taiwan: From Hard to Soft Authoritarianism?" *China Quarterly*, no. 99 (Sept. 1984): 481–99.

————. "National, Regional and Local Politics." In Emily Ahern and Hill Gates, eds., *The Anthropology of Taiwanese Society.* Stanford: Stanford University Press, 1981.

Winckler, Edwin, and Susan Greenhalgh. "Elite Political Struggle: 1945–1985." In Winckler and Greenhalgh, eds., *Contending Approaches to the Political Economy of Taiwan* (q.v.).

Winckler, Edwin, and Susan Greenhalgh, eds. *Contending Approaches to the Political Economy of Taiwan*. Armonk, NY: M. E. Sharpe, 1988.

Woo, Jung-en. *Race to the Swift: State and Finance in Korean Industrialization*. New York: Columbia University Press, 1991. See also Woo-Cumings, Meredith.

Woo-Cumings, Meredith. "National Security and the Rise of the Developmental State in South Korea and Taiwan." In Rowen, ed., *Behind East Asian Growth* (q.v.). See also Woo, Jung-en.

Woo-Cumings, Meredith, ed. *The Developmental State*. Ithaca: Cornell University Press, 1999.

World Bank. *The East Asian Miracle: Economic Growth and Public Policy*. Oxford: Oxford University Press, 1993.

———. *World Development Report, 1987*. New York: Oxford University Press, 1987.

———. *World Development Report, 1991*. Washington, DC: World Bank, 1991.

Wu, Chyuan-yuan. "The Politics of Financial Development in Taiwan." Ph.D. diss., University of Pennsylvania, 1992.

Wu Derong. "Guojia, shichang, haishi jingji guanzhi?" (State, market, or economic governance?). *Xianggang shehui kexue jikan* (Hongkong Journal of Social Sciences) 1 (Spring 1993): 176–200.

Wu Huilin and Zhou Tiancheng. "Shi jie Taiwan zhongxiao qiye zhi mi" (Solving the riddle of Taiwan's SMEs). In Chen Mingzhang, ed., *Taiwan zhongxiao qiye* (q.v.).

Wu Ruoyu. *Zhanhou Taiwan gongying shiye zhi zheng jing fenxi* (The political economy of Taiwan's postwar public sector). Taipei: Yeqiang, 1992.

Wu Sanlian. *Wu Sanlian huiyi lu* (Memoirs of Wu Sanlian). Taipei: Zili wanbao wenhua, 1991.

Wu Yingchun. "Hanguo bandaoti ye weihe chaoqian?" (Why has the South Korean semiconductor industry been ahead?). *Tianxia* (Commonwealth), Aug. 1, 1985.

Wu Zunxian. *Rensheng qishi* (Seventy years of life). Taipei: Wu Zunxia wenjiao gongyi jijinhui, 1993.

Xia Qiyue. "Lun waihui maoyi gaige de jiben wenti" (Basic problems in the reform of foreign exchange and trade). *Taiwan jingji yuekan* (Taiwan economic monthly) 18, no. 5 (1958): 6–9.

Xiao Quanzheng. *Taiwan diqu de xin zhongshang zhuyi* (Neo-mercantilism in the Taiwan area). Taipei: Guoce yanjiuyuan, 1989.

Xiao Xinhuang. "Jiedu Taiwan zhongxiao qiyejia yu da qiyejia de chuang-ye guocheng" (The entrepreneurial process of Taiwan's small, medium, and big businessmen). *Zhongguo shehui xuekan* (China Journal of Sociology) 16 (1992): 139–68.

Xie Guoxing. *Qiye fazhan yu Taiwan jingyan: Tainan bang de gean yanjiu* (Corporate development and the Taiwan experience: a case study of the Tainan group). Taipei: Zhongyang yanjiuyuan, Jindaishi yanjiu-suo, 1994.

Xie Guoxiong. "Wangluoshi shengchan zuzhi: Taiwan waixiao gongye zhong de waibao zhidu" (Network style of production organization: the subcontracting system in Taiwan's export-oriented industries). *Zhongyang yanjiuyuan, Minzuxue yanjiusuo jikan* (Journal of the Institute of Ethnology of the Academia Sinica) 71 (1991): 161–82.

———. "Yinxing gongchang: Taiwan de waibaodian yu jiating daigong" (Invisible factory: subcontracting workshops and cottage labor in Taiwan). *Taiwan shehui kexue jikan* (Taiwan: A Radical Quarterly in Social Studies) 13 (Nov. 1992).

Xing Muhuan. *Taiwan jingji celun* (Views on Taiwan's economy). Taipei: Sanmin shuju, 1993.

Xingzhengyuan. Tai-Min diqu gongshangye pucha weiyuanhui, ed. "Zhonghua minguo liushinian Tai-Min diqu gongshangye pucha bao-gao" (Report on the industrial survey of the Taiwan and Fujian areas, 1971). Taipei, 1973.

———. "Zhonghua minguo qishinian Tai-Min diqu gongshangye pucha baogao" (Report on the industrial survey of the Taiwan and Fujian areas, 1976). Taipei, 1978.

Xu Jiadong and Guo Pingxin. "Woguo de yinhang zijin peizhi xiaolü fenxi" (Analysis of the efficiency of money allocation in our country). In *Taiwan jinrong fazhan huiyi* (Conference on Taiwan's financial development). Taipei: Zhongyang yanjiuyuan, Jingj yanjiusuo, 1984.

Xu Shijun et al. *Woguo weixing gongchang tixi zhi tantao* (A study on the satellite factory system in our country). Taipei: Xingzhengyuan, Yanjiu fazhan kaohe weiyuanhui, 1979.

Xu Xueji. *Minying Tangrong gongsi xiangguan renwu fangwen jilu, 1940–1962* (Forging the future: an oral history of the Tangrong Iron Co., 1940–1962). Taipei: Zhongyang yanjiuyuan, Jindaishi yanjiusuo, 1993.

Xu Youxiang. *Zouguo bashi suiyue: Xu Youxiang huiyi lu* (Going through eighty years; reminiscences of Xu Youxiang). Taipei: Lianjing, 1994.

Yan Jili. "Shi lun yingxiang zhongxiao qiye touzi de yinsu" (Factors influencing the investment in the SMEs). In Chen Mingzhang, ed., *Taiwan zhongxiao qiye* (q.v.).

Yan Junbao. *Taiwan diqu yinhang fazhan sishinian* (Forty years of development of banks in the Taiwan area). Taipei: Zhonghua zhengxinsuo, 1991.

Yang Aili. *Sun Yunxuan zhuan* (Biography of Sun Yunxuan). Taipei: Tianxia, 1989.

Yang Yahui (Ya-Hwei Yang). "Jinrong zhengce yu gongye fazhan" (Financial policy and industrial development). In *Chanye fazhan he chanye zhengce yantaohui lunwenji* (Collected essays from the Conference on Industrial Development and Policy). Taipei: Zhonghua jingji yanjiuyuan, 1993.

———. "Taiwan: Development and Structural Change of the Banking System." In Patrick and Park, *The Financial Development of Japan, Korea, and Taiwan* (q.v.).

Ye Wan-an. "Jinrong zhengce yu jingji fazhan" (Financial policy and economic development). *Taibei Zhonghua xuebao* 11, no. 1 (1984).

———. "Taiwan gongye fazhan zhengce de yanding yu shishi" (The formulation and implementation of the industrial development policy of Taiwan). *Taibei shiyin yuekan* 14, no. 12 (1983).

———. "Taiwan jingji sheji jigou de yanbian" (The evolution of Taiwan's economic planning agencies). Speech given at the Institute of Economics, Academia Sinica, Taipei, 1995.

———. "Yixie zhongda jingji zhengce de beijing ji juece guocheng, 1–3" (The background and policy process of some important economic policies, 1–3). Speeches given at the Institute of Economics, Academia Sinica, Taipei, 1995.

Yearbook of the Republic of China, 1953.

Yin Naiping. *Zhongxiao qiye rongzi wenti yu caiwu jiegou gailiang zhi yanjiu* (A study of the issue of industrial finance of the SMEs and the improvement in their financial structure). Taipei: Jingjibu zhongxiao qiyechu, 1990.

Yin Yunpeng and Xia Ruijian. *Juecezhe* (Decision makers). Taipei: Tianxia, 1983.

Yin Zhongrong. "Dui dangqian waihui maoyi guanli zhengce ji banfa de jiantao" (Reflections on the policies and practices of foreign exchange and foreign trade). In idem, *Wo dui Taiwan jingji de kanfa* (q.v.), vol. 2, pp. 130–49.

———. "Jinrong xianzhuang yu Taiyin duice" (The current financial situation and the policy of the Bank of Taiwan). In idem, *Wo dui Taiwan jingji de kanfa* (q.v.), vol. 3, pp. 102–5.

———. "Lun bensheng zhi lilü" (The interest rates of our province). In *Wo dui Taiwan jingji de kanfa* (q.v.), vol. 2, pp. 121–24.

———. "Lun youzi yu heishi lilü" (Idle funds and the interest rates of black market funds). In *Wo dui Taiwan jingji de kanfa* (q.v.), vol. 3, pp. 20–23.

———. "Qunian de jinrong yu wujia" (Last year's finance and price). In *Wo dui Taiwan jingji de kanfa* (q.v.), vol. 3, pp. 113–19.

———. "Taiwan de jinrong yu Taiwan yinhang de zeren" (Taiwan's finance and the responsibility of the Bank of Taiwan). In *Wo dui Taiwan jingji de kanfa* (q.v.), vol. 3, pp. 24–39.

———. "Taiwan gongye zhengce shini" (Taiwan's industrial policy). In *Wo dui Taiwan jingji de kanfa* (q.v.), vol. 2, pp. 8–19.

———. "Taiwan tonghuo pengzhang zhi kongzhi" (The control of Taiwan's inflation). In *Wo dui Taiwan jingji de kanfa* (q.v.), vol. 3, pp. 190–96.

———. *Wo dui Taiwan jingji de kanfa* (My views on Taiwan's economy). 4 vols. Taipei: Council of US Aid, 1959–61.

———. "Woguo jinrong shiye" (Our country's financial sector). In *Wo dui Taiwan jingji de kanfa* (q.v.), vol. 3, pp. 120–67.

"Yu Guohua pinjie shenme huo weiliu?" (Why was Yu Guohua urged to stay?). *Gongshang shibao,* Jan. 22, 1982.

Zhang Jun. *Chuangzao caijing qiji de ren* (People who made the economic miracle). Taipei: Zhuanji wenxue, 1994.

———. "Jianli zhongxiao qiye quanmian fudao tixi zhi yanjiu" (A study on establishing a comprehensive guiding system for the SMEs). In Chen Mingzhang, ed., *Taiwan zhongxiao qiye* (q.v.).

Zhang Maogui. *Shehui yundong yu zhengzhi zhuanhua* (Social movements and political transformation). Taipei: Guoce zhongxin, 1989.

Zhang Rongfa. *Zhang Rongfa huiyilu* (The memoirs of Zhang Rongfa). Taipei: Yuanliu, 1997.

Zhang Zonghan. *Guangfu qian Taiwan zhi gongyehua* (Industrialization in Taiwan during Japanese rule). Taipei: Lianjing, 1980.

Zhao Jichang. *Caijing shengya wushi nian* (Fifty years as an economic official). Taipei: Shangzhou wenhua, 1994.

———. "Taiwan zhongxiao qiye zhi fudao wenti" (The guidance of Taiwan's SMEs). *Taiwan yinhang jikan* (Bank of Taiwan Quarterly) 34, no. 3 (1983).

Zheng Jiazhong. *Sixiang qi, Taiwan jingji: yige jizhe yanzhong de caijing shinian* (Taiwan's economy: from a reporter's point of view over the past ten years). Taipei: Shibao wenhua, 1988.

Zheng Youkui, Cheng Linsun, and Zhang Chuanhong. *Jiu Zhongguo de ziyuan weiyuanhui* (The National Resources Commission in old China). Shanghai: Shanghai shehui kexue, 1991.

Zhengxin xinwen (Zhengxin news). Various issues.

Zhongguo guoji shangye yinhang. "Zhongguo guoji shangye yinhang banli chukou daikuan jielue" (The Bank of China's brief report on export loans). Taipei, 1977.

Zhongguo shibao (dianzi ban) (China Times), electronic edition, Mar. 19, 1999.

Zhonghua zhengxinsuo. *Taiwan diqu jituan qiye yanjiu* (Business groups in the Taiwan area). Taipei, 1974.

———. *Taiwan diqu qiye jituan yanjiu* (A study of business groups in the Taiwan area). Taipei, 1985.

Zhongyang xintuoju. "Qing bodai xintaibi eryi yuan kuochong Zhongyang xintuoju maoyi fudao zhongxiao waixiaoshang jielue" (Brief application for NT$200 million for the expansion of trade fund of the Central Trust of China for guiding the export-oriented SMEs). N.d. (1970s?).

Zhongyang yinhang. "Ge yinhang zhongdian fangkuan fenxi baogao (jiezhi 1973 nian liuyue)" (Analysis of the key loans of all banks at the end of June 1973). Taipei: Zhongyang yinhang, 1973.

Zhongyang yinhang. Jingji yanjiuchu. *Zhonghua minguo Taiwan diqu jinrong tongji yuebao* (Financial statistics monthly for the Taiwan area, Republic of China). Jan. 1965.

Zhou Tiancheng. "Quanli bianchui de zhongxiao qiye" (The SMEs in the power periphery). In Xiao Xinhuang, ed., *Jiepou Taiwan jingji: weiquan tizhi xia de longduan yu boxue* (Dissecting Taiwan's economy: monopoly and exploitation under the authoritarian regime), Taipei: Qianwei, 1992. See also Chou, Tien-chen.

———. *Taiwan chanye zuzhi lun* (Industrial organization of Taiwan). Taipei: Ershiyi shiji jijinhui, 1991.

———. "Taiwan jinrong guanzhi yu jingji fazhan: shuangyuanxing jinrong tizhi yu erfenhua shichang jiegou" (Financial control and economic development in Taiwan: the dual financial system and the dichotomous market structure). *Taiwan yinhang jikan* (Bank of Taiwan quarterly) 45, no. 1 (1994): 222–40.

———. "Taiwan waixiangxing zhongxiao qiye de tese yu xingcheng yuanyin" (The characteristics and causes of Taiwan's outward-oriented small- and medium-sized enterprises). *Taiwan yinhang jikan* (Bank of Taiwan quarterly) 50, no. 3 (1999): 116–29.

Zhou Xianwen. *Riju shidai Taiwan jingjishi (2)* (Taiwan's economic history under Japanese rule, 2). Taiwan yanjiu congkan (Series on Taiwan Research), no. 59. Taipei: Taiwan yinhang, 1958.

Zhu Peilian, ed. *Shu Yunzhang xiansheng nianpu* (A chronological biography of Mr. Shu Yunzhang). Taipei: Zhongyang yanjiuyuan, Jindaishi yanjiusuo, 1992.

Zhu Yunhan. "Guazhan jingji yu weiquan zhengzhi tizhi" (Oligopoly and authoritarianism in Taiwan). In *Jiepou Taiwan jingji: weiquan tizhi xia de longduan yu boxue* (Dissecting Taiwan's economy: monopoly and exploitation under the authoritarian regime), ed. Xiao Xinhuang. Taipei: Qianwei, 1992. See also Chu, Yun-han.

Zi Gu. "Taiwan jingji yu Riben" (Taiwan's economy and Japan). In Taiwan yinhang, Jingji yanjiushi, ed., *Riju shidai Taiwan jingji tezheng* (The characteristics of Taiwan's economy under Japanese rule). Taipei: Taiwan yinhang, 1957.

"Zongtong zhuchi caijing huiyi jilu (1–12), yijiuqiba nian liuyue liuri zhi yijiuqiba nian shiyiyue ershiba ri" (Minutes of the economic meetings chaired by the president, nos. 1–12, from June 6, 1978, to Nov. 28, 1978). In *Li Guoding dang'an* (Li Guoding archives). Taipei: Zhongyang yanjiuyuan, Jindaishi yanjiusuo.

"Zongtong zhuchi minying gongye zuotanhui jilu, yijiuqiba nian qiyue zhi yijiuqiba nian bayue" (Minutes of the private sector meetings chaired by the president, from July 1978 to August 1978). In *Li Guoding dang'an* (Li Guoding archives). Taipei: Zhongyang yanjiuyuan, Jindaishi yanjiusuo.

Zysman, John. *Governments, Markets, and Growth: Financial Systems and the Politics of Industrial Change.* Ithaca: Cornell University Press, 1983.

Index

Harvard East Asian Monographs
(* out-of-print)

Harvard East Asian Monographs

Harvard East Asian Monographs

Harvard East Asian Monographs

Harvard East Asian Monographs